KU-324-515

Information Technology Impact on the Way of Life

Organized by
FAST Programme
Commission of the European Communities
National Board for Science and Technology

Information Technology Impact on the way of life

A selection of papers from the EEC Conference on the
Information Society held in Dublin, Ireland,
18-20 November 1981

Liam Bannon, Ursula Barry and Olav Holst
Editors

Organized by
National Board for Science and Technology, Ireland
and
Commission of the European Communities,
FAST Programme

Published by
Tycooly International Publishing Ltd.
Dublin

The Conference was organized by the National Board for Science and Technology, Ireland, and the Commission of the European Communities, FAST Programme. Publication arrangements by Commission of the European Communities Directorate-General Information Market and Innovation.

EUR 7997

Joint Copyright © 1982. ECSC, EEC, EAEC, Brussels and Luxembourg, and NBST, Ireland.

Legal Notice
Neither the Commission of the European Communities, the National Board for Science and Technology, Ireland, nor any person acting on behalf of the Commission or Board is responsible for the use which might be made of the following information

All rights reserved. No part of this publication may be reproduced, stored in a retrieval system or transmitted, in any form or by any means, electronic, electrostatic, magnetic tape, mechanical, photocopying, recording or otherwise, without the prior permission in writing from the publishers.

Published by:
Tycooly International Publishing Ltd.,
6 Crofton Terrace,
Dun Laoghaire,
Co. Dublin, Ireland
Telephone: (+353-1) 800245/6
Telex: 30547 SHCN EI

Cover illustration by courtesy of
Strategie Journal, Milan, Italy
Cover design by Ailish McShane

Typeset by Photo-Set Ltd., Dublin and
printed by Cahills Printing Ltd., Dublin, Ireland

ISBN 0 907 567 34 7 Hardback
ISBN 0 907 567 35 5 Softcover

Contents

Part IV: New Technology and the Changing Role of Women

Part V: The Changing Media — New Forms and Uses

Foreword

This book contains a selection of papers presented at the Dublin EEC Conference on the Information Society, entitled *Information Technology: Impact on the Way of Life,* which was held in Dublin, Ireland, 18-20 November 1981. The objective of the Conference was to discuss the impact of the new information technologies on the way of life of individuals and social groups, with a view to developing policy options and priority areas for research and development. Over 200 researchers, public administration officials and industrialists from Europe, North America and Japan took part in plenary sessions and workshops over the three days. The Conference was organized by the National Board for Science and Technology, with the co-operation of the FAST Programme of the European Communities.

The FAST (Forecasting and Assessment in the field of Science and Technology) Programme is an experimental programme set up by the European Commission to identify the critical issues affecting the economic and social development of the European Community over a thirty-year time period (1980-2010). The Dublin Conference was one of several projects sponsored by the 'information society' sub-programme of FAST, which also has sub-programmes on 'work and society' and the 'bio-society'. The results of these research projects have particular relevance to Ireland, given its rapid change from an agricultural to a manufacturing economy. The National Board for Science and Technology has contributed to the formulation of European Community policy on Research and Development concerning the information society. It is actively involved in the development of information networks between researchers in all member countries of the EEC as a means to encourage research and disseminate findings on the social effects of the new information technologies. The publication of this book is one example of these activities.

Mel Healy
Economic and Social Division
National Board for Science and Technology

Dublin, 1982

Editors' Preface

This book consists of papers presented at a conference on the social impact of the new information technologies, held in Dublin, Ireland, 18-20 November 1981. The editors have selected these papers from the extensive and wide-ranging material presented during the three days of the conference.

The focus of the papers is on the impact of the new information technologies on the nature of daily activities and lifestyles. The papers thus address such themes as the content and the organization of work, shopping, entertainment activities, media usage, transport and social communications. The editors have provided an introductory paper to serve as a guide to some of the key issues raised and an epilogue which draws some implications from the viewpoints expressed.

We feel that this collection of papers brings together a set of exciting and stimulating contributions to the debate on the social impact of information technology — a debate that is critical insofar as we are examining a technology which is entering so many different areas of daily life, transforming human activity in the school, the home and the workplace. We are particularly pleased that a number of the selected papers contain empirical findings on the effects of the new information technologies.

It was decided not to publish a full Proceedings volume for a number of reasons. These included the difficulty of fitting all the papers into a coherent framework, the very different treatments of the issues evident in the papers, the varying level of detail and the overlap in topics discussed. We feel that the selected papers give an indication of both the range of topics and the variety of viewpoints which were expressed at the Conference. There are thus many disparities between the selected papers, in terms of style, length and viewpoints, but this can be seen as an asset rather than a failing. It may help to give some of the flavour of the actual Conference which was marked by very different opinions being expressed on many of the issues debated.

We would like to thank all those who contributed to the success of the Conference, particularly the staff of the National Board for Science and Technology, Dublin. We would also like to express our appreciation to all our speakers, respondents, chairpersons and rapporteurs for their contributions. We hope that the results will be of interest to all our readers.

Olav Holst
FAST Programme
Commission of the
European Communities

Liam Bannon
and Ursula Barry
National Board for Science
and Technology

Reflections on the Social Impact of New Information Technologies

Liam Bannon and Ursula Barry

National Board for Science and Technology, Dublin

INFORMATION TECHNOLOGY is today recognized as the technological development which is transforming the economies of Western Europe. The term 'information technology' is used to refer to a wide range of technologies which restructure and reorganize the spheres of production, distribution and circulation. Breakthroughs in computing and telecommunications technologies are transforming a whole series of products and processes, thereby altering the traditional labour-intensive nature of certain areas of economic activity.

NEW INFORMATION TECHNOLOGIES: THEIR APPLICATIONS

THE APPLICATIONS of these technological developments can be grouped into four main areas:

(1) The introduction of computing power into a wide spectrum of work processes across the different sectors of production, bringing about a new level of automation in these sectors (for example, in the automobile, chemical, printing, food, textile, engineering and agricultural industries). The development of microelectronics components that are small, cheap and reliable make it possible to integrate computing power into many different types of capital equipment used in manufacturing industry. Some writers have distinguished between an earlier period of automation in the 1950s and this

new phase associated with information technology. This distinction arises from the nature of the application of microelectronics within manufacturing processes, which is capable not only of transforming the equipment and machinery of the factory, but also the role of human labour in production itself. The new computerised machinery can incorporate many of the elements of human intelligence and knowledge into its own stored programmes, thus restructuring both the organization and content of work processes.

(2) The convergence of telecommunications and computer systems caused by a number of technological developments, principally the use of digital rather than analogue techniques for message transmission and switching. 'Telematics' is one term used to refer to this new field. The traditional governmental agencies responsible for postal and telecommunications services are confronted with enormous problems concerning the regulation of new commercial products and processes in the telematics field. Commercial firms themselves find that they are rapidly coming into conflict with each other over 'legitimate' spheres of interest — witness the involvement of IBM (the United States computer giant) in satellite communications systems and the organizational restructuring of AT&T (the major domestic telephone company in the US) as it prepares to provide computing and related services.

The speed and capacity of new transmission media (such as satellites at a global, and optical fibres at a local level) are such that vast amounts of data are capable of being transmitted across the world in seconds. The development of computer networks allows for the collection, collation, integration and dissemination of information on an unprecedented scale. This has far-reaching implications for such issues as personal privacy and corporate confidentiality. On a different level, it poses further problems for Governments that wish to ensure the integrity of their State apparatus, faced by powerful multinational corporations with an extensive information network that may contain sensitive socio-economic data spanning continents. This issue of transborder data flows is only beginning to emerge on the international stage but it is likely to become a major issue, especially for many Third World countries who are not in a position to control the flow of information to or from their countries.

(3) The development of a wide range of equipment capable of transforming the office environment. While automation has transformed the production processes both in agriculture and industry throughout the past 150 years, the spheres of circulation and distribution have undergone little change. Microelectronics allows for the development of highly complex, distributed processing systems that can support 'the integrated office', whereby all office procedures are co-ordinated and rationalised, with continuous monitoring of all transactions. Capital investment in the office arena is growing rapidly, resulting in the reorganization of work in such traditionally labour-intensive sectors as banking and social services.

Such developments have been interpreted by some as a beneficial development for employees, with the new office equipment allowing individuals to augment their skills and reduce repetitive work. An alternative view stresses the exact opposite, claiming that the most likely results of the introduction of the new technologies will be the elimination of jobs and the compartmentalisation of office work into routine, deskilled operations that allow for greater supervision and control. This issue will be examined in greater detail later.

(4) The development of new microelectronics-based consumer products and systems linked to, the media and general entertainment and recreation activities — the 'leisure' industry — comprising such items as microelectronics-based video games, video-cassette recorders, videodiscs, videotex services and personal computer systems, all of which have created completely new market areas in a relatively short time. These products are affecting the very nature of current social practices, how we spend our time and how we organize our daily activities.

THE INFORMATION SOCIETY?

THE POTENTIAL for wide-ranging change in the nature of daily life is thus apparent from the scope of applications of these new technologies. The pervasive nature of the technology has led some commentators to argue that our society is undergoing a change as profound as that of the industrial revolution, giving rise to a 'post-industrial' society (Bell, 1973; Masuda, 1980).

One of the major reasons for positing such a profound change in the nature of society rests on an analysis of the percentage of workers employed in the handling, processing, transfer and storage of information. Porat (1976), in a major study on the composition of the US economy, argued that over 50 per cent of the labour force were employed in the information sector, producing 45 per cent of the US gross national product in 1967. While there are many criticisms directed at his definition of information-related work, few will disagree with the view that 'information' plays an increasingly important role in economic activities. It is this and similar kinds of studies that have led some people to the concept of a 'post-industrial' or 'information' society, where information and knowledge are key resources.

Other analysts have chosen to study the impact of the technology without positing either a revolution or a new society. This is not to say that the significance of the technology in changing how we produce and how we consume has been underestimated. Rather, they argue that unless the diffusion of information technology is accompanied by a fundamental transformation in the social, economic and political relationships which shape societies, then it cannot be considered as revolutionary. Valaskakis (Chapter 1) puts his point thus:

> *If the essence of the contemporary transformation was the passage from a manufacturing to an information society, then that metamorphosis would be less than earthshaking.*

Valaskakis proceeds to argue that information-related activities were dominant in fifth century Athens, medieval Florence and other historic societies; thus, the dominance of information activities is not in itself revolutionary. He argues that information technology is a new industrial wave rather than a post-industrial wave and that microelectronics is a new industrial technology. Thus, he sees the changes occurring as being firmly *within* the logic of capital-labour substitution and, therefore, at the very heart of the concept of industrialisation.

Those who speak of revolutionary societal change tend to put forward a futuristic vision, based not only on the widespread use of information technology, but also on structural changes in the very organization of society itself. Masuda (Chapter 3) describes his vision in the following manner:

> *In the global Information Society, all citizens will be linked to each other by a global information and knowledge network, directed towards global consciousness, overriding differences in culture, interests and nationalities.*

Masuda's futuristic view is not restricted to those people actively involved in the information industry or in information services; he is, in a sense, describing a New World Order. He predicts a global education system, the end of illiteracy, world peace and human happiness.

The debate on information technology is not, therefore, concerned so much with the significance of the technology *per se* but rests more on the issue of the social and economic impact of the diffusion of these technologies. Many writers argue that the economic and social structures of European societies will remain virtually intact, despite the widespread application of information technologies. Some go further and argue that the power relations and inequities in the current system of social order will be exacerbated. Robins (Chapter 5) takes this view:

> *Information Technology is the culmination of processes set in motion by Taylorism and Fordism: particularly the extension from the factory to the social totality of (managerial) rationalisation and the centralisation and monopolisation of knowledge/information/skill.*

From the discussion so far, there are two points at issue. In the first instance, does information technology carry a potential for change that can be characterised as revolutionary? Secondly, what is the nature of these changes and how will they affect or be affected by the different actors in European societies? These are some of the questions addressed in this book.

In the authors' view, the criteria used to determine whether new economic or technical advances actually contribute to human growth and development are often not explicit and depend, to a large degree, on the socio-political framework adopted. The same technology is heralded by one group as the key to a future 'full-of-promise', while others regard it as stifling human creativity and self-expression. This disparity of views is not necessarily a negative phenomenon since it merely demonstrates that technological development cannot be examined or assessed without the use of theoretical frameworks determined by the value-systems of different authors. The failure of an author to describe this framework explicitly does not imply that the results are 'value free'. This should be borne in mind when perusing the writings collected here. Let us now take an overall view of the themes discussed by the various authors.

DISCUSSION THEMES

Technology and Societal Change

One of the few but important points of agreement to be found in this book is that the nature of societal transformation is determined by the complex interaction of various agents of economic and social change. Technology is thus only one factor amongst a number of others influencing the nature of societal change. Other factors (such as population changes, the level of economic activity, environmental conditions and political attitudes) also have a key role in determining our future. Within the technological sphere, the new information technologies are clearly recognized as the most significant technological element which will contribute to the process of change during the next few decades.

However, the importance attributed to the technological component within this process of social change varies considerably. Some authors consider technology as being of paramount importance, arguing a position of 'technological determinism', best exemplified in the following statements from Masuda (Chapter 3):

. . . societal technology has become the axial force that has brought about the transformation of human society . . . The basic framework of new human society should be moulded by the fundamental characteristics of the new societal technology.

In this perspective, each period of history over the past two centuries has been characterised by technological developments, such as steam power, electrical power and the computer revolution. Technological developments are thus seen as the motors of change. A contrasting view is put forward by Dover (Chapter 19):

Another difficulty which arises when attempting to forecast the effects of new technology on society is that society is subject to change from other sources. It will not be a static society; many social forces are at work concurrently with technology to bring about change. Rising population and other demographic changes, changed expectation levels, changing sectoral configurations in employment or unemployment, land-use changes, the

distribution of wealth, resource depletion, political stability and many more
– all will work through to alter society.

A further viewpoint, mentioned though not elaborated, argues that technology is an integral part of the social process and should therefore be viewed as a 'social relation' (Braverman, 1974; Robins and Webster, 1980).

The discussion in the present book concentrates on the social and economic context in which technology is used, rather than the design or constitution of technology itself. In this sense, critical importance is given to the choices and decisions made in the development, implementation and use of information technologies. The notion that information technology has its own inherent logic of development is rejected by most authors, who turn to an examination of the dominant social relations within which strategic decision-making takes place.

Howard Rosenbrock (1981) argues that the history of technological development is marked by a choice between two distinct paths. The first sees technology as a tool designed to complement and enhance human skills. The second attempts to exclude human intervention by increasing control of the work process through automation and the use of scientific management techniques. In Rosenbrock's view, it is the second path which has been almost universally adopted to date. Thus, far from technology determining the nature of society, the very nature of technology has been determined by certain dominant interests within society.

There are many reasons given for this. Some authors, such as Robins and Garnham (Chapters 5 and 24, respectively), point to the degree of control held by a very small number of multinational corporations over the development of technology and see this as the key factor. According to this view, these dominant interests have determined that Rosenbrock's second path would be the one that was to be followed. To change this situation, they argue that the crucial issue is not how do we adapt to, respond to, or educate for, technical change but rather how do we transform the process by which technical change is determined. On this point, Cronberg (Chapter 20) argues that half the population — women — have been virtually excluded from the design and development process.

Many other authors take the design of the technology as given and for them the element of choice surfaces in the manner of integration of the new technologies, their rate of diffusion and the exploitation of their potential.

Centrality of Work

Much of the discussion on the impact of the new information technologies has tended to focus on the potential changes in the nature and organization of work activities in the 'formal' or money economy. Gershuny (1979) characterises this economy in terms of the flow of money and commodities between the formal production system and households. Labour from households enters the formal production system and wages are received in exchange. In industrial society, the wage and salary have been the key mechanisms by which the majority of people obtain income. Many analysts argue that in the future, the formal economy will no longer be able to play such a fundamental role in defining people's status, income group, interests, social relations, attitudes and opinions.

There are a number of underlying trends which support this statement. For instance, a substantial proportion of the population in Western Europe have *never* entered the formal labour force (unemployed youth), while another section of the population have left, or have been forced out, through compulsory early-retirement schemes or factory closures. It is also acknowledged that many of those made redundant are unlikely ever to return to the formal labour market. This has caused a sharp rise in the level of unemployment, quite unprecedented in Western Europe. Besides the very high level of unemployment, there has been a marked change in the composition of those unemployed. Previously, unemployment tended to be confined to those in particular sectors of the economy or to a certain social class structure within society. The current crisis has resulted in people from all sectors and from different socio-economic groups joining the growing ranks of the unemployed. This has had a profound effect on the consciousness of society as a whole, as it makes the unemployment problem more immediate, more permanent and more visible throughout all levels of society.

Such measures as shorter working hours or 'work-sharing' initiatives, suggested as a means to spread the available work more evenly amongst those seeking employment, may have some effect in the short term, but are unlikely to be sufficient to stop the growing wave of structural unemployment that many observers foresee in the coming decade. The destructive nature of such developments on society at large are commented on by MacBride (Chapter 7):

> *There is nothing more soul-destroying or damaging to the fabric of society and family life than unemployment and dependence on State welfare benefits. It is utterly unjust, as the man or woman who is thrown onto the unemployment scrapheap has no alternative – they are merely the victims of developments over which they have no control. The dignity of the human being who is unable to earn his living or to work is severely damaged and unemployment is one of the factors in the break-up of family life.*

With the role of the formal work system being increasingly called into question, there is the possibility of a new social reality evolving, one in which people may characterise themselves not in terms of a job in the formal economy, but according to their role, activity or political perspective; on the other hand, they may reject the categorisation process entirely! Such a shift from a society in which social acceptability and legitimacy is primarily established through a job in the formal economy to a society where this is no longer possible, or even desirable, represents a major challenge to all the social actors in our society.

Such a transition will probably take place in an uneven fashion throughout Western Europe over the next decade. It may occur with less disturbance in countries with a strong rural tradition, where pre-industrial norms and values still exist, in contrast to highly industrialised countries where the market and wage labour predominate. Toffler (1980) sees the whole ethos of industrial society (with its emphasis on specialisation, standardisation, centralisation and bureaucratisation) as being an abberation and he believes that the current difficulties of Western societies are caused by the inevitable upheaval and self-examination that occurs when a new societal ethos is emerging.

A new view of women and their contribution to society is one aspect of this new ethos. In this regard, Morrissey and Drew (Chapter 21) discuss the implications for women of a radical shift in the concept of work and the organization of the household. In their view, formal employment has never played the central role for women in industrial societies as it has for men — rather the work of women (domestic labour) has been undervalued. They take the optimistic view that the coming information society will mean "more humanitarian work, greater flexibility in the use of time, work sharing inside the house and home, and an integration of work and leisure".

The diminution in the importance of formal work activities, previously mentioned, has corresponded to an upsurge in the activities, organization and importance of what is often referred to as the 'informal' economy. Gershuny (1979) defines three major types of activities that take place in this economy: activities connected with the household, the community and the 'underground'. This latter category (the underground) covers a wide range of activities, from theft to tax evasion and moonlighting (jobs on the side). A number of factors, including lifestyle changes and government taxation and welfare policies, are cited by Gershuny as contributing to the growth of this sector of the economy.

The informal economy is of concern in the present context because it refers to a host of activities that may become even more widespread due to the further shrinking of job opportunities likely to occur in the 'formal' economy. It is thus probable that governments will look for ways of incorporating such activities into a possibly expanded and reorganized socio-economic framework, rather than simply trying to suppress them. Certainly, the current policies of ignoring such activities in the compilation of many economic and social statistics cannot be sustained in the long term.

These views on the changing nature of our society imply a displacement of the wage and salary as the primary means by which wealth is distributed. Can the Welfare State continue to function in its present form when an increasing proportion of Western European society is not involved in the formal economy, but is dependent on the State for an income? This raises the question of how wealth is created, owned and distributed in different societies. Is the informal economy to function as a major source of income for the unemployed or will the role of the State become even more significant and central to the distribution of wealth, as it is in the provision of services? It is impossible to adequately address such fundamental and wide-ranging issues here but, in the authors' view, they are critical to a full consideration of the changing role of work in society.

A further factor influencing the nature and role of formal employment is examined by Cronberg, and Espejo and Ziv (Chapters 20 and 17 respectively). The possibilities for a more diffuse or decentralised work organization arising from the new technologies are looked at, which allow for work to be efficiently carried out at home or in neighbourhood work centres. The changing nature of office organization, for example, enables employees to link up to central office resources and activities, while simultaneously making their input from remote locations. Cronberg argues that this decentralisation of work, based on the home or community work centres, could lead to a re-vitalisation of local areas, both urban and rural. However, she warns that such centres could become ghettos if the work is routine and monotonous and if the workers have no means of influencing society as a whole.

On a more speculative note, several writers have commented on the changes in the social patterns of the work environment, caused by increased human-machine interaction, for example in the use of VDUs for extended periods. In these situations, the person has reduced face-to-face contact with other workers, as more work tasks and work-related communications are mediated by machine. The consequences of such changes for the psychological well-being of the individual are as yet little understood, although it is evident that the socialisation of work has been a major historical development linked to communal and collective activity, serving an important human need. This social role of the workplace is emphasised by Cullen (Chapter 6):

> *The workplace is not only a source of human productivity, which may be greatly increased by our information technology. It is above all else a social context, relying very heavily on human support networks.*

Work and Human Development

The enhancement of human creativity and self-expression is one of the most important considerations in evaluating any process of social change. Thus, in considering the societal changes brought about by the introduction of the new information technologies, it is of interest to discover the extent to which the new tools free us from drudgery and promote flexibility and creative self-expression. Several authors address the question of the effects of the new technologies in the workplace — issues such as skill enhancement or degradation, the nature of job tasks, job complexity and overall job satisfaction are discussed. Since many of the authors are relating the outcome of actual empirical research projects on the social impact of information technology, their results merit attention.

If one were to summarise the research studies, the main finding would be that the application of microelectronics does not have any uniform impact on the skills and tasks of workers, in either the office or the factory. Indeed, examples of both deskilling and skill-enhancing effects can be provided. As Boddy and Buchanan (Chapter 12) state:

> *Technology can be used to replace or to complement human capabilities. The consequences of a particular application depend partly on the*

capabilities of the technology and partly on the way in which work is organized around the technology.

In their case studies, Boddy and Buchanan found a management desire to "reduce human intervention and contribution by replacing people and their knowledge and skills with machinery". Thus, along with the economic objectives — reducing costs and raising productivity — management had introduced information technologies with a view to increasing the "predictability, reliability, consistency and controllability of operations".

This desire on the part of the management to eliminate the human factor in many industrial operations is carried to the limit in the projected case of the 'fully automated factory'. Leaving aside the implications of this development on skills and the potential displacement of labour, Sorge, Hartmann, Warner and Nicholas (Chapter 9) raise serious doubts on the validity, and even the economic viability, of such an approach from a corporate viewpoint:

We interpret the fascination with the automated factory as another incorrect trend extrapolation. It is again founded on past experience with the expansion of homogeneous mass markets and the existence of a consistent and stable demand for specialised products. The present phase of technical advance is less characterised by stable, specialised mass markets but more differentiated and shifting market patterns, which invariably create the need for direct and skilled human intervention because standard solutions are either too costly, too complex or liable to failure because of unanticipated variety.

Thus, Sorge *et al* foresee "the continued presence of directly intervening production operators on the shop floor". The goal of a fully automated factory is, in their view, a short-sighted and ultimately weak management policy that is based on the increasing division of labour, specialisation, de-skilling and bureaucratisation. They argue that this Tayloristic approach to production work should be rejected in favour of an approach that builds on craft-workers' skills and flexibility at all levels in the work process. They point to a number of German plants where this new approach is in operation, while admitting that the general implementation of such an approach may be difficult due to the rigid corporate strategies and personnel policies of many companies.

The different approaches taken by management itself and the resistance by some to the very introduction of the new technologies is certainly one factor which influences the conditions under which information technology is introduced and used. Wilkinson (Chapter 13) argues that the processes of development and diffusion of the technology reflect the influences of different social actors. For this reason, research results on the impact of information technology in the workplace may at first appear contradictory. This may be explained by the intervention of different social actors in its design and implementation. Wilkinson describes this process:

They (microelectronic applications) have no uniform 'impact' but depend on the social and political intentions of managers and engineers and also on the way workers respond, adapt and try to influence the outcome. The various stages in the process of innovation of design, trial, implementation and debugging – all provide junctures at which people can (and do) intervene to influence the process of technical change.

The difficulty in arriving at overall conclusions on the effects of the technology is argued also by Francis, Snell, Willman and Winch (Chapter 15). In their view, the effects observed in their research depend on the organization of work around the technology. Their case studies identified a range of effects of information technologies, yet the establishment of direct casual links was extremely difficult. With respect to management orientations, they conclude that:

Our evidence so far is that labour-process-type arguments, that managements choose particular technologies partly to deskill and exercise tighter control over labour, gain only limited support. We did not find a great deal of evidence either of this intention by management or of this effect. Though there appears to be some tendency in this direction, there are also many countervailing pressures.

On a more general issue, a number of commentators have raised their voices concerning the general mismatch between human abilities and the nature of jobs, as Rosenbrock (1981) notes:

The skills and abilities of people are a precious resource which we are misusing and a sense of urgency and fitness for purpose should drive us to find a better relation between technology and human ability.

In his book, Cooley (1980) takes up this point, focusing specifically on what he sees as the deskilling effects of the new technologies. He has been critical of computer-aided design (CAD) systems, arguing that many of these systems reduce the creative capacity of the designer. In his view, the new technology tends to restrict the design process to the manipulation of a limited number of standard elements, while the tacit knowledge and experience of the designer is being continuously devalued. This raises deeper questions concerning the obsolescence of skills and the logic behind the quest for objectification and quantification of human abilities. These are important issues, yet they are only briefly mentioned in this book. We turn now to an examination of the impact of information technologies on daily activities outside the formal work environment.

The Leisure Era

It is of interest that in a book about the social impact of the new information technologies, there is no detailed pronouncement on the forthcoming 'age of leisure'. In the authors' opinion, the whole concept of a 'leisure society' is seriously flawed. Aside from the question of the desirability of such a society, societal trends do not indicate a major increase in leisure time for most of the population. An insight on this topic is given by de Gournay (Chapter 25):

We do not believe that the post-industrial society corresponds to the stage at which work will be reduced and idleness and play predominate, although in actual fact it does lead to a real reduction in formal working hours . . . the organization of leisure activities remains closely dependent on the socialised conditions created by work – this is why non-working women have no leisure. In short, leisure only exists as the negative of work and, as a social phenomenon, it has only assumed its full importance and significance in societies where work has been set up as the sole dominant value, to the exclusion of all others, whether religious, family or community.

As a result, those who 'consume' leisure are precisely those in society that work in the formal money economy and therefore have money to spend on leisure activities, such as travel, recreation or entertainment. In addition, the socialised nature of work lends itself more easily to the organization of other leisure activities, such as sport.

Television-viewing is a very popular non-working-time activity for a large number of people. New information technologies have expanded the range and scope of television through such devices as video-cassette recorders, video-disc machines, video games, and teletex/videotex services. This expanded complex of television services is regarded by some as a positive development, allowing for greater choice and diversity. Garnham (Chapter 24) argues that, on the contrary, the new developments may polarize viewing audiences into upper- and lower-income groups. The upper-income group would pay extra for a number of specialised services (such as Pay TV) and thus would have a greater choice and flexibility; but the lower-income groups would, he believes, receive a more homogenised and lower quality service. To avoid this, Garnham advocates that the attempt to move more and more services from the public into the private sphere, commercialising areas of human activity previously outside the control of the market, be resisted. It is interesting to note that Thompson (Chapter 8) puts forward precisely the opposite view — that if a new 'wealth-creating information economy' is to come about, it is essential to move more information services into the private sphere. Several papers are critical of the content of recreational and general cultural amenities and services currently available. Mattelart (Chapter 23) comments on the passive nature of media usage, citing the example of radio as a technological innovation which could potentially have developed as a two-way technology but, in practice, has failed to do so.

The development of two-way TV or the capacity to make home-video films are often cited by those who claim that the new technologies allow for greater participation in the media. Critics state that the apparent control of the consumer is more illusory than real and that the predominant mode of use of the new technologies is that of passive consumption of pre-packaged products. It will be interesting to observe whether this trend continues or whether people will begin to become active producers in the new media — as with Citizens Band (CB) radio, for instance. In this regard, a recent survey carried out by the JVC Company in the United States estimated that only 20 per cent of video-cassette recorder (VCR) sales involve a video camera, a prerequisite for producing home-video films. This and other information on the use of VCRs is given in an interesting research paper by Baboulin, Mallein and Gaudin (Chapter 28). They challenge the view that VCRs revolutionize media usage:

All the qualitative surveys show that as soon as the VCR is used, it becomes a
banal product taking its place among the normal domestic durable goods.

They note that a close link exists between the use of television and the VCR, characterising the user as a 'rational' television viewer and movie fan; yet surprisingly, no significant change in the amount of television-viewing among VCR users was demonstrated in the surveys. Examining the video-cassette market, they point out that 60 per cent of video-cassette sales in France are for pornographic films, the remainder being for 'classic' films and special interest films.

Knulst (Chapter 27) reports his research findings on media use in the Netherlands, stating that the nature and extent of media usage derives more from the characteristics of the users than the technological possibilities offered. This corresponds to the data in the Baboulin *et al* study on the nature of VCR-users, who come from specific sectors of society (30-35 years of age, in the management or professional class, married city dwellers and so on). Knulst indicates that leisure activities become more varied in periods of economic growth, although certain activities (such as attendance at public performances) have declined in absolute terms.

At a more fundamental level, de Gournay (Chapter 25) questions the value systems which we employ when selecting our free-time activities. For instance, she notes that the time a child spends playing an individualistic video game necessarily implies that there is less time available for other, more social pursuits. She points out that even the benefit accrued through knowledge and familiarity with the new technology must be weighed against the potential alternative benefit from the pursuit of other pastimes, like dancing or painting. Such thoughts serve as useful antidotes to the somewhat utopian fantasies of many writers when they discuss life in a leisure society.

In conclusion, the concept of leisure appears to be of limited usefulness in describing the observed changes in our society. The new information technologies have, and will continue to have, an important effect on the new services and products that will be available for recreational and entertainment purposes. Whether this implies that there will be greater opportunity for genuine human development and creativity is, at this stage, an open question.

Power and Control

The question of ownership or control of technology is raised by several of the authors, though rarely is this their main concern. It is somewhat surprising that this topic has not featured more prominently. However, the changing nature of our society, the break-up of traditional power blocks, the increasing fractionation of social groups, coupled with the emergence of pressure groups and 'single-issue' movements — all render it imperative that the nature and distribution of power in our society be taken fully into account in an analysis of specific technological developments.*

Garnham (Chapter 24) points out the degree of concentration of power in the 'cultural' field held by a very few multinational corporations:

> The culture industries are characterised by a high level of oligopilistic control, not only in national markets but across the world market. In the record industry, seven firms control 90 per cent of the US market and 70 per cent of the world market. In Britain, four groups control over 80 per cent of daily newspaper circulation.

One of the problems that occurs when the market is dominated by either multinationals or governments is that independent groups find it virtually impossible to affect the market in any substantive way. Indeed, the argument can be made that the market itself is an inappropriate vehicle for conveying the real needs of people, as pointed out by Bianchi, de Cugis and Falaguasta (Chapter 22):

> Needs must be distinguished from wants and desires, which express themselves in the market as demands. We can distinguish the pursuit of wants through the market system from the pursuit of wants through social policy; free markets take wants as given, whereas social policy must attempt to characterise the needs it is designed to meet.

This comment, that the market as it currently operates is inadequate, receives support from MacBride (Chapter 7), who notes: "It is not so much the consumers as the producers that decide what the market requires." Perhaps the most critical view of all comes from Robins (Chapter 5):

> Information technology heralds a further stage in the subordination of social needs and values to technological rationalisation and the logic of the market.

Whilst admittedly there are some opposing views on this question, they are not articulated by many of these authors. Perhaps Thompson (Chapter 8), in his discussion of a new information marketplace, comes closest to putting forward a positive view of the market, although he points out the major restructuring and rethinking required before such an information marketplace would become a reality.

We now move from the level of the marketplace to consider the use of power within an organizational context. Reference has been made to studies which show that management have tended to introduce new technology in order to further control the operation of work activities. This policy is in conflict with that of other groups, such as the trade unions, who have been increasingly arguing for more job autonomy and greater industrial democracy in the running of companies. This argument does not revolve around the introduction of new technology *per se,* but rather on the kind of technology and how it will affect current skills and employment levels. In this regard, it is

---

*The FAST Programme (Forecasting and Assessment in the field of Science and Technology) of the European Community has funded a study on the implications of information technology on the nature of power and participation in society, under the Information Society sub-programme. Details of the FAST Programme are given in Appendix II of this book.

interesting to note the increasing demand by trade unions and other workers' organizations for much greater participation in all aspects of the design of new systems. Such a participative approach is most advanced in the Scandanavian countries, although trade unions in other countries are increasingly adopting similar stances. The restructuring of traditional work patterns that this new approach demands will not take place easily. However, the failure of management to adapt will cause increased industrial unrest, resulting in increases in absenteeism and labour turnover, as Hedge and Crawley (Chapter 11) point out.

New information technologies do not of themselves give rise to the centralisation or decentralisation of daily activities. Some writers, in analysing the potential of telematics, have noted a possibility for greater decentralisation in the organization of work (Martin, 1978). A number of authors in this book point out that a distinction should be drawn between the delocalisation of activities and their decentralisation. The physical diffusion of activities (for example, working at home or in neighbourhood work centres) could, in theory, allow for greater decentralised decision-making (Espejo and Ziv, Chapter 17; Bannon, Chapter 18). But one is certainly not a logical consequence of the other. On the contrary, other writers note that telematics allows for the integration and centralisation of vast amounts of information, thus paradoxically allowing for the further centralisation of power and decision-making. What we can conclude is that the technology is not a barrier to the organization of activities in a flexible manner. Mattelart (Chapter 23) discusses this issue on a more theoretical note:

> Decentralisation is only one word but it covers a wide range of processes. It can mean an attempt to reorganize power structures in order to legitimise from the periphery rather than from the centre, from the micro rather than the macro. It can and does mean the search for new forms of expression and interaction and the search for new democratic forms. At the level of communications technologies, it can and does mean an active user, no longer confined to the consumer function.

Addressing the issue of power and control at a general societal level, many commentators believe that the need for flexibility in response to changing economic conditions will require a devolution of authority, forcing social organizations to decentralise. On the other hand, it is possible that continued rigidity will lead towards more open and direct conflict between social groups, undermining attempts to achieve social consensus.

CONCLUSIONS

THE DISCUSSION THEMES outlined have been selected on the basis of the authors' perception of the critical issues raised in this collection of writings. It can be seen that there is little unanimity in the method of analysis or the nature of the conclusions drawn regarding these issues. A few general comments may be made at this point concerning themes which were somewhat neglected in this collection but, in the authors' view, merit further study.

There is a lack of comparative data on the social effects of the technologies in different regions of Europe. While the majority of contributions state, or assume, that the rate of diffusion of information technology does not occur in a homogeneous fashion, this has not been reflected in actual research programmes. There is, on the contrary, a tendency to view societal development as proceeding along a convergent or linear path, not only within Europe but on a global scale. An integrated analysis, examining technological change in the context of different geographical regions, systems of production and cultural patterns (within an uneven process of economic development) is required if the specific nature of European development is to be understood. In this sense, the societal impact of technological change itself reflects the contradictory, unequal and, at times, polarized nature of social and economic development on a world scale.

This lack of comparative data is of particular concern in the Irish context, where research on the social impact of microelectronics is in its infancy. The size and relative importance of the services sector in the Irish economy implies that it is a particularly critical area for study since it is the key area for the diffusion of the technology.

The impact of information technology on particular classes and class factions receives relatively little attention in the present book. Contributions tend to gravitate towards an examination of different segments of daily life, such as work or urban organization, rather than towards an analysis of individuals within specific socio-economic categories. In this respect, the research project described by Scardigli, Plassard and Mercier (Chapter 2), which presents scenarios outlining the different possible paths which may lie ahead for European society, could form a basis for more particular analyses of specific European regions and socio-economic groups.

In one of these scenarios, inequalities are aggravated, tensions heightened and there is a risk of a more authoritarian state emerging. In another, the state intervenes to counteract class divisions and redistributes wealth in a context of rapid economic growth. The countervailing tendencies which would give rise to such contrasting developments are influenced by a wide range of factors, including governmental policies, corporate strategies, the level of public involvement in the decision-making process, social movements and overall economic developments.

Clearly, debate and discussion on the societal effects of information technology are in their early stages. The technology which is being examined is penetrating a wide range of current social practices as well as opening up new ones. Such issues as the content and organization of work and leisure activities, and the scope they allow for creativity, are of crucial importance in our society and will ultimately be determined by society at large, at all instances of social and political organization. Thus, it is extremely important that those in the research community and in administration make their findings and analyses widely accessible, at all levels of society, to encourage this critical debate.

References

Bell, Daniel (1973) *The Coming of Post-industrial Society.* Basic Books, New York (Revised 1976).
Braverman, H. (1974) *Labour and Monopoly Capital: The Degradation of Work in the Twentieth Century.* Monthly Review Press, New York.
Cooley, M. J. E. (1980) *Architect or Bee? The Human/Technology Relationship.* Hand and Brain Publications, Slough.
Gershuny, J. I. (1979) *The Informal Economy: Its Role in Post-industrial Society.* Futures, Vol. 11, No. 1, pp. 3-15.
Martin, James (1978) *The Wired Society.* Prentice-Hall, Englewood Cliffs, New Jersey.
Masuda, Yoneji (1980) *The Information Society as Post-industrial Society.* Institute for the Information Society, Tokyo.
Porat, M. U. (1976) *The Information Economy.* Ph.D. Dissertation, Centre for Interdisciplinary Research, Stanford University, California.
Robins, K. and Webster F. (1980) *Information is a Social Relation.* Intermedia, Vol. 8, No. 4, July.
Rosenbrock H. (1981) *Engineers and the Work that People do.* IEEE Technology and Society, Vol. 9, No. 3, pp. 14-18.
Toffler, Alvin (1980) *The Third Wave.* W. Collins, London.

PART I

Perspectives on the Information Society

There is much variety of opinion expressed by the experts on the nature and extent of the changes likely to result from the diffusion of the new information technologies.

Kimon Valaskakis examines the very concept of the 'Information Society', its origins and parameters. He defines a new concept of 'informediation' to characterize the process by which the new information technologies tend to become mediators in many spheres of daily activity.

Victor Scardigli, Francois Plassard and Pierre-Alain Mercier discuss the relationship between daily life and technology and then provide a set of outline scenarios, with alternative views both on the nature and significance of the impact of these new technologies in shaping European society.

A vision of the future information society is given in the short contribution by Yoneji Masuda, someone who has greatly influenced policy development in Japan concerning computerisation. This vision contrasts with the more pragmatic approach of Johan Martin-Löf, who describes current legislative and planning developments with regard to the new technologies, drawing from his wide administrative experience as chairperson of the OECD Working Party on Information, Computers and Communications Policy.

Kevin Robins elaborates a political perspective which places the new information technologies within the framework of a 'scientific management' philosophy, as espoused by F. W. Taylor. Robins argues that this logic has characterized the whole history of automation.

The health and psychological well-being of the individual is discussed by John Cullen, providing an interesting contrast to the more familiar approaches to the issues of technological change.

On a more general level, Sean MacBride highlights some major issues in the arena of international communications, drawing from the recent UNESCO report on world communications, and also comments on specific aspects of Irish social and economic policy. Gordon Thompson questions the usefulness of traditional economic concepts in explaining the nature of an information economy.

Finally, Kimon Valaskakis has prepared an extensive bibliography, which we have included at the end of Part I as a guide to further reading, particularly within North American literature on the subject.

CHAPTER 1

The Concept of Informediation:
A Framework for a Structural Interpretation
of the Information Revolution

Kimon Valaskakis

The GAMMA Group, Canada*

THE CONCEPT OF INFORMEDIATION

BY NOW, almost everyone is aware of the existence of a 'revolution' in computers and telecommunication equipment and has probably experienced some of its effects. This is particularly true in the First World where the so-called 'information technologies' are advancing by leaps and bounds. However, in spite of the near ubiquity of the chip and its wide penetration, the structural significance of this seminal event in the history of mankind is, to a large extent, missed or misunderstood. Strangely enough, it is the experts in the field, rather than the layman, who are more likely to wrongly assess the profound meaning of this major transformation because the experts are too close to specific applications of the chip to view the overall picture in perspective.

As a result, there are widely diverging interpretations of what the revolution is really about. In particular, one can detect at least three major views of the information revolution which differ fundamentally in scope and content. These various 'diagnoses' then lead quite naturally to diametrically different 'prognoses' and policy recommendations. The purpose here is to provide support for what is called the *structural* view of the information revolution by introducing the concept of 'informediation' and then using it as a framework for the assessment of its implications on the quality of life. As such, this is an 'issues' rather than an empirical discussion and purports to provide a new perspective to interpret the change society is going through. But before developing this concept, it will be useful to review the various perceptions of the 'revolution'.

*The GAMMA Group is a Canadian inter-university 'think-tank', specializing in forecasting and planning studies. This research was supported by grants from the Canadian Social Science and Humanities Research Council and the various contributors to GAMMA's ongoing Information Society programme.

The Micro-Sectoral Perception: The revolution concerns the communications sector

This view is understandably prevalent among people within the communications sector of society, who will tend to subsume the various innovations under the generic term of 'communications technology' and then appropriate the revolution to their field. This temptation is, incidentally, very strong in Canada because this country possesses an extremely advanced communications infrastructure and has produced (and is producing) world-class communications equipment, such as the *Telidon* videotex machine. However, the danger with this interpretation is that the communications sector, in itself, is usually a small fraction of general economic activity. This is even truer of the telecommunications sector — itself a part of the communications sector. To include the changes under the rubric of 'communications' may be just identifying the tip of the iceberg.

Another version of the micro-sectoral interpretation is to focus on some specific application of microelectronics technology, like office automation, new services in the home or video cassettes, and look at the entire revolution from that vantage point. The resulting perception will necessarily be narrow and much more of a worm's eye, than a bird's eye, view of the event.

The Macro-Sectoral View

Moving up the scale from specificity to generality, we now encounter the macro-sectoral approach which involves equating the revolution to the growth of one major sector of the economy to the detriment of others. This approach was most eloquently advanced by Marc Uri Porat (1976) in his pioneering study *The Information Economy,* where he defined an enlarged 'information sector' in the United States and concluded that about 45 per cent of the GNP was generated by it and that it employed over 50 per cent of the US labour force. The 'Information Society', which is the result of these changes, has become the rallying concept in most international studies inspired by Porat's approach. If information processing is the principal economic activity, then we are in a post-industrial, rather than an industrial, society.

While this view is very attractive, it is somewhat incomplete. If the essence of the contemporary transformation was the passage from a manufacturing to an information society, then that metamorphosis would be less than earthshaking. After all, there have been many information societies in the past and the event is not a novelty in the history of humanity. The ancient Egyptian religion-dominated society, fifth century Athens, medieval Florence, Oxford and Cambridge or Elizabethan England — all offer instances of societies or social units where information generation and communication in various forms was a central, if not dominant, feature of their activities. Surely today's revolution is significantly different from what prevailed in those societies in at least some respects. But what are these respects? What is the central indicator of revolutionary change in the techno-social sphere?

The Structural View: Changes in the modes of production, consumption and the way of life

The structural view of the information revolution is that it not only affects a sector or two of society, but it transforms its very roots. At the basis of societal organization is an economic infrastructure which is the result of the interaction between the technical mode of production and its socio-political manifestations. The technical mode of production reflects the state of the arts, the dominant technology and the attendant factor-proportions in the production function (resources, labour, capital and social organization). The socio-political manifestations of this infrastructure are the power relations, social hierarchies and ways of life embedded in that mode of production. When this mode is profoundly transformed, it has a 'domino' effect, altering almost all social relations.

In only two countries has the structural interpretation of the micro-electronics revolution prevailed, not only among intellectuals but also at the policy level. These two are Japan and France. Japan's 'Information Society' blueprint was first conceptualized in the 1960s and '70s. Since then, the Japanese have been faithfully implementing the changes which they continue to describe in English as relating to 'information'. One wonders what the exact Japanese term is and whether it conveys nuances and subtleties that the English word does not have. In the case of France, the key concept is not 'information' but the French *informatisation,* which literally means 'computerisation'. *L'informatisation de la société* thus conveys a structural perception which the sectoral 'information society' does not. However, even the French term is somewhat misleading as it lays too much emphasis on the computer side of the equation. In order to bring in the telecommunications side, the term *télé-informatique* or *télématique* is used (Nora and Minc, 1980). But once again, the sectoral pitfall looms ahead: many authors now make trivial the term *télématique,* as being merely the combined 'sectors' of computers and telecommunications rather than a society-wide 'process'.

Because of the importance of a structural view, the concept of 'informediation' was developed at GAMMA. It was originally coined by Fitzpatrick-Martin (1979), who developed its basic framework in a paper entitled *Social Implications of the Information Economy.* The present author is here enlarging on the original idea, with the usual caveats that whatever interpretations he advances that may be at variance with the original author's framework engages only his responsibility.*

Basically stated and as used in this discussion, informediation may be defined as: the process by which an increasing number of human activities in

*The fact that the original author is also my wife only increases the possibilities of diverging interpretations!

all fields, including agriculture, industry, commerce and communications, are being either *mediated* or taken over by *high technology information machines.* Three points require clarification here. First and foremost, the process of informediation is not confined to communications activities. If it were, it would be a relatively trivial concept, merely stating that communications are increasingly mediated and no longer direct — a true statement but not particularly surprising. Secondly, 'mediation' implies some form of interposition by the information machine which may go as far as the complete replacement of the human being. Thirdly, the mediation must be accomplished by information machines.

Admittedly, the concept of an information machine is not easy to define. Broadly speaking, an information machine may be said to process information and be teleologically guided by some equilibrium state or some kind of system-homeostasis. As such, the information machine is a cybernetic instrument with non-neutral feedback loops and is to be contrasted to a Newtonian machine whose *modus operandi* is controlled by the laws of physics, not logic. A Newtonian machine has levers and pulleys; an information machine has logic gates. The process of informediation is therefore different from ordinary automation. The capital-labour substitution is no longer mechanical, with energy-capital substituting for human labour, but cybernetic since it is now information-capital substituting for human endeavours. This point will be expanded later.

A final clarification to avoid making the term 'informediation' trivial is to emphasize that the information machine in question (whether hardware, software or firmware) must embody a high technology component. After all, a pencil is a crude information machine. To claim that we are being informediated because we write with pencils on paper, rather than with our fingers in the sand, is to so generalise the concept as to drastically reduce its usefulness. Accordingly, we are limiting it to high technology information machines only, which possess a cybernetic *modus operandi* and, by definition, exclude more primitive information tools.

Having defined the basic concept of informediation, its implications may be examined according to the following headings: its domain, extension, degree and scope, both at the individual and societal levels. From an analysis of these factors, conclusions will be drawn in the form of an agenda of issues to be investigated empirically in order to assess the impact of informediation on the quality of life.

THE DOMAIN OF INFORMEDIATION

THE DOMAIN of informediation covers the types of activities likely to be affected by the new technologies and, as the latter develop, its domain necessarily increases to encompass a broad spectrum of human endeavours. In this connection, the current technological revolution is in sharp contrast with the earlier ones. The nineteenth century Industrial Revolution involved a substitution of energy-capital for labour. Energy-machines (initially the steam engine and later, the internal combustion engine and electrical generator) began to take over mechanical and energy-intensive tasks, hitherto performed by human beings and domestic animals. Since the energy output of a full-grown man is quite small compared with that of other animals, such as horses or cattle (it being estimated that eight hours of physical labour would produce the energy equivalent of one horsepower per hour), the substitution was certainly a welcome one. Man has never prided himself on his physical prowess. As a result, the physical automation that ensued covered a limited number of activities, gladly eschewed by human beings.

What is striking about informediation is that it invades territories previously considered untouchable, such as activities involving the human brain. Indeed, the new information machines are now replacing three types of activities requiring cerebral input. The first is perceptual. Cathode-ray tubes (CRTs) and the other video instruments are extending, modifying and altering human perception. The second is conceptual. The pocket calculator and the desk computer are now replacing many of the conceptual 'thinking-type' functions hitherto considered irreplaceable. The third is motor, where robots are taking over physical activities requiring skill and co-ordination and which, again, were previously thought to be the sole domain of human beings.* A further point of interest is that there is no clearly definable limit to the expansion of this new domain. The older view, that computers will only perform trivial tasks and not thinking functions, is becoming more and more untenable — unless one defines thinking tautologically as something only humans can do. The new field of artificial intelligence seems to indicate that the domain of informediation is more limited by the human brain's inventive capacity than the inherent capabilities of computers.

This extended domain of informediation has two important implications. Firstly, it further emphasizes that an informediated and an information society may not be identical. For instance, an economy may be still heavily dominated by the manufacturing sector, accounting for a large proportion of the GNP, and yet be extremely informediated if advanced industrial robots do all the work. Indeed, one of the consequences of informediation might be jobless-growth in manufacturing, with information machines producing the output. Conversely, an information society possessing a strong information sector need not be informediated. A society of poets, artists, novelists and philosophers could produce and consume information in great quantities and high quality and yet use low or intermediate communication technologies, which will escape our definition of informediation. A poem on a scroll, a painting on a canvas, a paperback book or a philosopher's peregrinations do not necessarily require data banks, computers or videotex machines.

---

*I owe this particular formulation of human functions to my GAMMA colleague, Scot Gardiner, whom I wish to thank for his contribution.

The second implication concerning the domain of informediation is to cast doubt on the hypothesis of 'post-industrial society'. It has become very fashionable to describe our contemporary period as being at the threshold of post-industrial society. Now if 'industrial' is meant to describe a sector of the economy where raw materials are transformed into finished goods, then a move away from that type of transformation may indeed be termed post-industrial. However, if 'industrial' is viewed as any *process* of transformation, not merely confined to material goods, and if that process is defined as a mode of production involving high capital-intensity and above all high-technology inputs, then we can speak (as indeed many do) about the 'industrialization of agriculture', an 'industrial strategy for the cultural sector', an 'industrial strategy for office automation' and so on. In this context, informediation is a *new* industrial wave, not a post-industrial wave. Whereas in Toffler's *The Third Wave* (1980), the computer revolution is seen as the third important event in the history of humanity (agriculture and manufacturing being the other two), this alternative view argues that the computer revolution is a third 'industrial' wave.* The point is not semantic, it is substantive. At stake may be 're-industrialization' versus 'de-industrialization'. The Japanese are re-industrializing by using the new technologies in an industrial mode, while the Europeans and North Americans may be involuntarily de-industrializing by not quite realising the domain and potential of what we call informediation.

A perusal of economic history will, in fact, support the contention that microelectronics is a new industrial technology. There have been not one but many industrial revolutions in the past. In fact, whenever a significant enough change has occurred in the technology of production, the term 'industrial revolution' has been used. The passage from steam engine to internal combustion, from internal combustion to electricity, from iron to steel, from one-crop agriculture to crop-rotation, from vacuum tubes to transistors, from transistors to microprocessors — all herald minor or major industrial revolutions. Almost all of these changes also imply an increasing capital-labour substitution, with the human being progressively liberated from more and more tasks. The informediation revolution would therefore be the latest instance of capital-labour substitution, which is the very heart of the concept of industrialization.

THE EXTENSION OF INFORMEDIATION

IF INFORMEDIATION increases its domain, it also increases its extension, which may be measured in terms of time budgets. In other words, given a quantum of

*A description of multiple industrial revolutions can be found in David Landes' *The Unbound Prometheus* (1969) and in the works of the Italian economic historian, Carlo Cippola, who talks of the neolithic revolution as an 'industrial' revolution.

time available to human beings on a periodic basis (a day, a week, a month or a year), what proportion of that time is now informediated? This is somewhat different from the question of domain. Although more activities may be informediated, they may in fact take less time than previously, as for instance calculations with a pocket calculator. This may free the individual's time for alternative uses. In turn, some of these uses may be informediated and others may not.

What is needed is an in-depth empirical analysis of the temporal extension of informediation using time budgets, but with the proviso that the empirical investigation must be carefully thought out. Ordinary time-usage studies may yield misleading results because they often omit to consider the existence of multiple concurrent activities. For instance, it is possible to watch a show on television, while playing computer chess with a stand-alone computer and perhaps even carrying on a casual conversation all at the same time. How is this time usage to be counted? As human conversation, as passive information reception (the television show), as active informediation (the computer chess-game) or as all three? The time-usage study must probably be tempered and weighted by the *quality* of time use, including attention spans and dominant activities. In particular, the hypothesis to be tested is whether informediated activities are making increasing demands on our *attention spans* in a given time period or whether they are relegating certain activities to the threshold of unconscious automatic reflexes, thereby freeing our conscious thoughts for other endeavours. For instance, activities such as driving are, for the experienced practitioner, uses of time that do not preclude other complementary activities, such as listening to music, carrying on a conversation or enjoying the scenery. The more driving is informediated, the more these other complementary activities will be available within, of course, the limits of safety. In the case of flying, this point is even more striking. Computer-directed flying allows modern jets to proceed on automatic pilot literally from runway to runway. Again, the result of these improvements is to decrease the attention span required for a given task and make it available for another one.

The research strategy emerging from this realization is that studies on the extension of informediation should, in fact, measure attention spans in time usage rather than merely count the number of hours or minutes in a given day taken over by informediation.

THE DEGREE OF INFORMEDIATION

INFORMEDIATION, as previously defined, is the interposition of an information machine in a human activity. The degree of that interposition will affect the intensity of the attention spans described in the previous section.

Conceptually, at least four such degrees can be identified:

(a) Informediation: Degree Zero (Person/Person)

At this level, there is no informediation at all. There may be mediation by Newtonian machines but no interposition by high-technology information machines. Eating with a knife and fork, working with a hammer, writing with a pencil — all are activities of zero informediation, together with the totally unmediated activities of, for example, walking barefoot, talking with a friend or shaking hands.

(b) Informediation: Degree One (Person/Machine/Person)

In this first level of informediation, one or more high-technology information machines are interposed in a human activity in such a way that there develops a Person/Machine/Person interface.

A telephone exchange, a radio or television broadcast, an interactive videotex communication: these are examples of a flow of information that is mediated by high-technology machines. It is, in fact, this classic model of Encoder/Code/Decoder which has inspired the early information-theoretic conceptualisations forming the very basis of systems and computer theory.

The Degree One informediation is, of course, vulnerable to the distortions, or noise, of the information machine but, by the same token, the machine may amplify, embellish, emphasize or highlight certain informational inputs, thus improving communication.

(c) Informediation: Degree Two (Person/Machine)

This second level of informediation goes beyond telecommunications by eliminating the person-to-person communication and introduces instead a bilateral and autonomous person/machine interface. This specific interface demonstrates that the technological revolution is not merely a communications revolution. The development of stand-alone computers for home or office use, and the penetration of computers into all fields of human activities, make this second level increasingly prevalent. The researcher consulting his electronic data-bank terminal (affectionately known as *Eddy* at GAMMA), the hobbyist with his *Apple* or *Pet,* the chess player with his *Boris* or *Igor,* and the video-arcade fanatic shooting up the *Space Invaders* or the *Galaxians* — all are experiencing level-two informediation. They need no other human being for that experience which is complete in itself, a one-to-one relationship between man and machine.

(d) Informediation: Level Three (Machine/Machine)

The final and most ominous level of informediation is the situation where the human being is cut out altogether. What was previously a human activity is now completely replaced by cybernetic machines. Yet the activity has continuing implications for human beings.

Two classic examples will illustrate this third level. The first is electronic mail. Today, word processors are programmed to send form-letters to various correspondents, either through the regular mail or via the electronic route. We are at the threshold of a situation where communicating word processors will send form-answers to form-letters in a totally informediated mode of correspondents, with no human input at all.*. This correspondence, although devoid of human input, could lead to major decisions affecting humans. The second case concerns robots. A completely 'robotized' factory, including robot workers, robot quality controllers and robot supervisors, is an even more ominous (yet quite real) instance of total informediation of the third type. The next stage might be self-reproducing robots or 'Turing' machines, with potentials and consequences best left to the imagination, but already abundantly alluded to in science-fiction novels.

THE SCOPE OF INFORMEDIATION: WHAT IS THE IMPACT ON QUALITY OF LIFE?

THE MESSAGE so far is quite clear. At the heart of the contemporary technological revolution is the ubiquity of informediation, the emerging dominance of cybernetic machines and their invasion of all human activities. Central to this process is the importance of the person-machine interface. For better or worse, we will have to deal with cybernetic machines and the effect of that present and prospective interaction has only just begun to be fathomed. The catalogue of effects is wide and far-reaching but may be organized into five main groups:
 (1) The Technophobia/Technomania Continuum;
 (2) Reality Blur;
 (3) The Future of Human Labour;
 (4) Political Implications; and
 (5) System Vulnerability.

The Technophobia/Technomania Continuum

The range of possible interfaces between the person and the machine have been intensively studied at GAMMA (Gardiner, 1980 and 1982). There are two undesirable extremes and an optimum golden mean. The extremes are technophobia and technomania, with an ideal in-between situation of ergonomic symbiosis.

---

*A variation of this theme is the case of the professor who was tired of repeating his course year after year. He therefore taped it and sent out the tape to the class every Wednesday and Friday. One day, he was curious to find out how the class was reacting and decided to see for himself. What did he discover? A docile receptive class? No, thirty-five tape-recorders instead! His expected second-level informediation (his tape-recorder and their ears) had given way to the third-level — tape-recorders all round.

Technophobia is the adverse reaction to machines, a process of technological alienation, which manifests itself by full rejection or partial resistance to machines by their potential users. Akin to mathphobia, technophobia may be rooted in rational or irrational motives and may be experienced by either individuals or groups. Among the reasons explaining technophobia are:

(a) lack of understanding of how the machine operates;
(b) fear of manipulation by the machine;
(c) fear of replacement by the machine;
(d) fear of de-skilling;
(e) fear of de-humanization;
(f) fear of excessive dependence;
(g) fear of exploitation by the owners of the machine, if other than the user;
(h) boredom brought about in using the machine;
(i) health hazards, real or imagined;
(j) fear of imminent obsolescence of that particular machine;
(k) inability or unwillingness to break old habits and learn new ones;
(l) opportunity-cost of learning how to use the machine. The learning cost involved before one can use a new information machine might be extremely high in terms of time and effort. Poorly written operating manuals and unnecessary complexity in machine design may deter users from learning to operate the machine. Simpler technologies might be as effective and, therefore, the opportunity-cost of learning a new machine language may be judged as too high.

At the other end of the person-machine continuum is **Technomania,** an excessive love (if not lust) for information machines. A generation of 'techno-freaks' and 'computer junkies' may be one result of the spread of informediation, with attendant consequences as potentially deleterious as technophobia.

Among the causes and manifestations of technomania are factors often exactly opposite to the ones explaining technophobia, such as:

(a) blind faith in the power of the machine — the computer can do no wrong, any error is human error;
(b) discounting Murphy's Law which states that 'anything that can go wrong will go wrong': technomaniacs usually refuse to believe in that possibility;
(c) lack of attention to unintended consequences related to the use of the machines, such as health hazards or environmental deterioration;
(d) a proliferation of artificial and often semi-fictitious needs where the technomaniac develops an increasing dependence on the machine, believing it to be essential to the satisfaction of his most basic needs. For instance, the modern office's dependence on the telephone has now become so great that its absence effectively paralyzes the senior management. At the lower levels, increasing dependence on the word processor makes typists unwilling to use ordinary electric

typewriters, again paralyzing the office when the machines malfunction.

The happy medium of **Ergonomic Symbiosis** is a harmonious and effortless complementarity between person and machine. We have evidence that such ergonomic symbiosis exists in person-machine interfaces which preceded our contemporary informediation. The virtuoso sportsman (be he a golfer, skier, tennis player, hockey player or swordsman) learns to use the instrument of his trade in ergonomic perfection. This is also true of the accomplished violinist, painter, sculptor or racing driver. Why should it not be true of the systems-analyst, computer-graphics artist or electronic-music composer? Somewhere between the excesses of technophobia and technomania lies an informediation at the service of humanity, acting as an auxiliary memory or an intelligence-amplifier, a skills co-ordinator or a creativity enhancer. Some will advocate that every human being should develop a close and intense complementarity with his or her personal computer. Just as Jean-Luc Godard suggested in 1968 — that true democracy meant every citizen should have his film-camera as an auxiliary eye to allow him to experiment with his creativity — it is conceivable that, in 1988, a similar plea will be made for the personal computer which will then seem like another natural extension of man.

Reality Blur

Another set of consequences related to the diffusion of informediation is the increased probability of Reality Blur, which may be defined as a progressive blurring of the distinction between truth and fiction, reality and fantasy, actuality and potentiality. As cited in the previous case of the technophobia-technomania continuum, there are at least three versions of reality blur, two undesirable and one desirable. The two undesirables are 'fiction is truth' and 'truth is fiction' and the desirable one is 'optimum pedagogical simulation'.

Fiction is truth

The first version of reality blur is mistaking a fictitious situation for a real one. This has already happened with our existing media. The theatre in classical Greek and Elizabethan times had acquired a significance and influence larger than life. The characters of Hamlet, Othello or Ulysses are often more vividly embedded in the audience's consciousness than the next-door neighbour. It has always been the purpose of Art to enlarge and transfigure life and to achieve what is known in dramatic circles as a 'willing suspension of disbelief'. In a proscenium stage, the audience is asked to think of itself as secretly witnessing, through an invisible fourth wall, what is happening on the stage bounded by three walls. Only by this voluntary acceptance of the dictum 'fiction is truth' can the audience emote with the performers.

In the plays of Luigi Pirandello (such as *Henry IV, Six Characters in Search of an Author, It's so if you think so),* the reality blur is the principal purpose of the author who seeks to engulf the audience in a box of illusions. Similar intentions are found in Jean Genet's *The Balcony,* Shakespeare's play within the play in *Hamlet* or the Japanese *Rashomon,* which is a short story describing six versions of the same event with the true version never being clarified.

With the advent of high-technology media (such as the cinema, stereophonic sound and colour television), the fiction-is-truth idea has attained new heights. Children, even of adolescent age, will willingly suspend disbelief concerning the existence of their super-heroes (Batman, Superman, The Incredible Hulk, Spider Man or The Six Million Dollar Man). Grown adults too will let themselves be taken in. There are countless examples documented in North American research studies of television-viewers writing to a station to obtain medical advice from *Dr. Kildare,* inquire about *Mary Tyler Moore's* health or offer hypotheses as to who shot JR in *Dallas.*

At the extreme, 'fiction is truth' can lead to criminal activity. The attempted assassination of President Reagan in 1981 was inspired by the film *Taxi.* Many burglaries, violent crimes, rapes or larcenies are often seen on the media first and imitated in real life later. In the recent novel by Trevanian, *Shibumi,* the author refuses to describe in detail a lethal Japanese martial art for fear of indiscriminate imitation, claiming that a detailed account of how some paintings were stolen from a museum, described in an earlier novel, led to the very same crime being committed a few months after the book's publication.

With the advent of informediation on levels two and three, the danger of 'fiction is truth' becomes even stronger. The information machines are increasingly anthropomorphic: Boris the chess computer; Big Mac the word processor; Eddy the electronic data-bank processor. Already, one firm is marketing a chess computer with a robot-arm, another has created a flesh-like female playmate capable of performing certain sexual acts. With talking cars (the *Datsun Maxima*) already here, talking houses just around the corner and full television holography not too far away, all the ingredients for the complete illusion of 'fiction is truth' will be available. The breakdown of one of our most cherished distinctions, between Truth and Fantasy, may be imminent. The likely consequences, at this stage, are anyone's guess.

Truth is Fiction
The second version of reality blur is not taking a real situation seriously enough, believing it to be fictitious. Many documented instances of this have already been collected. Two examples will serve as illustrations:

(a) Television news broadcasts in the evening are usually preceded and followed on a typical night by various serials carrying with them the usual dose of violence and crime. It is small wonder then that when the news reports real violence, crimes or natural disasters, the viewers shrug them off with a reverse suspension of disbelief. This time, they refuse to believe the truth, preferring to switch channels and pretend it was all fiction.

(b) There have been many cases of violent crimes being committed in full view of hundreds of witnesses who refuse to intervene. Part of the reason for this is fear but another part is reality blur, where the witness is not completely sure whether he is watching truth or fiction. The long hours of television-watching have made him completely *blasé* about it all. He could not care less.

Optimum pedagogical simulation

As in the Technophobia/Technomania case, somewhere between the extremes of reality blur there is a desirable use of informediation for an optimum simulation of events. In particular, informediated simulation can be used as a very powerful teaching device to allow the student to identify with the actors of the scenario he is studying and to learn from that identification. What constitutes optimum simulation without the excesses of dangerous reality blur is, however, not easy to define and must be based on explicit, socially acceptable, value judgements.

The Future of Human Labour

The future of human labour in an informediated world is obviously a topic of the highest priority and would require a chapter to itself. Suffice it to say that, in the present context, informediation at level-three (i.e. machine/machine interface) raises the possibility of the total obsolescence of human labour. Whether this possibility need be viewed as a Cassadrian scenario or whether, on the contrary, it opens up a desirable vision of a leisure society — a sort of Athens without slaves — is too complex an issue for discussion here. The only conclusion worth noting is that the impacts are by no means predetermined and that unconditional pessimism is as imprudent and unjustifiable as unconditional optimism.

Political Implications

Similarly, the political implications of an informediated society are too wide to discuss here. However, the basic *problématique* can be stated as follows:
(a) Informediation is likely to seriously affect the distribution of power within a given society. Social groups may find their positions changed as a result of the introduction of the new technologies. In particular, the control of carriage and content, the issue of computer literacy, the differential impact on women and the control of the production and distribution systems are all extremely important topics to investigate.
(b) Informediation is likely to seriously affect the distribution of power between different societies. A New International Information Order may or may not emerge; but whatever happens, power relations between states are likely to be greatly affected by industrial advantage, transborder data flows, loss of cultural sovereignty, etc.
(c) Informediation is likely to considerably alter the political process itself. Ordinary representative democracy may well be replaced by a tele-democracy

(or a tele-dictatorship for that matter), where control of the electronic highway may confer control of the political process itself.

System Vulnerability

Finally, this brief survey of possible impacts of informediation would not be complete without mentioning the issue of vulnerability. Informediation brings with it both an increased dependence on machines and an increased interdependence of events. The degree of vulnerability of an informediated society has already been presaged by the vulnerability of our electrical society. Dependence on electricity, especially in North America, has rendered society extremely vulnerable. In the US or Canada, a prolonged black-out is tantamount to a disaster. The Great Black-Out of the mid-1960s demonstrated this vulnerability, where heating and cooling systems, lighting, mass-transit and communications systems all failed at the same time. Economic development brings with it a vulnerability which poverty does not. The US bombed parts of Vietnam yet did not subdue that country, because bombing the Ho Chi Minh Trail was an exercise in futility since there was nothing to bomb. On the other hand, a few well-placed bombs in about six power-generating stations in North America could literally paralyze the continent. The rich may get richer but they also get more vulnerable!

Informediation adds another layer of vulnerability to the electrical grid system. This is particularly true of the High-Interconnection or *Telematique* version of the Information Society (Valaskakis, 1979), where all systems are interconnected. It is less true of a decentralized, stand-along computer society with multiple built-in redundancies. The inventory of topics related to the system vulnerability of an informediated society covers at least the following:
  (a) threats of malfunction, industrial accidents and the operation of Murphy's Law and its many corollaries;
  (b) threats of natural disaster;
  (c) threats of sabotage resulting from terrorism or industrial disputes;
  (d) computer-fraud and embezzlement; and
  (e) external threats (hostile actions by enemies, war by computer error).

CONCLUSIONS

A CONCEPTUAL FRAMEWORK has been constructed in order to assess the social impacts of the information revolution — a framework whose central feature is the idea of informediation, with its domain, extension, degree and scope, summarized in Figure 1. Informediation carries with it a structural, rather than a sectoral, view of the revolution and invites the analysis of linkages, spin-

Figure 1

Informediation as the Central Process resulting from the Microelectronics Revolution

Definition: The process by which an increasing number of human activities in all fields are being either mediated or completely taken over by high-technology information (i.e. cybernetic) machines

Domain:
(1) Perceptual activities: video, audio, telecommunication instruments
(2) Conceptual activities: calculators, computers, artificial intelligence machines
(3) Motor activities: robotics

Extension:
(1) Proportion of total time spend in informediated versus non-informediated activities
(2) Attention-spans and intensity or consciousness in the informediated versus non-informediated activities

Degree:
Level Zero: Person/Person Interface
Level One: Person/Machine/Person
Level Two: Person/Machine
Level Three: Machine/Machine

Scope:
(Influence on
quality of life)
(1) Technophobia/Ergonomic Symbiosis/ Technomania
(2) Reality Blur
(3) Future of Human Labour
(4) Political Implications
(5) System Vulnerability
(6) Miscellaneous Special Effects

offs, spill-overs and unintended impacts. At the same time, it provides a principal indicator to monitor the many expected changes in the socio-economic system. Above all, it generates an agenda for research which is both wide and yet integrated, since it always relates back to the central theme of the interface between humanity and its latest technology.

Our preliminary assessment as to the impact on quality of life must necessarily be conditional: it all depends how the technology will be used. As previously mentioned, the prognosis is mixed, with both unconditional pessimism and unconditional optimism unwarranted. But, in the opinion of this author, although mixed, the balance is likely to be positive — perhaps in the ratio of 70 to 30 per cent, beneficial to detrimental effects. In the history of human kind, the latest quantum jump of informediation is yet another step in *Homo sapiens'* management of his environment. But this time, there are fewer foreseeable ecological drawbacks than in earlier industrial waves because information-intensive machines consume less energy and pollute much less than conventional machines. In some senses, informediation is both a Pandora's box of promises and threats and a Promethean hope of liberation from certain types of material bondage. The productivity increases, qualitative improvements and human potential of the technology will, hopefully, overshadow the negative impacts. But we must remain vigilant and take nothing for granted.

References

Fitzpatrick-Martin, Iris (1979) *Social Implications of the Information Economy.* Information Society Project, Paper No. 1-5, GAMMA, Montreal.

Gardiner, W. L. (1980) *Public Acceptance of the New Information Technologies: The Role of Attitudes.* Information Society Project, Paper No. 1-9, GAMMA, Montreal.

Gardiner, W. L. (1982) *Psychological Approaches to the Person/Machine Interface.* GAMMA, Montreal.

Landes, D. S. (1969) *The Unbound Prometheus: Technological Change and Industrial Development in Western Europe from 1750 to the present.* Cambridge Univeristy Press.

Nora, S. and Minc, A. (1980) *The Computerization of Society* (A translation of *L'Informatisation de la Société).* MIT Press, Cambridge, Mass.

Porat, M. U. (1976) *The Information Economy.* Center for Interdisciplinary Research, Stanford University, California.

Toffler, Alvin (1980) *The Third Wave,* William Morrow, New York.

Valaskakis, K. (1979) *The Information Society: The Issue and the Choices.* Information Society Project: Integrating Report, GAMMA, Montreal.

CHAPTER 2

Information Society and Daily Life

Victor Scardigli, Francois Plassard, Pierre-Alain Mercier

Centre d'Etudes Sociologiques, Paris

Laboratoire d'Economie des Transports, Lyon

IN THE LAST FEW YEARS, there have been many predictions that the development
and application of new electronic and information systems will give birth to
'revolutions' in technology and thus cause important changes in daily life,
leading to the establishment of an 'Information Society' in many developed,
and even developing, countries.

In specifying the potential impact of the new information technology, we
must avoid two pitfalls: firstly, an oversimplistic technological determinism
and secondly, an underestimation of the possibilities of change linked with
these technologies. The first danger lies in overemphasising the technological
characteristics of the new goods or services in terms of their impact on daily
habits. The second leads to a refusal to even contemplate a future world with
characteristics different to the present.

In order to avoid these two difficulties, a three-stage approach was adopted
in our study.* The goal of the first stage was to specify the areas affected by the
new technologies and to determine the habits of daily life most susceptible to
change. Since it is not possible to reduce the interrelations between technology
and society to a simple relationship of causality, the aim of the second stage
was to construct three models of interaction, describing possible individual
behaviour with the assistance of some particularly contrasting hypotheses on
the social penetration of the new technologies. Finally, the third step (in which
the actual scenarios are played out) attempts to integrate these three models
into Western European society in the year 1995, on the basis of hypotheses
about the political and economic evolution of these societies.

This research refrains from a projection of the future since it is unlikely that
any one or other of the scenarios described will occur. But the issues
considered during this study show that certain types of social, economic and

*The preparation of this research has been assisted by Alain Bonnafous, Anne Charreyron, Jean-Michel
Cusset and Daniele Patier-Marque.

37

industrial policies orientate European societies toward appreciably different situations. In this sense, the study could serve as a basis for defining the objectives of the various social actors engaged in the process of computerising society.

NEW TECHNOLOGIES AND DAILY LIFE

THE FIRST HYPOTHESIS of this research is that the features distinguishing the information society of 1995 will be arrived at by using already known techniques or a 'given technology'. But the question remains of defining how this technology will be applied.

The second hypothesis is one of a partial rigidity of daily life: it will not be possible in the space of 15 years to drastically disrupt the daily activities of individuals and families. However, certain practices appear, through analysis, to be relatively flexible and these are likely to be the most seriously affected.

The New Technologies of Information

The products arising from the new information technologies emerge at the meeting point of three technological currents. Firstly, the generalisation of digitalisation brings about a great number of new technological applications which appear strongly interconnectable, even substitutable. In the second place, the opening of new markets (specialised or general) corresponding with these innovations increases the possibilities of transmitting information. This increase in diffusion and circulation capacity allows for an increase in the quality of the messages as well as the multiplication of their number, the latter presenting a growth in the possibilities of choice for the user, the creation of new types of service or the installation of two-way systems. Finally, these advances have been made possible by miniaturisation, improvement of performance and lowering of costs. One may ask, nonetheless, whether these tendencies are of an exponential nature or is there not a possible slowing-down in cost decrease.

The technical advances mentioned lead to products arriving on the market with almost identical characteristics. Even though they are the historical product of three distinct networks (radio/television, telecommunications and computers), these products become very closely linked and even substitutable. This increasing substitutability of equipment and networks, all functioning according to the same logic, makes it particularly difficult to classify, let alone distinguish between, the new goods and services. The barriers that separate them become more and more fluid and questionable.

A classification according to the branches of origin provides a succinct presentation of the new electronic and computer science applications and corresponds best to the users' view of the new goods and services.

Electronic Media and Audio-Visual Techniques: This sector of radio-television already constitutes an important part of leisure activity and the numerous applications of the new technology only constitute a development of existing markets. The principal contributions of the new technology are an improvement in quality of programmes, multiplication of programmes, establishment of a market of taped programmes and development of two-way communications.

Technical advances have led to a development of the possibilities of reproducing taped programmes (video-tape, stereophonic and high fidelity), as well as an improvement in the quality of the broadcast and the reception of radio programmes. At present, the sound and visual quality of televised programmes is improving and, in the near future, the quality of the picture and comfort of reception will increase with the commercialisation of giant and flat screens.

The multiplication in the number of programmes is a direct consequence of the improvement in performance of the hertzian networks and of the development of cable networks. These developments can be seen in the increased number of national channels; at a later stage, this leads to an extension in the capacity of reception of sets, resulting in an exposure to more worldwide information and thus the possible development of cultural problems; at an even later stage, the introduction of language-specific programmes can be attained with the help of decoders.

The development of the mass media gradually transforms the television screen into a simple means of reproducing programmes, either previously taped by the users from televised broadcasts or put together by actors independent of the network or even self-made with a video camera. The explanation for the video-recorder getting off to a slow start in Europe may be the low proportion of European homes with colour sets and the multiplication of incompatible recorder standards. Most video-recorders continue to be used simply for the recording of televised programmes, to be replayed at a later time. As for the video-recorder — its characteristic of 'passive equipment' places it in the category of traditional leisure goods, similar to the gramaphone for example.

Technical progress has allowed the public to move from its traditional role of being a passive receiver to that of a broadcaster, either by access to the broadcast (Citizen Band, free radio and independent television networks) or by development of two-way systems within the network. At present, these possibilities of interaction are only used in a limited way. The new forms of communication now offer a greater choice of programmes, a system of payments related to the number of programmes and a possibility for the broadcaster to know at any given moment the size of his audience; eventually, this may lead to instant public referenda.

Telecommunications: From the point of view of the general public, the improvement in telecommunications began with the development of the network. Besides improvement in quality, new services are already available or will be in the near future: televised conferences, video and audio conferences and, ultimately, mass videophony. Other services surpass the framework of traditional telecommunications: televideo-alarm, telemetering, telesurveillance, remote control and so on. Faced with an underutilisation of networks, administrative bodies are trying to develop new services linked to the distribution of numerous apparati, such as telephone-answering systems, telecopiers and teleconferences.

Computers: A great decrease in the cost of hardware has led to the appearance of the computer on the domestic market. Initially confined to gadgets (small calculators, watches or electronic games), private consumption is now in the process of exploring the microcomputer. It will probably be used only for games at first; then other uses will appear, transposing professional methods to the home, for example, in organizing the household budget. Awaiting discovery will be other specific uses, of which we know only the areas of application at present (teaching, education, family history, etc); the specific content has yet to be developed.

New products arising from the fusion of the three networks: Three products, resulting from the simultaneous use of the computer, telecommunications and television, concern the daily life of households: videotex, teletex and the electronic transfer of funds.

Future implications of videotex are related to the worldwide interest in this type of communication, which uses animated pictures of the televised type. The transmission of these texts, displayed on the screen, necessitates an abstraction and weakening of the message. The future of videotex depends on its content (that is, on the social use which will be made of the process). At present, its content is being researched. From the union of the televiser and the telephonic receiver, a sort of world domestic terminal will be developed, permitting a form of direct communication, between the home and the daily environment. But it is too early to say precisely what the final form will be.

Teletex results from putting machines for the treatment of texts into contact with the telecommunications network. An analysis of the actual contents of the mail between private citizens shows that an increasing proportion is suitable for data processing (or is already processed) — for example, publicity or mailing material or the administration of banking correspondence. Leading on from this is the direct transmission of data, in the form of coded impulses, decoded with the aid of a domestic terminal or equipment available at the local post office. Here is an example of the eventual development of an office application to the domestic field. Mass telecopy and teleprinting are other new methods of correspondence, the innovation consisting essentially in the immediate, or semi-immediate, character of data transmission.

The electronic transfer of funds is one of the potential uses of the interactive videotex but it goes far beyond the traditional framework. The practice is already underway in the banking profession, with credit cards and systems of automatic withdrawal of funds.

Application to other areas of daily life: Miniaturisation and the low cost of electronic components has led to a worldwide penetration of computers (albeit limited) and telematics into numerous sectors of daily life. Such components are already solidly implanted in cine- and still-cameras, invading the area of toys, tending to transform the car and household appliances, thereby supplanting electro-mechanical programme planners.

This introduction should lead to an improvement in the working of various apparati, using generalised programmes based on more automation relieving the user of knowledge which has become obsolete because it is transferred to the software of the machine. One can also see that the apparati will be better adapted to various tasks that must be performed, thanks to the increasing possibilities of programming. If this evolution leads to an increasing ease of use, it will also mean a greater dependence by the user on the manufacturer who will determine the mode of operation.

The areas of application of new technology in daily life

So far, we have described the areas of daily life which are likely to be transformed by the new information technology. However, the relationship between daily life and new technology is not as evident as the promoters of the new goods, or even the authorities, would lead us to believe. In fact, with the majority of these products, supply comes before demand and the technical discussion on the characteristics of the products takes the place of any analysis of social demand. These technical arguments are twofold. On the one hand, since these new technical capabilities have appeared, it is necessary to utilize them so as not to be behind the times; on the other hand, their use allows one to do more, better and with less effort than before, and thus can only lead to greater happiness. The information society then appears as an extension of the consumer society.

Such singular references to objects are made without any reference to a way of life which is certainly one of consumerism, but which can only be understood when placed in a social context. This social context is made up of patterns of activity which have undergone great changes over the past twenty years and are likely to undergo further changes in the coming fifteen-year period, given the fact that they involve areas affected by new information technologies. Shopping purchases, leisure activities, transport and communications appear to be activities that are doubly sensitive in daily life: they are, on the one hand, the main target for the manufacturers of new equipment; on the other hand, they appear to be the aspects of daily life which are currently changing. If the areas of potential application of new technology can be relatively well seen, it is no less true that the daily lives of individuals and households are organized around certain structures which give it its coherence.

Shopping Activities: During the last twenty years, shopping behaviour has been profoundly transformed: the appearance of supermarkets, the disappearance of many small businesses and the longer term stocking of goods in the household, utilizing refridgerators and even freezer units. Although shopping serves to satisfy our fundamental needs (for nourishment, clothing, etc), the actual manner in which we carry out these activities is likely to change in the future.

It is important to distinguish between everyday shopping and occasional buying. The behaviour patterns of the former can be attributed to the composition of the household, the type of home and the kind of shopping centres or services available in each residential area. Mail-order sales have achieved an advanced level of penetration in the area of occasional buying, the area most likely to adopt the techniques and systems of video-distribution. This area is particularly indicative of likely future changes.

For a long time, mail order services were primarily aimed at a rural clientele, those far from large commercial centres and also less mobile than today. During the past ten years, one can observe a considerable evolution in the distribution of clientele by socio-occupational status: the most affluent classes of the population are now interested in this form of purchasing, one that they neglected over the last fifteen years. Removing the necessity to travel is considered as the most important factor by the customer (50 per cent), followed by the absence of the influence of the salesperson (34 per cent), being able to buy without being fussed (33 per cent) and economic prices (22 per cent). Compared to mail-order, ordering by telephone offers certain advantages: knowing if the article is available, being able to obtain appropriate information, thus avoiding ordering incorrect items, and the feeling of having a personal contact with the supplier.

Leisure and Television: The great reduction in working time experienced by Western European society has resulted in an equivalent growth of free time. Moreover, all studies carried out on a worldscale show that whatever the level of development and the forms of political and economic organization, 90 per cent of free time is devoted to leisure activity. Although the range of possible leisure activities is extremely broad, only a few are widely practised: television, radio, listening to records and reading. The choice of different activities is often simplistically explained: there are leisure activities for men and women or the way one's leisure time is spent depends on the level of education. Television, as an instrument of mass leisure, partially escapes these distinctions. On average, those who watch it spend about 2 hours per day. Only retired people and non-working women have a viewing time higher than those of other categories. It is important to consider whether new technology will give rise to increased television viewing.

Transportation and Telecommunications: The new technology is likely to cause drastic changes in the field of communications. These technologies are viewed by some as allowing for a renewed communication between individuals or groups. Others view the new forms of communications as a substitute for physical movement.

The appearance of new video technologies gave rise to the idea of a return to community living. However, by themselves, they are incapable of developing new communication techniques; witness the relative failure of a number of experiments with communal TV. It is impossible to discuss what this new world might look like, given that we do not know how already existing technologies, such as the telephone, are used. A recent study at Lyon showed that three-quarters of household communication concerns family or friends, whereas searching for information and reservations only represented a little more than 5 per cent. If this pattern of household telecommunications activity is reproduced in the future, the new technologies, such as the 'picturephone', will receive only limited use. As for journeys, the majority of those occurring in urban areas are related to work (40 per cent) and shopping (20 per cent). The new technologies of communication, allowing these activities to be performed from the home, can thus lead to a reduction in travel. This travel reduction can have different and opposing consequences. On the one hand, new travel needs may appear where others are no longer required: this would happen where the individual is socially adept, in accomplishing a certain number of things in given time periods. On the other hand, when the constraints of travelling to work or to pick-up young children disappear, a retreat to the home results. This is why non-working women without children, although young, have a behaviour pattern similar to retired people. The additional attraction of the television and the decrease in many outdoor activities may lead to a reduction in social relationships, especially when we note that, in the main, they occur at the same time as other activities and appear as optional.

An Integrated View of Daily Life: Viewing daily life with respect to the new technologies or its principal activities may hide the fact that, above all, it is a complex set of habits which relate to a certain value system. Changes can only occur if these habits are modified, thus affecting the organization of daily life. But from studies on the interrelationships between the daily activities of individuals, we know that there is a rigidity to these activities, making them less susceptible to rapid change.

It is clear that working hours structure the greater part of the day. This role of working time is replaced for the non-working population (especially women) by housework; these activities are spread out over the day — beyond what is necessary, as if to justify the presence of women at home during normal working hours. In fact, time-budget studies show that professioinal working women, with children at home, also have more outside-the-home activities than other women.

There are certain interrelationships between leisure activities, social intercourse and television viewing. Firstly, they show a certain substitutability. It is above all people who do not watch TV and who do not engage in leisure activities who take part in social relationships. Forty-one per cent of those who watch television engage in social activities, as against fifty-six per cent of those who do not watch television. The development of new patterns of activity linked to the diversionary nature of television viewing may well accentuate the impoverishment of other social communications which have already taken place as a result of the development of television.

MODELS OF INTERACTION

THE TWO HYPOTHESES presented previously (the existing technology and the rigidity of daily life) need to be supplemented with a third. While the technology of the products of the Information Society can be considered as understood, the supply characteristics on the contrary remain uncertain. The development of these technologies can only result from an interaction between the policies of procedure and the behaviour of users. Such interaction takes place in a wide variety of circumstances. The simplest methodological response to this difficulty therefore, consists in outlining several broad possibilities, models of interaction which will, in reality, be required to combine together according to circumstances or according to alternative hypotheses. Three models of interaction are presented and possible combinations of these models are envisaged, specifying four scenarios for Western European society. The models are described in the following manner: Model 1 (Integration) is distinguished by an active search for autonomy and for fulfilment of the personality by the individual. This attitude allows them to overcome the destruction of the social network of society and allows new forms of socialisation and solidarity to emerge. Model 2 (Disfunctioning) expresses the attachment of others to the way of life of traditional societies. These people retain their individual rights and their rights concerning the use of technology. In Model 3 (Subjection), daily life is invaded by the new technologies which are not controlled; as a result of this situation, communal life disappears.

Model 1: Integration

In this model, innovation develops in response to the needs of individuals who respond positively to information and microelectronic technologies in their daily lives. Well-off, educated, capable of using to their own advantage the possibilities offered by modern technology, they actively seek progress through market consumption as a means of assuming the modern relation of that individual with the world, with others and with himself.

This behaviour corresponds, on the supply side, to a general distribution of electronic and computerised goods and services, both in the form of networks and 'stand-alone' electronic systems. All these techniques produce free-flowing, quality information, which is quite responsive to the needs of households. The programmes are simple to learn and use; they eliminate errors, incorporate many diversified skills and take account of national and regional peculiarities. Without going into detail, it can be said that daily life in this model is characterised by a depreciation of domestic duties, the return to a new socialised existence and the emergence of the individual.

Certain duties characteristic of traditional society (preparation of meals, washing-up, child care) are endured as chores or drudgery, because they are not profitable, because they are not skilled and because they have no recourse to a technology which requires scientific and technical competence. To perform these tasks in the new society, individuals use all the resources offered by new technology; they hand-over responsibility for selection of meals and the storing of general information on family happenings to the home computer; they rely on the potential of TV and video to manage or supervise the children; they perform most of their shopping by electronic means.

This technology, far from aggravating the damage due to industrialisation and urbanisation, is used to compensate for this damage and to re-create a web of social networks and support. The new technologies can be used flexibly: teleshopping does not eliminate local commerce. In the same fashion, the telephone allows faraway family or friendly ties to be maintained and to keep local associations alive. Taping of TV programmes allows people to defer viewing and thus preserves family relationships. In this context, the individual behaves as a basic social unit of society. The new services and equipment give him the mobility and autonomy demanded by his new roles. Tele-information and reservation systems, available either in the home or in the neighbourhood centre, credit cards and electronic transfer of funds — all permit the individual to save time and also to organize his use of time while not having to worry about the constraints of normal opening hours. Telework in workshops near home and information retrieval capabilities in the home allow a minority of individuals to alleviate the separation of work life and non-work life.

In all these activities, the individual seeks happiness and personal fulfilment. But in this quest, he emphasizes those activities that he wishes to practice and knows where and how to find the information that he needs. This attitude prolongs the work ethic as internalised by industrial man; happiness and fulfilment of the individual are certainly the ultimate goal of daily life, but work (the accumulation of goods or services) remains the means of attaining this objective.

This model of daily life might characterise an evolutionary stage in the industrialised world. The hypothesis would be that all societies which are set-up from the economic order evolve towards a 'general technological-market, consumer society', where one finds an interposition of the technology between man and his physical and human environment.

Model 2: Disfunctioning

In this model, culture and technology form two separate worlds due to the refusal of individuals to fully rationalise daily activities and time use. Electronics and computing systems do not respond to a socially constituted need, so they remain 'gadgets' without real influence on daily life. Lacking demand, the new technology is imposed by the bias of a market which depends on the state. But the electronic networks, mainly centralised and specialised, are not always compatible due to incomplete standardisation. The computer programmes remain complex and abstract, with alphanumeric data predominating over more natural data.

In spite of the aggressiveness of the merchants on the supply side and of massive promotion, the new services hardly affect daily home-life. Videotex is hardly ever used for long-distance buying or obtaining practical information; cash money keeps its symbolic quality to the detriment of electronic forms of money and the spread of centralised file systems and electronic identity systems is accorded a hostile reception. These new services, although intended to make life easier, imply various constraints and a new attitude that very few households are ready to accept. The difficulties of access to information discourage many households, due to a query system that is too rigid in the formulation of questions. Besides, the responses are more suited to the needs of those who conceived the programmes than of the general population. Further apprehension and difficulties are felt by many households as they cannot refer to any existing habits or practices when using these new systems. In these conditions, lack of confidence in the machine means that individuals continuously verify information furnished by it and try to maintain direct human (non-mediated) contacts. Fear of computer filing leads to deviant behaviours, with some people not heeding answers given by the system and others knowingly furnishing false information to the system.

Another whole sector develops parallel to the official sector of the economy. It is characterised by a different rationale, one that is not computerised. The 'underground' economy takes up a large part of many people's daily lives and is totally free of control or direction from official sources. This behaviour results in a general return to domestic tasks, due to both the attachment of women to their traditional functions and to a desire to preserve family intimacy in reaction to the electronic invasion of daily life. The rationalisation of many activities gives rise to a hostile attitude which reflects fear of losing control of one's life and environment.

Although supported actively by the public authorities, computer-aided instruction and teaching (CAI and CAT) have limits which explain their slow development. The difficulties of access and poor quality of programmes (especially for subjects that are difficult to reduce to a simple logic) cause a lowering of educational standards amongst pupils and an accentuation of inequalities. As for adults, hopes that arose from the introduction of CAT into training courses have not materialised.

The domain of leisure activity reflects the suspicious attitude towards the multiplicity of standards and the apathy engendered by the repeated broadcasting of the same programme acts as a brake to equipping households with electronic systems and leads to a set back in the use of audiovisual technologies. The development of an alternative parallel sector leads to a search for leisure activities mainly outside the technical sphere, for activities in which all the senses are used and not just hearing and seeing. The search for a non-media-oriented lifestyle leads to a certain disenchantment with electronic games and a revival of clubs and neighbourhood associations.

Model 3: Subjection

This model is characterised by the primacy of supply over demand. The manufacturers create a demand which does not correspond to a socially constituted need. The new technology has transformed the population into uprooted, helpless, powerless individuals who passively accept this imposed 'modern' way of life. The individual is dispossessed of his traditional abilities by the machine: cooking, accounting, administrating, playing, learning. Excessive urbanisation and the destruction of traditional patterns of support result in a new reliance by the individual on his home, which is supported by numerous other goods and services. These goods and services develop to the detriment of traditional cultures, which are also being undermined by the standardisation of many activities and destroyed by the transfer of skills from man to machine.

The sectors of daily life, largely existing outside of the market up to this, are progressively integrated into the area of market consumption, leading to a global decline in the informal sector of the economy and to a reduction in real socialisation. But along with this growth in consumption, the new technologies bring poor content and tend to reproduce activities rather than assist in the creation of new ones. The diffusion of information technology activities originates in the sectors of consumption currently affected, leisure activity and household amenities in particular. In the area of leisure, they are used for automation, to facilitate or improve activities, rather than for creating and personalising activities. The computerisation of domestic activities is hardly visible so as not to frighten the user, who has not, as a result, any possibility of understanding how the new apparatus works or functions. These machines are programmed in an increasingly standardised manner which forces the individual to adapt to a new mode of consumption. This certainly helps to accomplish particular tasks and save time, but this extra time is usually absorbed by passive consumption of new 'mediated' leisure activities.

This model, is thus characterised by a separation between the possibilities caused by the consumption of new goods and services and a global level of culture, which is insufficient to allow individuals to master the concepts and significance of these new models of consumption. It implies a relation of subjection, incomprehension and passivity toward the new technology.

FOUR EUROPEAN SCENARIOS

OUR ANALYSIS of information technology and of the characteristics of daily life has allowed us to pinpoint several typical models of behaviour. This work shows that certain characteristic variables will determine the profile of tomorrow's computer society. Thus, the way in which family chores will be performed, the nature of the educational system, the role of the home and the separation between work and outside-work activities form the first group of factors that will play a determining role. But the passage to an eventual information society will be strongly influenced by economic factors. The scarcity or abundance of energy resources, the pattern of growth, the level of unemployment and the variation in State revenue will either encourage or prevent certain changes. Finally, the role of the producers of new information goods and services and the choice of State policies will be determining factors in orienting tomorrow's society in one direction rather than another.

The combination of these variables can give rise to a great number of scenarios. Only four are explored here, as representative of tomorrow's world. When saying 'representative model' we are more or less implying a caricature. The scenarios which we present are not to be taken as images of society which are realistic tomorrow. They are an attempt (without making any forecasting claims) to identify the social impacts of certain behaviour patterns and certain political policies. Two of them (1 and 3) are scenarios which imply attitudes of resignation or policies of *laissez-faire;* the other two (2 and 4) are impulsed by the State. Table 1 outlines the principle characteristics of each with a tentative description.

Scenario 1 — Crisis without change
Scenario 2 — Living with the crisis thanks to the new technology
Scenario 3 — Resumption of a new and vigorous growth cycle
Scenario 4 — Information society as a result of economic growth

Scenario 1: Crisis without change

General characteristics: In this first scenario, computerisation affects only goods for which there exists an obvious demand. Profitable sectors develop rapidly while others stagnate or regress. Leisure technologies, electronic toys, regulatory and surveillance technologies develop rapidly, but do not diffuse through the whole population, giving rise to great disparities (i.e. the dual society).

The Behaviour Patterns of different groups in the population: The behaviour patterns of the young, the retired and women particularly reveal a fragmented social structure. The persistence of widespread unemployment isolates a great number of young people for whom entry into the work force is becoming more and more difficult. Their low incomes lead them to develop other independent activities related to the new technology, such as Citizens Band radio — deviant

Table 1

Four Scenarios for the year 1995

Variables	Scenario 1	Scenario 2	Scenario 3	Scenario 4
Variables	Crisis without change	Living with the crisis, thanks to technology	Resumption of growth cycle	Growth towards Information Society
Growth	Zero	Zero	Upturn	Upturn
Energy	available but constraints	critical shortage	less dependency	less dependency
Work	high unemployment	high unemployment; equally shared M/W	decreasing unemployment	decreasing unemployment
Income	steady or lowering disparities	steady or lowering but reduction of inequalities	increasing disparities	increasing; reduced inequalities
Domestic tasks	mostly women	different sharing; new service activities	unchanged M/W sharing	relieved by the State and by ready-made goods
Educational policy	unchanged	spreads new values and social change	technological new elites	generalized familiarity with new technology
Home functions	unchanged	intensive sociability	unchanged	functional
Division work/non-work	identical	identical	evolves under technological pressure	evolves
Role of State	compensations	chief actor of change decentralization	liberalism	Welfare State and control of the inner market
Technological development	only profitable sectors	supply meets social demand	logic of supply	world logic of supply

and sometimes fraudulent use of telematic networks. These leisure activities do not involve official information channels for two reasons: the information networks are not intended for these young people and they ignore them more or less systematically. Although banking networks are well developed and easily accessible, they have limited access for these people due to insufficient income.

This leads one to a model of disfunctioning, where a few technological toys function in parallel with a whole informal system which provides young people with satisfaction of their essential needs and socialisations. The lowering of the retirement age for the purpose of freeing jobs results in a growing number of individuals with much greater free time available, but with less income than when they were active. This free time is largely spent on leisure activity, but income constraints incline retired people to domestic leisure activities, by preference, due to their low cost — television viewing remains the major activity, the use of other video-related services being dependent on income level and familiarity with technical equipment. Information networks are used regularly by the well-off to search for light entertainment. Retired people must use automated banking networks to collect their pension, but a continuation of their previous habits leads them to make large cash withdrawals.

The current evolution of the labour market reveals a bipolar tendency regarding women's work; on the one hand for reasons of security, more and more women are joining the labour market, but unemployment continues to affect them more than men. Therefore, a steady ever-growing number of women stay at home voluntarily or out of necessity. Those who remain by choice tend more toward 'integration' type behaviours, while those who stay at home out of necessity tend more towards passive consumption. It is active working women who have the most need to organize and rationalise their time, even more so for those that have young children at home. Their salary alleviates in part income restrictions and permits them to use electronic appliances. Their more limited leisure time reduces the importance of passive activities (such as TV) and the constraints of work or school lead them to participate more in activities outside the home, resulting in greater integration with these.

The Possible Tensions: This scenario of a society divided is based on tensions between generations and regions. The increasing use of electronic goods does not resolve the problems of work for the young and new technologies do not accomplish the integration of retired people. Autonomous, even contradictory, societal practices thus develop between these two groups and the active population. In regional terms, intolerable tensions may appear, especially in areas with high unemployment levels: advertising and business offer more and better toys and gadgets for use in everyday life while a significant number of people find themselves unemployed, feeling excluded from this social evolution in which they cannot participate.

Furthermore, as the use of electronics develops solely according to criteria of profitability and the marketplace, the difference in amenities between inner cities and suburbs merely reproduces the present situation regarding services and transportation. The rural environment will witness the mushrooming of country homes, fully equipped with electronic products and belonging to the well-off sectors of the population who belong to the model of integration (Model 1), whereas the locals with lower incomes and a more traditional culture will be excluded in part from this information society.

Scenario 2: Living with the crisis thanks to new technology

General Characteristics: West European societies have been solidly entrenched in a no-growth phase and the scarcity of energy resources remains a crucial issue. Rather than endure this situation, public authorities decide to take advantage of the situation to move towards new forms of social organization, mainly utilising the new technologies of information. These latter are no longer put into operation with profit objectives, but rather with social aims. This policy assumes a major intervention by the State and other key actors.

Daily Life: The division between work and non-work remains identical to that of today. But there is a willingness to share jobs more equally between men and women. Available 'manpower' is utilised to provide new services connected with education, child care and the aged — tasks which are not necessarily rewarded financially. Those who work do so in a manner quite similar to today. But the introduction of robots aims less at productivity enhancement than at eliminating more tedious tasks.

Education plays a crucial role because it is in the school that one wishes to spread the use of new technologies and to attempt to promote adherence to a new set of values. Energy scarcity leads to rationalising transportation — on the one hand, priority activities are defined and, on the other, electronic substitutes are widely used to reduce commuting. Public terminals (free or very cheap) are available at numerous places. Confronted with the difficulties in commuting, people set up social networks based on physical proximity — (blocks of flats, neighbourhoods, villages); distant relationships are maintained using tele-networks. Socialised child care develops. Electronic appliances are restricted to preparing meals. On the contrary, all types of energy-saving devices are used (heating control, use of electricity, etc). Leisure activity at home retains considerable importance, centering around the television and its attachments. Difficulties of transportation result in new life being given to neighbourhood and village leisure activities.

Tensions and Risks: Weak or even zero growth leads to difficulties in allowing more open access to the new technologies. This scarcity of resources leads to equipping densely populated zones before sparsely populated zones, thus accentuating present inequalities. Such general access to technologies replacing traditional activities leads to a generation gap. Difficulties for old people in adapting are attenuated by the help given them by unemployed people and specially trained people.

The most serious risk remains without doubt the major intervention of the State. The fact that it is the engine of change can lead as much to a totalitarian regime as to a revival of harmony. This risk of 'electronic dictatorship' can be avoided if autonomous intermediary influences are encouraged to emerge, thanks to the free circulation of information amongst all the electronic networks. This scenario corresponds, in the optimistic hypothesis, to the progressive and generalised diffusion of Model 1 to all social categories and, in the pessimistic hypothesis of Model 3, to more accentuated subjection.

Scenario 3: Resumption of a new and vigorous growth cycle

General Characteristics: A return to growth opens new possibilities for investment and allows a redistribution of income to take place. But the absence of social reform leads to the appearance of an information society with a new elite. The development of new technology leads to slight social mobility from traditional sectors to more dynamic sectors and a certain redistribution of power.

Daily Life: Daily life is modified by the deep impact of new technologies whose development corresponds more to the logic of profit maximisation than that of social demand. Work-at-home is more common but involves the mere performance of tasks while responsibilities are held in the firm. This 'working in the home' helps to overcome problems linked to the education of children, but women remain confined to their domestic role. Leisure activities develop rapidly under the influence of increasing incomes and more free time. Television attachments and related product services develop in an anarchistic fashion due to aggressive competition between producers, with programmes becoming more and more worldwide. Education of children and adults by computer-aided teaching remains unequal, its aim being to select elites needed by the dynamic sectors, oriented towards the world market.

The Risks: The risks are those of a society whose aim is to increase wealth. New products are circulated first and above all to wealthy sectors of the population and to the dynamic sectors which produce them. The cultural level of the population remains linked to income. There is a great risk of simultaneous diffusion of Model 1 in higher cultural level classes and of Model 3 (or better, Model 2) in other classes.

Scenario 4: The Information Society as a result of growth

General Characteristics: The upturn of growth permits an acceleration in the introduction of new technologies as much by market forces as by State intervention. The State, in contrast to the preceding scenario, plays an important part in defining priorities for industrial strategy and in the use of new technology. In addition, there is a definite willingness to reduce inequalities in access to these technologies.

Daily Life: The upturn of growth allows professional women to find a job. The extra wealth allows the public or regional authorities and associations to create jobs in the service sector designed to relieve women of domestic and child-care tasks. Technology is systematically used to reduce these tasks, both for families and for public authorities. The lifestyle of women in general tends toward similar behaviour to that of women active in the labour force. The traditional values of the woman at home are replaced by that of the organized efficient woman who uses ready-made and standardised products, permitting her to have more leisure time. Home is more and more functional and becomes a key place for the sending and receiving of information.

The shopping sector undergoes important changes. Stocking by tele-purchase and teleordering becomes common. The only sector which remains autonomous is that consisting of small shops which serve as last-minute 'emergency' shopping areas and for supplying goods needing viewing and fitting (fashion and luxury goods). The wish to have all individuals on an equal footing regarding technology leads to policies of compulsory study of the new information technologies, as previously was the case in learning to read and write.

The Risks: This type of society gives rise to an ambiguity as regards sociability. This scenario may indeed lead either to a focus on the family or couple or to a rise in the status of individuals, within a wide network of relations. The scenario also leads to an antagonism between the development of strategic sectors required by a logic of expanding world markets and the way new technologies are used by the State. One of the possible methods of resolving this contradiction might lie in the setting-up of two totally separate sectors, protectionist on the one side and international on the other.

CONCLUSIONS

THE SCENARIOS, briefly presented, have allowed the authors to highlight a few key points. Firstly, the tendencies in the development of society which we can observe at present are not sufficient to specify precisely the characteristics of tomorrow's society. Certainly, the length of the working day will be reduced and leisure will be increased; on the other hand, shopping practices which have considerably changed in the last twenty years will change even further. But, we have no basis to predict future behaviour patterns.

The choices made by different social actors will determine those patterns. First of all, the State, by deciding on its administrative, educational and industrial policies, will decisively affect the changes which will occur. Secondly, on the supply-side, the role of producers will be dominant. Finally, the social acceptance or rejection of the information technology will depend on the action or inaction of the consumer as a new power group.

There are three major questions about social practices which are impossible to answer at present. However, the changes occurring at this level will be a critical influence on the nature of tomorrow's society. What will be the place of women at work? How will men and women divide up domestic tasks? How will the separation of work and outside-work activities finally evolve?

CHAPTER 3

Vision of the Global Information Society

Yoneji Masuda

Institute for the Information Society, Tokyo

WHAT IS THE INFORMATION SOCIETY?

HUMANITY is at present in the midst of a societal transformation from an Industrial Society to an Information Society. There are two historical hypotheses for the Information Society. The first is that technology has become the axial force that has brought about the transformation of human society. Societal technology is epochal: it is a technology that has spread throughout society and from it a new type of productivity has rapidly expanded, with a deep societal impact, sufficient to bring about the transformation of human society. Historical examples can be cited — hunting technology and society, agricultural technology and society, industrial technology and society.

The second historical hypothesis is that the basic framework of new human society should be moulded by the fundamental characteristics of the new societal technology. It is precisely this new technology that is information technology. The coming Information Society will be unprecedented compared with traditional society because information technology is based on unique computer and communications technology, which is an invisible and non-material producing technology.

The prescription of the Information Society will fundamentally embody three special characteristics of information technology. Firstly, information is non-consumable, non-transferable, indivisible and accumulative; its most effective processing and distributing system is joint-processing and shared utilization by citizens. This means that information basically comes under the heading of 'utility goods'. Secondly, the value of information is to eliminate uncertainty and to improve the ability of mankind to make optimum action selection. Thirdly, the origin of the societal impact of information technology

55

is (a) replacement of mental labour (intelligent automation); (b) amplification of mental labour (knowledge creation, problem-solving and opportunity development); and (c) system innovation (transformation of the societal system).

The framework of the Information Society will be as follows:

(1) the information utility (computer-based public infrastructure), consisting of information networks and data banks, will become the symbol of society;

(2) the leading industry will be the information industry as a quaternary group and systems industries will be formulated as a matrix of the industrial structure;

(3) the political system will become a participatory democracy — the politics of autonomous management by citizens, based on agreement, self-constraint and synergy;

(4) the social structure will be made up of multi-centered and complementary voluntary communities;

(5) human values will change from material consumption to the satisfaction of goal achievements;

(6) the most advanced stage of the Information Society will be a high-mass, knowledge-creation stage, the final goal of which would be a Global Information Society.

The Global Information Society is not a dream

The Global Information Society is not merely desirable but a realistic concept of the ultimate stage of the Information Society. There are three powerful arguments for this assumption.

The first is that globalism will become the spirit of the times in the future Information Society. This thought is rooted in the global crises of shortage of natural resources, destruction of the natural environment, population expansion and the serious North-South economic and cultural gap. The second is that the development of a global information network, utilizing communications satellites and linked-up computers, will promote mutual exchanges of information and deepen understanding that will override national, cultural and other differing interests. The third is that the production of information goods will exceed material goods in total economic value and the economic system will change from a competitive, profit-seeking system to a synergistic, social contributory system.

GRAND DESIGN OF THE GLOBAL INFORMATION SOCIETY

A DESIRABLE AND FEASIBLE grand design of the Global Information Society can be boldly pictured as follows:

(a) *Establishment of a World Information Organization (WIO):* The main aims of the WIO will be to ratify an international treaty on the joint utilization of communications satellites, to formulate a long-range global information policy and to promote the standardization of equipment and software.

(b) *Formation of Global Information Utility:* Any ordinary citizen in the world will be able to obtain all necessary information readily, at low cost, at any time and at any place in the world. The participation of citizens in originating useful information and in forming data banks will be essential.

(c) *Development of Global Education System:* The level of literacy of the world population will be above 90 per cent and a universal world language, distinct from Esperanto, would ultimately be developed.

(d) *Development of Global Medical Care System:* This system would eliminate leprosy, malaria and other endemic diseases and the practice of birth control would become universal.

(e) *Simultaneous Resolution of Industrial and Information Gap:* The simultaneous introduction of sophisticated and carefully conceived industrial and information technologies would narrow the dual gap between North and South and would contribute indirectly to the emergence of a global ecosystem.

(f) *Establishment of Global Watch-dog Institute:* By utilizing inspection satellites and a world simulation model, early warning signs or trends toward global crises of human life would be quickly detected and the information spread accurately to all citizens at once.

(g) *Flourishing of Global Voluntary Informational Communities (GVIC):* Communities that have information space functionally bound together by voluntary information networks will have an important role in the Global Information Society. The most needed and feasible GVIC would be non-smoking, zero-population growth, anti-nuclear weapons or similar GVICs.

TWO MAJOR CHALLENGES FOR THE FUTURE

HUMAN BEINGS must bear and overcome two major challenges to actualize the grand design of the Global Information Society. One is the battle for Information Democracy, which is the most critical objective condition for avoiding Orwell's *1984* and to enable the desirable Global Information Society Plan to flourish.

Information Democracy consists of four development components. The first level of Information Democracy is the protection of privacy. The nature of this is negative — the human right to keep one's private life private from others. The second level is the right to know. This is more positive and it guarantees the right of citizens to know all kinds of governmental confidential information such as would seriously affect the citizens. The third level is the right of use. This means that every citizen can freely have access to all Information Utilities and Data Banks, at low cost and from any place, at any time. The fourth level is the highest level of Information Democracy — the right to participate directly in the management of the Global Information infrastructure, such as the World Information Organization, a Global Watch-dog Institute, and critical decision-making at all levels (global, governmental and local).

The successful establishment of these four information rights could pave the way to the most favourable environment for citizens to solve global issues voluntarily and to enlarge their own opportunity for the potential future of each person.

The second challenge to be met is Global Intelligence, the most critical subjective condition. Global Intelligence means the adaptative capability of citizens against rapidly changing global conditions. Intelligence is the human ability to adapt one's manner to the rapidly changing environment. It is an intelligence rooted in, and acquired from, the accumulation of knowledge and many experiences of failure and success. Thus, intelligence is basically the capability of rational selection of human action in solving problems. Intelligence starts at the personal level and develops to the higher and wider level of group intelligence. Among a group, personal intelligence will be combined and harmonized toward the common goal of changing the social environment. This is Social Intelligence.

The final developmental stage would be Global Intelligence. This would be acquired on the mutual global understanding, recognition and mission, directed toward the solution of global problems. If ordinary citizens, living in different states and belonging to different cultures, can adopt the same manner and action for a specific global problem, it means Global Intelligence is at work. For example, if people could quit smoking and eliminate lung cancer, by their own self-awareness and self-regulation rather than by enforcement of law and power, this would be a real actualization of Global Intelligence. In Industrial Society, there is no absolute need for such intelligence because, fundamentally, material consumption does not need that kind of human ability, which belongs in the realm of social instincts. The only thing that matters in an industrial society is how to develop the purchasing power of the consumer.

The emphasis on the importance of Information Democracy and Global Intelligence cannot be too great for attaining the future desirable and feasible Global Information Society.

CHAPTER 4

Some Policy Issues in the International Debate

Johan Martin-Löf

Ministry of Industry, Sweden

Information Technology Development — how it drives the issues

There is a very rapid development in microelectronics which improves the capacity of computers and also impacts on telecommunications. Computers have taken over more and more human activities, starting with the handling of numbers. This first happened in science and engineering, then crept into our administration, control of communications and process control, and right now, it is penetrating the manufacturing industry.

Computers have taken over our words — starting with information retrieval as one of the first major applications, they have reformed printing and are now coming into the office in the form of office automation.

Computers have taken care of our images — first by recognizing or analysing our images, a typical application being character recognition. Machines can read the bottom line of cheques and perform medical analysis of X-ray pictures; remote sensing of the earth is based on very powerful and complicated image analysis. Another application is the generation of images, for example the generation of artificial pictures of things that exist only in software. You can look at an object that does not exist except in the mind of the designer and you can use image generation to operate control systems. For example, there are aircraft pilots flying into a completely synthetic world: they can land on an airfield that is not visible except on their screens and when they come down through the clouds it is actually there.

Finally, the computer can take over our voice; voice input into computer information systems is underway, as is voice output. This has important applications in education and in aids for the handicapped.

All these applications have impacts on society and the individual. With the rapid development of electronics, the impacts of this technology have many facets and the timescale is different in each case. In contrast to computers, the human capacity for information processing remains fairly constant; we have eyes, ears and hands whose capacity will not develop very much. But the capacity of the human memory is still very impressive in comparison to present-day memory technology.

The Public Debate

Technological development leads to promises — there will be new opportunities for the development of goods and services. But we also perceive threats because our existing structures are in danger and the human being has always felt threatened by changes, especially rapid ones. The threats look far more real than the promises. It is fairly simple to examine a branch of industry and say what particular sectors, companies and individuals will be affected by technical change. It is also easy to pinpoint and make credible the jobs that will be affected. The promises are far more difficult to visualize because the whole innovation must be projected in order to say that in five years, we will have an industry in a particular place producing a new product. Thus, the critics have an easier task in substantiating their criticism than the promoters have in furthering their cause, because the latter is inherently more elusive. A further aspect is that promoters can often be suspected of having a vested interest in encouraging development. Alas, we live in a world of sensationalism — an information world where those who cry loudest get the headlines and, no doubt, the negative aspects get better headlines than the positive ones.

The general economic effects of the development of information technology have attracted much interest. It seems clear from marco-economic studies at the national level that the effects have been minor compared to those resulting from other issues, such as energy prices, general world recession, gloomy economic conditions and so on.

If we proceed to the micro-economic level, it is quite clear that productivity is greatly improved in some sectors. Particular sectors will be hit at different times by the onrush of the new technologies. And in those sectors, employment changes may be large. But this is a sort of 'spotty' effect which will appear from time to time in different sectors. There are some typical international examples: the watch-making industry was hit by the micro-chip almost overnight, similarly the mechanical cash-register industry.

As a general observation, many theoretical studies may be too simplistic if they neglect secondary effects. If, in the present set-up of an enterprise, you change one element (for example, the replacement of office typewriters by word processors), you may easily predict rather dramatic changes. But in actual fact, the primary change generates other side-effects which will often counteract the initial effects to an extent which is hard to predict. An example of this is the banking sector in Sweden, which has been heavily computerised over the past 15 to 20 years, with minor employment impacts, although productivity has risen dramatically. One key reason for this is that the banks have taken on a lot more work and executed it more profitably than before. Similarly with office automation — not only can you continue the office functions of yesterday, but this new equipment also provides opportunities to innovate. It is thus important to avoid simplistic forecasts.

Unemployment is a very serious issue, placing certain groups in society more at risk than others, such as the old, the unskilled and women. Women, particularly, seem to be in danger because they are concentrated in certain professions, more so than male labour. So, the preoccupation tends to centre on those groups. As long as we live in a competitive society with open trading, we are subject to competition and cannot shut our eyes to the new technologies — we had better try to employ them. The employment effects will be worst for those who neglect the new technologies. A general observation is that the gloomy economic outlook will, of course, make people in general sceptical to any change — good or bad.

Is the present development of Information Technology different from other types of technological changes in the past, or are we suffering from what has been termed temporal provincialism? Are we sitting down and thinking 'never before has humanity been subject to such intense pressures as today'? Are we just ignoring historical facts or is it really very different? These questions we must ask ourselves. The author does not venture the answers!

Issues in the International Debate

The United Nations is working on information technology in a very general sense. UNESCO is working on cultural aspects. The International Labour Organization (ILO) is studying the impacts of technology on the labour market. The Council of Europe is interested in the human rights' aspects of the new technology. The World Intellectual Property Organization (WIPO) is studying the intellectual property rights to software and programmes and how to protect such rights in this field. The Intergovernmental Bureau ot Informatics (IBI) is a step-child of UNESCO, comprising some 30 mostly developing countries, and is working towards creating awareness of the need for information policies in the Third World. They are planning a Conference in Cuba in June 1983. The International Telecommunications Union (ITU) works for the just distribution of communications channels. CEPT is the European Conference for Postal and Telecommunications Administrations, who are co-operating to develop our infrastructures. And there are also many non-governmental organizations, like the International Chambers of Commerce, trade unions and so on, who are working on information technology.

The OECD has been very active in this field. OECD membership comprises the European Communities, other Western European States, the USA, Canada, Japan, Australia and New Zealand. In essence, these countries form a group where information technology has become very important. Thus, the OECD is an appropriate discussion forum on new information technologies.

OECD work started in the Committee for Scientific and Technological

Policy (CSTP), which has been in existence for a long time. The CSTP started working in the information field in the 1960s by setting-up the IPG (Information Policy Group) in 1965 and the CUG (Computer Utilisation Group) in 1969. These two groups were merged into one Working Party on Information Computers and Communications Policy (ICCP) — a title which demonstrates that the English language lacks a word such as *telematique*. The author has had the privilege of chairing ICCP since it started. The Secretary-General of OECD has recently proposed that this Working Party be given committee status, a question which should be settled in the near future.

Economic analysis of information activities

An early study, started in 1977, by the ICCP was on the subject of the Economic Analysis of Information Activities. The results of this project have been published by the OECD. The study was an attempt to measure precisely the economic and employment impact of the implementation of information technology. An attempt was made to define what was called the Information Sector, by examining national employment statistics and taking out those people who produce information, process and distribute it, and those who manage the infrastructure. Admittedly, this is a wide definition and encompasses much more than those who deal directly with computers and telecommunications as much information handling is still done manually. But the value of the study lies in its being carried out on an international basis, using a common definition. The main observations were that an average increase had occurred of 6 per cent in information occupations over ten years and that nearly half of the economically active could be said to be working in the information sector. (The figures vary from country to country, between 25 and 50 per cent.) Another main conclusion of the study showed that the analysts could find no evidence that information goods and services would be an important factor in final demand; this means that households (the final consumers) were not seen as a major buying force for information technology in the 1980s to drive our economies.

A graph included in the report shows the share of information occupations over 25 years from 1950 to 1975 from about a dozen OECD countries. There is a steady increase which seems to be uniform over the whole OECD area. The absolute values can be debated since they depend on definitions of the information sector; but still, it is interesting to note the comparison betwen countries, with the US, UK and Canada fairly high on the scale, followed by Sweden, France, West Germany and Austria, Japan and Finland. However, this survey does not cover the whole of the OECD. Another graph from the study depicts the relative size of the sectors dealing with information, services, industry and agriculture. Tendencies seem to be quite uniform; the information and services sectors are growing, while the industrial and agricultural sectors are shrinking, the latter, very dramatically in several countries. Setting the information sector side-by-side with these others may seem somewhat artificial. It is, after all, a sector which straddles the others; but such a computational effort indicates the extent of our march into the information society.

Working conditions

Information technology has the advantage of eliminating many jobs that people do not want to do. But it may also create new jobs which are just as boring, monotonous and give people little satisfaction. Thus, planning the organization of jobs and the working environment is very important when new technologies are being introduced. Their arrival may reveal old deficiencies in an organization. The whole planning process should include employee participation since it is in the designer's best interest to take care of all the detailed skills that are present in an organization and this participation requires education. In other words, planning from the top down is too simplistic — a dialogue is needed between employer and employees.

Privacy

Privacy of the individual has been evoked as an issue in recent years due to the large administrative systems needed to deal with social security, taxation, medical care and so on. A particular issue has been the growing linkage between the public and the private systems. Another issue currently emerging is the risk or the possibility of monitoring the employee in his workplace. The new machines are powerful when it comes to collecting statistics on the individual's work performance.

There is now privacy legislation in several countries and draft bills in others. Such legislation really needs to be tailored to the national background. The attitude of those registered is another issue being brought into this question of legislation. The OECD has completed a negotiation to produce national guidelines for law-making in this area. The guidelines have been adopted by all OECD countries, except Australia, Canada and Ireland. The guidelines have the character of non-binding recommendations, attempting to strike a balance between the need for a free flow of information and the need to protect the privacy of the individual. It is important to view this as a dynamic area. Technology is rushing forward. The present-day legislation and guidelines are by no means a permanent solution and will need further discussion.

Vulnerability

Today, many critical societal functions are computerised. It is fairly easy to put a computer or a communications system out of operation or mishandle it.

This vulnerability is an issue in Sweden, where a number of external factors have been isolated, such as catastrophes, accidents, criminal acts and fraud, but also threats from political pressure groups. Such groups have blown up computer centres in France and Italy, purely to show their dislike of these symbols of the capitalistic system.

A large number of internal factors also contribute to the vulnerability of today's computerised society, such as the risk factor tied to confidential registers, the functional sensitivity of computers and their high concentration in particular areas. An electricity black-out in a capital city will shut down the majority of state functions. This has been highlighted recently in Tokyo. There is also a trend to integrate systems so that they depend on each other — thus, a difficulty in one system spreads like wildfire to the others. A large amount of data on all sorts of things are accumulated and this raises the question of privacy. It is clear that there is insufficient educational knowledge in many systems. The quality of hard- and software is sometimes deficient. The operation of a system may depend on a few key people, whose absence may mean disaster to the system. Documentation is often faulty, emergency plans deficient and there is an inevitable dependence on foreign suppliers for spares. Disturbance in trade may thus be quite a problem.

Transborder data flows

The transborder data flows of non-personal information is an emerging area of issues for debate in the OECD in the 1980s. One aspect is the trade in information bought and sold to data banks. There are systems which provide special services, like the SITA for airlines and the SWIFT fund transfer system for banks.* International trade in computer services is increasing rapidly with inter-company transactions and intra-company traffic within large international enterprises.

The basic objective is to protect the free-flow of information and to remove any barriers to this process. But there are some international preoccupations which should be remembered, such as national sovereignty (loosely defined) — if a very important part of a system is out of the country, is national sovereignty being eroded? There is a security aspect — if significant parts of the system are abroad, what if something happens such as a strike? Some governments are concerned that when data are transferred to other countries, jobs are also transferred and lost to the home market. And finally, the issue of privacy is always present. OECD work in the future on trade and services is going to be influenced to some extent by transborder data flows.

---

*International Society of Aeronautical Telecommunications (SITA); Society for Worldwide Inter-bank Financial Telecommunications (SWIFT).

Towards the future

It is obvious that information technology is penetrating all aspects of working life. There are also many technological possibilities on the domestic front but a major breakthrough remains to be seen here. The domestic market is a capricious one, for example the market for video-cassette recorders (VCRs) was dormant for a long time but has suddenly blossomed.

The speed of introduction will be dictated by the technical possibilities as well as the economic and social factors with the complicated interplay between them. International language and cultural barriers will remain. The bright future information society, described in Chapter 3, will first have to overcome such barriers. In conclusion, the author feels that information technology will develop more slowly than its promoters hope but that it will not be as bad as its critics fear.

CHAPTER 5

New Technology — The Political Economy of General Ludd

Kevin Robins

Department of Languages and Cultures, Sunderland Polytechnic, UK

A CRITICAL ATTITUDE is adopted here to information technology, a response that invokes provocatively, but seriously, the maligned name of Ned Ludd. There is a need to move behind the bland and abstract concept of Information Technology (IT) to the political and economic realities (both national and international) that are its essence. There is also a need for an adequate theoretical approach to technology, which entails the situating of current developments within the social history of technology in capitalist societies. On this basis, IT is seen not in terms of futurist utopias and technological revolutions, but as the culmination, on a social scale, of processes (rationalisation, the separation of mental from manual labour) set in motion by Taylor and Ford. It represents a further stage in the subordination of social needs and values to technological rationalisation and the logic of the market.

THE IDEOLOGIES OF FUTURISM AND POST-INDUSTRIALISM

THE REAL ISSUES underlying Information Technology (IT) have been clouded by an opportunistic surge of futuristic paperbacks and journalism, predicting the advent of a 'silicon civilisation', an 'information age'. In these texts, we are told that microelectronics offers solutions to the problem of administering complex societies; to the question of political participation (via the 'electronic plebiscite'); to ecological problems; to poverty and inequality (making "the humanistic dream of universal affluence and freedom from drudgery a reality", according to Christopher Evans). Technology provides an answer to the severe economic, political and social problems of the 1980s. IT provides

66

the infrastructure for a new decentralized, democratic and harmonious society that fully values the individual. Social ills may be remedied by more, and ever more, communication and/or information (Robins and Webster, 1981a).

Two intellectual strands sustain and inform this literature. The first, which has a long history, has been called "the rhetoric of the electrical sublime" (Carey and Quirk, 1970). This tradition of 'secular religiosity', anticipating a future electronic golden age, found its most celebrated exponent in McLuhan, the advocate of an "electronic integrated world" wherein there would be a "pentecostal condition of universal understanding and unity". The McLuhanite faith and rhetoric has received a great boost from IT. It is now easier to argue that we increasingly live in a 'shrinking world': in every sense, man around the world is again similar to primitive man in a single tribe, since 'accessibility' of information is almost universal (Higman, 1979). And the head of *Prestel,* no less, can argue "that telecommunications development will lead to increased interpenetration, increased interdependence, tending towards McLuhan's 'global village', towards the planetary 'common brain' of Teilhard de Chardin" (Reid, 1978).

The second intellectual current is the more technocratic and managerial theory of post-industrialism, centrally associated with the work of Daniel Bell. Bell (1979) argues that post-industrial society (which he also calls the 'information society') is marked by the centrality of knowledge/information: "Knowledge and information are becoming the strategic resource and transforming agent of the post-industrial society." Moreover, innovation and change now derive from the codification of theoretical knowledge. For Bell, IT is the crucial lever of planned social control and change, the key to managing and administering complex societies: "The computer is a tool for managing the mass society, since it is the mechanism that orders and processes the transactions whose huge number had been mounting almost exponentially because of the increase in social interactions" (*ibid*).

THE REALITY OF MULTINATIONAL CORPORATIONS

BEHIND FUTURIST ACCOUNTS, there is a reality seldom mentioned but which undermines both millenarian and technocratic optimism — the reality of multinational corporations (like IBM, AT&T, RCA, Xerox, as well as oil giants like Exxon), who are engineering the 'information revolution'. As traditional industrial sectors — telecommunications, computing, electronics — converge, so large corporations, hitherto operating in discrete areas, become locked together in turmoil like a nest of vipers. The struggle is unleashed to lay the 'information infrastructure' that will underpin the 'electronic home' and the 'office of the future'. The prizes are rich. It is not possible, or necessary in the context of this discussion, to give details of this economic struggle (Robins and Webster, 1979 and 1981a). The important point is to ask, given the overwhelming presence of multinationals, in whose interests and for what purposes is Information Technology being developed? The past history of these corporations gives little promise that they will have democratic interests at heart in the future. Their goal is profit maximisation and market dominance. Against the futurists and post-industrialists, Schiller (1981) points out that "contrary to the notion that capitalism has been transcended, long-prevailing imperatives of a market economy remain as determining as ever in the transformations occurring in the technological and informational spheres." For the likes of IBM, IT represents just another series of exchange-values which by no means correspond to real social needs. It is necessary, then, to contest Parker's belief (1976) that "the issue is not who owns or operates the hardware facilities. the issue is whether the facilities, however owned, are accessible for use by all members of the society." the issue, in fact, lies not in the *use* of technologies, but in their *constitution.* IT has been shaped by multinational corporations — without democratic participation and consultation — to express specific corporate values and priorities. There is no reason to believe that IT will not reinforce, and aggravate, existing inequalities at both the national and international levels.

CRISIS, TECHNOLOGY AND CAPITALIST PLANNING

THIS CURRENT PROCESS of corporate restructuring is not occurring in a vacuum, but in the context of economic recession and crisis. Faced with the decline of manufacturing industries (notably automobiles) and their re-location in Third World countries, metropolitan capitals are turning to IT as the basis of a new and profitable cycle of accumulation (in both capital and consumer goods). As such, it is important not to consider Information Technology in isolation: it is one of a number of new technologies, including nuclear power and biotechnology, that will form the basis of superprofits in the 1980s and beyond.

The motive force for this economic reorganization comes from the multinationals and the iron logic of capitalist growth. But, increasingly, it is orchestrated by state mechanisms, anxiously striving to co-ordinate an economic uplift. Within this process of crisis-management, technology plays an even more important role as the development of science and technology represents an increasingly important counteracting influence to the tendency towards crisis and collapse in the developed capitalist countries. Technology becomes in fact the privileged mode for resolving economic stagnation and social tensions, insofar as it materialises new cycles of consumption. The state — in its Keynesian form, as planner — becomes integrally involved both in the orchestration of production and consumption, and in the financing, co-ordination and planning of technological growth, indeed in the very shaping and constitution of technologies. This has an important implication: "The acceleration of scientific and technological progress forced by developed capitalism's tendency to crisis signifies an increase in the pace of the development of the productive forces and rapidly advances the socialisation of production" (Hirsch, 1978). There is a complex interrelation of technological development and this socialisation of production (as social capital), with the state playing a key role. According to Panzieri (1980):

> The capitalist development of technology, as it passes through the various stage of rationalisation, involves more and more sophisticated forms of integration – a continual growth of capitalist control. The basic factor in this process is the continued growth of constant capital with respect to variable capital. In contemporary capitalism, as is well known, capitalist planning expands enormously with the transition to monopolistic and oligopolistic forms, which involves the progressive extension of planning from the factory to the market, to the external social sphere.

With the socialisation of production, the command relation of capital — with technology as its privileged mode of existence — moves inexorably beyond the factory to the social totality. IT will play an important role in this process.

It is just this extension of capitalist domination and rationalisation that is reflected — in de-politicised form — in the post-industrialist conception of a planned, administered, cohesive and technocratic social organization. There is indeed a rational kernel to the ideological shell.

A KNOWLEDGE ECONOMY: FROM TAYLOR TO POST-INDUSTRIALISM

COMMON TO MOST DISCUSSIONS of Information Technology is a view that technology is a neutral phenomenon. Recent research on the labour process — by Braverman, Gorz and others — suggests that in fact contemporary technologies incarnate the social relations and values of capitalist society. IT is thus constituted to mediate and express the unequal social relation between capital and labour: information is a social relation (Robins and Webster, 1980). In the factory and office, IT will be introduced not just to increase productivity and profitability, but to ensure management control of the labour process — Fordism and Taylorism clearly exemplify this tendency. IT will render administrative and political processes more efficient but it also promises centralisation and social control (data banks, files and so on). And in the leisure sphere, it will offer choice and flexibility but this will be expressed through an augmentation of the commercialisation, standardisation and privatisation that already characterise the 'culture industry'. This is to argue that the quest for efficiency and profitability is inseparable from the tightening of the ratchet of social control and rationalisation.

The methodical and conscious application of this principle of technological subordination was instituted by Taylor and Ford, who, at the factory level, sought to maximise efficiency and rationality, whilst simultaneously (re)asserting managerial control over the workforce. A central means to this end was to 'capture' the traditional skills/knowledge of workers: the "deliberate gathering in, on the part of those on the management side, of all the great mass of traditional knowledge which in the past has been in the heads of the workmen" (Taylor). With Ford, this knowledge was to be invested in machinery.

With the socialisation of capitalist production (which necessitates capitalist planning), this same process set in motion by Taylor and Ford — entailing the tendential separation of mental from manual labour — is extended to society as a whole. Knowledge, information and skill is 'gathered in' from the margins and peripheries of society, to be centralised, 'codified' and monopolised by Bell's 'knowledge elite'. Popular access to this social resource may be controlled and restricted. And when social knowledge is made available, it is hawked as a commodity and subject to the dictates of the market: knowledge/information becomes an exchange-value. Knowledge is indeed power — and profits.

Thus, Taylorist forms move from the factory to the social totality (the social factory): Taylor's monopolisation of knowledge within the plant becomes the tendency to hierarchial control of all social knowledge. It is precisely this scenario that is celebrated and endorsed in the post-industrialist notion of a 'Knowledge/Information Society'. In this sense, we can see the theorists of post-industrialism as the direct ideological successors to Taylor in the era of social capital. This lineage is quite apparent in the work of Drucker (1969), who argues that "knowledge, during the last few decades, has become the central capital, the cost centre and the crucial resource of the economy." Indeed "the productivity of knowledge has already become the key to productivity, competitive strength and economic achievement." Drucker then reveals the starker reality behind the knowledge society: "The most important step towards the 'knowledge economy' was, however, Scientific Management", which understood that "the key to productivity was knowledge, not sweat". Scientific Management "has proved to be the most effective idea of this century. It is the only basic American idea that has had worldwide acceptance and impact."

The post-industrialist and futurist idyll of a harmonious and bountiful future — ultimately a managerial and consumerist utopia — was also anticipated by Taylor (and Ford):

> *In short, what Taylorism offered – certainly within the plant and ultimately, according to its author, in all spheres of government and social life – was the elimination of scarcity and constraint . . . the heralded change from power over men to the administration of things . . . Ostensibly Taylor's factory*

could become the nucleic building block of a post-bourgeois world or at least a secure managerial one (Drucker, 1969; Maier, 1970).

THE POLITICAL ECONOMY OF GENERAL LUDD

INVARIABLY THE NAME of our eponymous 'hero' is used to disparage those who criticize or oppose technological innovations. 'Mindness Luddites' are lampooned as Canutes before the tide of progress. The point to be made here is that behind this labelling of 'deviant' behaviour, there lurks an *implicit* theorisation of technology. Technology is conceptualised not as a social relation, but as a thing — a thing with a life of its own. It is a reified, hypostasised and abstract force that subordinates people to its own inscrutable logic. Moreover, this technological determinism — or technological fetishism — serves to obscure, and sanction, the equally constraining economic logic of the multinational corporations.

The alternative conceptualisation of technology here presented demands a different interpretation of Luddism. It has been shown by Thompson (1968) that the Luddites were not frenzied bigots, mindlessly opposed to new machinery as such. Rather, they were resisting social changes — mediated through technology — that were imposed from above and which had repercussions on their whole way of life. They were aware, in a very concrete sense, that technologies incarnate social relations. As such, Luddism represented a refusal to meekly suffer the ravages of the new *laissez-faire* economy. It was the attempt by workers to reassert control over their own lives, to impose social and moral priorities upon the inhumane system of industrial capitalism. As Thompson states:

> *It was Marx who saw, in the passage of the 10 Hour Bill (1847), evidence that for 'the first time . . . in broad daylight the political economy of the middle-class succumbed to the political economy of the working class'. The men who attacked Cartright's mill at Rawlfolds were announcing this alternative political economy, albeit in a confused midnight encounter.*

Luddism, then, in this affirmative sense, must be seen in terms of the *critique* of technology (Robins and Webster, 1981b). It does not imply a return to machine-breaking. Rather that, because technology (increasingly and more extensively) infuses the very texture of our daily lives and because it expresses a particular structure of social relations, it is necessary to rigorously scrutinize and question both its exploitation and its constitution. By the political economy of the working class (of General Ludd) is meant the self-assertion of the subordinate party within the social relations of capitalism and the affirmation of *its* values. This is the assertion of an alternative set of criteria to assess technology: the criteria of use-values rather than exchange-values. Against the quantitative justifications of rationalisation or the increase in consumer goods, it is necessary to juxtapose the quality of life and real social needs. Specifically, in the case of Information Technology, the term 'information' must be subjected to critique. IT is invariably justified on the basis of administrative criteria: it is needed to cope with the 'information explosion' of recent years. But information is also a political issue (whose interests does it serve?). And there is a critical (Luddite?) spirit at large that brings out this social and political dimension by refusing to accept information at face value: "I don't think there is any information overload. I think there's an anti-information overload. I would say that we are inundated with increasing amounts of garbage information" (de Sola Pool and Schiller, 1981).

References

Bell, Daniel (1979) The Social Framework of the Information Society. In *The Computer Age: A Twenty-year View,* M. L. Dertouzos and J. Moses, Eds., MIT Press, Cambridge, pp. 172, 193-194.

Carey, J. W. and Quirk, J. J. (1970) *The Mythos of the Electronic Revolution.* The American Scholar, Spring and Summer.

de Sola Pool, I. and Schiller, H. I. (1981) *Perspectives on Communications Research: An Exchange.* Journal of Communications, 31, 3, Summer, p. 21.

Drucker, P. (1969) *The Age of Discontinuity.* Heinemann, London, pp. ix, 248, 254-255.

Higman, H. (1979) The Information Society. In *Telecommunications: An Inter-disciplinary Survey,* L. Lewin, Ed., Artech House, Mass., pp. 232-233.

Hirsch, J. (1978) The State Apparatus and Social Reproduction. In *State and Capital,* J. Holloway and S. Picciotto, Eds., Arnold, London, pp. 79-80.

Maier, C. S. (1970) *Between Taylorism and Technocracy.* Journal of Contemporary History, 5, 2, p. 32.

Panzieri, R. (1980) The Capitalist Use of Machinery. In *Outlines of a Critique of Technology,* P. Slater, Ed., Ink Links, London, pp. 48-49.

Parker, E. B. (1976) *Social Implications of Computer/Telecommunications Systems.* Telecommunications Policy, December, p. 20.

Reid, A. A. L. (1978) *New Telecommunications Services and their Social Implications.* Phil. Trans. R. Soc. Lond., A. 289, p. 181.

Robins, K. and Webster, F. (1979) Mass Communications and Information Technology. In *The Socialist Register 1979,* R. Miliband and J. Saville, Eds., Merlin Press, London.

Robins, K. and Webster, F. (1980) *Information is a Social Relation.* Intermedia, 8, 4, July.

Robins, K. and Webster, F. (1981a) Information Technology: Futurism, Corporations and the State. In *The Socialist Register 1981,* R. Miliband and J. Saville, Eds., Merlin Press, London.

Robins, K. and Webster, F. (1981b) *New Technology: Luddism and the Critique of Political Economy.* Mimeograph.

Schiller, H. I. (1981) *Who Knows: Information in the Age of the Fortune 500.* Ablex, Norwood, N.J., p. 2.

Thompson, E. P. (1968) *The Making of the English Working Class.* Penguin, Harmondsworth, pp. 603-604.

CHAPTER 6

Impact of Information Technology on Human Well-being

John Cullen

Irish Foundation for Human Development and Department of Psychiatry, University College, Dublin

A FEATURE OF RECENT discussion in biological sciences has been the increasing prominence which information is seen to have in living systems. Whether one is considering the transmission of DNA encoded messages across generation boundaries or the coping of whole organisms with environmental flux, it is clear that life is essentially about information. It is an informing process and the information society we live in has had, and will continue to have, effects at levels which range from subcellular to that of the human community. The information matrix is a continuous one and our sharing in it is as ecologically significant as our relationship to air or water. The management of its technology will be no less difficult than the management of other ecosystems' features.

There have been many conferences and government-initiated enquiries and reports on the possible impacts of the new information technology on human life and well-being. Most of these studies develop interesting and new insights about how our societies may evolve and how our relationships to, for example, work, power or centralized bureaucracy may undergo radical change. A particularly far-reaching perspective is developed by Nora and Minc (1980) in their report to the President of France. It is a humane and balanced document but, nevertheless, it does not achieve much more than these precious, intuitive considerations. What is urgently needed is a taxonomy of effects of information technologies on human life and the development of methods for monitoring their impacts over time.

RANGE OF IMPACTS

RAPID SOCIO-ECONOMIC CHANGE of the type precipitated by our information technology involves, for participant human populations, an entry into new systems of coping and role demands which are at best only dimly understood. New responses are demanded explicitly, of course, from the populations by the planners and investors. There are, however, many more responses and adaptations which are never planned for and never explicitly demanded. They follow nevertheless and, by a gradual and largely unconscious shift in human behaviours, intrude in many subtle ways on traditional indigenous cultures and confront their value with new aspirations.

The processes involved are complex but they are not random. Systematic effects occur in the psycho-social networks of human behaviours. They work their way through the basic psycho-biological context of human life — the human life cycle and its social supports. Effects occur in the child, in the family and in the emergent adult at adolescence. They occur in men and women and in their dyadic relationships; there are effects on the value and authority vested in age and experience. Changes occur in personal control over work pace and place and in the scope for regulation of the pressure to which the individual is subject. Changes will occur in perceptions of belonging, contact with people and the nexus of roles and their ranked value in the community. New social goals will emerge, at least in those intermediate goals which are the reinforcers and motivators in everyday life. For example, will electronic currency be as effective a reinforcer or motivator as 'cash in the hand'?

THE POSSIBILITY OF MONITORING

DESPITE THEIR MULTIPLICITY and complexity, it is argued here that these effects may be monitored and that they are beginning to be measurable. Sensitive indicators are available and methodology in the biomedical and in the psycho-social sciences has advanced enough to give reliable descriptions of change in these kinds of dimensions of the life cycle. These data-based and descriptive foundations will provide the platform from which the main thrust of the monitoring task will proceed. The central task is to assemble, update and re-update a clear picture of the 'change' profiles and to seek ways to make this available to serve insights, coping and value-based decision-making at every point in the process for the planner, investor and everyone in the population. The raising of consciousness about these change processes is crucial for health and well-being.

The monitoring of human impact has been greatly enhanced by the enormous power of modern electronic data processing. A few decades ago, the possibility of correlating large amounts of data about large numbers of interacting variables was indeed slim. The author's early research days involved the use of a mechanical calculator, borrowed by the UK Medical Research Council from the Royal Air Force and subject to frequent enquiries from headquarters about its well-being! Despite its valued status, it could achieve nothing that the modern schoolboy's pocket calculator could not surpass. Modern multivariate analysis, factor analysis, ANOVA and time-series analysis — all permit epidemiological perspectives on risk to health and well-being which would not have been possible a decade or so ago. It is now possible to seek explanations of risk variance for some of the more serious risks to health and life in our time. For example, heart disease (and especially myocardial infarction) has a multifactorial aetiology. There are contributions to risk from dietary and body-weight factors, from lifestyle factors such as physical exercise and from habits such as use of tobacco, alcohol or other stimulants. In addition, risk alters with level of blood pressure, blood lipids and other biochemical factors. We also know that risk alters with social class, occupational class and grade, and with certain personality traits (Marmot *et al,* 1978; Orth-Gomer *et al,* 1980). These latter psycho-social risk factors are independent of lifestyle, dietary and similar physical risk factors, although they do, of course, compound them. It is now also clear that stress (or the load one one's adaptive capacity as measured, for example, by life-change events inventories) can substantially increase risk (Dohrenwend and Dohrenwend, 1974).

This array of components in a risk profile can only be monitored effectively with the same modern information technology that is itself contributing to change in many of the risk parameters it has helped to identify. This is the merest outline of some of the interacting variables in one area of human well-being. It can, however, serve as a paradigm for many other areas. The key point is that our capacity to monitor impact is enormously enhanced by modern data management facilities and the conceptual models of epidemiology, which can be tested and manipulated around the data. This facility has become available *pari passu* with the development and validation of psycho-social-monitoring techniques, such as the life-change events inventories previously mentioned.

At another level of analysis and detection, the microelectronic technology of physiological measurement is increasingly providing 'socially acceptable monitoring instruments' (SAMI) which are non-invasive, safe and tolerable. This allows continuous monitoring of physiological change in a variety of psycho-social environments, for example, situations of varied mental workload. Indeed, many situations that have arisen because of modern information technology are being monitored for impact on human well-being, using the very powers it has extended to us. This, of course, includes abilities to process and store large amounts of physiological information in 'real-time' in real-life situations.

Taken together, these two general dimensions of monitoring capability provide a very significant possibility for monitoring the impact of technology but they must be accurately directed. For this, we need to evolve checklists or check-out routines for major parameters of impact. For example, a life-cycle criterion should almost always apply, so that factors relating to age, developmental status and current concerns in life-tasks can be evaluated. So also must differential impacts on men and women be borne in mind. Then, effects may be sought in physiological and psychological responses or, more usually, in both together. Certain socio-economic or occupational groups may experience greater positive or negative effects; rate of sickness, absenteeism and other markers or indicators may draw attention to differential impacts or to special ones (DHSS, 1980; TUC, 1981). The basic knowledge on these issues is available to us now and we could begin to establish the kinds of check-out routines required.

IMPACTS ON WELL-BEING — SOME BENEFITS AND RISKS

THE STORAGE AND REDEPLOYMENT of information by electronic means has become commonplace in our lives. The use of pre-programmed 'chips' in for example, domestic appliances, has become almost universal and many applications are undoubtedly useful. They are, however, for the most part quite trivial. One has the impression that product development in this context is still enmeshed in old psycho-social constructs. At an industrial level and in the workplace generally, however, the picture is much more sophisticated. Information technology is eliminating many types of work by human operators which is monotonous, repetitive or mentally over-loading in a routine way. It is also, through its ability to design and implement control systems, beginning to reduce exposure of humans to hazards in the workplace by removing the human operator from the actual workface itself. These contributions to the improvement of working conditions are very real advances. The bad effects of monotony, especially in paced work under noisy conditions, has been well documented (Thackray, 1981) and these effects are detrimental at both psychological and physiological levels. Of course, information technology creates its own monotonies and linearities.

A sizeable amount of work has now been done on video display units (VDUs) and it is clear that the ergonomics of their operation is still far from fully checked out. There is a strong suspicion that they may have visual effects which are undesirable (Laubli et al, 1980). Recent Norwegian studies have suggested general skin or dermatological problems related to ambient ionization of the air and the build-up of static charges on the operator leading to attraction of dust particles (New Scientist, 1981). Thus, there are still unresolved issues about the new technology hardware and the person operating it. Clearly, it will be possible to improve certain aspects of these facilities (for example, by using liquid crystal displays). However, effects on other psycho-social aspects of human well-being may prove more difficult and these effects may interact with effects of an almost infinite capacity to generate and manipulate information loads. Studies of air-traffic controllers show deleterious effects of the time-pressured demand to handle high information loads for continuous periods (Rose *et al,* 1978). These studies look for long-term effects on the health and psycho-social well-being of these workers. There are also other experimental, laboratory-based studies on the acute effects of mental workload variability (Moray, 1979). Mulder (1979a) in Groningen has conducted extensive studies on mental load, mental effort and attentional demand. He has also measured changes in the cardiovascular system — in heart rhythm and blood pressure, which occur in response to mental load and information processing in human operators (Mulder, 1979b). These studies may be taken as representative of many others; the message which emerges is that the human operator incurs a physiological cost in mental information loading, just as in physical effort. Studies of ships' pilots show this very clearly, with elevations of heart rate associated with the mental effort of directing the docking manoeuvers, reaching as high as those produced in boarding the vessel from the pilot boat and, at times, even exceeding them (Shipley and Cook, 1979).

But there are more complex psycho-biological phenomena involved in all of this. It is now evident that while biological systems (such as the cardiovascular and endocrine systems) may be activated by information — and varied with its content, rate or novelty — these systemic changes may themselves also regulate the information-processing capacity of the brain, in turn to modulate information fluxes in the nervous system. Experimentally induced elevations of blood pressure have been shown to reduce information intake and processing rates in the nervous system. Adrenal hormones also have brain effects (Dewied, 1977). We are, thus, in a continuum of information fluxes which relate to events at the very core of our psycho-biological being. Considerations at this level may ultimately be more important for human well-being than inventive applications of information technologies.

Lest it seem that too exclusive an emphasis is being laid on the negative effects of these technologies, it is important to realize that such a profound extension of our information-managing capability must have a major contribution to make to human coping and adaptability. Cognitive skills and the information-processing capacities for developing mental world maps, contingency matrices and strategies for dealing with novelty are fundamental in our psycho-biological capacities for adaptively dealing with stress. The ability to manipulate large models in our heads is essential and we can now increasingly extend this manipulation outside ourselves. This must have enormous heuristic significance for coping with our increasingly complex, man-made environment.

The impact of information-channel configurations and the architecture of systems on social interactions is an area for urgent study. Some intuitive insights may develop lines of enquiry: many have commented on the personal isolation of the VDU operator and yet we have also seen the frustration of check-in clerks at airports when the system breaks down. There is clearly a need to relate to this information source in a personal way. Developmental psycho-biologists have developed profound insights into the source of this need for a personalized relationship to information sources. In its first attempts to come to terms with the incessant and, initially, many novel stimuli in the environment, the organism needs, above all, a stable relationship with a parent figure who will provide consistent, reliable and relevant information about sources of satisfaction, feed-back about performance and a map of the environment. In this context, it is said that 'primary trust' can develop. If this experience is not available, then such trust will not develop. Primary trust is the source of expectations that people are usually reliable, that long-term goals may be obtained even if short-term rewards may have to be sacrificed and, in the ultimate cognitive expectation, that there is a fairly predictable pattern to life experience. It also reinforces a trust in the bank of past experience or information — the life history of one's development out of which personal identity and autonomy is secured.

It is highly likely that child development will continue in this way for the foreseeable future at least. It has biological imperatives which are difficult to envisage being replaced. For example, breast milk is a highly important information source for developing immunity and also digestive and metabolic competence (Jelliffe and Jelliffe, 1979). Against this kind of developmental background, it is not surprising that much of human communication is validated consensually by all sorts of collateral information channels — by, for example, gesture, body tension, posture, eye-contact, touch or skin changes. Our cold-information systems of modern technology have defects in this area; we must recognize these and plan around them. Unless we do, there will be damaging impacts on human well-being, involving loss of personal worth, relevance and meaning in the workplace. Evidence of these effects is growing. The workplace is not only a source of human productivity which may be greatly increased by our information technology. It is above all else a social context, relying very heavily on human support networks. Without these supports, we will not only fall ill, physically and mentally — we will inevitably die (Lynch, 1977). Therefore, we must look at how we may achieve placing our information technology in a network of human social supports.

At a community level, our information technology promises an increase in good neighbourliness in 'the global village'. Unless we cope with the loss of livelihood for so many and the increased peripheralization of the under-privileged, culturally deprived and under-educated (such as the millions of migrant workers in our European Community), then this will intrude massive new cleavages in our social class structures. So also, the promise of new toys for *Homo ludens* may be premature if we do not seek to understand the role of play in the mammal and expecially in the human developmental years (Millar, 1981). Lastly, to return to an earlier concern and to maintain the stance that benefit and risk may be alternates in the same situation, it is probably true that, with enhanced epidemiologies of risk to well-being and health in our complex world, we may be increasingly "medicalizing' life. But this need not inevitably increase dependency because we are probably also vastly increasing our scope for personal intervention and real caring.

References

Dewied, D. (1977) *Pituitary adrenal system hormones and behaviour.* Acta Endocrin. Supp., 214.

DHSS (1980) *Inequalities in Health – Report of a Reserach Working Group.* Chairman: Sir Douglas Black, Her Majesty's Stationery Office, London.

Dohrenwend, B. S. and Dohrenwend, B. P. (1974) *Stressful Life Events – Their Nature and Effects.* John Wiley and Sons, N.Y.

Jelliffe, D. B. and Jelliffe, E. F. P. (1979) *Human Milk in the Modern World – Psychosocial, Nutritional and Economic Significance.* Oxford University Press, Oxford.

Laubli, T., Hunting, W. and Grandjean, E. (1980) Visual impairments in VDU operators related to environmental conditions. In *Ergonomic Aspects of Visual Display Terminals.* E. Grandjean and E. Vigliani, Eds., Taylor & Francis, London.

Lynch, J. J. (1977) *The Broken Heart.* Basic Books, N.Y.

Marmot, M. G., Rose, G., Shipley, M. and Hamilton, P. J. S. (1978) *Employment grade and coronary heart disease in British civil servants.* J. Epidemiol. Comm. Health, Vol. 32, pp. 244-252.

Millar, S. (1981) Play. In *Oxford Companion to Animal Behaviour.* D. McFarland, Ed., Oxford University Press, Oxford, pp. 457-460.

Moray, N. (Ed.) (1979) *Mental Workload – Its Theory and Measurement.* NATO Conference Series Vol. 8, Plenum Press, N.Y.

Mulder, G. (1979a) Mental Load, Mental Effort and Attention. In *Mental Workload – Its Theory and Measurement,* N. Moray, Ed., Plenum Press, N.Y., pp. 299-325.

Mulder, G. (1979b) *Sinusarrythmia and Mental Workload. Op. cit,* pp. 327-343.

New Scientist (1981) *Safety rules recognize new hazard in screens.* New Scientist, 13 August 1981, p. 393.

Nora, S. and Minc, A. (1980) *The Computerization of Society – A Report to the President of France.* MIT Press, Cambridge, Mass.

Orth-Gomer, K., Ahlbom, A. and Theorell, T. (1980) *Impact of pattern A behaviour on ischaemic heart disease when controlling for conventional risk indicators.* J. Human Stress, Vol. 6, No. 3, pp. 6-13.

Rose, R. M. Jenkins, C. D. and Hurst, M. W. (1978) *Health changes in air traffic controllers. A prospective study.* Psychosom. Med., Vol. 40, No. 2, pp. 142-165.

Shipley, P. and Cook, T. C. (1979) Individual vulnerability to occupational stress: some psychological and other findings from a study of ships' pilots. In *Response to Stress: Occupational Aspects.* C. Mackay and T. Cos, Eds., IPC Science & Technology Press, Guildford, pp. 9-24.

Thackray, R. I. (1981) *The Stress of Boredom and Monotony: A Consideration of the Evidence.* Psychosom. Med., Vol. XLII, No. 2, pp. 165-176.

TUC (1981) *The Unequal Health of the Nation – TUC Summary of the Black Report.* Trades Unions Congress, Congress House, London.

CHAPTER 7

Perspectives on the Information Society

Sean MacBride, S.C.

UNESCO

IT IS FORTUNATE that the awareness of the importance of communications and
its impact on development coincided with the development of the silicon chip.
This invention has reduced the space required for instrumentation to minute
proportions. Binary codes of transmission have created a new language and
virtually eliminated delay. These developments have multiplied the resources
available not only for information and entertainment, but also for medicine
and all branches of science; these developments have had, and will continue to
have, important results in social organization and development.

These new technologies, which originated in the industrialised countries,
have spread rapidly and have opened new horizons in many different fields,
particularly that of communications. Distance has ceased to be an obstacle
and a universal communications system, linking any number of points on the
planet, is quite realizable. Conversely, it is possible to envisage, instead of a
global system, a web of communication networks, integrating autonomous or
semi-autonomous decentralized units. The content of messages could be
diversified, localised and individualised to suit many different purposes,
Teleprocessing, or telematics, and the establishment of links and relays
between several satellites are likely to open up endless possibilities for
systematic integration.

The importance of these processes lies not only in the technical transmission
facilities, but more on the fundamental transformation they will impose on
society. Following the industrial revolution, man had to learn to handle the
information and communications systems that had been developed in that
period. Man has now entered into a new era, which will be increasingly
dominated by informatics. To adapt, it will be necessary to acquire the
capacity to switch rapidly from the present analogical techniques to various
forms of binary language. Dealing with some of these problems, the
International Commission for the Study of Communications Problems (of

which the author was Chairman) drew two main conclusions. Firstly, these changes represent an irreversible trend in the development of communications and science. And, secondly, there is basically interdependence, not competition, between the different types of media communication.

Nations which choose to concentrate on one technique should not do so to the detriment or neglect of another. While it is often said that we are entering the electronic age, there is no sign, for instance, of the demise of the printed media. Newspapers, magazines and books will continue for decades to be major sources of information, common knowledge and pleasure; efforts should be made to ensure that they continue to increase their quantity and improve their quality. Radio and television also need further expansion and large investment, above all, in developing countries. The same is true of the latest innovation in technology: all nations need to plan for the gradual introduction of the new technology. Developing nations, in particular, should make their plans as a matter of urgency, in order to share in the advantages of the new technology and adapt it to their special needs and conditions.

There is a justifiable view that technological progress is running ahead of man's capacity to interpret its implications and direct it into the most desirable channels. This view, expressed by many thinkers (particularly since the Second World War) is becoming more and more widespread. The gap is disturbingly evident in such areas as biology, genetics, nuclear physics and cybernetics. New technologies, advancing by their own momentum and often urged on by political pressure and economic requirements, impose themselves before they can be properly assessed or assimilated. Because of the speed of technological progress and the concurrent breakdown in all standards of public and private morality, the assimilation of new techniques elude both ethical guidance and social control. That great African thinker who is the Director-General of UNESCO, Amadou Mahtar M'Bow, quite rightly points out:

> Discovery now follows discovery at an ever-increasing pace not only because of man's need to create, but also under the stimulating pressures of economic demands. Technological innovation has become one of the incentives to production. What has declined is the mental and cultural ability of society to control the effects of progress. Man no longer endeavours to obstruct the forces of change, but he does not always succeed in containing them.

Albert Schweitzer, the Nobel Prize Laureate, said the same thing with a slightly different emphasis. He pointed out that: "Man has lost the capacity to foresee and to forestall the consequences of his own actions."

The discussion so far is not advocating a slowing-down in the utilisation of technological developments. Rather it urges that, concurrently with their utilisation, there should be a constant process of assessment of the moral and social implications that will result from the modern technology — an extremely important aspect of the 'micro-chip revolution'.

The use to which technology is put is seldom neutral. It is influenced by many political or financial considerations. It is therefore useful to know how decisions are taken concerning the main lines of emphasis that are given to innovations. It is also well to know who decides research and development policies. It is clear that the general public exercises little or no control over such decisions. In the final analysis, it is not so much the consumers as the producers that decide what the market requires. Technological developments demand careful scrutiny. Technical options may well increase the risk of manipulation, both at national and international levels. In the field of information, one may wonder sometimes whether the volume of information produced does not exceed the actual needs of a given society. This led the Commission for the Study of Communications Problems to emphasise that:

> It would seem especially important to socialise, so far as possible, the decision-making process (in other words, to associate multiple partners in decision-making, not leaving it merely to technocrats or bureaucrats), whether in regard to defining priorities, employment policies or production and supply possibilities. The fact that the governments in industrialised and developing countries alike are frequently ill-equipped to take decisions concerning new technologies deserves a mention. Governments all too often tend to leave the matter in the hands of technicians, giving them no directives in matters, judged a priori to be too complex or too highly specialised.

In the field of communications, the Commission took the view that there should be a systematic change from a system of disadvantage, or dependence, towards a system of self-reliance and the creation of more equal opportunities. Since communication is interwoven with every aspect of life, it is clearly of the utmost importance that the existing 'communication gap' be narrowed and eventually eliminated. With this end in view, the Commission made the following recommendation:

> We recommend that communication be no longer regarded merely as an incidental service and its development left to chance. Recognition of its potential warrants the formulation by all nations, and particularly developing countries, of comprehensive communication policies, linked to overall social, cultural, economic and political goals. Such policies should be based on interministerial and interdisciplinary consultations with broad public participation. The object must be to utilize the unique capacities of each form of communication, from interpersonal and traditional to the most modern, to make men and societies aware of their rights, harmonize unity in diversity and foster the growth of individuals and communities within the wider frame of national development in an interdependent world.

Leaving aside the information aspect of technology, let us pass to a related problem — electronic technology. Unemployment is a generalised problem affecting most countries today. But, Ireland (the author's country) is more vulnerable to it than most. We seldom analyse, or even admit, the real reasons for the unemployment and underemployment from which we suffer. This applies to our political parties, state bodies, employers and trade unions. Instead, we blame it on economic recession, world depression, inflation, bad employer/employee relations, excessive demand by the workers, inter-union rivalry, bad industrial relations — all the old clichés. In reality, the massive unemployment which disrupts our society and undermines our political development arises from four different causes. The first three of these causes are of our own making. The fourth cause is related to technology and the micro-chip revolution. These causes are:

(1) Inadequate development of our own natural resources, such as afforestation, agriculture, sea-fishing and land reclaimation, coupled with an inadequate assessment of the consumer requirements of our own population. There is also inadequate market research in regard to export possibilities. Three illustrations will suffice:

    (a) By reason of our climate and soil, timber can be grown in Ireland more rapidly than in any other country in Europe; yet we do not produce enough timber to meet our own requirements, much less to provide an exportable surplus of timber and timber products. This is the fact, despite the international forecasts predicting a serious timber and paper-pulp shortage reaching crisis proportions by the year 2000.

    (b) Ireland can produce excellent potatoes, yet our potatoe production is organized so inefficiently that it is necessary to import large quantities of potatoes. This is surely due to an inadequate assessment of our own consumer requirements and improper agricultural planning.

    (c) We are told that the Tuam Beet Sugar Factory is closing because of inadequate supplies and the low quality of beet grown in the area. Surely, this could have been remedied if there had been adequate foresight and planning.

(2) Some of Ireland's unemployment arises from our over-eagerness to attract foreign industries and sometimes 'fly-by-night' investors, who come to Ireland for easy and quick profits. In order to attract them, we provide very substantial financial inducements and the promise of more financial support and tax reliefs. In addition, we portray Ireland as a country of 'cheap labour', where workers are 'docile' and industrial relations are 'managed' by the Government. This, of course, is far from the truth; indeed, it is questionable as to whether or not we should aim at being a country of 'cheap labour and high profits for foreign investors'. Be that as it may, we have, as a result of such inducements, attracted some industries that wanted to make quick profits and some that were not viable. As a result, false hopes were created and as soon as the Irish Government subsidies and inducements were exhausted, the factories closed. Those disemployed were then added to the already high unemployment pool. It would be of interest to quantify the amount of subsidies and other inducements granted over the last 20 years to bolster up industries that ultimately shut down because they were not viable. Apart from the financial loss sustained as a result of these 'non-viable industrial adventures', the hopes raised by the opening of such factories led to a feeling of despondency when they closed.

(3) While Ireland's membership of the EEC has undoubtedly conferred some economic benefits, it has also been one of the causes of our unemployment problems. Our shops are flooded with imported consumer goods that we do not really need. The author favoured our membership of the EEC, firstly because it was the only way in which colonial Europe could adjust itself to the demolition of colonialism, so as to become a viable economic unit without relying on colonial exploitation. Secondly, because it offered a diversity of markets for Irish agricultural and industrial products. However, the question of membership may well have to be reconsidered should it preclude us from promoting the greater utilisation of Irish goods and thus lead to the closure of existing Irish industries.

(4) The final cause for the endemic and mounting unemployment from which Ireland and the rest of the world suffer arises from automation and the electronic technology. This trend will not decrease; on the contrary, with the help of the micro-chip revolution, it will increase and cause more and more unemployment. Even if it were desirable to do so, one cannot put back the clock. We have to face the reality of automation and electronic technology, which will continue at an increasing rate to replace human labour in a more efficient and less costly manner. There is no escape from this ultimate cause of massive unemployment.

Instead of blaming each other or the trade unions, workers, employers, banks, government or the political parties, let us now face the inevitable task of reorganizing our society and economy to cope with the revolution which is taking place. This could be done, on the basis of sharing whatever employment is available up to the point where everyone gets a fair share of commercial employment. This may mean working for a 'commercial' wage, maybe two weeks out of four or even every alternate month. By reason of the ultimate substantial reduction in 'commercial employment', everyone will have a considerable amount of leisure time — probably much more than most people would wish. The State and Local Authorities would then have the responsibility of providing work on socially desirable projects, remunerated at current rates of wages, for those who wish to earn more during the period in which they are not employed. Naturally, such a reorganization of the commercial work available, to ensure everyone got their fair share, is capable of endless variation. Similarly, planning and carrying out socially desirable projects opens up unlimited perspectives as to how the quality of life and productivity of people could be improved. These changes, induced by the new technologies, should be welcomed as giving an opportunity to reorganize society on the basis of Christian principles in which existing resources will be used justly and constructively for the common good.

There is nothing more soul-destroying or damaging to the fabric of society and family life than unemployment and dependence on State welfare benefits. It is utterly unjust, as the man or woman who is thrown onto the unemployment scrapheap has no alternative; they are merely the victims of developments over which they have no control. The dignity of the human being, who is unable to earn his living or to work, is severely damaged and unemployment is one of the factors in the break-up of family life. Instead of bemoaning change or paying vast sums of money in unemployment benefits, let us avail of the micro-chip revolution, and the resultant redundancies which exist and which will increase, to share out justly the available work and to undertake socially desirable work which will benefit the community as a whole. This is the real challenge. If we do not rebuild our economic structures on more just and Christian principles that will safeguard the economic liberty and dignity of the individual and his family, we can rest assured that another society will supervene, relying on Marxist concepts and based on an all-powerful socialist state in which the individual has no liberty.

CHAPTER 8

Ethereal Goods:
The Economic Atom of the
Information Society

Gordon B. Thompson

Bell-Northern Research, Canada

WHEN ADAM SMITH wrote about making pins, he was using this as a metaphor for the content of the industrial revolution. How could he know that the automobile would be a major content item of that revolution, or that pins would be completely insignificant? Similarly, there is little likelihood that we can identify the significant content items of a mature Information Economy. However, like Smith, we can explore possibilities that come about because of the unique characteristics of the new technology that will form the basis of the economy of an Information Society.

In one sense, Adam Smith had it easy. The good that was to be exchanged in his new industrial economy was little altered from the good that was the basis of the mercantile economy. The amount of processing involved in making the goods would be increased and the economics of production altered, but the good itself was basically the same. It was still a simple tangible one, with clear property rights. With the introduction of Information Technology, a non-tangible good has become available for exchange. This kind of good has disturbing characteristics that run against our traditional notions of property. Given this non-tangible good's recalcitrant market behaviour, it is small wonder that we have not stumbled on applications of information technology that are widely perceived as being wealth-creating. Little wonder our videotex systems have been somewhat disappointing.

To look towards such systems as a means of providing jobs in the manufacture of the hardware is to perceive the new information technology as just more industrial technology. The railroads were important not simply for the jobs created by making the engines, wagons and track, but rather because of the goods that were more freely moved about and the resulting impact on the marketplace. Similarly, we cannot expect the jobs that are created in making the information technology to be the major benefit. If tomorrow's information society is to be something better than what we have today, with our rather over-stressed industrial economy, we must go beyond the considerations of who makes the hardware or who collects for the haulage or storage. True, these are important in their own right, but they must not obscure the main issue. The wealth that is created through exchanges and other processes in using the hardware must exceed the costs of the hardware itself or else the whole system is a drain on an already overloaded economy. The pot of gold, the wealth generator or whatever we might choose to call it, of the information economy underlying the information society must be identified and a wide consensus developed concerning its reality. We must learn how to get rich by *using* the hardware instead of just making it.

The 'economic atom' of an information economy must surely be the 'ethereal good', the non-tangible, easily copied, almost self-replicating, good that we have in the past forced to behave, in market situations, as if it were some special kind of tangible good. This misfit has produced a number of externalities, like copyright and performing rights legislation. To successfully exploit the opportunities made available by our new technology, we must refrain from treating this new good (the ethereal one) as some kind of tangible good with a few odd characteristics that can be accounted for by tacking-on some new legislative fix. To follow this approach is to deny the potential benefits of the new technology. The ethereal good is a vastly different thing to our old familiar tangible one and, unless we thoroughly understand the differences, there is little hope that we will reap the benefits.

An ethereal good, for the purposes of definition, is one that is not tangible, not expropriable and can be copied easily, at a cost that is less than that of a *bona fide* version.

Unembodied information delivered as a stream of electrical impulses down a wire is an example of such an ethereal good. It is not tangible, in that it cannot be touched. Nor is it expropriable in that, although I can get back what I gave you, you may have made copies; so just getting back what I gave you is no insurance that you no longer have it. Such a good is clearly appropriable, but never expropriable with certainty. It is these unusual characteristics that lead to the two fundamental problems in dealing with ethereal goods, namely the problem of property rights and the difficulty of evaluation.

Real estate has long been the model for property rights and the language we use frequently demonstrates this long association. By the time of the great Code of Hammurabi, individual property rights were a well-established idea. John Locke defined how a proper government should aid in maintaining those rights. The history of property rights is a rich and long one. However, no such history exists where ethereal goods are concerned. What does exist is a comparatively short history that clearly shows the confusion generated by treating information as conventional property. This came about because information was generally closely bound to a physical embodiment, such as a book or a phonograph record. The physical embodiments became the economic surrogates for the information itself and thus it was the books and records that got counted and exchanged. The information, in effect, went along for free. Now that new technology has cut the umbilical cord linking information to a physical embodiment, this simple approach is no longer valid.

The two difficulties, property rights and evaluation, are closely connected. Property rights only become important when there is some value to the property. Tangible goods are rather easy to evaluate in comparison with ethereal goods. Webster's Dictionary (1978) defines *tangible* as (a) real; material; solid; and (b) able to be accurately valued. Both meanings have real significance; but the second definition is particularly important, for the non-tangible ethereal good is anything but easy to accurately value. The tangible good has the benefit of 'replacement cost' in its evaluation, simply because the tangible good cannot be copied easily. To force difficult copying onto the ethereal good is to deny its essence.

Just as Adam Smith wrote of pins, so I would like to write about music. The reader must bear in mind that music is only a metaphor for what might be the content that is exchanged in a mature information economy. Until about a hundred years ago, the majority of our great composers died in abject poverty. The full value of their work was not known until after their deaths. Clearly, they did nothing to increase that value by dying, for scarcity in music, as opposed to the graphic arts, is not a consideration. A song is an ethereal good, a portrait is not. The increase in value of their music was the result of a very slow social process involving a large number of people. The process was so slow that it took too long for the composers to benefit from it. Today, with modern technology, John Lennon did quite well! Three hundred years ago, he might have died of consumption instead of being shot as a celebrity. The attention we all gave the music that Lennon produced is how the value was built. Had we not been so attentive, it would have been of little value. The mere fact that modern communications has so altered the speed with which a composer can become a creator of ethereal goods of relatively immediate value clearly shows that the value of an ethereal good is not in the good alone, but is also rooted in the creation of a consensus of value perception in a very large number of people, which is, in turn, a function of the underlying or supporting technology.

Yet, when we analyse it, the value of any good is never inherent in the good itself but rather in the perception of those who consider the good. The difference between the tangible good and the ethereal one is in the quality of the consensus that exists about the value of the good. The tangible good has such a widely accepted, perceived level of value that we frequently associate the value with the good itself as if it were a fundamental characteristic of the good, rather than some mere attribute we have chosen to give it. The ethereal good, on the other hand, has to win its consensus of value — clearly illustrated by the popular 'hit parade' selection process.

Could not the process by which an author's works become popular be built into the structure of the new ethereal goods' marketplace? If it is true that communications brought a quickening of that process between Mozart's and John Lennon's time, then this is a reasonable direction to explore. The technological supporting infrastructure under an information society's ethereal goods' marketplace must contribute in a major way to the consensus process which that society uses to evaluate the goods in that marketplace. It is not enough to store, retrieve and haul the ethereal goods; accurate records of usage must be maintained and these must be aggregated and fed back to the users in a form that helps them perceive value in their subsequent selections.

If the value of an ethereal good is a function of the attention given to that good by the society, then to vest the entire property rights to that good in the hands of the author is perhaps a bit extreme. There is absolutely no guarantee that society at large will benefit maximally from an isomorphic relationship between an author's financial reward and the usage made of his works. In a recent radio broadcast, a popular author stated that he was embarrassed by the amount of his royalties. At the other end of the scale, many as yet undiscovered authors are denied the opportunity to get on with the process of learning their craft because they must work at another occupation to keep body and soul together. Separating the reward mechanism from the mechanisms through which evaluation is performed may be a major accomplishment, for the two can then be related in ways designed to optimize both the authors' and society's benefits from creative outpourings.

If a user perceives that he gets an increasing proportion of useless items from his activities in the ethereal goods' marketplace, he will perceive that the collection of goods in the marketplace has fallen in value and so he will be less willing to pay for the ethereal goods he uses. If, as a result of aids that are generated by intelligent algorithms hidden within the information technology infrastructure that underlies tomorrow's information marketplace, he increasingly finds that he is getting outputs that are relevant and useful, then his opinion of the value of the data base will rise. It is this opinion, when spread widely throughout society, that can create the wealth in an information society.

If the evaluation of the ethereal goods that form the basis of an information society is tied up in some information-technology-based, consensus-building system, then our old ideas of copyright and performing rights are quite inappropriate. Society's behaviour towards the theft of today's ethereal goods, compared to the way we react to the theft of tangible goods (and also our prohibition of the burglar tools for tangible goods but not for ethereal goods — for after all, that is what a tape recorder is) suggests that we do, at the behavioural level, recognize the essential difference between ethereal and tangible goods.

When a copy of a song is made from a broadcast, that song is receiving attention and its value is increasing, not decreasing. What is missing is that there is no indication to the rest of society that someone thought enough of that song to make a copy of it. That information may be of equal, or even greater, value than the miniscule cost of the copyright violation that such copying appears to involve. Even if that copy is given a limited distribution beyond the confines of the copier's home, it could well be that the data about the making of these copies (when added to similar data from across society) is at least as valuable as any royalty payment. Adequate sustenance and stimulation must be provided for society's authors, but that provision must not inhibit the spread of their works and the difficult task of proper evaluation. More satisfactory ways may exist than simply charging each user with a direct charge to be paid to the creator. Searching out and examining, and perhaps even simulating, such schemes is an important prerequisite to an information society.

Attention may be the rare good in an information economy and recording the way that attention is spent is likely the principal role of an information economy. The evaluation of a society's information is the most important task that any society faces. Up until now, we had to settle for processes that involved the evaluation of surrogates for information, the tangible goods that could be produced and sold using specific collections of information. Today, we can move towards marketplaces where ethereal goods can be dealt with *per se* instead of their surrogates, our old familiar tangible goods.

Selected Bibliography

Prepared by

Kimon Valaskakis

Barron, Iann and Curnow, Ray (1979) *The Future with Microelectronics; Forecasting the Effects of Information Technology.* Frances Pinter, London.

Bell, Daniel (1973) *The Coming of Post-Industrial Society.* Basic Books, New York. (Revised 1976).

Bell, Daniel (1977) *Teletext and technology.* Encounter, June.

Berger, G. (1973) The prospective attitude. In A. Cournard and M. Lévy (Editors). *Shaping the Future.* Gordon & Breach Science Publishers, New York, pp. 245-249.

Boorstin, Daniel J. (1978) *The Republic of Technology: Reflections on our Future Community.* Harper & Row, New York.

Boulding, K. E. (1965) *The Meaning of the Twentieth Century.* Harper & Row, New York.

Braun, Ernest and MacDonald, Stuart (1978) *Revolution in Miniature: The History and Impact of Semiconducter Electronics.* Cambridge University Press, London.

Brunel, Louis (1978) *Telecommunications: Des Machines et des Hommes.* Les dossiers de Québec science, Québec.

Burke, J. G. (1967) *The New Technology and Human Values.* Wadsworth, Belmont, California.

CAD/CAM Technology Advance Council (1980) *Strategy for Survival: Issues and Recommendations concerning the Implications and Impact of CAD/CAM Technology in Canadian Industry.* Department of Industry, Trade & Commerce, Ottawa.

Cartwright, Glenn F. (1980) *And now for something completely different: Symbionic minds.* Technology Review, October, pp. 68-70.

Chisholm, D. A. (1978) *Communications and Computers: Information and Canadian Society.* A position paper. Science Council of Canada, Ottawa.

Clark, Arthur C. (1980) *Electronic tutors.* OMNI, June, pp. 76-78, 96.

Computer/Communications Secretariat (1978) *The Growth of Computer/Communications in Canada.* Department of Communications, Ottawa.

Covvey, H. D. and McAlister, N. H. (1980) *Computer Consciousness: Surviving the Automated '80s.* Addison-Wesley, Reading, Mass.

Dreyfus, Hubert L. (1979) *What Computers Can't Do: The Limits of Artificial Intelligence.* (Revised Edition). Harper & Row, New York.

Ellul, Jacques (1974) *The Technological Society.* Knopf, New York.

Engberg, Ole (1978) *Who will lead the way to the "Information Society"?* Impact of Science on Society (UNESCO), July-September, 28 (3), pp. 283-295.

Evans, Christopher (1979) *The Mighty Micro.* (Entitled *The Micro Millenium* in US Edition). Victor Gollancz, London.

Fitzpatrick-Martin, Iris (1979) *Social Implications of the Information Economy.* Information Society Project, Paper No. I-5. GAMMA, Montreal.

Fitzpatrick-Martin, Iris (1982) *Women and Informediation: The Six Interfaces of Eve.* GAMMA, Montreal.

Gardiner, W. L. (1980) *Public Acceptance of the New Information Technologies: The Role of Attitudes.* Information Society Project, Paper No. I-9. GAMMA, Montreal.

Gardiner, W. L. (1980) *On Turning Development Inside-Out or (Better) on Not Turning Development Outside-In in the First Place.* Paper presented to the GPID Human Development Study Group at Bariloche, Argentina, December 1980.

Gardiner, W. L. (1982) *Psychological Approaches to the Person/Machine Interface.* GAMMA, Montreal.

Glass, Robert L. (1977) The Universal Elixir and other Computing Projects which failed. Computing Trends, Seattle, Washington.

Glass, Robert L. (1981) *Software Soliloques.* Computing Trends, Seattle, Washington.

Glass, Robert L. and DeNim, Sue (1980) *The Second Coming: More Computing Projects which failed.* Computing Trends, Seattle, Washington.

Glenn, E. N. and Feldberg, R. L. (1979) Proletarianizing clerical work: Technology and organizational control in the office. In *Case Studies in the Labour Process,* A. Zimbalist (Editor), Monthly Review Press, New York.

Godfrey, David and Parkhill, Douglas, Editors (1980) *Gutenberg Two: The New Electronics and Social Change.* (Second edition, revised). Press Porcépic, Toronto.

Goldman, R. D., Platt, B. B. and Kaplan, R. P. *Dimensions of attitudes toward technology.* Journal of Applied Psychology, 57 (2), pp. 184-187.

Gotlieb, C. C. (1978) *Computers in the Home: What they can do for us – and to us.* Occasional Paper No. 4. Institute for Research on Public Policy (IRPP), Montreal.

Gotleib, C. C. and Zeman, Z. P. (1980) *Towards a National Computer and Communications Policy: Seven National Approaches.* IRPP, Montreal.

Green, K. and Coombs, R. (1981) *Employment and new technology in Tyneside.* Futures, 13 (1), 43-50.

Gurstein, Michael (1981) *Videotex and Special Needs Groups.* Socioscope, Ottawa.

Harman, Willis W. (1978) *Chronic unemployment: An emerging problem of post-industrial society.* The Futurist, August, pp. 209-214.

Hetman, F. (1973) *Society and the Assessment of Technology.* Organization for Economic Co-operation and Development (OECD),Paris.

Hiltz, Starr Roxanne and Turoff, Murray (1978) *The Network Nation: Human Communications via Computer.* Addison-Wesley, Reading, Mass.

Huber, B. J. (1978) Images of the future. In *Handbook of Futures Research.* J. Fowles (Editor), Greenwood, Westport, Connecticut, pp. 179-224.

Hughes, T. P., Editor (1975) *Changing Attitudes toward American Technology.* Harper & Row, New York.

Illich, Ivan (1973) *Tools for Conviviality.* Harper & Row, New York.

Innis, Harold A. (1964) *The Bias of Communication.* (Second Edition). The University of Toronto Press, Toronto.

Jenkins, Clive and Sherman, Barrie (1979) *The Collapse of Work.* Eyre Methuen, London.

Jouvenel, B. de (1963) Introduction. In *Futuribles: Studies in Conjecture*. B. de Jouvenel (Editor). Droz, Geneva, pp. ix-xi.

Juneau, Pierre (1980) *National Information in the Global Environment*. Department of Communications, Ottawa.

Kling, Rob (1980) *Social analyses of computing: Theoretical perspectives in recent empirical research*. Computing Surveys, March, 12 (1), pp. 61-110.

Knelman, Fred (1980) *Energy and Information*. GAMMA, Montreal.

Kuhns, William (1971) *The Post-Industrial Prophets: Interpretations of Technology*. Harper & Row, New York.

LaForte, T. and Metley, D. (1975) *Public attitudes toward present and future technologies: Satisfactions and apprehensions*. Social Studies of Science, 5, pp. 373-398.

Lee, R. S. (1970) *Social attitudes and the computer revolution*. Public Opinion Quarterly, Spring, 34, pp. 53-59.

Lund, Robert T. (1981) *Microprocessors and productivity: Cashing in our chips*. Technology Review, January, 83, pp. 32-44.

Lussato, Bruno and Bounine, Jean (1979) *Telematique – Ou Privatique? Questions a Simon Nora et Alain Minc*. Editions d'Informatique, Paris.

Machlup, Fritz (1962) *The Production and Distribution of Knowledge in the United States*. Princeton, N.J.

Mander, Jerry (1978) *Four Arguments for the Elimination of Television*. William Morrow, New York.

Marien, Michael (1977) *The two visions of post-industrial society*. Futures, 9 (5), pp. 415-431.

Marsh, Peter (1981) *The Silicon Chip Book*. Abacus, London.

Martin, James (1971) *Future Developments in Telecommunications*. Prentice-Hall, Englewood Cliffs, N.J.

Martin, James (1978) *The Wired Society*. Prentice-Hall, Englewood Cliffs, N.J.

McDonagh, Eileen L. (1976) *Attitude changes and paradigm shift: Social psychological foundations of the Kuhnian thesis*. Social Studies of Science, 6, pp. 51-76.

McLean, J. Michael (1979) *The Impact of the Microelectronics Industry on the Structure of the Canadian Economy*. Occasional Paper No. 8. IRPP, Montreal.

McLuhan, Marshall (1964) *Understanding Media: The Extensions of Man*. McGraw-Hill, New York.

McLuhan, Marshall (1980) In *MacLean's* Magazine, 7 January 1980, pp. 32-33.

Menzies, Heather (1981) *Women and the Chip: Case Studies of the Effects of Informatics on Employment in Canada*. IRPP, Montreal.

Mesthene, Emmanuel G. (1969) *Technology and humanistic values*. Computers and the Humanities, 4 (1), pp. 1-10.

Michalos, Alex C. *North American Social Report: Comparative Study of QOL in Canada and U.S.A.* D. Reidel, Boston.

Minsky, Marvin (1980) *Telepresence*. OMNI, June, pp. 44-52.

Nilles, Jack M. *et al* (1976) *The Telecommunications-Transportation Tradeoff: Options for Tomorrow*. John Wiley, New York.

Nilles, Jack M. (1979) *Opportunities and threats from the personal computer*. Futures, 11 (2), pp. 172-176.

Nora, Simon and Minc, Alain (1980) *The Computerization of Society*. (A translation of *L'Informatisation de la Société.*) MIT Press, Cambridge, Mass.

Norman, Colin (1980) *Microelectronics at Work: Productivity and Jobs in the World Economy.* Worldwatch Paper 39. Worldwatch Institute, Washington, D.C.

Orcutt, J. D. and Anderson, R. E. (1974) *Human-computer relationships: Interactions and attitudes.* Behaviour Research Methods and Instrumentation, 6 (2), pp. 219-222.
Osborne, Adam (1979) *Running Wild: The Next Industrial Revolution.* McGraw-Hill, Berkeley, California.

Pergler, P. (1980) *The Automated Citizen.* Occasional Paper No. 14. IRPP, Montreal.
Plowright, Teresa (1980) *Social Aspects of Videotex Services: Proposed Research Directions.* Social and new services policy division, Department of Communications, Ottawa.
Porat, M. U. (1976) *The Information Economy.* Center for Interdisciplinary Research, Stanford University, California.

Rada, Juan F. (1979) *Microelectronics: A Tentative Appraisal of the Impact of Information Technology.* ILO, Geneva.
Rockman, Arnold (1980) *Notes on the coming of the wired heads.* Canadian Forum, December/January.
Roszak, Theodore (1978) *Person/Plant: The Creative Disintegration of Industrial Society.* Doubleday, New York.
Rule, J., McAdam, D., Stearns, L. and Uglow, D. (1980) *The Politics of Privacy.* New American Library, New York.
Russel, Robert A. (1978) *The Electronic Briefcase: The Office of the Future.* Occasional Paper No. 3. IRPP, Montreal.

Salisbury, R. F. and Lafrance, J. P. (1978) *The Future Development of Public Communications in Canada: 1976-1991 "Group" Needs in Canadian Communications.* GAMMA, Montreal.
Science Council of Canada (1979) *A Scenario for the Implementation of Interactive Computer-Communications Systems in the Home.* Science Council of Canada, Ottawa.
Science Council of Canada (1980) *The Impact of the Microelectronics Revolution on the Canadian Electronics Industry.* Proceedings of a workshop sponsored by the Science Council of Canada Committee on Computers and Communication. Minister of Supply and Services, Ottawa.
Serafini, S., Andrieu, M. and Estabrooks, M. *Post-industrial Canada and the new information technology.* Canadian Futures, 1, pp. 81-91.
Servan-Schreiber, Jean-Jacques (1980) *Le Defi Mondial.* Presses Select Ltée, Montreal.
Sheridan, T. B. (1980) *Computer control and human alienation.* Technology Review, October, pp. 61-67, 71-73.
Shriver, Donald W. Jr. (1972) *Man and his machines: Four angles of vision.* Technology and Culture, 13 (4), pp. 531-555.
Sindell, Peter S. (1979) *Public Policy and the Information Society.* GAMMA, Montreal.
Singer, Benjamin D. (1977) *Incommunicado social machines.* Social Policy, November/December, pp. 88-93.
Singer, Benjamin D. (1978) *Assessing social errors.* Social Policy, September/October, pp. 27-34.
Singer, Benjamin D. (1980) *Crazy systems.* Social Policy, September/October, pp. 46-54.

Tanny, Stephen M. (1978) *Post-industrial Canada.* Futures, February, pp. 44-52.

Tavis, Irene *A survey of popular attitudes toward technology.* Technology and Culture, 17 (4), pp. 606-621.

Tavis, Irene (1970) *The Computer Impact.* Prentice-Hall, Englewood Cliffs, N.J.

Techno/Peasant Survival Team (1980) *The Techno/Peasant Survival Manual.* Bantam, New York.

Teich, Albert H., Editor (1977) *Technology and Man's Future.* (Second Edition). St. Martin's Press, New York.

Thompson, Fred, G. (1980) *Computer Assisted Communication.* Department of Communications, Ottawa.

Thompson, Gordon B. (1979) *Memo from Mercury: Information Technology is Different.* Occasional Paper No. 10. IRPP, Montreal.

Toffler, Alvin (1980) *The Third Wave.* William Morrow, New York.

Uttal, Bro. (1981) *Xerox xooms toward the office of the future.* Fortune, 18 May 1981, pp. 44-52.

Valaskakis, Kimon (1979) *The Information Society: The Issue and the Choices.* Information Society Project: Integrating Report. GAMMA, Montreal.

Valaskakis, Kimon and Sindell, Peter S. (1980) *Industrial Strategy and the Information Economy: Towards a Game Plan for Canada.* Information Society Project Paper No. I-10 GAMMA, Montreal.

Weizenbaum, Joseph (1976) *Computer Power and Human Reason: From Judgement to Calculation.* W. H. Freeman, San Francisco.

Welles, Chris (1980) *We have seen the future of video and it sure looks like the same old wasteland. Is that their fault or ours?* Esquire, June, pp. 89-95.

Whiteside, Thomas (1978) *Computer Capers: Tales of Electronic Thievery, Embezzlement, and Fraud.* New American Library, New York.

Wicklein, John (1979) *Wired city U.S.A.: The charms and dangers of two-way TV.* Atlantic Monthly, February, 37, pp. 35-42.

Wooldridge, S. and London, K. (1979) *The Computer Survival Manual.* (First revised edition). Gambit, Ipswich, Mass.

Zeman, Z. P. (1970) *The Impacts of Computer/Communications on Employment in Canada: An Overview of Current OECD Debates.* IRPP, Montreal.

PART II

Information Technology in the Workplace

In the following chapters, changes occurring in the organization of work as a result of the applications of new technologies are examined, particularly in the office and factory environments.

Arndt Sorge, Malcolm Warner, Gert Hartmann and Ian Nicholas present some results from an Anglo-German research projected on computer numerical control (CNC) applications in manufacturing industry. They put forward a critique of the viewpoint that the trend is towards the fully automated factory.

Office communication systems are the subject of the study by Arnold Picot, Heide Klingenberg and Hans-Peter Kranzle. They use a variety of research instruments to examine the potential for electronically mediated communications to substitute for oral communications.

Alan Hedge and Richard Crawley argue for the importance of taking a socio-psychological approach to the design of new information technology systems and stress the need for the active involvement of all employees in the system-design process. The paper by David Boddy and David Buchanan bridges the office and factory environments, presenting a case study on each. Their concern is the impact of information technologies on the experience of work as viewed by different groups of employees. They conclude that it is management orientations rather than the technology itself which principally determines the nature of work organization.

Barry Wilkinson reinforces this point, while focusing on the nature of human tasks rather than the general organization of work. He believes that the interventions of different social actors profoundly influence both the way technology is used and its effects on work organization.

Michael Rader presents preliminary results from his extensive survey of German engineering companies, concerning the effects of computer-aided design (CAD) systems. He examines the issues of democratisation of design and deskilling, both in an historical and theoretical context.

Finally, Arthur Francis, Mandy Snell, Paul Willman and Graham Winch give some initial results from their study of computer-aided manufacturing plants, pointing to the difficulties in firmly establishing the nature of both job losses and changing skill levels.

CHAPTER 9

Computer Numerical Control Applications in Manufacturing

Arndt Sorge and Gert Hartmann

International Institute of Management, Berlin

Malcolm Warner and Ian Nicholas

Henley Management College, UK

OVERALL PERSPECTIVES

Common Factors and National Differences

All our results serve to stress the extreme malleability of Computer Numerical Control (CNC) technology.* There is no effect of the use of CNC as such. This underlines one of our conceptual points of departure which stresses that it is inadequate to consider a production technology as given and to observe the effects or constraints which follow from it. But this is not to say that technology is unimportant; its significance only unfolds through a continuous series of 'piecemeal' modification and innovation. This is part of a complex pattern of socio-technical design and improvement where technical developments interact with organizational and manpower developments. Thus, in the company context, the detailed technical specifications of the CNC system adopted are seen to reflect the influence of corporate and departmental strategies, existing production, engineering and organizational procedures and current manpower policies, all of which vary within a country and between countries.

*This research is part of a study financed by the Anglo-German Foundation for the Study of Industrial Society. A fuller version of this research may be found in *Microelectronics and Manpower in Manufacturing: Application of Computer Numerical Control in Britain and West Germany.* IIM, Berlin, 1981. (Research Report, Mimeo).

We have found solutions to CNC applications which are alternatively organizationally simple or complex; some stress functional differentiation, while others emphasize functional integration within positions or departments; in some cases, there is a strong element of skill, but with skill enrichment at the shop-floor level. None of these contrasting policies can be said to be more 'advanced' from the technical point of view. Yet, at the same time, it cannot be said that the application of CNC has been haphazard or the subject of accidental initiative.

There are a series of very clear 'logics' of CNC application. These different concepts are analytically distinct but they interact, and sometimes conflict, with each other. The factors involved in attempting to distinguish between the available alternatives are as follows:

(1) company or plant size;
(2) batch size or, conversely, the time needed to machine a batch;
(3) complexity of component, metal-removal technology and machine type;
(4) national institutions and accepted practices of management and the nature of technical work, training, status differentials, etc;
(5) socio-economic conditions of the present situation, regarding shortage of natural resources, limitation of mass markets, slow growth, market competition, etc.

Company Size

It has been shown that small plants often make a very unconventional use of CNC equipment and maintain unbureaucratic, simple organizational structures with programming-related functions tending to be less concentrated into specialised departments or positions. There is no systematic apprenticeship training in the plants, but a high degree of pragmatic and flexible 'learning' of how best CNC might be utilized. By contrast, large companies have adopted more systematic procedures with a greater division of labour, resulting in differentiating programming functions away from the shop floor into specialised departments.

'High technology' does not, by any means, signify greater bureaucratisation; the smaller plants combine a strikingly higher percentage of CNC machinery with personalised industrial relations, weak formal methods of organization and a great deal of traditional entrepreneurial, paternalistic and intuitive style; whereas the bigger plants are sometimes prevented from larger-scale CNC use by conventional organization and industrial relations of a more bureaucratic type. While the bigger plants are starting to incorporate CNC into apprenticeships and other training schedules in a more systematic fashion, this is unusual in the smaller plants. Small companies profit from the qualifications and expertise inherent to personnel who were trained or who worked in larger plants and, although this knowledge is not developed formally, they are ingenious in pushing ahead without organizational shackles.

Batch Size

Whilst plant size is associated with a greater differentiation of programming functions into separate departments, increasing batch size is linked with the greater differentiation of programming away from machine-operating, although not necessarily into separate departments. Nor is it necessarily taken away from the machine: there is a strong inclination for programme input on the machine not by the operator, but by a programmer, foreman or setter in small companies producing large batches. This is the case of an unbureaucratic but polarising division of labour and qualification structure. It is important to distinguish between bureaucratisation within the organization and the polarisation of skills. Increasing plant size is linked with the former, while increasing batch size is related to the latter. They interact, however, to bring forth organizational and qualification patterns as seen in Figure 1.

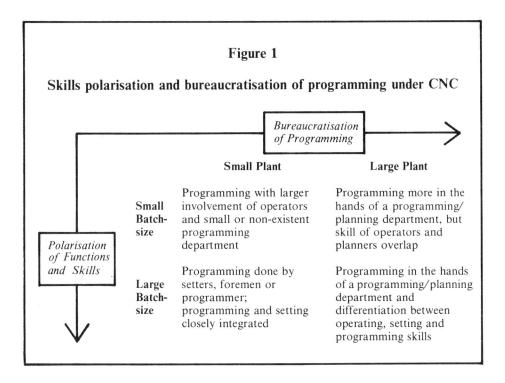

Figure 1

Skills polarisation and bureaucratisation of programming under CNC

	Small Plant	Large Plant
Small Batch-size	Programming with larger involvement of operators and small or non-existent programming department	Programming more in the hands of a programming/planning department, but skill of operators and planners overlap
Large Batch-size	Programming done by setters, foremen or programmer; programming and setting closely integrated	Programming in the hands of a programming/planning department and differentiation between operating, setting and programming skills

Bureaucratisation of Programming →

Polarisation of Functions and Skills ↓

The scheme in Figure 1 traces more or less 'ideal-typical' solutions, around which various modifications occur in working practice. It helps to summarize results which show that polarisation of functions and skills is very closely linked with batch size. This is, of course, also intuitive: the smaller the batch size, the greater the need for frequent conversion of machines with new tools, fixtures and component programmes and the less machine-setting expertise is differentiated from operating. Batch-size economies of scale thus involve a reduction of skills at the operator level.

Machine-setting and programme-related functions, however, overlap; the elimination of setting from machine operation also entails differentiation of programming-related functions from operating and it is often linked with a further differentiation between setting and programming.

Complexity of Component

The ideal-typical variation just described is modified by the metal-removal technology and machine type. This refers to a wide field of differences regarding numbers and types of tools, fixtures, materials, geometrical complexity of contours, standards of precision, type of machine and so on. Generally, the more time it takes to compile a programme, the more is programming differentiated from operating and for the two processes to occur in parallel. It is important to realise, however, that the central reason for differentiating programming and operating is not the innate technical superiority of a programmer, but the desire to achieve maximum machine utilisation.

But machine type does have an influence. A technologically advanced, horizontal machining centre, with automatic tool-changing facilities, is usually manned by a skilled operator because of the high costs involved in the machine itself, the necessary tooling and, frequently, the nature and complexity of the components manufactured.

Apart from any 'macros' or planning sub-routines, these machine types have increasingly sophisticated input systems which substantially simplify programming procedures. Thus, in this situation, the differentiation between planning and operating may not be particularly polarised. By contrast, on a simpler milling machine, the component is probably less complex; the programme is probably also less technically demanding but the operator may only be semi-skilled. In this instance, skill polarisation may be enhanced.

The time needed to make a programme is the central factor associated with different allocations of programming-related functions; the more time it takes to make a programme, the less is programming likely to occur on the shop floor. However, such a relationship presupposes that an operator cannot make a programme without the machine being idle. But this is only true to a limited extent. We have seen, for example, cases of operators drafting programmes after working hours at home. It is also possible on some machines to compile the programme for the next job while the present one is being processed.

The allocation of programming to groups of personnel, therefore, is not a simple objective choice: it is influenced by technical developments in electronic control and programming techniques, as well as operator-programming skills. In addition, both of these are subject to corporate and departmental strategy. Geometrical or informatical problems are increasingly made easier and quicker to solve, which reduces programming time continuously, on the basis of a part with a given design complexity. This holds, above all, in turning. With this trend, there seems to be emerging an increasing tendency for operators to perform programming-related functions, ranging from simple speed and feed modifications of previously compiled programmes to complete programme preparation on the shop floor. To that extent, the advance of CNC technology is depolarising by comparison with previous NC methods.

National Institutions and Cultural Practices

Just as CNC exercises different effects according to plant and batch size and type of cutting technology and machine type, so it also adapts to different societal environments. It is seen to adapt readily to different national institutions and cultural practices. Our study confirmed the existence of a series of pre-determined Anglo-German differences (Hearn, 1978).

The German companies, for example, distinguish less than those in Britain between specialised departments for production management, production engineering, work planning and work execution functions. Similarly, there is a consistently greater use of shop floor and operator programming in Germany: programming is seen as the nucleus around which the various company personnel — the managers, engineers, planners, foremen and operators — are integrated.

This general principle is seen to apply not only in terms of the selection of equipment and the utilisation of control system variants and so on, but also in the deliberate structuring of training, manning and organizational policies. These differences are reinforced by the CNC dimension, as are the different qualification structures which stress the craft-worker apprenticeship to a much greater extent in Germany. The greater separation of programming and operating in Britain ties in with the increasing differentiation of technician and worker apprenticeships, whereas technician training in Germany is invariably subsequent to craft-worker training and experience. In addition, whilst in Britain the planning and programming function distinguishes white-collar workers, it is much less so in Germany, where blue-collar workers are more extensively used for programming, both on the machine and in the planning department, and where rotation between the two groups is quite frequently observed.

National differences interact with company and batch-size differences: in Germany, the similarity between organization, labour and technical practices of small and large companies is greater than in Britain, where there appears to be a split between pragmatically flexible small plants and organizationally more segmented larger plants. Formal engineering qualifications at various levels are more common in Britain in larger plants whereas, often, they are not represented in small British plants. In Germany, by contrast, formal qualifications are common to small and large plants alike.

In both countries, there was a generally held perception that CNC operation was less distinctive for requiring 'information' skills than for advanced machining skills. Programming aids on the machine or in the planning departments are seen to be tools which help to control a process which has become ever more demanding from the point of view of precision, machining speeds, tools, fixtures and materials.

Cutting techniques and metal-removal skills still remain the focal points in production. CNC control systems may enhance the manner by which the machine is 'driven' but the mechanical processes themselves, the feeds and speeds and the precision and quality of the finished component, are where the major working problems and attractions alike reside.

Socio-economic Conditions

Thus, there are a series of 'logics' that have been moulded by separate historical, cultural and social developments. But there is a further logic of CNC application which is common to Britain and Germany. This extends from the relevant existing macro-economic factors, including competitive and marketing strategies, and also incorporates a very broad range of factors which affect enterprises but which the enterprises themselves attempt to influence.

The most generally stated competitive situation was one in which there was static or (more commonly in Britain) negative economic growth. Enterprises stated that they were seen, or perhaps being forced, increasingly to cater to small market 'niches' rather than to homogeneous mass markets. More individualised, custom-built products, with a greater number of product variants, were seen as being required. Product innovation, as part of this development, was tending to lead towards increasing numbers of components and component variants in production. Market expansion or maintenance of market share was only thought feasible with increased production variety.

In product design, there has also been a tendency for increasing component complexity. This is a result not only of increased product specialisation, but also is one of a number of ways whereby the overall manufacturing costs can be limited. There is a noticeable increase in both the number and complexity of 'cuts' to be performed on the component. Such a trend is observed to be dependent on, and causal to, the wider diffusion of NC machining and thus, the justification of NC machines has a *qualitative* element in addition to that derived from increases in productivity.

These kinds of complex and precise machining configurations would often not have been possible with conventional machines; thus the NC machine is a central, if not essential, element of effective production although its justification, particularly if associated with computer-aided design (CAD) facilities, is very difficult to express quantitatively.

Complex design of components is consistent with NC application but the greater variability of products and components is more specifically associated with CNC application. Perhaps generally, the two most important factors which lead to increasing CNC application within the manufacturing area are:

(a) the demand for more frequent and less time-consuming machine conversion from one batch to another, arising from the increased variability of products and components; and

(b) the inducement to minimise finished product stocks and work-in-progress which can be substantially reduced when the full potential for manufacturing 'families' of different, but similar, components is realized and/or advantage is taken of the opportunity to produce, in single manufacturing cycle, those sub-assemblies which comprise the final product.

Thus, market-oriented as well as financial considerations point in the direction of smaller batch sizes and more frequent conversion. This increased variability of batches, however, is not one which can be handled bureaucratically through a conventional increase in the division of labour. On the contrary, it implies increased flexibility right at the level of the machine and the operator; every CNC operator is likely to have to deal with a greater and more frequently changing range of jobs. Part of this transition is related to the increased sophistication of the machine-control system, by which more flexible change-overs and improvements in programmes can be achieved. But the crucial 'bottle-necks' are not observed to be information-processing and calculating skills: experience indicates that the most crucial problems refer to tooling materials, feeds, speeds, faults and breakdowns. Skills in handling these problems are most directly developed on the machine. It follows then that while programming skills are required, increasing emphasis needs to be placed on machining.

This tendency was shown in our study; companies, particularly those in Germany, are increasingly recognising the merits of an approach which relies strongly on craft-worker skills. This depolarising of skills and qualifications structures falls within the present logic of CNC development and application, not because it is a necessary consequence, but because CNC has been developed and applied along the lines of a socio-economic context which links economic success with depolarisation. There is a striking kinship between CNC and some of the craft trades and the renewed interest in companies, again particularly in Germany, to train and employ skilled workers.

Increased programming or programme-changing in the workshop also signifies an assimilation of status for blue- and white-collar workers. Planning and programming activities are less constitutive of status distinctions when they are rendered easier. It would, however, be extremely misleading to interpret this as another step towards the 'post-industrial' society, as 'information-processing' work or as a 'service' function, as so often happens.

Whilst it is true that workers are dealing with increasingly sophisticated information technology, this only concerns the *tools of their trade* rather than their *working goals*.

But there is another angle to the relationship between CNC and employment and we believe it to be the most important. The previous logic of socio-technical design has been geared to specialised, homogeneous mass markets, inflexible automation, an erosion of craft-worker skills and an increased emphasis on separate planning and programming activities. There has been a drift in the labour market towards white-collar occupations, information-processing, administration and different kinds of clerical work. The socio-economic context of CNC application, however, reverses this trend; there is an increased focus on craft skills and the levelling-out of the growth of indirectly productive employees. Re-orientation towards more flexible production engineering techniques, more relevant organization structures and related labour market and employment patterns (including the function of training) can be difficult for companies with rigid corporate strategies and personnel policies. Insofar as the application of CNC emphasises the need to regain flexibility in production, its successful diffusion can only occur in association with a re-orientation of company strategy and vocational career policies which are capable of responding to economic and employment problems.

FUTURE OF WORK

THE DISCUSSION OF work and employment under new technology has suffered from speculation where truisms, truths, half-truths and plain errors are strangely mixed. We suggest that the analysis of CNC application is of importance beyond the area of metal-working; it demonstrates the effects of technology under prevailing socio-economic conditions which are not restricted to CNC but which are more general in character and thus not limited to CNC. Some of these tentative findings are now discussed.

Initially we propose that it is possible to distinguish between different phases of microelectronics application and development. The first stage, generally recognised by a polarisation of qualifications and skills, emphasises not only a centralization of managerial decision-making but also the creation of separate data-processing departments and specialised informatic functions, including planning, programming and systems analysis. Manpower requirements from this phase still find expression in figures for most of the years of the last decade. This phase is marked by the impact of 'conventional' electronics and NC, but merely to extrapolate this trend for microelectronics is quite inappropriate.

In the second phase, a different picture emerges. Microelectronic applications, particularly some of the newer models, are notable not only for the dramatic increase in their degree of mechanical sophistication, but also for the reduction in the amount of intellectually demanding data-processing work necessary for their successful operation. They are not only much easier to 'drive' but also much simpler to 'instruct', even in the manufacture of highly complex components. But another effect is also apparent: with data-processing now more and more within the scope of the non-EDP specialist, the necessary technology becomes more widely diffused as, correspondingly, the demand for separately identified 'information workers' within the enterprise is diminished. But this process also has a secondary result: as this information-processing skill becomes more widely understood, it becomes less demanding in its own right; it becomes an integral part of the job and is a vehicle by which the vocational expertise of its users is broadened. In CNC, for example, this consequence is apparent in the increased emphasis and concern for proper tooling, improvement in cutting techniques, more adaptable fixtures and so on. Thus, paradoxically, advances in information technology, rather than reinforcing the technical zones, are not only providing new occupational opportunities, but also are enhancing the levels of potential development of 'traditional' skills.

In addition to these general considerations, some specific conclusions can also be drawn with regard to the foreseeable future of machining work. Here, the discussion is again beset by some ideas which can increasingly be viewed as obsessed with an extrapolation of past trends that, in many cases, have already been reversed. There is, for example, widespread fascination with the automated factory as the culmination of technical ingenuity. We think that this view is seriously misguided.

Further developments of CNC application, as observed at present, point in the following directions:

(1) CNC machines can be further mechanised by the automation of workpiece handing. This will allow workpieces to be fed automatically into the machine, where they are set, processed, extracted and provisionally stored. Different flexible manufacturing cells of this kind have already been exhibited at the 1981 European Machine Tools Fair and are perhaps most likely to be the next stage of wide application.

(2) Further steps of automation which will help to relieve the operator of some tasks are automatic workpiece measurement and adaptive control of the cutting process. These are expected to leave the experimental stage and be incorporated, on a comparatively large scale, into CNC machines in the not-too-distant future.

(3) The linking of machines, by automatic transport and feeding mechanisms, to form a successive chain of machining operations whereby workpieces progress from machine to machine without having to be handled by operators. Such flexible manufacturing systems have been the subject of substantial experimentation in a number of companies and development institutes, often financially assisted by governments. Logically, a flexible manufacturing

system is one step of automation beyond that of the flexible manufacturing cell since, rather than containing only one CNC machine, it links up two or more machines, usually of different types or having different tasks.

It is not difficult to construct a logic of development which emphasises the evolution towards production processes which become more and more automatic, culminating in the 'automatic factory'. This is often presented as the most advanced achievement of Japanese industrial efficiency. But, by and large, Japanese factories are not necessarily more automated than comparable European plants. One study, for example, has found that British companies may, in fact, be more automated than those in Japan, but that the efficiency of Japanese plants rests more on the meticulousness and dedication to detail of various employees, particularly operators, who are more charged with responsibility for quality of work. The usefulness of highly automated flexible manufacturing systems has also been questioned; there is evidence to suggest that they may not only be uneconomic, but also too complex to operate effectively on a continuous basis (Blumberg and Gerwin, 1981).

We interpret the fascination with the automated factory as another incorrect trend extrapolation. It is again founded on past experience with the expansion of homogeneous mass markets and the existence of a consistent and stable demand for specialised products. For traditional continuous production — whether, for example, continuous flow production (as employed in oil refineries, petrochemical plants and so on) or mass production (in the manufacture of motor cars) — technical advance, together with the intrinsic nature of the product, has led to highly automated, capital-intensive production facilities.

But it is also of interest to note the corresponding organizational tendency. In essence, it is one where production personnel have become fewer in number and consistently less involved in the overall manufacturing process. The picture, schematicaly presented in Figure 2, is one of deskilling, increased specialisation, centralization and the scaling-down of operator functions and their physical removal from the shop floor.

This view of automation, however, especially if generalized, is increasingly misleading. The present phase of technical advance is less characterised by stable, specialised mass markets, but by more differentiated and shifting market patterns which invariably create the need for direct and skilled human intervention because standard solutions are either too costly, too complex or liable to failure because of unanticipated variety.

The present trend of technical progress appears to combine productivity increases, including greater mechanisation and an increased dependence on electronic control systems, with the continued presence of directly intervening production operators on the shop floor; labour is not necessarily being driven away from the shop floor and the drift towards specialised planning and programming activities appears to be checked. It may, in fact, even be inappropriate to call this level of development 'automation'; instead, we have shown that the present phase of CNC application is more marked by greater interchange of personnel between production and planning departments and

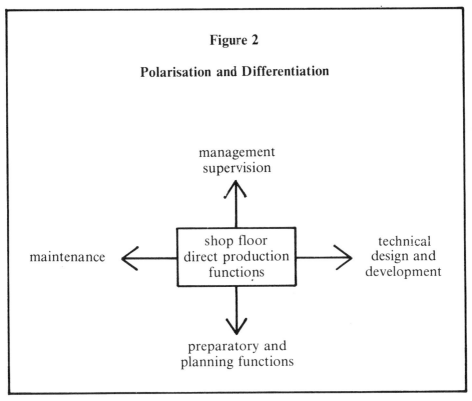

Figure 2

Polarisation and Differentiation

management
supervision

maintenance

shop floor
direct production
functions

technical
design and
development

preparatory and
planning functions

by the return of the planning and programming functions to the shop floor (Figure 3).

This evolution, however, depends on the prevailing socio-economic context, rather than on properties of the technology employed. A change of context will entail a change of technical development and modes of use. There will also always be a range of socio-technical options which can be taken up. This can be exemplified by the flexible manufacturing cell which, as previously mentioned, appears, after CNC itself, to be the next most widely applied production system.

Such a cell, from its technical properties, does not prejudge the attribution of qualifications, production organization and manning policy. It allows very different solutions, just like CNC. The common factor is that operators are relieved of workpiece handling. The question then is how this saving of work is made use of.

Different directions of socio-technical development can already be discerned. But the reasoning of a user may be as follows:

We already have machines which can be programmed whilst the previous batch is being processed. It was difficult, however, to make use of this facility because the operator had to spend too much time handling pieces and therefore, he could not do as much programming as was necessary. But now that he is relieved of the handling, is there not the possibility for him to take over planning and programming completely?

Alternatively, another user might conceive of a different solution:

Operators are now only needed for a limited number of 'machine-minding' functions: could we not increase the number of machines to which the operators or the production group is attached, especially if programming and machine-setting are performed, as scheduled, before the start of the batch by specialised setter-programmers.

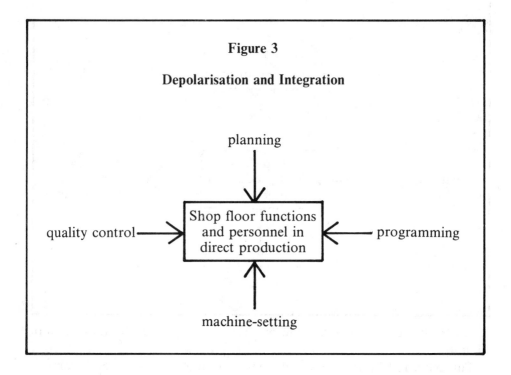

Figure 3

Depolarisation and Integration

We have observed both of these strategies and other intermediate solutions can also be imagined. We predict different solutions will again be developed; these will depend, just as much as under CNC machines, on prevailing national or company-specific organization and manpower patterns. Again, they will be strongly dependent on batch-size and production flexibility requirements. Thus, a more advanced stage of mechanisation does not necessarily imply automation in the conventional sense. In a context where increased flexibility and shorter batches are necessary, the opposite will be true.

SOCIO-TECHNICAL CHANGE AND EMPLOYMENT CREATION

THE DEBATE ABOUT MICROELECTRONICS has been marked by an underlying worry about decreased opportunities for employment. Whilst we did not find evidence to support the proposition that CNC, as the most important application of microelectronics in manufacturing, reduces the number of jobs available, it is still necessary to discuss its role in this most important area.

Unemployment is a cause for concern in both Britain and Germany, though in different degrees.

At the outset, however, we should state that we do not see any point in a discussion about job creation through the promotion of information technology or its application. Particularly in Britain, public debate has become marked by a kind of technology fetishism, where it is expected that promotion of a basic technology (such as microelectronics, software design, programming and so on) is a policy which is geared to the jobs of the future and will therefore create employment. One finds a more vocal, articulate and institutionalised commitment to an expressly defined microelectronics policy in Britain than in Germany. Our analysis, however, leads us to question such an approach. Whilst we do not dispute the value of widespread computer skills, a good supply of proficient design, software engineers and so on, we do not think that this will bring about an economic dynamism of sufficient strength to generate a noticeable quantity of employment.

This sort of industrial and labour supply policy by-passes the central problem of adaptation to current technical change. The most noteworthy feature of an information technology is that it reinforces the need for occupational skills and expertise of a 'non-informatic' type, which are simultaneously developed and expanded as the technology becomes more widespread. The present situation requires an emphasis on basic vocational skills and qualifications to cope with the prevailing socio-economic conditions.

The central point of attack for an employment-generating policy must be to strengthen the capacity of an economy to improve manufactured products, to achieve greater flexibility and variety in production and to be competitive through a more efficient utilisation of both capital and labour resources. Application of microelectronics, and CNC specifically, is no automatic remedy; it has to be carried out following a socio-technical approach specifically oriented to the desired objectives.

The revitalisation of manufacturing is an important part of such a strategy. It is paradoxical that there are increased manufacturing challenges, changing demands for production, traffic and communications, different energy generation and consumption infrastructures and so on — all co-existing with large-scale unemployment. A great deal of work needs to be done, primarily of an industrial nature. The institutional patterns for generating this type of work and employment (through craft and technical training and the corresponding occupational choices) however, have declined over the past phase of socio-technical evolution. The emphasis has been permitted to drift into clerical, white-collar and service careers and to stress greater importance and status for general education rather than vocational training. This has to be redressed in order to cope with the prevailing socio-economic situation.

Contrasts between the two phases are similar to those between Britain and Germany. Discrepancies in the strength of vocational training between these two countries are striking and this has been reflected in our study (Prais, 1981). There are major differences, particularly at the basic levels of qualification and in the emphasis on the practical versus the academic elements. Again, it is paradoxical that the institutional system for vocational training in Britain is being jeopardised at a time when it is particularly required (Maurice *et al,* 1980).

However, it would not be realistic to recommend a unilateral emphasis on strengthening training institutions. Their strength is a reflection of industrial performance as much as a factor which may increase it. Such an interaction shows the necessity to bring about an integrated approach which does not stress the importance of one field of action, such as training, to the detriment or neglect of others.

A training policy has to be linked with the increased promotion of industrial efficiency; the two factors are interdependent. Industrial efficiency, in turn, is increasingly dependent on the ability to combine flexibility with productivity increase — a combination of factors which have, in the past, often appeared to be opposites. They can only be combined under a distribution of skills and qualifications which is less polarised and in a type of company organization which emphasises cohesiveness across functional and departmental boundaries. These matters should be the concern not only of companies, but also of governments, training bodies and other industrial agencies, including the trade union movement.

A revitalisation of manufacturing is sensibly linked with an increased concern for engineering education, especially in the wake of the Finniston Commission and Report. Particularly in Britain, a more practical orientation to engineering education appears overdue. The most recent period of socio-economic development in education has emphasised higher scientific, academic and theoretical attainments. Proportionately, there has come about a neglect of basic and intermediate, vocational, practical and technical education and training. This now requires strengthening, particularly in Britain where it has always been weaker, and where the discrepancy with Germany has grown rather than decreased. It is of significance that in addition to Germany's generally higher productivity, its productivity tends to be relatively higher in those industries that are skill-intensive and particularly in those industries relying on the intermediate grades of skill (Prais, 1981).

There is one further and very important point to be made: there has to be a warning against the view of those who stress employment in 'information occupations' in the 'post-industrial society' as an extension of the 'knowledge industry' in schools, universities and scientific institutes. Such ideas are even used to interpret Anglo-German differences in formal qualifications: a higher percentage of formal qualifications in Germany is used as an argument to establish an immediate link between general education and productivity or efficiency. Such a view builds on the assumption that knowledge is the most important single input into modern productive systems, that we have become an information society in which the knowledge industry is the major growth area and that the bulk of the labour force have become information operatives. A factual knowledge of microelectronics applications in manufacturing exposes such a statement to be as sensible as considering a general practitioner in medicine to be a transportation worker because he goes to see patients by car. When policies are developed following this line of reasoning, further industrial decline will be the consequence and unemployment will increase. Special care has to be taken not to project the socio-economic logic of the years after the Second World War, up to the beginning of the 1970s, onto the development and application of microelectronics. A policy which continues this logic is bound to fail for there is no way around the need for increasing technical competence in industry. It has to be developed, from the bottom upwards, in every kind of manufacturing enterprise.

References

Blumberg, Melvin and Gerwin, Donald (1981) *Coping with Advanced Manufacturing Technology*. Discussion Paper, International Institute of Management, Berlin.

Hearn, D. A. (1978) *Shop Floor and Management Aspects of CNC Machine Tools*. Machine Tool Industry Research Association, Macclesfield, UK.

Maurice, M., Sorge, A. and Warner, M. (1980) *Societal differences in Organizing Manufacturing Units: A Comparison of France, West Germany and Great Britain*. Organization Studies 1, pp. 59-86.

Prais, S. J. (1981) *Vocational qualifications of the labour force in Britain and Germany*. Discussion Paper 43, National Institute of Economic and Social Research, London.

CHAPTER 10

Organizational Communication: The relationship between Technological Development and Socio-economic Needs

Arnold Picot, Heide Klingenberg and Hans-Peter Kränzle

University of Hannover, Federal Republic of Germany

SOME ASPECTS OF NEW OFFICE COMMUNICATION TECHNOLOGY AND THE WAY OF LIFE

AN EXPLORATION is undertaken here of the possible impacts that the new technologies of office communication might have on the structure of organizational communication.* Rapid progress in microelectronics has produced a variety of new technical communication channels for office use. Some of them (such as viewphone, video conferencing, integrated text and fax services) are only expected to enter the commercial arena of office communication in the future. At present, however, new channels are being implemented, or are about to be introduced, such as telecopy services (fax, facsimile), telephone conferencing, computer conferencing, electronic messaging and videotext. Their diffusion, however, is not very far advanced as yet. Some of the new technologies of this latter group are examined here, mainly new electronic channels for written (text) communication. These new media will enrich the spectrum of existing channels in organizational communication (face-to-face, telephone, classic mail, telex and sometimes telecopy contacts).

Availability of more facilities allowing electronic mediation of information will change the patterns of organizational communication. These changes and

*This research is part of an ongoing larger empirical project on office communication, sponsored by the German Department of Research and Technology (Bundesminister für Forschung und Technologie). Co-operation with and support from the participating organizations (Allianz-Versicherung, Olympia/AEG/T & N, and Siemens) are gratefully acknowledged.

114

their possible consequences deserve scientific attention. Most people spend a remarkable proportion of their lifetime working and communicating in organizations or communicating with organized institutions. It is widely accepted that our construction of social reality, as well as the modes of relating to each other, depend to a large extent on communication experiences made in everyday-life (Berger and Luckmann, 1966). Therefore, possible structural changes in organizational communication patterns, caused by new office communication technologies, could affect the way of social life. Furthermore, the quality of social life also depends on the effectiveness and efficiency of organizations. As far as those are affected by new office technology, indirect impacts may occur on the way of life.

MAJOR PROPOSITIONS ON THE IMPACTS OF NEW OFFICE COMMUNICATION TECHNOLOGY

THE POSSIBLE CONSEQUENCES of the availability of new text-oriented, electronic media can be divided into three contrasting groups. They represent different schools of thought about the functions of technologies and organizations in society.

Proposition I: Revolutionary and advantageous changes in Office Communication

According to this proposition, new electronic text media would not only replace the old text communication channels of mail and telex (thus enabling written organizational communication to become faster and more efficient), but furthermore, this technological development would substitute the new media for a large proportion of oral communication in organizations (especially telephone and face-to-face contacts, regarded as particularly time-consuming and costly). Assuming a task-oriented, rational perspective on organizational communication, a diminution of face-to-face and oral communication in favour of telecommunication and written information is felt desirable since most verbal communication tends to be somewhat lengthy. According to Marill (1980, p. 185):

> *The phone also shares a problem with all speech communication: the information density of speech is very low. Generally, the electronic transmission of speech requires about 60,000 bits per second. These 60,000 bits of speech carry about the same information as 15 characters of written text . . . . But you can transmit 15 characters directly as text by transmitting only 120 bits of information, rather than 60,000 bits of speech. If you insist on transmitting speech, you are transmitting 500 times too many bits. And*

these bits have to be paid for. In a very fundamental sense, speech is not an economic medium of communication. (See also Merrihue 1960, p. 179; Turoff, 1973).

New electronic text media seem to share all the desirable properties necessary to overcome the shortcomings of oral communication. They are fast, they document the information content and they provide these qualities at low costs and over almost any distance between sender and receiver (Uhlig *et al,* 1979; Panko, 1980).

New structural configurations for innovative, organizational decision-making could emerge (Witte, 1976; Szyperski, 1979, p. 161 f). By means of new communication technologies, decentralized autonomous groups could pursue their work effectively without risking organizational disintegration (Witte, 1977 and 1980, p. 1055 f). Thus, organizational functioning could become much more independent from location restrictions (Goddard, 1971), even including 'working at home' (Goldmark, 1972). Eventually, the technological development could lead to a more effective reconciliation of individual needs and organizational demands. Such prospects are, of course, attractive. They nourish expectations of a rapid development of market demand for new communication technologies.

Proposition II: Modest changes in Organizational Communication

However, one quickly thinks of an analogue to these predictions. The Management Information System (MIS) — euphoria of the 1960s and early '70s — made many similar promises which for the most part remained unfulfilled. That movement was also driven by a rational approach trying to match demand and supply of information in organizations with the help of upcoming new information technology (Argyris, 1971; Kirsch and Klein, 1977; Feldmann and March, 1980). Therefore, one hesitates to fully accept the view of a technological revolution of office communication.

Scepticism derives from two interrelated sources. Social, psychological and related research underline the functional importance of non-verbal aspects in face-to-face communication. Developing of a 'social meaning' and establishing social relations would require such contacts (Watzlawick *et al,* 1967; Argyle, 1969). In organizational communication, requirements of that kind are manifold, such as developing trusting relationships among members, co-ordinating the information for performance of complex and dynamic tasks, creative solving of complex problems, motivating members or evaluating performance.

On the other hand, recent economic theories of organization show that firms are mainly concerned with situations heavily involving these functions and, thereby, with sensitive communication problems. The emergence of business organizations can be explained by market failure considerations. Those economic exchanges (transactions) are carried out within the firm and would be too complex and too expensive for market co-ordination (Arrow, 1974; Williamson, 1975; Picot 1981). Market exchange principally demands the possibility of codifying goods, services and conditions involved. When this is not feasible (or only at extremely high costs), and if the intended exchange should still take place, the parties involved integrate and build some sort of (hierarchical) organization. Thus, the internal organization of business firms handles the more complicated transactions of an economy. Typically, these internal transactions call for an information exchange which only to a lesser degree can be translated into, for example, written codes. Consequently, symbolic interaction and social presence (oral and face-to-face communication) are inevitable and most important requisites for a successful goal achievement in organizational communication. In the field of external communication, the new technologies could also replace the old text media which — according to this theory — cover a larger proportion of the whole external communication. Thus, transactions with the environment could be facilitated.

Given this second proposition, one would expect that new communication technologies will substantially replace existing text communication channels (mail and telex) and will only marginally affect channels of oral communication (telephone and face-to-face). However, to that extent organizational communication could become faster and better organized. Taking the organization as a whole, these changes would be incremental rather than revolutionary. In addition, development of future markets would be relatively slow.

Proposition III: Social and Economic Hazards

Yet, one may also argue that there are dangers involved with the upcoming new communication technologies. The business world could widely adopt the expectations of the first proposition, hoping for a more rational control of organizational behaviour. It could design organizational communication systems, making extensive use of the new technologies and permitting transmission of task-oriented information almost exclusively through new technical channels. The consequences could be harmful in several respects: co-ordination of complex tasks and solving of difficult problems would decline. Even if a Tayloristic redesign of jobs had been undertaken in advance, adaptability to external change would decrease. In any case, social structure of organization and need-fulfilment of members would suffer, since there would be less chance of developing trusting social relations. That is why isolation of individuals could increase. Similar arguments are advanced by Weizenbaum (1980 a and b) on the social impacts of information technology.

RESEARCH QUESTIONS

IN ORDER TO FURTHER EXPLORE the empirical justification of the expectations so far delineated, one should try to answer the following questions.
(1) What general attitudes do managers show towards new office technologies in general? Answers to this question could point to problems or opportunities that the new office communication technology will face when entering organizations.
(2) What determinants influence the choice of communication channels? In accordance with Pye and Young (1980, p. 7), we feel that the "next step forward in the hierarchy of predictive methodologies is to take individual selection acts and seek the empirical determinants of choices." Improving our empirical knowledge about channel decisions will result in a better understanding about the extent to which new channels will replace old ones. Reflecting our previous discussion of socio-emotional and rational functions of organizational communication, it seems useful to subdivide this problem into two components (Communication Studies Group, 1975, p. 18):
    (a) cognitive (rational) determinants of channel selection;
    (b) affective (emotional) determinants of the selection act.
    Answers to these questions will help us to clarify under what task-oriented as well as affective-conditions channels (in particular, new text-oriented electronic media) are likely to be accepted as a communication tool in organizations. Only then can we tackle the next question:
(3) What potential for substitution between channels can be observed in organizational communication and what changes in communication patterns do people demand?
    Having shed some empirical light on these questions, we will be able to draw some general conclusions with respect to the three previously mentioned propositions about the impacts of new organizational communication technologies.

DESCRIPTION OF THE FIELD STUDIES

THESE RESEARCH QUESTIONS are included in a larger research programme, sponsored by the German Department of Research and Technology. This project aims at an assessment of the impacts of new office communication technology on organizational structure and job characteristics, evaluating the new teletex technology in several field experiments (Picot and Reichwald, 1979).

Teletex Technology

Teletex, as a new electronic communication service of Western European and many overseas countries, will be officially available during the next 3 years, starting from 1982. The teletex system belongs to the family of electronic mail or electronic messaging systems. It integrates features of an electronic word processing device with an advanced and comfortable electronic telex machine. Its main characteristics are:

(a) by means of electronic storage and automatic dialing, the functions of word processing (typewriting) and text communication operate independently;

(b) accessability and compatibility to the national and worldwide well-established telex system, increasing the new service's attractiveness as a communication tool for the business world and public administration;

(c) high transmission speed (2,400 bits/sec), more than 30 times faster than the old telex system and transmission of a keyboard's standard repository of symbols;

(d) simple standard layout (CCITT standards), with a mandatory printer and a modest storage capacity, so that the device could be affordable on a large scale (quick market penetration and surmounting critical mass limits); screen and other additions optional.

Teletex does not yet provide integration with other computer services nor allow device-independent operation. However, other electronic mail/message/conference systems do not as yet offer (inter)national compatibility of equipment and networks.

Sample

The field study consists of 4 sub-organizations in two large private companies (insurance and electrical manufacturing), with some thirty locations spreading all over West Germany and West Berlin. Eighty teletex stations (preliminary versions of the teletex technology only allowing internal organizational use between one organization's stations) were installed, supplemented by telecopy (facsimile) facilities.

Six hundred and forty users, having access to these stations, take part in the investigations, about 40 per cent thereof being technical and scientific personnel and 60 per cent holding positions in business, finance and other administrative functions. A breakdown by hierarchical level shows that approximately 50 per cent are lower level managers, 40 per cent middle level managers, and 10 per cent high level managers. One hundred and fifty operators, mainly secretaries, are included in the study.

Method

In order to answer our questions and control other factors as precisely as possible, a rather complex package of research instruments had to be developed, containing some 20 different tools. These range from expert interviews and various questionnaires for managers and secretaries, on simple structured, self-report measures (checklist crossing in order to assess certain frequencies of information and communication) to objective measures (counting of mail, telex, teletex contacts, etc). More detailed information about the research instruments is available on request from the authors.

RESEARCH RESULTS

THE FOLLOWING RESULTS represent the initial analyses of the data collected in the field. As collection of data was completed only very recently, the preliminary character of the reported findings should be stressed.

Attitudes towards New Office Technology in general

Based on attitudinal questionnaire data (n = 629 users and 147 operators), we found an interesting contrast between a favourable general attitude towards technological innovations in offices (Proposition I) and a sceptical view of the specific personal consequences to be faced when technological change in offices occurs (Proposition III).

On the one hand, a large majority of managers and secretaries (about 80 per cent) articulated a positive opinion on new office technology in general, especially on its contribution to more effective task performance. The majority (52 per cent) do not fear substitution of their labour or major deskilling of jobs. At the same time, higher educational requirements were expected to be needed in order to cope with technological changes (70 to 80 per cent).

On the other hand, there exists a widespread fear of unfavourable consequences for the personal work situation. Most respondents (about 60 per cent) were afraid of an increasingly impersonal work atmosphere, an increase in written communication and growing bureaucratic structures, all caused by new office technology.

These findings seem valid since they were obtained in an organizational environment already well-equipped with decentralized office technology, allowing individuals to base their judgements on analogous experiences.

Following the first preliminary results from a factor analysis (PCA with VARIMAX-rotation),* no clear attribution was to be found as to whether the

---

*All factor analyses were computed by the SPSS subroutine 'FACTOR'. Further details about these analyses are available on request from the authors.

expectation of increasing written communication would be related to the expectation of increasing impersonal co-operation or rather to the expectation of better task performance.

Choice of Communication Channels

Cognitive Determinants of Channel Selection

As a first step, we put together a list with possible work-related problems faced by organizational communication. These requirements had been collected from textbooks and discussions with practitioners. The list was extensively pretested, leaving 21 items which seem to have general significance as criteria shaping the process of organizational communication. Then, we asked managers to evaluate each requirement's general work-related importance on a 3-point scale. The results are summarized in Table 1.

Table 1

**General evaluation of communication requirements by users
(3-point scale; n = 477)**

very important	1.0	
	1.1	unambiguous understanding of content
	1.2	speediness
	1.3	certainty of exact wording/certainty of information reaching the wanted receiver
	1.4	availability of channel/capability of quick response/ capability of quick feed-back/transmission of difficult content/short composition time
	1.5	easy processing by receiver/short transmission time/ resolving disagreement/capability of documentation
	1.6	identification of sender/transmission costs
	1.7	comfort/circular letters/transmission of small information volume
	1.8	transmission of large information volume/protection from faking
	1.9	confidentiality
less important		
	2.0	
unimportant	3.0	

Unambiguity, speediness, exact wording and 'reaching somebody' seem to be the most important criteria to be met in order to solve communication problems in organizations. On the other hand, confidentiality and protection from faking do not play the role one would expect given recent public debates in Europe.

In the next step, we asked users to rate the six channels available to them (telephone, face-to-face, mail, telex, telefax and teletex) on a six-point scale (1 being the highest rating), considering each channel's capability to fulfil the criteria mentioned above. Initial, and as yet preliminary, factor analyses of the data for each channel show that there might be four major factors involved when evaluating task-oriented functions of communication channels:

Factor A: *Promptness,* comprising items: speediness, comfort, capability of quick response and transmission of small information volume.

Factor B: *Complexity,* comprising items: resolving disagreements, transmission of unambiguous content, transmission of difficult content and certainty of reaching the wanted receiver.

Factor C: *Confidence,* comprising items: confidentiality, protection from faking and identification of sender.

Factor D: *Accuracy,* comprising items: exact wording, capability of documentation, easy processing by receiver and transmission of large information volume.

These factors explain between 90 and 100 per cent of the answer variance, depending on the type of channel. Their order of contribution to variance explanation changes from channel to channel; factor C, however, never exceeds a third rank.

It is our contention that managerial promptness, semantic complexity, interpersonal confidence and administrative accuracy represent four basic problems to be overcome by organizational communication. According to these factors, we listed the communication requirements and their mean ratings with regard to each channel. This should allow us to find out possible channel preferences with respect to the four basic dimensions.

Table 2 condenses the results and also shows the order of channel preference found when communication problems associated with one of the factors occur. When looking at the rankings, the distances represented by the differences of the means should be kept in mind. These rankings reflect managers' perceived effectiveness of channels with respect to each of the four basic communication issues. Tasks whose complexity or whose social characteristics (such as leadership) demand clarification and development of interpersonal relationships (Factors B and C) seem to require face-to-face contacts. In situations involving urgency, comfortable transmission and less complex contents (Factor A), the telephone is preferred, followed at some distance by electronic text media and face-to-face contacts. In communication situations where the information is well defined and subject to more or less programmed documentation or processing on the receiver's side (Factor D), text media are preferred, followed by face-to-face contacts and the telephone.

Table 2

Task-oriented evaluation of communication channels
(6-point scale)

channel item/factor	telephone (n = 326)	face-to-face (n = 316)	mail (n = 337)	telex (n = 328)	fax (n = 332)	teletex (n = 324)
speediness	1.3	4.1	4.2	2.2	2.1	2.2
comfort	1.4	3.6	3.5	3.0	2.6	2.9
transmission of small information volume	1.7	4.7	3.5	2.0	2.4	2.5
capability of quick response	1.4	2.9	4.5	2.5	2.5	2.5
short composition time	1.3	3.4	3.9	2.8	2.7	3.0
short transmission time	1.6	4.4	4.2	2.4	2.4	2.3
A "promptness" weighted average	1.4	3.8	4.0	2.5	2.4	2.6
rank	①	⑤	⑥	③	②	④
resolving disagreement	2.1	1.2	4.0	4.0	3.8	3.7
unambiguous understanding of content	2.6	1.6	2.6	3.2	2.7	2.8
transmission of difficult content	3.0	1.5	2.8	3.8	3.0	3.1
certainty of reaching the wanted receiver	1.6	1.3	2.9	3.1	3.1	3.0
B "complexity" weighted average	2.3	1.4	3.1	3.5	3.1	3.1
rank	②	①	③	⑥	③	③
confidentiality (during transmission)	2.9	1.3	2.3	4.4	4.2	4.1
protection from faking (during transmission process)	3.6	2.2	2.1	3.2	2.5	2.8
identification of sender	2.8	1.5	1.9	3.0	2.5	2.7
C "confidence" weighted average	3.1	1.7	2.1	3.5	3.1	3.2
rank	③	①	②	⑥	③	⑤
capability of documentation	5.1	4.9	1.5	2.1	1.6	1.7
certainty of exact wording	4.0	3.2	1.6	2.2	1.7	1.7
easy processing by receiver	4.3	4.2	2.0	2.4	2.1	1.8
transmission of large information volume	4.3	3.2	2.2	3.3	3.1	2.2
D "accuracy" weighted average	4.4	3.9	1.8	2.5	2.1	1.8
rank	⑥	⑤	①	④	③	①

Scale: 1 = very good . . . 6 = very bad

Though these results are produced by quite different methods, they are consistent with other theoretical and empirical literature in the field (Short *et al,* 976, p. 62 f; Johansen *et al,* 1978, p. 390 f; Schulman and Steinman, 1978; Johansen *et al,* 1979, p. 21 f; Rice, 1980).

Affective Determinants of Channel Selection

The affective side of channel selection was covered by a pretested list of sixteen adjectives, covering affective as well as cognitive components of attitudes. We asked managers to rate each of the six channels with respect to these items on a five-point scale; we also asked them to fill-in the questionnaire in an emotional, affective way. After analysing the data in factor analyses, we came up with the following results, almost identical for all sub-organizations investigated.

There are five basic factors (dimensions) describing and guiding emotional judgements of communication channels in organizations. These factors are the same for all channels, explaining between 87 and 100 per cent of the answer variance. Their order of contribution to variance explanation changes from channel to channel:

Factor I: *Stimulation,* comprising items: active, creative, happy and energetic.

Factor II: *Comfort,* comprising items: simple, quick and comfortable.

Factor III: *Dependability,* comprising items: exact, secure and reliable.

Factor IV: *Formality,* comprising items: standardized, bureaucratic and regular.

Factor V: *Privacy,* comprising items: confidential, personal and secret.

We suggest that these factors represent relevant, mainly affective aspects of channel evaluation.

Table 3 shows the weighted averages of the mean ratings of related items for each factor. For instance, the value of 3.3 for mail in Factor II (comfort) is the weighted average of the values this channel received for the adjectives simple, quick and comfortable in both organizations. With a value of 3.3, this channel is perceived to be somehow 'not comfortable' — on our 5-point scale, **5** represents the lowest value (not appropriate) and **1** the highest value (appropriate). Thus, values indicate the extent to which related emotional aspects are attributed to communication channels. The circled figures indicate the ranking of a channel with respect to the evaluation features represented by a factor.

Whereas face-to-face communication ranks highest, associated with 'stimulation' and 'privacy', the telephone is highly preferred for 'comfortable' communication. Text media score highest when 'dependability' and 'formality' are involved. One should note the remarkable distance between text-oriented media and oral media on the factors of 'stimulation' and 'formality', also the leading position of the telephone on the factor 'comfort'.

Finally, users were asked for an overall affective judgement (on a six-point scale, **1** ranking highest) how much they liked using each channel, regardless of

Table 3

Affective evaluation of communication channels (5-point scale; n = 241)

Factors	Channel	telephone	face-to-face	mail	telex	fax	teletex
I stimulation	weighted average	2.6	2.3	3.1	3.3	3.5	3.1
	rank	(2)	(1)	(3)	(5)	(6)	(3)
II comfort	weighted average	1.4	2.4	3.3	2.4	2.1	2.3
	rank	(1)	(4)	(6)	(4)	(2)	(3)
III dependability	weighted average	2.5	2.1	1.9	2.0	1.9	1.9
	rank	(6)	(5)	(1)	(4)	(1)	(1)
IV formality	weighted average	4.0	4.1	2.9	3.1	3.2	3.2
	rank	(5)	(6)	(1)	(2)	(3)	(3)
V privacy	weighted average	2.3	1.5	2.0	3.8	3.9	3.3
	rank	(3)	(1)	(2)	(5)	(6)	(4)

Scale: 1 = appropriate . . . 5 = totally inappropriate

the task or situation involved. In all organizations, the telephone and face-to-face contacts were most popular, ranking highest with an overall mean value of 1.6 and 2.0 respectively. There is a remarkable affective gap between these two channels and the group of text-oriented channels, the first being mail (4.0), followed by fax (4.1), teletex (4.2) and telex (4.6).

It is interesting to note that the telephone ranks highest above face-to-face contacts. This may be due to its easy availability, combined with its effectiveness for prompt and varied day-to-day communication. (See also the importance of the telephone with situations involving Factors A or II.)

Potential Of and Demand For Substitution

In order to assess the potential of substitution between channels in organizations, we first need information about the distribution of channel use. Using a self-reporting measure, we studied some 16,000 contacts. Roughly, we found the following structure:

Average number of contacts per day: 30

External/internal contacts: 43% intradepartmental,
                                                           45% interdepartmental,
                                                           12% external

Distribution over channels   39% telephone, 42% face-
(before implementation of teletex):   to-face, 16% mail,
                                                           3% telex/telefax

Contacts perceived as urgent: 40%

A break-down by channel and communication partner for one sub-organization is given in Table 4, other sub-organizations showing similar patterns. These findings underline the enormous significance, both relative and absolute, of oral communication in organizations, previously reported by Mintzberg (1973, p. 38 f) and Weinshall (1979, p. 3). If the high proportion of telephone and face-to-face communications indicate that the majority of communications within the organization are concerned with handling difficult problems, then the findings seem consistent with Proposition II. However, according to Proposition I, the high volume of oral communication could also point to a high potential for substitution, if a high proportion of tasks, currently handled by oral channels, were efficiently replacable by new text media (i.e. strongly related to Factor D).

Table 4

Breakdown by channel and communication partner (manufacturing departments of one organization, n = 9,204 contacts, n = 165 users)

Channel / Contacts	telephone	face-to-face	mail	telex	fax	
Intradepartmental	22%	73%	5%	0%	0%	100%
Interdepartmental	53%	28%	15%	3%	1%	100%
External	46%	11%	32%	10%	1%	100%

We therefore investigated the possibilities of substitution between channels using different approaches. We asked managers to give general judgements on a possible replacement of their oral and mail channels by other channels. Preliminary analysis of the data (though still needing some additional checking) indicates a perceived potential of substitution, represented in Table 5. The figures in that table cannot be added by row since, for instance, a face-to-face contact replacable by mail can, in many cases, also be replaced by telephone. However, managers' judgements show that electronic text communication media (teletex, fax, telex) could replace at least 5 per cent of face-to-face contacts, 12 per cent of telephone contacts and 18 per cent of mail contacts. Thus, new text-oriented channels could play a major role replacing telephone contacts — especially if the high absolute volume of phone contacts is kept in mind — and in replacing traditional mail. But it must be noted that substitution could also work in the other direction (moving from written to oral or from telephone to face-to-face communication).

Table 5

Subjective assessment of potential channel substitution (n = 96)

Replaced channel \ Replacing channel	telephone	face-to-face	mail	telex	fax	teletex
. . . percentage of **face-to-face** contacts could be replaced by . . .	28%	—	13%	2%	2%	5%
. . . percentage of **telephone** contacts could be replaced by . . .	—	20%	16%	9%	5%	12%
. . . percentage of **mail** contacts could be replaced by . . .	15%	13%	—	7%	10%	18%

These findings are corroborated by a more detailed substitution analysis. Managers were asked to thoroughly describe their recent channel uses and to account for possible substitution through electronic text channels. Initial and still very incomplete data analysis shows that about 8 per cent of more than 1,000 face-to-face contacts analysed are perceived as suitable for new electronic media (teletex and/or fax). Managers mention the following main reasons for denying the possibility of greater substitution: discussion needed, group meeting necessary, exchange of difficult ideas or acquisition of background knowledge.

A comparison between actual use of communication channels and desired use can serve as an indicator of managers' demand for substitution. As Table 6 shows, respondents will want more face-to-face contacts, a decrease of telephone and standard mail communication and an increase in use of fast, new electronic text media (the latter reflecting some good experiences with the

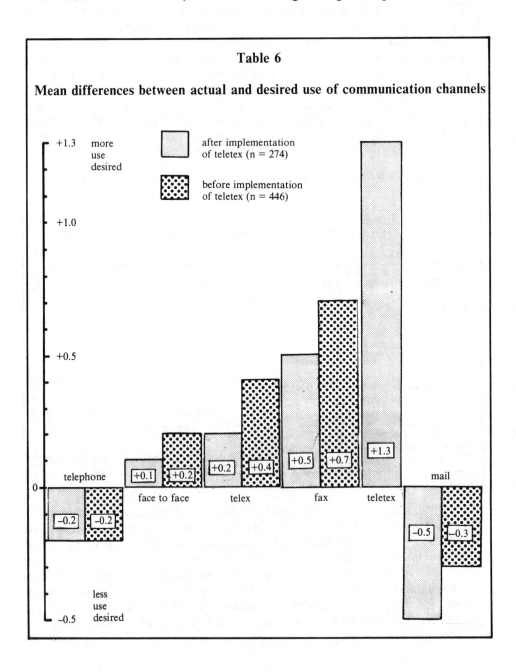

Table 6

Mean differences between actual and desired use of communication channels

new channels). However, no overwhelming demand for further expansion of the new media is seen when looking at this result in combination with the foregoing analysis.

DISCUSSION

WATZLAWICK, BEAVIN AND JACKSON (1967) show convincingly that any human communication process addresses aspects of information content as well as aspects of social relations between sender and receiver. Proportions of content-oriented (task) problems and of relation-oriented (interpersonal) issues vary, depending on contingencies. Furthermore, the authors distinguish between two basic modes of communication: digital (coded) communication, mainly using languages and writing as tools, and analogue (symbolic) communication, working with non-verbal signals as a means of message transmission, such as gestures, facial expressions, voice modulation, physical and environmental symbols and other associative analogues ('metacommunication'). Whereas many matters of content (not all!) can be transmitted by coded communication, most aspects of interpersonal relationship (not all!) require symbolic communication. Coded (digital) information can be telecommunicated in cases where the contents are not too complicated. Analogue communication eludes telecommunication for the most part and, thus, demands the social and physical presence of partners.

Reviewing our research experience, we feel that these concepts provide a good basis for interpreting our results. The findings about choice and substitution of channels seem also to support assumptions underlying other authors' view (Short *et al,* 1976). Referring to these theoretical and empirical foundations, one can predict impacts of new electronic text media confronting socio-economic needs of organizational communication.

Telecommunications technology in general and new text-oriented media in particular can primarily take over those transfers of information which can be coded and whose content is not too complex. New technologies can transmit those communication problems faster, cheaper and probably more reliably than channels previously used for that purpose. Hence, they could replace old text-oriented channels (mail and telex). As far as telephone and face-to-face contacts were used for handling such kinds of information exchange, they could also be replaced.

However, theory suggests, as does our data, that this type of information exchange does not prevail in organizational communication. The core of intra-organizational activity comprises processes heavily concerned with complicated contents and/or with social relations, such as co-ordinating complicated tasks, solving complex problems, developing innovative strategies, monitoring and evaluating barely tangible performances and motivating people. These and similar activities involve complex contents.

Moreover, they affect and require trusting social relations. Consequently, they cannot be properly maintained by using telecommunication technology. In this context, it seems worth noting that in Japanese companies — whose efficiency is, *inter alia,* attributed to a high degree of mutual trust and the sharing of beliefs (Ouchi, 1980) — face-to-face communication is reported to be remarkably high (Pascale, 1978).

Thus, the new text-oriented and technically powerful communication technologies will only, to a minor degree, keep the promises initially expressed in Proposition I because much of the work-related, information activities cannot be properly handled by the new media. Our data on general attitudes towards new office technology show that some fears of the kind suggested in Proposition III do exist. An overenthusiastic deployment of the new technologies, without taking account of the social character of organizational structure and performance, could be harmful. This would not only hinder individuals' need satisfaction, but in many cases the organization's viability would be endangered due to the rigidity and sterility of its communication structure and its lack of ability to adapt to change. These problems can be avoided if an open, participatory planning and implementation strategy concerning the new communication technology for organizations is adopted. Favourable attitudes towards new office technology as such seem to guarantee a fruitful process of communication development.

Thus, in conclusion, Proposition II seems to provide a good description of the possible impacts that new communication technologies might produce. The extent of channel subtitution previously outlined will surely lead to improved organizational co-ordination and performance. The organization's information-processing capacity increases, thereby facilitating growth and regional expansion of activities. Some characteristics of office jobs will change, along with the changes in text-oriented communication technology and its integration with EDP. However, as far as communication technology is concerned, if the social and economic needs mentioned are taken into consideration, there will be evolutionary, rather than revolutionary, impacts on our way of life.

References

Argyle, M. (1969) *Social Interaction.* Methuen, London.
Argyris, C. (1971) *Management Information Systems: The Challenge to Rationality and Emotionality.* Management Science, Vol. 17, pp. B 275-B 292.
Arrow, K. J. (1974) *The Limits of Organization.* W. W. Norton, New York.
Berger, P. L. and Luckmann, T. (1966) *The Social Construction of Reality.* Double-day, New York.
Communication Studies Group (1975) *The Effectiveness of Person-to-Person Telecommunications Systems.* Research at the Communications Studies Group. Long Range Research Report 3, University College, London.
Feldman, M. S. and March, J. G. (1980) *Information in Organizations as Signal and Symbol.* Paper presented at the annual meeting of the Western Political Science Association in San Francisco, March 27-29.
Goddard, J. B. (1971) *Office Communications and Office Location: A Review of Current Research.* Regional Studies, 5, pp. 263-280.
Goldmark, P. C. (1972) *Tomorrow we will Communicate to our Jobs.* The Futurist, April, pp. 55-58.
Johansen, R., Vallee, J. and Collins, K. (1978) Learning the Limits of Teleconferencing: Design of a Teleconference Tutorial. In *Evaluating New Telecommunications Services,* M. C. J. Elton, W. A. Lucan and D. W. Conrath (Eds.). Plenum Press, New York and London, pp. 385-398.
Johansen, R., Vallée, J. and Spangler, U. (1979) *Electronic Meetings: Technical Alternatives and Social Choices.* Addison-Wesley, Reading, Mass.
Kirsch, W. and Klein, H. (1977) *Management-Informationssysteme II.* W. Kohlhammer Stuttgart.
Marill, Th. (1980) *Time to Retire the Telephone?* Datamation. August, pp. 185-186.
Merrihue, W. V. (1960) *Managing by Communication.* McGraw-Hill, New York.
Mintzberg, H. (1973) *The Nature of Managerial Work.* Harper Row, New York.
Ouchi, W. G. (1980) *Markets, Bureaucracies and Clans.* Administrative Science Quarterly, Vol. 25, pp. 129-141.
Panko, R. R. (1980) *The EMS Revolution.* Computerworld, August 25, In Depth, pp. 1-12.
Pascale, R. T. (1978) *Communication and Decision-making across Cultures: Japanese and American Companies.* Administrative Science Quarterly, Vol. 23, pp. 91-110.
Picot, A. (1981) *Transaktionskostentheorie der Organisation.* Mimeo. Universität Hannover, West Germany.
Picot, A. and Reichwald, R. (1979) *Untersuchungen der Auswirkungen neuer Kommunikationstechnologien im Büro auf Organisationsstruktur und Arbeitsinhalte – Phase 1: Entwicklung einer Untersuchungskonzeption, Eggenstein-Leopoldshafen.* Fachinformationszentrum Energie, Physik, Mathematik GmbH.
Pye, R. and Young, J. (1980) *Do Current Electronic Office System Designers meet User Needs?* Paper presented at Stanford University, International Symposium on Office Automation, March 26-28.
Rice, R. E. (1980) Impacts of Computer-mediated Organizational and Interpersonal Communication. In *Annual Review of Information Science and Technology,* M. Williams (Ed.), Vol. 15, Knowledge Industry Publication, White Plains, N. Y.
Short, J., Williams, E. and Christie, B. (1976) *The Social Psychology of Tele-communications,* Wiley & Sons, London.
Schulman, A. D. and Steinman, J. I. (1978) Interpersonal Teleconferencing in an Organizational Context, In M. C. J. Elton, W. A. Lucas and D. W. Conrath (Eds.) *Evaluating New Telecommunications Services,* Plenum Press, New York, London, pp. 399-424.

Szyperski, N. (1979) Computer-Conferencing — Einsatzformen und organisatorische Auswirkungen. In O. Grün and J. Rössl (Eds.) *Computergestützte Textverarbeitung,* R. Oldenbourg, Munchen, Wien, p. 151-174.

Turoff, M. (1973) *Human Communication via Data Networks.* Computer Decisions, pp. 25-29.

Uhlig, R. P., Farber, D. J. and Bair, J. H. (1979) *The Office of the Future: Communication and Computers.* North-Holland, Amsterdam.

Watzlawick, P., Beavin, J. H. and Jackson, D. D. (1967) *Pragmatics of Human Communication.* A Study of Interactional Patterns, Pathologies and Paradoxes. W. W. Norton, New York.

Weinshall, Th. D. (1979) General Introduction. In T. D. Weinshall (Ed.) *Managerial Communication: Concepts, Approaches and Techniques.* Academic Press, London.

Weizenbaum, J. (1980a) Where are We Going? Questions for Simon. In T. Forester (Ed.) *The Microelectronics Revolution.* Basil Blackwell, Oxford, p. 434-438.

Weizenbaum, J. (1980b) Once More, the Computer Revolution. In T. Forester (Ed.) *The Microelectronics Revolution,* Basil Blackwell, Oxford, pp. 550-570.

Williamson, O. E. (1975) *Markets and Hierarchies: Analysis and Antitrust Implications.* Free Press, New York.

Witte, E. (1976) Die Bedeutung neuer Kommunikationssysteme für die Willensbildung im Unternehmen. In H. Albach and D. Sadowski (Eds.) *Die Bedeutung gesellschaftlicher Veränderungen für die Willensbildung im Unternehmen, Schriften des Vereins für Socialpolitik,* Neue Folge, Bd. 88. Duncker & Humblot, Berlin, pp. 305-320.

Witte, E. (1977) *Organisatorische Wirkungen neuer Kommunikationssysteme.* Zeitschrift für Organisation, 46, pp. 362-367.

Witte, E. (1980) Kommunikationstechnologie. In E. Grochla (Ed.) *Handwörterbuch der Organisation.* C. E. Poeschel, Stuttgart, col. 1048-1055.

CHAPTER 11

Employee and Organizational Responses to Information Technology: A Socio-psychological Approach to Systems Design

Alan Hedge and Richard C. Crawley

Applied Psychology Department, University of Aston in Birmingham, UK

DEVELOPMENTS IN INFORMATION TECHNOLOGY will have the greatest effect on those work situations where information must be processed, stored or transmitted. Thus, the impact on traditional heavy industries (such as steel and mining) and production industries (oil, chemicals and engineering) will, even by the 1990s, probably be less dramatic and obvious than the impact on information industries, such as banking, insurance and education (Barron and Curnow, 1979). However, all organizations must process information at some stage of their operations and hence, none of them will be totally immune from the effects of this technology. A socio-psychological approach to understanding, guiding and managing technological change is outlined in this chapter, together with an examination of the impacts of information technology on employees and the possible implications for life in the 1990s.

A SOCIO-PSYCHOLOGICAL APPROACH TO TECHNOLOGICAL CHANGE AT WORK

THERE ARE SEVERAL overlapping models for conceptualising ways in which organizational characteristics interact with employee behaviour. These are relevant because it has been shown that technological change affects employee

133

behaviour by modifying these characteristics. Firstly, the theory of socio-technical systems focuses on the organization of work groups and examines patterns of employee-employee and employee-technology interactions (Trist *et al*, 1963). This approach argues for the joint optimisation of the social and technical sub-systems within an organization and implies their simultaneous design, as distinct from the traditional sequential approaches to systems design of scientific management, classic ergonomics and early industrial psychology. The concept of organizational choice (Trist, 1971) is central to this approach since it places the onus on the organization to specify a form of system that takes into account both the needs of employees (the social system) and the technological goals (the technical system).

This approach has been criticised by Steele (1973), however, for ignoring the physical environment. He suggests a related approach — socio-physical organizational design — in which emphasis is placed on studying the interrelations of the social and spatial environments at work. This approach appears to be especially relevant to office environments where spatial and other environmental factors seem to affect productivity (Hedge, 1980; Magnus, 1981), as well as attitudes and reactions to work.

Finally, the job characteristics model (Hackman and Oldham, 1976 and 1980) examines those characteristics of individual jobs that are associated with intrinsic motivation and satisfaction. This postulates that people will experience intrinsic job satisfaction to the extent that they learn (knowledge of results) that they have performed effectively on a task that they feel to be worthwhile (experienced meaningfulness) and for which they feel personally responsible (experienced responsibility). These three experienced psychological states are a function of the levels of skill variety, task identity, task significance, autonomy and feedback in the job. Many studies have pointed to the importance of socio-psychological factors in systems, job and environmental design (Srivastva *et al*, 1975), both for the individual and for the organization. Typically, the consequences of failing to take these factors into account are increased rates of absenteeism, turnover, industrial disputes and, for the individual, dissatisfaction with the job, reduced intrinsic motivation and problems of health and well-being.

The three models thus described can be integrated into a socio-psychological systems framework for understanding, guiding and managing the impact of information technology (see Figure 1). However, to use this approach effectively demands the development of appropriate techniques and methodologies with which to investigate the impact of change on systems, jobs, people and the work environment. Although there are existing techniques for measuring these variables, it can be argued that they fail to analyse systems and jobs at an appropriate level of detail and also that they lack integration. Typical of existing approaches is the Job Diagnostic Survey (Hackman and Oldham, 1975) which, while measuring some general characteristics of people's jobs and their reactions to them, fails to analyse the actual tasks and required skills in any way or the interactions between jobs.

Recently a methodology has been developed which begins to overcome

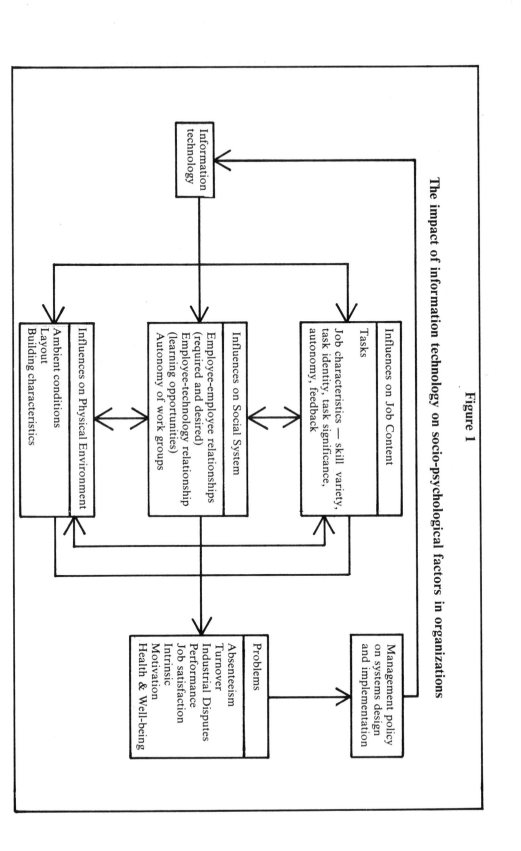

Figure 1

The impact of information technology on socio-psychological factors in organizations

these problems (Crawley, 1981). This method involves the use of task analysis (Annett *et al,* 1971), combined with Repertory Grid (Fransella and Bannister, 1977), to produce affective ratings of tasks within jobs in a form appropriate to the requirements of system design. However, there is still considerable scope for developing integrated methodologies in keeping with the socio-psychological approach previously presented.

THE ORGANIZATIONAL IMPACT OF INFORMATION TECHNOLOGY

FOR MANY ORGANIZATIONS, the information technology revolution is already underway (Wohl, 1980). Looking ahead, this will lead to the widespread introduction of word-processing systems over the next few years. Of particular interest from the present authors' point of view is that it is expected that this change will necessitate major revisions to organizational design, personnel staffing and work structure. Above all, it is claimed that word processors, together with other electronic office equipment, will vastly increase office productivity. This has several implications.

It is important to make a general distinction between those employees doing secretarial work (including low-grade clerical and administrative support work) and those involved in managerial work. This is because we anticipate a marked difference in the impact of new technology on these activities. To further emphasise this distinction, we choose to label the former as 'passive users' and the latter as 'active users' of new technology. To illustrate these differences in impact, two examples will suffice.

Passive Users — Impact of Word Processors on Secretarial Work

There has been considerable conjecture on the effects of word processors on secretarial work and staff. Typically, it is reported that staff will resent and react against word processors (*Which,* 1981). It has also been suggested that in certain situations (the clerk/typist), the word processor may lead to a 'de-skilling' of work and possibly even create greater social isolation at work (Damodaran, 1980). Certainly, the possibility of health problems attributable to operating word processors has resulted in a great deal of attention being paid to even the minutiae of their design (Mackay, 1980). However, there are as yet relatively few published studies on the actual impact of introducing this technology.

Over the past few years, several departments at the University of Aston in Birmingham, UK, have introduced various kinds of word-processor systems. In general, existing secretarial staff have been retrained to operate these in addition to their other secretarial duties. Recently a survey has been completed which has compared the content and characteristics of the secretarial jobs now performed by word-processor operators and traditional secretaries.* The survey looked for possible differences in work motivation, job satisfaction, health and general work attitudes between the two groups. To obtain these data, three measures have been used — a one-month, detailed diary of secretarial tasks; a questionnaire on health and attitudes to work and to word processors; and the Job Diagnostic Survey, developed by Hackman and Oldham (1975), as a measure of job characteristics, job satisfaction and motivation. The results for the measures of job content do indeed show a distinct difference between the work performed by word-processor operators and traditional secretaries (see Figure 2). Although the word-processor operators in the University do spend some time using conventional electric typewriters, the vast majority of documentation and text revision which they undertake is now done on word processors (see Figure 3). However, both groups of secretaries still spend approximately the same proportion of time on non-text activities. Thus, the word processor in this case has primarily replaced conventional typing activities, rather than fundamentally changing other aspects of the job. This is also probably the reason why no significant differences appear between the two secretarial groups on any of the other measures investigated. For the University of Aston, at least, the introduction of word processing has not yet created any major problems or dramatically changed levels of job satisfaction, work motivation or work attitudes.

Similarly, a study by Krois and Benson (1980), using the Job Diagnostic Survey, compared the jobs of word-processor operators, traditional secretaries and administrative support personnel. Briefly, they also found that in general there were no major differences in job satisfaction or work motivation between any of these staff. Interestingly, they conclude that factors such as job satisfaction appear to be far more strongly influenced by the unique characteristics of different organizations than by changes in job content arising from using word processors. This is consistent with other findings on redesigning jobs (Hackman and Oldham, 1980).

Active Users — Impact of Information Technology on Managers

Unlike secretarial staff who, as we have seen, spend a substantial amount of time transcribing information, managers typically need to search for and react to information, frequently using this as a basis for decision-making and problem-solving. Thus, the impact of information technology on management will primarily derive from the effects of providing better information bases, in terms of accessibility, quantity and probably quality of information. In this respect, the effects might generally be expected to be similar to those previously predicted for the impact of computers on management. Indeed, the five major effects listed by Whistler (1966) still seem appropriate (see Table 1).

*The authors wish to thank Major M. Hayward for his invaluable assistance with the Word Processor Survey.

Figure 2

Comparison of the job content of the non-WP (word-processing) and WP secretaries at the University of Aston in Birmingham, UK

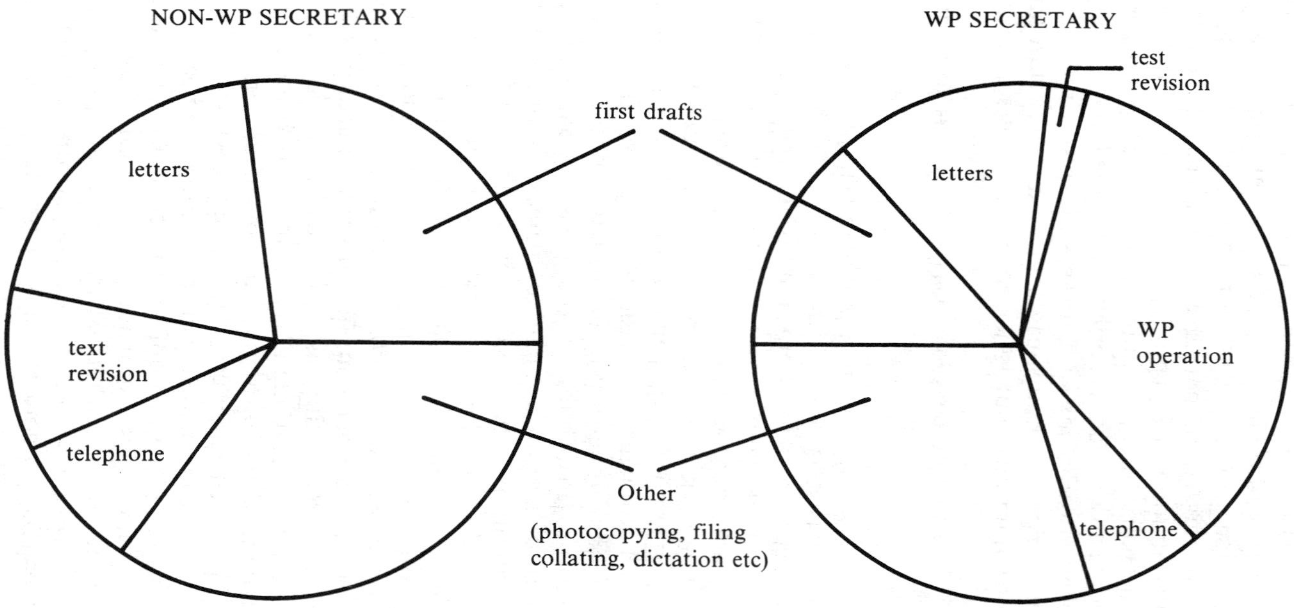

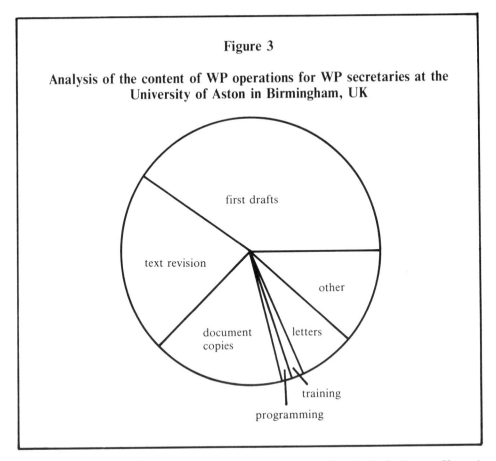

Figure 3

Analysis of the content of WP operations for WP secretaries at the University of Aston in Birmingham, UK

However, even today many managers have remained relatively unaffected by computers. In fact, in many organizations both computers and data-processing staff are segregated from other management. Several factors seem to have contributed to this schism between computers and management: (a) the hardware requirements (such as dust-free, air-conditioned rooms); (b) the software requirements (knowledge of programming language); (c) the information bases (primarily numerical); (d) the professional emergence of computer system specialists; and (e) the considerable shortfall in the education of managers on the operations and potential of computer systems.

The authors believe that the new information technology will have a much more immediate and permanent impact on management than large computers have, because the hardware now readily handles text needs, it requires no special environmental conditions and it does not require that the user possess any sophisticated knowledge of a programming language. But once again, there is a marked dearth of published work on the direct effects of new technology on the jobs of managers.

To learn more of these effects, we have discussed reactions to the introduction of new technology with the senior management of a small, progressive company (150 employees). This, taken in conjunction with other case-study information (Birchall and Hammond, 1981), has highlighted what is felt to be two extremely important problem areas. Firstly, there seems to be general agreement that the introduction of information technology markedly accelerates the pace with which decisions have to be made by managers and thereby, introduces more time-pressure into the job. This seems to be a direct result of the greater accessibility of more comprehensive information bases, the more frequent use of aids to decision-making (such as forecasting models) and the ability to monitor organizational performance and gain more rapid feedback on it. A second problem, which seems to frequently conflict with and exacerbate that of time-pressure, concerns certainty in arriving at a decision. Since managers are now placed in a position where they are able to ask a broader range of "What if…?" questions (Hopkins, 1980), there seems to be a marked tendency to overestimate the range of information required, thereby creating a self-induced situation of information overload (O'Rielly, 1980). Indeed, Kaufman (1973) has found that many managers still appear to work on the basis of 'more information is better', rather than concentrating on making better use of the information already available.

Table 1

The impact of computers on management

(1)   Decision-making can be rationalised and there is a greater access to quantified information
(2)   The scope of decisions is enlarged since more information is available
(3)   The level at which decisions are made within an organization may change
(4)   The rhythm of planning decisions may change
(5)   Decisions are now made by man-machine and not just man-man systems

Source: Whistler (1966)

The worrying point is that such problems of overload can be potent sources of occupational stress (Cooper and Marshall, 1978). This is certainly true for those managers with whom we have spoken, for they invariably report feelings of greater pressure and stress for the reasons mentioned. Thus, it is conceivable that such problems may ultimately lead to a deterioration in the performance, health and well-being of many managers unless the necessary steps are taken to rectify the problems, at both the system-design and implementation stages.

DEVELOPMENTS TO THE YEAR 2000

THERE IS LITTLE QUESTION that many of those employed in the information sector will experience major changes to their jobs; far more debateable is the extent to which these changes will affect their lifestyles. One possibility presented by information technology that has given rise to considerable public and press interest is that of working at home: office automation may imply office dissolution (Peltu, 1980). This suggestion certainly has many attractive features, especially for those employees affected: for example, they would have greater autonomy in terms of work organization and supervision; greater flexibility of working hours; and more flexible integration of work and domestic arrangements. Many situations can be envisaged where, for example, work targets might be remotely set to be tackled at the employee's convenience, where staff need be present at a central office only for a 'core period', thus enabling organizations to save substantially on office costs.

While this prospect might be extremely attractive to employees, we feel that such a development is unlikely to be either widespread or rapid for a variety of reasons. Set against the potential savings on overheads, management may have to consider problems of information security created by unsupervised work stations in people's homes. Moreover, working at home would produce an immediate loss of direct supervisory control by management over its employees. There is evidence that, despite the obvious benefits that can accrue from delegating responsibility for supervision and work scheduling to employees themselves, management is often unwilling to lose direct control. Blackler and Brown (1980, p. 325), reporting on recent developments in the job and system redesign projects in the *Volvo* factory, noted:

> *Senior managers told us they were convinced significant production savings could be achieved by dock assembly. Yet they felt that such methods were less reliable . . . Perhaps above all, they were largely suspicious of a production method that allowed workers to complete their quota before the end of the working day and they wished this 'slack' to be controlled.*

A final point with respect to working at home is that office buildings typically function as more than just workplaces. They represent status symbols, reflecting the prestige of organizations and, as such, help to provide a cohesive image to employees, potential clients and the general public.

On balance, we do not feel that information technology will dramatically change the lifestyles of people at work, though it may well change other aspects of their lives. Insofar as changes to their lives at work will occur, there will probably be a continuation of factors already in evidence, for example, increases in managerial stress or changes to the level of job satisfaction. What distinguishes information technology from most previous technological developments is its enormous flexibility and accessibility. This allows systems to be closely tailored to optimise organizational goals, job requirements and employee needs, but only providing that organizations consider all of these factors well in advance.

However, it is abundantly clear that at present most organizations still lack any general policy or strategy for managing technological change. In consequence, there is a real danger that the piecemeal acquisition of electronic office systems will result in technology determining, rather than fulfilling, the requirements of organizational change. Moreover, if information systems design remains the prerogative of technical specialists (such as computer scientists), then experience has shown that very often these systems are designed in such a way that the employees, and ultimately the employer, suffer (Mumford *et al,* 1972).

In order to avoid these problems, it is essential for management to recognise that it must plan and direct change on the basis of a prior systematic analysis of the organization's needs at every level. Furthermore, current experience in the field of socio-technical systems design also suggests the need for the practical involvement of those employees to be affected by technological change in all stages of the design process (Elden, 1979; Hawgood *et al,* 1978). To the extent that such participation takes place, it will arguably represent the most revolutionary change to people's lifestyles at work.

References

Annett, J., Duncan, K. D. Stammers, R. B. and Gray, M. J. (1971) *Task Analysis.* Department of Employment Training Information, Paper 6, HMSO, London.

Barron, I. and Curnow, R. (1979) *The future with Microelectronics.* The Open University Press, Milton Keynes, UK.

Blackler, F. H. M. and Brown, C. A. (1980) Job redesign and social change: Case studies at *Volvo.* In K. D. Duncan., M. M. Gruneberg and D. Wallis (Eds.). *Changes in Working Life.* John Wiley, London.

Birchall, D. W. and Hammond, V. J. (1981) *Tomorrow's Office Today: Managing Technological Change.* Business Books, London.

Cooper, C. L. and Marshall, J. (1978) *Understanding Executive Stress,* MacMillan, London.

Crawley, R. C. (1981) *Air Traffic Controller Reactions to Computer Assistance.* Unpublished PhD Thesis, University of Aston in Birmingham, UK.

Damodaran, L. (1980) *Wordprocessing: occupational and organizational effects.* Management Services, June, pp. 4-18.

Elden, M. (1979) Three generations of work-democracy experiments in Norway: beyond classical socio-technical systems analysis. In C. L. Cooper and E. Mumford (Eds.). *The Quality of Working Life in Western and Eastern Europe.* Associated Business Press, London.

Fransella, F. and Bannister, D. (1977) *A Manual for Repertory Grid Technique.* Academic Press, London.

Hackman, J. R. and Oldham, G. R. (1975) *Development of the Job Diagnostic Survey.* Journal of Applied Psychology, Vol. 60, No. 2, pp. 159-170.

Hackman, J. R. and Oldham, G. R. (1976) *Motivation through the design of work: Test of a theory.* Organizational Behaviour and Human Performance, Vol. 16, pp. 250-279.

Hackman, J. R. and Oldham, G. R. (1980) *Work redesign.* Addison-Wesley, New York.

Hawgood, J., Land, F. and Mumford, E. (1978) A participative approach to forward planning and systems change. From *Lecture Notes in Computer Science 65: Information Systems Methodology, Proceedings Venice 1978,* Springer-Verlag, Berlin, pp. 39-61.

Hedge, A. (1980) Office design: user reactions to open-plan. In R. Thorne and S. Arden (Eds). *People and the Man-Made Environment: Building, Urban and Landscape Design related to Human Behaviour.* University of Sydney, Sydney, p. 57-68.

Hopkins, A. (1980) *The Boardroom Computer.* Management Today, June, pp. 132-142.

Kaufman. H. (1973) *Administrative Feedback.* Brookings, Washington, DC.

Krois, P. A. and Benson, P. G. (1980) *Word Processing and personnel.* Personnel Journal, Vol. 59, No. 12, pp. 992-995, 1008.

Mackay, C. (1980) *Human factors aspects of visual display unit operations.* HMSO, London.

Magnus, M. (1980) *Work environment: its design and implications.* Personnel Journal, Vol. 60, No. 1, pp. 27-31.

Mumford, E., Mercer, D., Mills, S. and Weir, M. (1972) *The human problems of computer introduction.* Management Decision, 10, pp. 6-17.

O'Rielly, C. (1980) *Individuals and information overload in organizations: is more necessarily better?* Academy of Management Journal, Vol. 23, No. 4, pp. 684-696.

Peltu, M. (1980) *New life at home for office workers.* New Scientist, Vol. 85, No. 1200, pp. 1004-1008.

Srivastva, S., Salipante, P. F., Cummings, T. G., Notz, W. W., Bigelow, J. D. and Waters, J. A. (1975) *Job Satisfaction and Productivity,* Case Western Reserve, University Press, Cleveland.

Steele, F. I. (1973) *Physical Settings and Organization Development.* Organization Development Series. Addison-Wesley, Reading, Mass.

Trist, E. (1971) *Critique of scientific management in terms of socio-technical theory.* Prakseologia, 39, pp. 159-174.

Trist, E. Higgin, G., Murray H. and Pollock, A. P. (1963) *Organizational Choice,* Tavistock, London.

Which (1981) *How to make friends and influence staff.* Which Word Processor, Vol. 2, No. 1, pp. 23-24.

Whistler, T. L. (1966) The Impact of Advanced Technology on Mangerial Decision-making. In J. Steiber (Ed.) *Employment Problems of Automation and Advanced Technology: An International Perspective.* MacMillan, London, pp. 304-317.

Wohl, A. (1980) *A review of office automation.* Datamation, Vol. 26, No. 2, pp. 117-119.

CHAPTER 12

Information Technology and the Experience of Work

David Boddy and David A. Buchanan

Department of Management Studies, University of Glasgow, UK

INTRODUCTION

THE APPLICATIONS of information technology are described and analysed here in two case studies. The first case, completed in 1980, concerns the development of word processing in an engineering consultancy organization. The second, completed in 1981, looks at the application of computerized production measurements and controls in a biscuit-making factory.

Information technologies are distinguished from mechanical and electro-mechanical devices by their ability to combine the following features in single or closely linked pieces of equipment:

(1) capture information — gather, collect, monitor, detect and measure information;

(2) store information — convert information to digital form and retain it in some form of permanent memory which allows the information to be retrieved when required;

(3) manipulate information — rearrange and perform calculations;

(4) distribute information — transmit, move and display information electronically;

(5) control operations — which happens in three ways:

    (a) the equipment gives the operator rapid and relevant feedback information to make control of the equipment or process more effective;

    (b) the equipment is taken, under computer control,' through a predetermined sequence of operations;

    (c) deviations from equipment or process performance standards are measured and corrective action initiated by the computer.

Information storage, manipulation and distribution happen inside the equipment, without human intervention beyond activating the procedures, and operate with high degrees of predictability and reliability. Information capture, the receipt and interpretation of distributed information, and operations control — all have different characteristics. They concern the links between the device and the world beyond it. They rely on conventional engineering technologies and on human intervention; they constitute sources of unreliability, error and flexibility; and they are areas of choice in work organization design.

The aim of this discussion is to generate tentative answers to the following questions:

(1) What factors influence management decisions to use informatioin technologies?

(2) What factors influence management decisions about the organization of work around the new technology?

(3) How do these decisions affect the roles of operators of the new technology?

Data were collected in each case from three main sources. Firstly, relevant company documents were studied. Secondly, semi-structured interviews were held with employees at all levels concerned with the new technology. And finally, the research findings were fed back to the respondents to check their accuracy, completeness and emphasis.

INFORMATION TECHNOLOGY IN THE OFFICE

THIS CASE STUDY concerns the development of word processing in an engineering consultancy firm. Word processors have three main components:

(a) a video-display screen with a keyboard;

(b) a central processing unit with internal and external memory; and

(c) a printer (called a 'daisy wheel' printer from the shape of the print element).

There are five distinct capabilities of word processing which are as follows:

Information capture: as the video typist (the term used here, in preference to 'word processor operator') hits the terminal keys, the words appear temporarily on the video-display screen and are sent by the central processor to the machine's storage device.

Information storage: text is stored either in the machine or on some form of portable storage medium (usually magnetic disc, tape or card) and the text can then be retrieved and reproduced any number of times without retyping.

Information manipulation: once stored, the text can be edited before it is committed to paper; the typist can correct mistakes as they appear on the screen and can edit the draft once the author has checked it.

Information distribution: information stored for one machine can be read, edited and printed on another compatible machine and text entered on one device may be transmitted by telephone line or other wiring directly to other machines.

Operations controls: all typing, or printing, is done under computer control; the typist gives the computer instructions on what to type and how to type it, by entering page format and other print instructions along with the text.

In larger installations, several typists can share one or more printers and one or more central processing units. These are called 'shared logic' systems, where the central processor controls the queue of materials waiting to be typed.

The organization studied in this case was a Glasgow engineering consultancy which had developed its own shared logic, word-processing system. The company employed about 500 people. Consultancy work was presented to clients in written technical reports, which usually had several authors and went through several revisions. Before the introduction of word processing, each group of specialist consultants had a secretary and one or two copy typists. Reports were typed on conventional electric typewriters; secretaries and copy typists worked close to each other and to the authors of the reports.

The company formed a 'Typing Services Working Party' in 1977 to examine the benefits of word processing. The minutes of the Working Party indicated that the decision to adopt word processing had been influenced by three factors:

(1) the objective of increasing typists' productivity and reducing the number and cost of the typing staff;
(2) the enthusiasm of two managers closely concerned with computing and typing for the word-processing technology;
(3) the need to replace obsolescent typesetting equipment.

Pressures arising within the company were more powerful than those arising outside. The decision was not prompted by competition and the equipment that was obsolescent in 1977 was still operating in 1980. The role of 'champions' or 'promotors' in stimulating interest in, and encouraging adoption of, technological change was a key factor.

The Working Party decided to establish two word-processing centres in which all the video typists would be grouped, with a supervisor in each. The centres were the responsibility of a Technical Services Manager, whose line of authority extended down through a word-processing Section Head, a Typing Services Co-ordinator and the two Supervisors to the nine video typists. This arrangement was strongly influenced by the perceived need to control more effectively the flow of work to and from the typists. Other advantages of grouping were easier training, flexible staffing, less cable and fewer printers. It was recognised that typists would lose contact with authors who would not easily be able to follow the progress of their typing through the system. This re-organization of the typists was therefore determined by management objectives for the control of typing work. There was nothing in the technology of word processing that dictated this pooling arrangement.

Copy-typing and word-processing staff, as a percentage of technical staff, fell from 8.3 to 4.5 per cent between December 1975 and June 1980; 28 typists worked for 338 authors in 1975 and 16 worked for 352 authors in 1980. The overall reduction in support staff, however, was small and their percentage of the company's salary bill did not fall. The typists' output increased dramatically. Copy typists produced 5.8 pages a day on average whereas the video typists produced 40.5 pages a day. The overall effect on typing productivity was difficult to assess. The typists' output had risen but the time that authors waited for reports to be typed was not reduced; they also felt that more time was spent correcting drafts.

The two centre supervisors and nine video typists were interviewed to discover how their jobs had been affected by the word-processing equipment. Their individual experience with the system ranged from three weeks to two years. All were internally recruited, trained copy typists. Training on word processing was informal and on the job.

In some respects, video typing was less skilled than conventional copy typing. Little or no paper handling was required. The keyboard touch was light. Corrections were simple and the fear of making mistakes at the bottom of a page, which slows the conventional typist, did not arise. The video typist did not have to be concerned about the paper edges and line lengths as the computer positioned text on the paper. The keys on modern terminals are closer together, involving less finger stretching, and the keyboard is flatter, more comfortable and less painful on the wrists. The terminals are quieter than typewriters and, although the printers are noisy, they were kept in a separate room. Through experience with a group of authors, the copy typist build up knowledge of their handwriting, technical terms and report-layout needs and preferences. The video typists in the word-processing centres could neither acquire nor exploit this knowledge.

But the video-typing job required more skill and knowledge than conventional typing in three respects. Firstly, the video typist had to learn the codes for formatting and editing text and be able to assess the appearance of printed text from the format codes attached to the input. As the system developed, this knowledge had to be updated. Secondly, the job required more concentration and was physically more demanding than conventional typing. Thirdly, the system editor on the computer could cause files to be lost and erase the work of others if not used carefully, thus much of the training concerned file management procedures. The overall pattern of skill and knowledge required by the typist had therefore changed.

Overall, the variety of the video typists' job was less than they had experienced as copy typists. Each video typist worked for several different groups of authors who had different report styles and preferences. In this respect, variety had increased. But the video typists spent almost all of their time in one location, entering and editing text. Most of the preparatory and auxiliary tasks concerning the operation of the printers, the collating and delivering of work to the authors, were carried out by the supervisors. The typists could vary their work by switching between input and editing tasks, and by dividing long and monotonous reports between them. But the copy typists could vary the pace and intensity of the work to a greater extent. There were natural breaks for setting-up the typewriter and contacting authors to clarify their requests. One video typist stated that "there is now pressure to keep working" and another said that she felt like a "zombie", constantly typing with infrequent breaks. The system was interactive, prompting responses from the typist, and the screen was always 'live'. The video typist was thus subjected to a form of machine-pacing and was likely to work for longer periods than a copy typist without a change of activity. Apart from lunch, the video typists had two official 15-minute breaks, in the morning and afternoon, and the lighting and seating in the centres were carefully planned.

Copy typists, working for one group of authors, normally followed a job through to completion. The video typists felt that it was satisfying, after they had done a long job, to watch the printer producing perfect copy; but this rarely happened in the video centres as successive drafts were often done by different typists. This loss of identity with the whole job was reinforced when a large job was divided among several typists, when the typist did not know the author whose work was being typed and when the typist did not know when she was typing the final copy.

The copy typists had dealt directly with the authors. To give a particular job priority was a matter for negotiation between the author, the group and the copy typist. These negotiations had become a major component of the jobs of the centre Supervisors, the Typing Services Co-ordinator and the Section Head. Although typists could share longer jobs, control over work scheduling passed to management, who acted as a buffer between typists and authors. The typists felt, however, that they had more control over the quality and appearance of the end product through the word-processing system. An item that was 're-typed' carried its corrections without the introduction of fresh errors, as may be the case with conventional re-typing of a document. Producing better quality reports was evidently a source of satisfaction.

Feedback to the video typist was limited because she could not see on the screen the precise format of the copy to be typed and had to judge the appearance of the printed text from the accompanying format codes. There was no instant 'hard' copy. The typist had to wait until the printout was complete to check that the text and format instructions had been entered correctly. The printers were in a room separate from the centres and typists did not always see their work being printed. The centre Supervisor often collated the printouts and delivered them to their authors. This lack of feedback on performance impeded learning the system. Feedback from authors was also absent when editing was not given to the typist who did the input.

Management tried to encourage interaction between typists and authors but the equipment and the change in work organization inhibited this. Authors were given written instructions which declared that all discussions about their requirements should take place with either the Supervisor or the Typing Services Co-ordinator. Negotiations over job priority often involved the Section Head and sometimes managers and directors. At this stage, the Supervisor would not normally know which typist was going to do the job. The instructions encouraged authors to contact their typists, but authors did not usually know which typist was doing their work and the typists no longer controlled those aspects of the typing that were interesting to the authors: the amount and timing of the work done. The formal rules and re-allocation of control led the authors to the Supervisors and higher levels of management.

There were also physical and technological barriers between typists and authors. The typists were geographically remote from the authors, who did not know what the video typists' job involved and were uncertain about the capabilities and constraints of the new equipment. Rather than checking spelling and format problems with authors, typists would 'have a go' because corrections were easy. The capabilities of the equipment reduced the need to get the typing right first time.

The combination of these organizational, physical and technological barriers meant that authors and typists did not develop or retain the personal, informal working relationships of the previous copy-typing system. This loss of contact was regretted by both typists and authors.

INFORMATION TECHNOLOGY IN BISCUIT-MAKING

THE SECOND CASE STUDY concerns applications of computerised production measurements and controls in a biscuit-making factory. The organization studied in this case was the Glasgow branch of one of the largest biscuit manufacturers in Britain, employing about 2,000 people in 1981. The factory had 15 production lines, each making a different type of biscuit. This case concerns the 'Number 4' line which made one of the company's most popular and profitable products.

Management were constantly looking for ways to improve the performance of all the lines in the factory and the company had a specialist group whose function was to monitor developments in process control which could be applied in biscuit-making. Biscuits were made in three stages: mixing, baking and wrapping. The mixing stage was controlled by computer. Flour arrived in bulk tankers and was pumped into storage silos. Recipes for each biscuit-type were stored on computer paper tape. The required amounts and types of flour were pumped from the silos into automatic weighing vessels and the computer controls then fed the flour, along with the correct amounts of water and sugar, to the appropriate mixing machine.

The operators in the computer control room had an illuminated wall display called a 'mimic board', showing a plan of the process for each line. At the start of each shift, the 'doughman' (or mixer operator) checked with the control-room operators that the correct recipe tape was loaded and made sure that enough sundries — ingredients added in small quantities — were available. The doughman then pressed a call button to start the mixing cycle. When the computer had delivered the water and flour to his mixing machine, a light came on to tell him he could start the mixer. The sundries (including salt, syrup and various chemicals) were added by the doughman during the process which was interrupted by the computer at the required times. Each mix took about 20 minutes, with three interruptions. During each mix, the computer refilled the storage units above the mixing machine and the cycle was ready to start again as soon as the previous mix was over. A dough sample was then passed through the oven to test it. If the dough passed the 'oven test', it was emptied into a trough and taken by conveyor to the cutting machine. The dough was flatted to the correct thickness by passing it through rollers, adjusted by a machine operator. The flat dough sheet then passed through a cutter which stamped out the biscuits. The biscuits were baked as they travelled on conveyor through a 100-metre-long oven for about 4 minutes. As they came out, an ovenman checked the thickness or 'bulk' of each batch. If the bulk was wrong, the ovenman would adjust the oven temperature to correct it. He could also control the colour and moisture content of the biscuits. Too much moisture reduced the shelf-life of the biscuits; too little made them fragile. After leaving the oven, the biscuits went through several loops on the conveyor to cool them.

The biscuits were next fed into an automatic wrapping machine which counted a pre-set number of biscuits, wrapped them and sealed the packet. Each packet then passed, still on the conveyor, over a checkweigher which pushed light-weight packets off the line. The wrapping-machine operator saw an instant digital display of the weight of each packet as it crossed the checkweigher. If the weight was wrong, she could adjust, within limits, the number of biscuits that the wrapping machine put into each packet. Summary information about packet weights also appeared on a video display unit in the ovenman's area. Packets were finally boxed and loaded on pallets for despatch.

To achieve the highest quality and lowest cost of the end product, therefore, several production variables had to be controlled, such as the composition of the dough, the biscuit bulk, shape, colour, moisture content and the final packet weight. The company's policy was to develop ways of controlling these variables by machine, and in particular by computer, to reduce human error and labour costs. Local management had considerable freedom to use the computerised systems they felt appropriate to improve productivity. Managers throughout the company, however, avoided the word 'computer' and used specific machine names or the term 'process control equipment'.

The company's first production computer was installed in 1971 to control the mixing process. The computer also recorded the amounts of raw materials used, which allowed management to accurately calculate stock losses; it also displayed information about faults in the weighing equipment and blockages in the pipework. Thus, the system had the information capture, storage, manipulation and distribution features discussed earlier. This is also an example of operations control by the computer, taking the equipment through a predetermined sequence, with human intervention restricted to activating the cycle and assisting the transfer of materials to the next stage of the process.

In this case, the jobs most radically affected by information technology over the past ten years in the biscuit factory were those of the doughman and the ovenman. The doughman was previously responsible for getting the flour, with the help of other manual workers. Mixing was done in open 'spindle' mixers, which were vats with devices resembling domestic food mixers. When he could see and hear the dough, the doughman could tell by the appearance, sound and feel whether it was too dry or too wet, or lacking some other ingredient, in which case he could simply add what was required. This job used to be done by time-served master bakers.

With the introduction of the computer, the doughman's job became repetitive, with a cycle time of around 20 minutes, and was classed as semi-skilled. His main tasks were now to start the mixing machine (by pressing a button when the light came on), to add the sundries when the computer interrupted the mix, to pass a sample of each mix to the ovenman and to empty the finished mix into the trough and onto the conveyor for the machineman. The mixing vessel was enclosed and the doughman had to leave it only to collect more sundries. When the mixing machine or any of its control gear failed, electronic technicians were needed to track down the cause and repair it. The doughman sometimes forgot to add the sundries, such as syrup or fat, and this was only discovered when the mixing was over or past the oven test.

The skilled and varied craft of the doughman had thus been replaced by the computer and management preferred the job title 'mixer operator'. The comments of some production managers illustrate this change:

> There used to be more variation in the things they did. Now they seem to lose all interest. There are some who have been here longer than the computer and they've really switched off. I've seen it happening to new people coming in as well.

> We found that one of the reasons they forgot to add sundries was that they were talking to 'visitors' from other parts of the factory. So now we keep people out of their area unless they're there for a reason.

> It affects our ability to get foremen and managers from the operators. They don't want to get out of the rut.

> The problem with the whole mixer set-up seems to be that the new generation of operators don't appreciate as fully as before the consequences of what they do. It's all so automatic, they have difficulty visualizing the effects of, say, half-a-minute extra mixing time on later stages in production.

Talking about their work and how it had changed, two doughmen stated:

> It's very repetitive. The computer controls it. We just press the button. If something goes wrong, it's more difficult to fix.

> We used to have much more humour. You had your own group of manual

workers with you doing the manhandling and this gave a lot more fun. The computers make it much easier, but if it breaks down, we can't do it by hand.

It also takes the responsibility off us. They can't blame the doughmen. If we had to weigh it ourselves, it would be our fault if anything went wrong.

It's much less interesting, more routine, very little scope for human error now. Initially, it's more skilled, till you get to know the set-up, then there's a fair amount of boredom. Except when something goes wrong.

The ovenman was responsible for baking biscuits that had the correct bulk, weight, moisture content, colour, shape and taste. This was complex because action to correct a deviation from standard on one of these variables affected the others. The job, therefore, was to balance these biscuit features so that they were acceptable at all times. The training time for ovenmen was 12 to 16 weeks. Every mix had different properties. Some flours absorbed more moisture than others; some doughs were soft and others were tough. Constant checking was necessary to ensure consistency of output. The ovenman checked the biscuit bulk and weight manually, at least once during the baking of every mix, and checked their colour and shape visually.

Biscuits are sold in packets by weight, which is stamped on the packet. Legislation allowed the company to sell a small proportion of packets that were light in weight, down to a standard minimum. Legislation did not prevent the sale of heavy packets, which gave the customer free biscuits. The amount of excess biscuit going to the customer was called 'turn of scale'. This term reflects the time when biscuit packets were weighed by hand on a scale with a pointer which could be deflected from the vertical (turned) by heavy packets. A computer-controlled 'turn-of-scale package' was installed in the Glasgow factory in 1979 to reduce the turn of scale on Number 4 line, which was over 3 per cent. The conventional electromechanical checkweigher that it replaced worked slowly and kept no records of packet weights. Operators and managers knew whether packets were over or under weight but not by how much. The problem with the conventional checkweigher was that it did not give the operators direct and rapid feedback nor did it indicate the degree of deviation from performance standard.

The turn-of-scale package was developed by the company's engineers. For one line, the cost of the package was about £20,000 at 1978 prices; it consisted of four components:

(a)   a checkweigher with a microprocessor controller;
(b)   a mini computer which recorded the packets' weights and controlled the display of information;
(c)   a visual-display unit to display packet weight information for the individual ovenman's line; and
(d)   a printer with keyboard for requesting and printing out information.

In the new system, packets still passed over a checkweigher. The weight of each packet appeared on a light-emitting diode display on the front of the machine and the computer recorded the weights of all packets. The computer analysed this information in various ways. Management had access to production-performance information that was not previously available and production, quality control and cost-office records were produced automatically. The computer also gave summary information on the state of production to the ovenman through the video-display unit next to his oven-control panel. This information was updated every two minutes and included:

(a) the average weight and standard deviation of accepted packets for the past two minutes of production;

(b) a graph plotting the number of packets produced against standard weight;

(c) the number of accepted packets for the shift so far;

(d) the number of rejected packets for the shift so far; and

(e) the average packet weight for the shift so far.

Most of the deviations from standard were controlled by the ovenman who could change the characteristics of the biscuits being baked by carefully adjusting the oven-temperature controls. The turn-of-scale package gave him information that he did not have before, at a speed and in a format that enabled him to take rapid corrective action. The turn-of-scale package thus incorporated information capture, storage, manipulation and distribution capabilities.

The ovenman felt that the new system had reduced the pressure on him. When production was running smoothly, management kept out of his way. The new package was also used to settle disputes about responsibility for turn of scale; the ovenman felt that it protected him from unfair accusations. He also felt that the package had increased the challenge and interest in his job because it gave him a goal that he could see and influence. This was reflected in the bonus-payment system and he felt that he had the additional satisfaction of knowing that he was cutting waste and costs. One of the process supervisors explained the effects of these changes as follows:

There is now no need for a physical check. The new package highlights problems, making it easier to make corrections quicker. The operators are continually on top of the job. The pressures on the operators have been reduced. The package acts as a double check for the ovenman. It's an assistant, a second opinion. More people can now see what is happening and are aware of the state of production and level of performance. The checkweigher is an instant reminder of the need to take corrective action. If things start to go wrong, we can regain the situation faster. Before, those unforgiving minutes were lost. Another effect of this spread of information is that nobody can fiddle because everybody has a clearer idea of where the problem lies when things go wrong.

Commenting on how his job had changed, the ovenman said:

Management want a straight graph on the video, showing minimum turn of scale. We're working to finer tolerance now. That's what our job is really all about. The equipment does all the work and our job is essentially to make sure that it is doing everything correctly. But when everything is computer-

controlled and the computer breaks down, the manual skills will still be needed and there will be nobody around who has them. And when everything is interlocked, in the way that this plant already is, problems arise when things start to break down.

Technological innovation in the plant had led to more consistent output, quantity and quality, by reducing product-handling and the opportunities for human error. The turn-of-scale package was not justified beforehand solely on financial grounds. One of the main argument for its introduction was a 'theoretical' one, based on its potential to improve production control by generating performance information quickly. Turn of scale on the Number 4 line fell from 3.5 per cent in 1977 to 1.8 per cent at the end of 1980.

CONCLUSIONS

WHAT FACTORS INFLUENCE management decisions to use information technologies? Firstly, the role of promoters or champions in encouraging technological change was important in both cases. Internal pressures for change were thus more significant than events in the organizations' environments. Secondly, all the changes discussed were justified at some stage on cost and productivity grounds. Thirdly, there appears to have been a management desire to reduce human intervention and contribution by replacing people, their knowledge and skills with machinery. Along with the economic objectives therefore, information technologies were perhaps introduced to increase the predictability, reliability, consistency, controllability or manageability of operations. Fourthly, different management levels and functions appear to accept new technology for different reasons. Top management seek return on investment; middle management seek improved operating control; supervisors want smoother work flow, fewer problems and less frustration. The information that a computerised system produces can be used in different ways by production and quality-control management and by accountants.

What factors influence management decisions about the organization of work around the new technology? The re-organization of the typists into two word-processing centres was determined strongly and directly by management's perceived need to control the flow of work to and from the typists; weakly and indirectly, it was influenced by the technology of word processing. It was felt that typing support would thus become more flexible, with supervisors handling competing priorities for typing work between different groups. These advantages were felt to outweigh the problems created by the loss of contact between typists and authors.

Although the roles of individual biscuit-making operators had changed, the overall organization of their work remained substantially intact. Their case is however comparable with that of the typists in one respect. The equipment that gave the operators more control over the baking process also gave management more control over the operators. The doughman had less discretion and influence over the mixing process and any errors made by the ovenman were revealed faster than before.

How do these decisions affect the roles of operators of the new technology? The assumption, 'as technology does more, people do less' is not generally true. Technology can either replace or complement people. Robots and automatic washing machines replace, musical instruments and conventional metal-working lathes complement human abilities.

The ovenman's case demonstrates complementarity. The turn-of-scale package gave him accurate and rapid information about the state of production that enabled him to control the baking line more effectively. This is described as complementarity because:

(1) The ovenman still had to decide what corrective actions were necessary to control the line, using information not previously available.

(2) The information capture, storage, manipulation and distribution features of the turn-of-scale package helped him to improve performance in his area of discretion — operations control.

(3) The ovenman was given a visible goal that he could influence and which made his job more interesting and challenging.

The video typists demonstrate unfulfilled complementarity. The word processor is a tool that complements the skills of the typist in the presentation of text. The video typist can visualize, create and experiment with different ways of presenting a given piece of text. In the case described here, however, the form of work organization that accompanied the introduction of word processing disrupted this complementarity in the following ways:

(1) Although the typing operations were computer controlled, the information-handling features of the system gave the typist the ability to develop a new area of discretion — information manipulation.

(2) Typists were remote from authors who were not fully aware of the facilities and constraints of the technology.

(3) Typists were not able to develop and use knowledge of individual authors' needs and preferences.

(4) Control over work scheduling was transferred to management.

(5) Typists did not follow jobs through to completion.

So while the typists enjoyed working with the new technology, they felt that the work re-organizaton had considerably reduced their job satisfaction. The authors were also unhappy about the new arrangements.

The doughman suffered a radical loss of craft skills as the computer replaced the need for human intervention in the mixing process, leaving him with the 'residual' tasks of pressing a button to start the cycle, adding small ingredient quantities and emptying the dough out at the end of the cycle. Overall process control was supervised by control-room operators remote from the mixing area and the doughman was thus left with no area of discretion. This led to what may be described as a distancing effect which had the following characteristics:

(1) operators had no understanding of the machinery or the process;

(2) operators could not visualize the consequences of personal action or inaction;

(3) operators could not trace sources or diagnose causes of process and equipment faults;

(4) specialised maintenance staff were required;

(5) there was no manual or mechanical back-up system;

(6) operators became bored, apathetic and careless;

(7) operators rejected responsibility for breakdowns;

(8) operators developed no knowledge or skills through their work experience that made them promotable, thus management lost a source of supervisory recruitment.

These may be features of many computerised and 'nearly automated' tasks. This distancing effect may be overcome, however, by reconsidering the organization of work around the biscuit-making process as a whole. One option would be the establishment of a 'line team' to replace the existing rigid and fragmented task allocations. It may also have been possible at an earlier stage of technological development to consider siting the computer mixing-control equipment in the mixing area, to be operated by the doughman. The point is that, as with the video typists, the information technology did not uniquely determine the organization of work that accompanied it.

Summary of Conclusions

(1) Promoters within organizations are a necessary prerequisite of process innovation.

(2) Information technologies are introduced to meet several management objectives concerning costs, productivity and system reliability.

(3) Different management levels and functions accept and use information technologies for different reasons.

(4) The organization of work around information technology is determined more by management orientations than by the technology itself. The two components of management thinking that appear to have the strongest influence in this respect are:

    (a) the desire to reduce human intervention and error, and

    (b) the desire to control work flow and operators more closely.

(5) Technology can be used either to replace or to complement human capabilities. The consequences of a particular application depend partly on the capabilities of the technology and partly on the way in which work is organized around the technology.

(6) The three applications described here illustrate:

    (a) complementarity, where the ovenman was given information not previously available that enhanced his ability to control the

operations of biscuit baking;
(b) unfulfilled complementarity, where video typists were unable to fully exploit the information manipulation capabilities of word processing because of the form of work organization;
(c) replacement, where the craft skills of the doughman were made redundant with the introduction of computerised mixing control.
(7) The residual role of the operator in a nearly automated system can be a 'distanced' one in which:
(a) the operator has no understanding of the equipment and machinery;
(b) the operator cannot assist with repairs or give manual backup; and
(c) operators become apathetic, deskilled and unpromotable.

CHAPTER 13

New Technology and Human Tasks: The Future of Work in Manufacturing Industry

Barry Wilkinson

Technology Policy Unit, University of Aston in Birmingham, UK

INTRODUCTION

OVER THE NEXT TWENTY YEARS, perhaps the most difficult problems facing managers and trade unionists in Britain (and throughout Europe) will be to come to terms with the host of industrial and commercial applications of microelectronics. Not the least important of these problems is the forms of work organization to be established around the new technology. Systems of payment, relations between individual employees and groups of employees, shiftworking patterns and, in particular, the tasks carried out by workers are all likely to change dramatically.

No attempt will be made here to predict the precise way in which work organizations will change over the next twenty years. Neither will the author try to forecast changes or depict scenarios. Rather, on the basis of some of my recent case studies on the introduction of new manufacturing technology in the engineering industry, an attempt will be made to point out how managers, engineers and workers can (and do) become involved in directing the 'impact' of the new technology. In other words, the discussion will not predict what the typical shop-floor worker will be doing in twenty years time, but it will show how he can intervene and influence what he does.

Background

Previous work has tended to treat aspects of work organization as related in a simple deterministic manner to the 'type' or 'level' of technology employed. Two authors immediately come to mind — Blauner (1964), with his optimistic view of the 'free and in-control' worker, characteristic of automated processes, and Bright (1958), with his pessimistic view of the decline of skills associated with increased technological sophistication. But much policy-oriented research, at least until recently, has been equally guilty of a strong measure of determinism. For instance, a series of OECD studies in the 1960s considered the 'problems of adjustment' to technical change — the worker having to be guided through the transition from a 'craft' to a 'technical' system of work, which had both positive and negative consequences (Touraine *et al,* 1965). Positive consequences included better working conditions and less physical effort, while the most important negative ones were the elimination of many traditional craft skills and the possible disruption of informal work groups. 'Adjustment techniques' to overcome any worker opposition could then be employed, such as 'consultation' and 'participation'. Both the need for change in the first instance and the form the change takes are presented as 'givens' and, if pushed, the economic arguments of the forces of competition and 'one best way' are fallen back upon.

Similarly, the early studies from Sussex University's Science Policy Research Unit (SPRU) on the relationship between technology and skills in the engineering industry used a simple deterministic model (Bell, 1972). Assuming that the physical characteristics of the technology determined the skill requirements of firms, they suggested that if the diffusion rates of technology could be forecast and the skill requirements of each type of technology assessed, then future changes in training needs, arising from changes in technology, could also be forecast. Individual firms, and more importantly national training boards, could then plan more accurately their training programmes with an improved knowledge of manpower requirements in the future. Management policies, when discussed at all, have been treated merely as 'obstacles' to the development of new technology and its associated skill structures.

Today, these deterministic models of change are occasionally being challenged — though the vast majority of researchers probably would not challenge their neo-classical basis. For instance the SPRU researchers have begun to identify the obvious flaws in their analysis. As Senker *et al* (1976) point out:

> It does not seem reasonable to assume that management policies merely delay the impact of technological change on skill structures . . . the skill structure of a particular . . . organization is a function of manpower, training and job design policies, as well as of the economic and technological characteristics of the organization's activities.

They go on to suggest that "future research should be designed to take into account the extent to which both technological change and skill structures are affected significantly by company policies" (*ibid,* p. 51). However, judging by some of the research carried out since then, the old assumptions have not been properly abandoned. For instance, Swords-Isherwood and Senker (1978) have explained Britain's poor performance in innovation simply in terms of the reluctance of UK management to undertake new responsibilities. In doing so, the 'logic' of innovation is returned, presumably to some abstract system in which managers simply stand in the way or 'resist' rather than play an active part.

In this discussion, managers, engineers, workers and so on are construed not as the mere 'messengers' of innovation nor as the 'resistors' of change when the 'logical' development of technology does not occur. Rather, participants in change are seen as active political beings whose interests and ideals provide a creative input to the direction the technical and social organization of work takes. In doing this, it shows how various interested parties influence the direction changes take and thus, hopefully, how changes might be better directed in the future.*

MICROELECTRONICS IN MANUFACTURING

THE FIRST THING to be noted about microelectronic technology is that we cannot talk about a *general* impact. Microelectronics find an enormous diversity of applications in virtually every sector of the economy and talking about the effects of the new technology in, for instance, the accounts department alongside the effects on the shop floor, makes little sense. As with the 'impact of automation' in the 1950s and 1960s, the issues raised are of a different order in different sectors. (This, no doubt, was one of the main reasons why people like Blauner and Bright could come to virtually opposite conclusions — they were using exemplars from different industries.) Thus, when we talk about the various stages in the process of innovation of conception, design, trial, implementation and debugging, it should be borne in mind that we are referring throughout to particular *applications* of microelectronics, not microelectronics in general.

In manufacturing, there is already a tradition of automation — the control of machinery and manufacturing processes by computers and electronic devices has a history of at least 35 years. What microelectronics has done is firstly, to increase the range of processes which can be automated — in particular more complex work and smaller batches can be dealt with — and secondly, to decrease the costs of control devices to such an extent that they have long been overtaken by the costs of the 'hardware' — the machinery itself. Of course, by taking manufacturing processes as a whole, we are in danger of overextending the diversity of possible exemplars, thus restricting our attention to those processes characterised by the use of discrete machines and machine operators (generally batch rather than mass production). Machine tools provide an obvious example but applications to die-casting

---

*The displacement effects of the new technology are not discussed in this study. The author concentrates solely on the character of work which remains.

machinery, plating equipment, rubber-moulding machines, mechanical-handling machines and so on have similar enough implications to be considered together. My case studies in the West Midlands' engineering industry presented many applications of this type and, with this region being Britain's manufacturing base, they are probably the most important type of application.

DESIGN OF TECHNOLOGY

BEFORE DISCUSSING the debugging and implementation of the new technology, which represents the major concern of the case studies, it is worth pointing out the vital importance of the design stage. The recent work by Nobel (1979) in America is especially important here. He traces the design of numerically controlled (NC) machine tools back to the Second World War and points out that, in the initial stages of development, there were two types of NC system. A 'record-playback' system involved the machinist making the first-off of a batch of components in the normal way, using the machine's manual controls. The machine's control system would record the movements used by the operator, so that the rest of the batch would run automatically. The second system, what is now conventional NC equipment, involves the preparation of a paper tape by programmers, encoded on which are the instructions for the movements of the machine tool. Placed in the machine's control cabinet, the operator simply has to load the machinery and press the 'on' button — the rest is automatic. According to Noble, there were no convincing economic advantages in favour of one control system over the other. Rather, the second type was developed out of social and political considerations. This system meant that control over the quantity and quality of production could be taken out of the hands of the skilled machinist on the shop floor and placed in the office — the new white-collar programmers being more conformist with management aims. The first system meant that all the traditional skills of the machinist would be maintained. The 'deskilling' effects of NC systems then are not related to 'technical necessities' — the choice of system does not represent the engineer's dream of the 'one best way'. Rather, the 'deskilling' route was chosen by management in an attempt to take control from what was considered a problematic workforce.

More recently Howard Rosenbrock, John Boone and others at the University of Manchester Institute of Science and Technology (UMIST) Machine Tool Division have begun to examine the possibilities of designing an NC system for operator programming on the shop floor. Already a prototype NC lathe, which is programmed at the machine's own computer control, has been successfully demonstrated and, in fact, is claimed in many respects to be economically superior. The intention now is to extend the control system to a whole 'flexible manufacturing system' (FMS), which involves a robot as well as two machine tools. The hope is to allow the development of a 'computer-aided craftsman' rather than a semi-skilled machine minder. At the same time as these more ambitious experiments with FMSs go on, commercial applications are being sought and we must now await the response from industry.

Before moving on to the way NC and other control systems have actually been utilised in individual manufacturing firms, it is worth noting that for some computer applications, the 'design' stage is perhaps even more important. I refer to new computer systems for a range of administrative and office functions. Here the hardware — the computer machinery — has little significance. It is what the computer does, as determined by the systems designer, which is all-important — the writing of the software. An instance from one of the case studies is provided by the introduction of a new shop-scheduling system to replace the old progress-chasing system of shop-floor-production control. By re-allocating the tasks of the progress clerks 'geographically' from the previous 'functional' division of labour, all the skill and knowledge, and the integrity and satisfaction in work that goes with it, has been eliminated. Instead of chasing all the parts necessary for the building of a machine or group of machines, the clerk now simply arranges for the work in his section of the machine shop to be allocated in the order dictated by a computer print-out. There can be no doubt that alternative, more skilled and interesting systems could have been 'computerised' and indeed the firm has now tacitly acknowledged this with recent considerations of another system with very different implications. Hedberg and Mumford (1975), among others, have focussed on computerised administrative systems and in particular have looked at the way the values (or 'models of man'), employed by computer systems designers, can influence the type of work they create for the user of new systems.

DEBUGGING AND IMPLEMENTATION

WHEN NEW ELECTRONIC control devices are applied to manufacturing processes, important implications for the nature of work tend to be 'built-in' to the machinery. As Noble and Rosenbrock point out, social choices have already been made during design. However, individual 'adopting' firms still have to choose between available options and, even then, there remains a degree of choice in organizing work around the new technology. The debugging and implementation phases of innovation are particularly important, since it is here that new working practices become established and 'institutionalised' as the various parties negotiate the change. The way choices were made and the way working practices evolved in my case studies will now be discussed (Wilkinson, in press).

The criteria for choice among alternative machinery on the market (where alternatives existed) were of course generally highly technical — referring to costs, suitability to production needs, payback periods, and so on. However, some firms did recognise the effects new systems might have on work organization — if only after experience with other automated machinery — and occasionally, there were indications that the choice among alternative options was coloured by considerations of the type of work they implied. For instance, in one firm (a machinery manufacturer) production engineers, supervisors and higher managers were divided on whether to move in the direction of operator-programmable NC machine tools (manual data input or MDI machines) or remain with conventional tape-controlled NC tools.* The choice they identified was not simply a technical choice, to be technically determined, but rather a social choice between shop-floor control over production (operator-programming, MDI) or office control (office programming, conventional NC). In fact, it was a production engineer who best summarized the options: "The firm has to go one of two ways. We can either retain skill on the shop floor and have manual data input or transfer skill into here with more tape control machines." Another firm (a plating company) attempted to influence the way work would be organized by the computer-control supplier, arranging the layout of equipment in the factory so that the electronic controls for the plating lines would be located in a separate room, access to which was denied to operators. Management complained that previously operator-control over the pace and quality of work was abused by some who would take longer than necessary to make their work easier or sometimes produce goods of a higher quality than was necessary (thus wasting time and materials) and so on. Direct management control over production quantity and quality was to be secured by replacing manual controls by automatic electronic ones — to be set only by managers and one or two select personnel. In the words of the managing director, a major reason for automation was to 'deskill' an 'unreliable' workforce.

During the implementation and 'debugging' stages of innovation, however, the people on the 'receiving end' of technological advance (the workers) may attempt to impose their own interests on working arrangements. Workers are generally assumed — by management as well as others — to be interested only in the monetary compensation they might receive for allowing the smooth introduction of new processes. However, the idea that workers can be simply 'bought off' is a gross and inexcusable oversimplification. Workers interests are always wider and failure to take them into account inevitably means management designs will not be achieved. In the plating company, for instance, during the debugging of the new systems, it was necessary to make occasional use of a manual override until the computer programmes were perfected. Operators *still* use the manual override frequently in order to

---

*The recent availability of MDI machines could represent a marked change in direction of design philosophy to that identified by Noble (1979). Whether it 'takes-off' is yet to be seen.

control their own work pace and also the quality of finish on goods. Now that debugging is almost complete, these practices have become institutionalised and managers have had to revert to the old styles of close supervision in order to maintain management control and standards. In another firm which found similar unwanted working practices becoming institutionalised during debugging, the next set of machinery to be introduced will be 'productionised' (their phrase) away from the shop floor in a specially built new development area. Only when machinery is ready for full-scale and uninterrupted production will workers see it. The time-study man can then time the job with work methods *pre-arranged* by development staffs. Any influence workers may have on their own work arrangements is thus eliminated. Only management interests are 'built-in' to the work organization.

At the machinery manufacturing firm mentioned, the NC machinery introduced over the last few years has been mainly conventional — tape-controlled/office-programmed. However, there is a tape-editing facility on these machines for the proving of tapes, which is carried out during the production of the first of a batch. As one can imagine, there is some dispute as to who carries out the editing, the arrangements tending to be negotiated between individual operators and programmers with each new programme. Being generally supported by shop-floor supervisors, operators have so far tended to win this 'battle for control'. Some operators have in fact learned — with no formal training — how to programme their machines at the machine's editing panel, thus usurping the role of the programmer altogether. The editing facility is, however, limited and the programming of more complex parts can be carried out at machines only when fitted with MDI systems. (In some other firms, operators are not allowed to tamper with programmes in any way and the editing panel is locked by programmers after they have proved their own tapes.)

Supervisory support for operators comes largely on the grounds that skill should, wherever possible, be maintained on the shop floor — 'after all, this is where production is carried out!' The foremen and supervisors in this firm are mainly skilled machinists themselves and the tradition of craft skills they have grown-up with obviously strongly influences their views. Some other managers in the firm have a clear preference for eliminating all shop-floor control of production and replacing the skilled worker with semi-skilled operators who are easier to replace. Management control of production would then be directly through the programmers, who are presumed to be more sympathetic to management aims. These experiences on the shop floor feed back, of course, to the 'choice of technology' stage, influencing the decisions taken on conventional and MDI NC systems and although this is not strongly reflected in official capital justification documents, production engineers did identify the influences during interviews.

CONCLUSIONS

ELECTRONIC CONTROL of manufacturing processes has been increasingly implemented in firms over the last few years. With microelectronics becoming cheaper and their range of possible applications being extended, we can expect to see more and more applications in the years ahead. However, they have no uniform 'impact' but depend on the social and political intentions of managers and engineers and also on the way workers respond, adapt and try to influence the outcome. The various stages in the process of innovation of design, trial, implementation and debugging — all provide junctures at which people can (and do) intervene to influence the process of technical change. They are in fact generally unacknowledged areas of policy-making which have the profoundest influence on the nature of modern work. In order to direct the future of human work in desireable directions — that is, in order to maintain and extend the dignity and satisfaction that comes from control and the development and execution of skills — managers and engineers, as well as workers and their representatives, must be made aware of, and come to terms with, the ways they can influence their own future. It is hoped that this discussion has helped lay bare the myth of the machine by showing how engineers, workers and managers do become involved as active agents, rather than presenting them as the passive recipients of innovation's own logic. The problem now is to openly acknowledge the social and political issues and to place them on the negotiating table.

References

Bell, R. M. (1972) *Changing Technology and Manpower Requirements in the Engineering Industry.* Sussex University Press, Sussex.
Blauner, R. (1964) *Alienation and Freedom.* University of Chicago Press, Chicago.
Bright, J. R. (1958) *Automation and Management.* Harvard Business School, Boston.
Hedberg, B. and Mumford, E. (1975) The Design of Computer Systems: Man's Vision of Man as an Integrated Part of the Design Process. In E. Mumford and H. Sackman (Eds.) *Human Choice and Computers,* North Holland, Amsterdam, pp. 31-60.
Noble, D. (1979) Social Choice in Machine Design: The Case of Automatically Controlled Machine Tools. In A. Zimbalist (Ed.) *Case Studies in the Labour Process,* Monthly Review Press, New York, pp. 18-50.
Senker, P. *et al* (1976) *Technological Change, Structural Change and Manpower in the UK Toolmaking Industry:* Engineering Industry Training Board, Watford, p. 51.
Swords-Isherwood, N. and Senker, P. (1978) *Automation in the Engineering Industry.* Labour Research, Vol. 67, No. 11, pp. 230-231.
Touraine, A. *et al* (1965) *Workers' Attitudes to Technical Change.* OECD, Paris.
Wilkinson, B. *Technical Change and Work Organisation.* Technology Policy Unit: PhD Thesis, University of Aston, Birmingham (In Press).

CHAPTER 14

The Social Effects of Computer-Aided Design: Current Trends and Forecasts for the Future

Michael Rader

Department of Applied Systems Analysis, Karlsruhe Nuclear Research Centre, Federal Republic of Germany

THE SOCIAL EFFECTS of computer-aided design (CAD) have been the focus of an empirical study conducted by a group of social scientists at Karlsruhe Nuclear Research Centre's Department of Applied Systems Analysis. The project was started in late 1977 and is scheduled to be completed by the end of 1982. The project is funded almost exclusively from the research and development of the Nuclear Research Centre. There has been no sponsor to determine the direction of the research work. However, there is some interchange with a project management team, also located at Karlsruhe, responsible for the administration of a scheme by the Federal Ministry for Science and Technology to promote the diffusion of computer-aided design. This scheme was started in 1973 and has since been terminated as an individual project, although CAD is still promoted within the confines of a programme encompassing a wider range of manufacturing technologies.

THE AIMS OF THE PROJECT

WHILST THE PROJECT is concerned with the social effects of CAD in the widest sense of the term, we have concentrated on a number of central issues:
(a) *Effects on skills:* which skills at present required for design endeavour will become redundant and which new skills will be required?
(b) *Effects on design methods:* this issue is in many ways related to the above.

Will the use of the computer in design force designers to modify their methods to adapt to the computer's requirements or will the computer merely prove a tool which can be applied within the framework of well-established design methods?

(c) *Effects on employment:* are redundancies to be expected as a consequence of widespread diffusion of CAD? Which professions are most likely to be affected? Will new jobs be created to any significant extent?

In order to assess the full effects of CAD on firms and their employees, we have developed a model, encompassing three main aspects as follows:

(1) *The innovation aspect:* what are firms' reasons for the adoption of technologies such as CAD? Who are the people involved in this process? Which departments take the initiative and where does resistance come from and for what reasons?

(2) *The implementation aspect:* what are the steps employed to introduce the technology into the firm once the decision to adopt has been taken? This involves such matters as information policy, training, initial areas of application, organizational changes and employment effects. Effects at this stage may best be described as transitional.

(3) *The impact aspect:* by this is meant the stage at which the application of a new technology becomes routine and the effects make themselves felt on an everyday level. It is at this stage that we may correctly assess the effects on employment, skills, organization, design methods and so forth.

A final issue — the effects of CAD on the products themselves — is not fully dealt with here due to the nature of the products manufactured by the firms chosen for closer review. One interesting side issue which will be discussed, however, is that of lay participation in design with the aid of computers.

A Note on Methods and the current status of the project

The greatest part of the information for the project has been collected by means of interviews, but the observation of people at work is planned for a future stage. Information gathering has not been confined to the effects of technology but also included technical trends and the context within which CAD is employed. Thus, it is hoped that causes can be attributed to the effects observed. Recent work has included interviews with mid-level management staff in 41 medium-sized engineering companies, 32 of them CAD users and 9 of them non-users. Ten to twelve were selected for closer scrutiny in order to assess the actual impact of CAD. The project consisted of a number of component parts and several reports have been prepared.

Briefly, the main components of the study may be summarized as follows:
(1) A pilot study in 14 firms belonging to various branches of industry. This pilot study has provided the basis for further research and has helped to bring the main issues into focus. The results have been published in several publications (Bechmann *et al,* 1978; Bechmann *et al,* 1979; Wingert *et al,* 1980).

(2) A fact-finding visit to Great Britain in order to get acquainted with current developments and with the state of discussion on CAD (Rader and Wingert, 1981).

(3) A series of interviews with all the major manufacturers and distributors of CAD components operating in the Federal German market. The results of this survey have been published along with a report on future developments in the field of CAD prepared by a project member and an information scientist working for the project on a contract basis (Duus and Gulbins, 1981).

(4) A series of 41 interviews with mid-level management staff in medium-sized engineering firms, 32 of them using CAD and 9 of them not. An interim report is being prepared, partly for distribution to the firms to secure their further co-operation and partly to provide users and companies contemplating the introduction of CAD with information on experience gathered by others.

(5) Interviews with specialists responsible for writing CAD software. Work on these interviews has been completed and transcriptions prepared. Possibly, additional interviews may be conducted if the need arises.

(6) A large-scale survey among lower-level staff working with CAD in 10-12 firms selected from the main sample. We have secured the firms' co-operation and are in the process of developing instruments for investigation.

RESULTS FROM THE PROJECT

Effects on Employment Level

The CAD applications reviewed in the project are still very much at the experimental stage. Experience has shown that with the introduction of a new technology, additional labour is generally required and permanent employment effects are felt only when the technology reaches the stage of routine application. In addition, measuring employment effects simply by comparing figures before and after the application of a technology fails to take into account such effects as an increase in the volume of work accomplished by the same number of employees and dispensing with contract labour. Shortage of labour and the removal of bottlenecks from the design department were primary factors in the introduction of CAD into the firms reviewed. Table 1 presents an overview of the firms' ten most important motives. These indicate the firms' expectations with regard to effects, as opposed to the actual effects.

At the time of the pilot study, a number of firms stressed the shortage of skilled labour available for the design department, giving this as one major reason for the necessity of CAD. The recent review of engineering firms has presented a very similar picture, despite a general deterioration in the employment situation. In this respect, our results are very similar to those produced by Sussex University's Science Policy Research Unit (SPRU): "In the last year or so of recession, the long-standing shortage of draughtspeople has disappeared in many — but not all — areas, but computer-aided draughting has generally been introduced in the context of, and sometimes in response to, skill shortage" (Arnold, 1981). In the Federal Republic of Germany, much publicity has recently been given to employers' complaints that school-leavers are most reluctant to enter engineering professions, an argument that could be used to lend support to the introduction of computer-aided design systems requiring little engineering skill on the part of the user.

Table 1

Firms' Ten Most Important Motives for the Introduction of CAD (Based on 31 Interviews in 30 Firms)

Ranking of Importance	Motive	Average value on 4-point Scale [a]	Standard Deviation [b]
1	Cutback in the time required for a certain task	3.52	0.89
2	Improvement of the basis for decision-making	3.33	0.76
3	Quality improvement	3.26	0.58
4	Removal of bottlenecks in the design department	3.23	0.76
5	Relief of staff from routine tasks	3.21	0.83
6	Cutbacks in costs in the design department	3.20	1.03
7	Increased flexibility	3.19	0.87
8	Cutback in production costs generally	3.14	0.99
9	Gaining a technological advantage over competitors	2.96	0.88
10	Increase in company turnover	2.90	0.97

[a] 4 = very important; 3 = important; 2 = not very important; 1 = unimportant.
[b] The standard deviation may be regarded as a measure for the degree of agreement on any one item on the list. The smaller the standard deviation, the greater the agreement in the assessment of an item.

In the firms covered by our project, 26 new jobs had been created to work with CAD, as opposed to 1 case of actual and 2 of expected job losses. The case of actual job loss involved 23 people, so there is great potential for large-scale redundancies. The jobs created were mainly for university graduates or engineers from polytechnics. In addition, 18 employees were transferred from other tasks to work with CAD. Job losses have occurred in departments not using CAD, such as production preparation, product testing and fitting.

Even if draughtspeople have not as yet been directly affected by job loss, it is fairly obvious from the data in Table 1 that firms do expect an increase in productivity in return for the investment in CAD. Besides an increase in the volume of work accomplished and dispensing with contract labour, CAD may also give a clear competitive edge to companies using it (Arnold, 1981), thus leading to job loss for non-users. There is little in our own data to support this statement, but disadvantages from non-use are only just beginning to make themselves felt.

Statements from the manufacturers and distributors of CAD equipment in the Federal Republic of Germany in some cases suggested radical cutbacks in the number of draughtspeople. In a number of instances, people interviewed expected a restructuring of activities, with draughtspeople being replaced or retrained as detail designers. One representative of a manufacturer expected the demand for the 'classic' designer to decrease by as much as 50 per cent. From this data, however, no clear pattern emerges and the statements are based more on educated guesswork than actual experience.

The expected effects of computer-aided design on employment may tentatively be summed up as follows:

(1) There will probably be little direct job loss in the form of dismissals in the design office. The jobs of people leaving firms may not be re-occupied. The immediate effects will probably be felt by contract labour. In addition, there may be some job loss in firms not using CAD.

(2) There is likely to be some job loss in neighbouring departments, such as production preparation, product testing and fitting. This is due to the greater accuracy of the computer and its potential for the simulation of critical situations which would otherwise require trials with models or prototypes. CAD programmes also often incorporate such features as parts lists.

(3) Initially, some new jobs may be created for highly skilled personnel to work with CAD systems. The number of these jobs is not likely to be very great. In the firms reviewed, new jobs were created for no more than 3 people except in one case, where 6 new jobs were created to deal with CAD.

(4) There may eventually be a reduction in the number of 'classic' designers of up to 50 per cent. The demand for various types of designer will be subject to shifts.

(5) At present, there has been little evidence of the introduction of shift work or flexitime to ensure better use of computer capacity but this may come later.

Effects on Skills

Although this is a very central issue in our research, it is also an area of uncertainty. The most common thesis currently being employed to describe the effects of the computer on skills is that of bi-polarization: very few highly qualified jobs are created, with the remainder becoming increasingly fragmented and requiring few skills. On the one hand, this leads to an increase in the intensity of work, particularly of decision-making; on the other hand, a vast amount of skills are wasted. To examine if this is really so, we shall be drawing on several sources: interviews with experts on CAD; mid-level management interviews; statements by manufacturers and distributors of CAD equipment; and statements by programme developers. Unfortunately, with the exception of some university graduates or engineers, we have not yet been able to ask those people who will, by all accounts, be most affected by the introduction of CAD. This is projected for the next stage of our study.

The questionnaire used to interview mid-level staff included a number of questions on skill requirements. A first indicator is the training level of staff currently working with CAD. At present, the majority of programmes are being used by users or groups of users, at least one member of which has university education or an engineering degree from a polytechnic. Only in 7 out of the 36 programme-applications reviewed did all the programme operators have less training (i.e. technicians and draughtspeople). Finite element methods,* which are generally considered difficult and practically cannot be calculated without computer aid, were in every case used by staff with higher training levels. Draughtspeople and technicians generally operated the simpler draughting programmes.

We also asked whether computer aid had made tasks easier or harder to accomplish than by conventional means. Surprisingly enough, the majority of respondents were of the opinion that the computer had made design work more difficult. This was the case for 10 out of 31 applications. In a further 6 cases, work was perceived as easier and in 4 cases, no change was felt to have taken place. For the remaining 11 applications, respondents were of the opinion that tasks before and after the introduction of the computer were not directly comparable. This applies especially to finite element methods. In addition, if we breakdown the assessments by programme, we find that the majority of cases in which work is deemed more difficult after computer application are also accounted for by finite element method programmes. Table 2 presents an overview of the knowledge considered necessary to operate the programmes reviewed.

From Table 2, we see that only a very elementary knowledge of programming techniques is necessary to use the programmes, apart from the very obvious case of job control language. The results also suggest that the introduction of computer-aided design might require learning new design methods.

Further evidence on this subject was gathered by asking if any previously required skills had become redundant and whether new skills were required. In the majority of cases (21 out of 36), respondents did not reckon that any skills would become redundant. Three others were of the opinion that draughting was becoming an obsolete skill and another three thought the same about calculation. Perhaps the most radical statement, cited by four respondents,

---

*Finite element methods are employed to calculate distortion in objects caused by various conditions of strain. For this purpose, the objects are divided into a finite number of simple geometric elements, such as rods, triangles, quadrangles and pyramids. The computer and programme guarantee the correct combination of elements into a mathematical model and its calculation under the conditions described.

was that experience would no longer be necessary. Opinions on the new skills necessary to apply CAD were more divided. Backing-up the impression previously stated, seven respondents thought that working with CAD required learning new design methods. Twelve respondents mentioned the obvious, saying that users would have to learn to use the computer. Another ten respondents said that CAD users would have to acquire the skill of abstract thinking. Finally, seven respondents considered that no new skills would be required.

Table 2

Skills and Knowledge needed to operate programmes
(Based on data for 36 applications in 31 firms)

Amount of knowledge/skill required

Skills/Knowledge	None	Moderate	Great	Unchanged	Don't know/ No reply
General knowledge on EDP*	12	13	8	0	3
Command language	4	7	22	0	3
Programming ability	25	5	2	0	4
Programme logic	11	11	7	1	6
Knowledge of design object	5	19	7	0	4
Design methods	7	7	10	8	4
Organization	5	9	7	8	7

*Electronic data-processing

Asked how they thought computers would affect the quality of working life, especially with regard to work load in the design office, eleven reckoned that there would be no change and one expected a general improvement. In two cases, both positive and negative effects of the computer were envisaged. One respondent saw an increase in routine activities and sixteen expected an intensification of activites, caused no doubt by the necessity to provide the computer with input at a given time. On the whole, respondents felt that users would need greater concentration, that work would be intensified and require a higher degree of diligence and planning than conventional design.

Some indication of the degree of skill required to operate CAD programmes may be given from the amount of use thought necessary for a user to have full command of the programmes as opposed to merely being able to operate them. Obviously, this depends to some extent on the frequency of use within a given period. The answers covered a range of up to three years, so that we may assume that, once again, this depends on programme characteristics and varies accordingly. Well over half the programme applications (63 per cent) required less than six months' experience for their command and over twenty per cent required less than one month. At the other extreme, seven programme applications were seen as requiring one to three-years' experience for their command.

Another pointer to effects on skills, and especially the fragmentation of work as a consequence of CAD use, is the organization of CAD applications within the firms. Whilst the division of labour encountered was not in itself dramatic, it could prove the first step on a road to fragmentation of tasks and deskilling. Two alternative stategies may be employed: will CAD be used by people doing the design work or will groups of specialists be created to deliver results on a customer-order basis? Both kinds of arrangement were encountered in practice. It is difficult to imagine what the eventual outcome of such division of labour will be. At present, it seems that the division leaves designers' jobs untouched, but it seems likely that it can only be effective in the long run for isolated tasks such as complicated calculations (e.g. finite element methods) or draughting, where a firm has several design departments for different products. As these tasks are integrated into large-scale, computer-aided design systems (and this is the intention of most firms), this division of labour should disappear and be replaced by a new division — providing input, interpreting results etc. or dealing with individual projects from start to finish. The present division of tasks could influence the degree to which individual professions are affected. For instance, the creation of a CAD group outside the design office could lead to the long-term disappearance of designers in a firm. On the other hand, leaving CAD in the design office could mean that it will be operated by people originally trained as designers. This is an area where we can only guess at the outcome.

The manufacturers and distributors of CAD equipment in the Federal Republic of Germany were also asked how they thought the technology would alter the quality of working life for the people using the equipment. I shall quote some excerpts from their replies:

> *There will be a demand for designers with the ability to 'get along with' CAD. This entails an upgrading of skills through abstract thinking at the screen.*

> *More rapid thinking and decision-making will be necessary. The smaller graphic representation at the VDU screen will cause strain on the eyes.*

> *A higher degree of mental strain caused by work at CAD stations will require amended arrangements for breaks in work.*

> *There will be a new division of labour: designers will now only prepare sketches and draughtspeople will do the detail work at the screen.*

> *A general increase in skills will be necessary.*

From these answers, it would appear that effects of programmes on skills are not a central area of concern for manfufacturers. A large number of manufacturers' and distributors' representatives did not answer the question at all and some evaded the real issues.

The CAD programmes reviewed were generally fairly widely distributed and by this criterion successful. In the main, they had originally been developed at universities, although in some cases they were being distributed by commercial companies formed especially for this purpose. Without exception, they had been developed by specialist engineers with a knowledge of programming, rather than information specialists. This was considered an advantage by most of the discussants, since information scientists lack the specialist information to deal with the problems involved in the manner that designers are accustomed to. Most of the programme developers were agreed on the necessity for adaptability to the requirements of users with varying degrees of experience. In two cases, the programmes were intended for use by operators with little specialised knowledge or skills. In one of the cases, a specialist qualification was, somewhat paradoxically, also deemed necessary. Generally, however, the discussants were agreed on the importance of some knowledge in the area covered by the programme.

To close this discussion on the matter of skills, I shall quote the opinions of some experts who have a great deal of experience with CAD. Hatvany, Newman and Sabin (1977), for instance, describe design as an act of decision-making, with lower-level decisions increasingly being incorporated in CAD programmes. Thus, "much of the basic decision-making power has gone into the hands of those who write the design programmes." This can lead to the rejection of programmes, if designers do not accept the competence of those writing the programmes. This lends support to the argument of the developers, who say that programmes should be written by engineers rather than information scientists.

Arthur Llewelyn, formerly of the CAD Centre in Cambridge (UK), claims that computers can be used to simulate more situations than a designer could encounter in real life. To prove his point, he quotes the example of bridge-building: the engineer is provided with a display representing a pictorial skeleton of the bridge. By varying the loadings, the engineer may, on the display, immediately see the stress and strain patterns in parts of the bridge. He may simulate various kinds of situation by varying the weight and size of objects moving across the bridge, testing them against safety limits. In real life, this may be done very expensively by putting sensors into the bridge and monitoring. Llewelyn's claim is that, in half an hour, even experienced engineers (with twenty or thirty years' experience in building bridges) could play with more problems on the screen than they had experienced in their whole lives (personal communication, in Rader and Wingert, 1981, p. 63). This can, however, only be the case if there is sufficient confidence in the computer programme applied and this in turn can only be true if the person using the programme has sufficient experience with the kind of real-life situation that is being simulated. In addition, the programme must be sufficiently clear for the user to be able to judge whether its 'workings' coincide with his idea of the way things should be done. Finally, even the experienced designer must find the time to play through the situations he has not yet experienced. An example of the kind of thing that can happen if programmes are used by inexperienced operators is provided by Mike Cooley (personal comm., *ibid,* p. 64). "The igniter in the after-burner of aero engines is roughly the same size as a car's spark plug. In the design of an igniter using CAD, the decimal point was erroneously shifted one place to the right, with the result that the igniter was built ten times too big by deskilled workmen. Some skilled workmen put the igniter on the designer's desk as a sort of joke. But he didn't even realize the igniter was ten times too big!"

Finally, I shall quote two important findings from our pilot study:

(a) Firstly, there is a change in the manner in which one's own work is planned. The use of the computer necessitates a change-over from planning during work to planning before work.

(b) Secondly, since real advantages may be gained from CAD only when a certain degree of integration is achieved, the organization of work must take the shape of a chain of linked steps, each of which must be completed before tackling the next step (Wingert *et al,* 1980, p. 55).

This could force designers to employ different methods to those used previously and will almost certainly bring about an end to idiosyncratic working styles. Whether this is a good thing remains to be seen and is certainly a subject for debate. There is, however, little in the results of our present survey to support the impressions from the pilot study and we shall have to postpone final judgement on the matter until results from the survey among lower-level staff are available.

To sum up, on the admittedly patchy and preliminary evidence, CAD will affect skills and working life in the following ways:

(a) At present, most CAD users have a fairly high level of formal education. This might change as the technology becomes more established.

(b) There is some evidence of a bi-polarisation of skill requirements, depending to some extent on the characteristics of the programmes applied. Staff on the level of draughtspeople or below are likely to be deskilled, especially where draughting programmes are applied. Above this level, an upgrading of skills seems likely.

(c) Only a minority of programmes require much design experience for use. There is a danger of application by users who may formally be able to provide the correct input, but who neither understand the problems involved nor can fully interpret the output. This matter will be dealt with presently.

(d) it seems likely that design methods will change, even if the computer does not take over the entire design process.

(e) CAD can only be used to add to experience if the user has some knowledge of the real-life situation being simulated.

CAD AS AN INSTRUMENT FOR DEMOCRATIZATION OF DESIGN

AN INTERESTING ASPECT of computer use in design is its potential as an instrument to enable user participation. This is one way in which CAD could affect all our lifestyles. The use of CAD in this context is being pioneered by the ABACUS group, headed by Professor Tom Maver at Strathclyde University, Glasgow (Maver, 1970 and 1976). The group has developed a set of programmes, designed for use in architecture, but Maver believes the method could be employed with equal success in any field of design endeavour, "whether or not the products of the design activity are artifacts (cars, toothbrushes, TV receivers) or social systems — educational, medical or political" (Maver, 1976, p. 318).

Certainly, most people would agree that democratization is a good thing and would readily be able to point out examples where the computer could be fruitfully employed to this end. Participation in environmental planning is one example that immediately springs to mind: the computer could be employed in much the same manner as described for bridge-building in Llewelyn's example, this time using graphic representations of environments not yet in existence.

The ABACUS group's experience with user participation was on the small-group level, employing a programme called PARTIAL with the following characteristics (Watts and Hirst, n.d.):

(a) The user can set up a preliminary brief, in the form of a space budget, and gain feedback on the brief;

(b) The user can define the relevant performance features (e.g. cost, energy consumption) and define average values against which feedback can be sought;

(c) The user can generate and manipulate a layout using graphic manipulation commands.

Experience with the programme was generally successful. However, one or two problems emerged, arising partly from the design not being conducted in the user's own terms of communication. Additional problems were created by users apparently feeling obliged to stick to 'guidelines' incorporated in the programme and not making use of the option to correct earlier design decisions. This shortcoming could be overcome by repeated use of programmes to add to users' confidence, thereby enabling them to take fuller advantage of the range of options offered by the programme.

The ABACUS group's programmes involve experts to assist in the design process. However, the group is not primarily concerned with the effects user participation will have on the skills of these experts. Indeed, it is a declared goal of the group to demystify expert knowledge such as that of the architect. At the same time, certain privileges will be diminished, but whether this will also lead to a reduction in bargaining power or to deskilling remains to be seen. This will depend to a large extent on the amount of expert knowledge which may successfully be transferred to the computer, a matter that will be dealt with briefly at the end of this discussion.

The other main point of interest is the feasibility of a participative approach to design in mechanical engineering. At present, none of the firms examined in our project are attempting such an approach or have plans to do so. Indeed, evidence of attempts to involve users in the design of the CAD systems themselves is very scant, although there are strong arguments in favour of such approaches (Mumford; Wingert et al, 1980; Kubicek, 1979). Participation was confined largely to providing information on the systems and, in a few cases, to taking designers along to demonstrations.

Many of the firms did, however, produce machines which were tailored individually to customers' requirements. Because of the high production costs involved, some firms were attempting to cut back tailoring in favour of standardized products, sometimes on the basis of 'assembly kits'. It seems feasible for customers to participate in design, by drawing on a stock of standardized parts. Obviously, the user has knowledge of the attributes required to perform the tasks the machine is designed for, whilst the designer has greater knowledge about the behaviour of the machine under extreme conditions encountered while performing certain tasks. If the computer can be used to enable communication between these two groups, in finding a compromise between requirements and constraints, both would benefit.

There are a number of barriers to participation. For instance, there may be tasks too complex to communicate to the user, even with the aid of the most sophisticated computer programmes. We must first decide who is to represent the user, since each and every user of mass-production consumer goods will hardly be able to participate in their design. There may be certain legal, ethical or moral barriers to user participation in every area, so certain fields may be taboo. It also seems very likely that user participation will first be introduced in areas of the greatest public interest and concern, so that areas possibly more important in their effects on our everyday lives will be omitted. We also encounter the problems of responsibility for results if something goes amiss. The more complicated (and, in scientific terms, controversial) the process for decision-making and the more serious the possible consequences of faulty design, the more reluctant people will be to participate in the process. This again narrows down the areas where participative approaches to design may be employed. If user participation serves to deskill people or merely to diminish certain privileges, by selecting areas for participation, we shall be handicapping some professions, whilst sparing others.

Finally, although computers are generally regarded as a very advanced technology, by their use in the area of design, we may be encouraging conservatism. Innovations generally come about with the aid of something we call 'genius' or 'creativity'. This is something that happens in the minds of people and which is not fully understood. It is an area where the computer has not yet taken over. Attempts are being made to unravel the mystery surrounding this area (see Feigenbaum, in Rosenbrock, 1980; Rosenbrock, 1981 a and b); although there is debate about whether it is at all desirable to do so (Cooley, 1980). This is an area where the human being is superior to the computer, so if we wish to take advantage of this superiority, we must ensure that this creativity can always be incorporated into our computer programmes.

CONCLUSIONS

To CLOSE, I shall briefly discuss some of the central issues involved when examining the effects CAD will have on the lives of people. At present, relatively little empirical evidence can be cited on the way things will develop since, for one thing, our own research is still in progress. Another fact that has clearly emerged is that CAD is not yet so fully developed that its full effects may be felt, at least in engineering. More sophisticated systems are available for the electronics and automobile industry.

Even from our relatively scant evidence, two possible tendencies for the development of CAD may be identified. During the course of the history of technology, there have always been paths available where technology could take one of two alternative courses. Referring to these alternatives, Rosenbrock (1981a and b) has suggested that there are, in fact, two kinds of machine: one kind designed to make existing skills more productive, the other designed to eliminate skill wherever possible. Rosenbrock demonstrates his point by contrasting the 'spinning jenny' and the 'spinning mule', invented by James Hargreaves and Samuel Crompton respectively, with the 'self-acting mule' invented by Richard Roberts. In the first instance, the machines were intended for the inventors' own use and designed to extend the skill of the user, making it more productive. They also retained human control over the process and did not require the spinner's task to be fragmented. In the second instance, the machine was designed to eliminate skill, principally to save the high wages paid to the hand 'spinner' and to release the employer from the domination through strikes that the spinner exercised on account of his skill and knowledge. The remaining productive tasks not transferred to the machine were deskilled and fragmented.

Throughout the history of technology, machines of this second kind have continually asserted themselves in competition with those of the first kind. A recent example, the case of the 'numerical control machine' versus 'record-playback' techniques, has been examined in depth by Noble (1979). Competition between the two approaches may also be found in computer technology: in the Federal Republic of Germany it is becoming common to distinguish between 'master' and 'slave' systems (Mertens and Griese, 1971; Kubicek, 1979 and 1981). In cases where the user is the master, the computer is intended to assist the user, relieving him of tedious routine tasks. His knowledge and skill in performing the task would be such that he would be at liberty to disagree with the computer if some important factor had not yet been incorporated into the computer programme. In cases where the operator assumes the role of a slave or servant to the machine, a training course in the computer system and its area of application would suffice to use the system efficiently. The quality of the work produced by the computer might even improve when compared with work produced by conventional means. However, the operator would no longer have the skills and knowledge to disagree with the computer (Rosenbrock, 1981a).

Quite apart from the unpleasant personal consequences this would imply for job satisfaction, it could easily lead to far more serious consequences, as Josef Weizenbaum has pointed out. In one case, a computer tape simulating a nuclear attack by a Russian submarine was inadvertently played into the control system of the North American Air Defence Command (NORAD), almost leading to a World War. In another instance, the US Federal Bank raised the interest rate on the basis of faulty computer data (*Manager Magazin,* 1980). Both examples illustrate our almost blind reliance on computer systems that very few people, if any, really fully command. In an area such as design, the consequences of too great a reliance on the computer as a result of de-skilling and fragmentation of work may not generally be quite so devastating, but it requires no great imagination to think of examples where faulty data used to erect buildings or bridges could lead to loss of life.

As in the historical examples just quoted, the introduction of computer-aided design could serve to fragment skills and to eliminate the necessity of skills, a process described as the Taylorization of intellectual work (Bechmann *et al,* 1978; Bechmann *et al,* 1979; Cooley, 1980; Kubicek, 1981; Rosenbrock, 1981a and b). One might argue that it would be a good thing if human beings no longer had to work and machines did the work for them. However, this would seldom appear to be the outcome of the mechanization of work. The object would seem to be to force human beings into a subordinate role to the machine and to control them through technology. Cooley (1980, p. 17) quotes an example of the kind of statements used to create an atmosphere for this. In the *US Journal of Accountancy,* advice was given on how to introduce the computer into the idiosyncratic working environment of accountants: "If you have got disgruntled employees, you should not allow them to start in case they might abuse the computer." Rosenbrock (1981a and b) cites an example of a similar attitude where robots are not used for certain tasks on the grounds that such tasks fail to take full advantage of the robots' ability. Instead, these tasks are given to women, apparently with no great concern about a possible mismatch beteeen their abilities and the tasks they were asked to perform.

Cooley (1980, p. 28) feels that developments in the area of intellectual work (such as design) are repeating those already completed in the area of manual work (such as skilled craftsmanship). In his opinion, computerisation of design represents an attempt to adapt intellectual work to the principles of predictability, repeatability and quantifiability, which are central notions in Western scientific methodology. Taylor's 'scientific management' is one outcome of this. However, the efficiency of such methods is subject to grave doubts, as Rosenbrock (1979) has correctly asserted: "Without the close interplay of manual work in experiments and mental work in their interpretation, it is inconceivable that science could have developed. No society which separated manual work could have given rise to it. Nor could science long survive such a total separation. In this respect Scientific Management is anti-scientific."

Rosenbrock (1981a) sketches out the alternative application of the same programme by partly trained computer operators and by medical practitioners. In the case of application by the practitioners, negative effects may be fully avoided and the computer may be used to enhance skills. In a similar vein, Kubicek (1981) describes the Statistical Package for the Social Sciences as a 'master system' — one where the user may be master and not a servant. In both cases, the programmes may, however, be applied by people with little knowledge of the problems incorporated in the programmes. Rosenbrock himself has developed computer software designed to enhance the skill of the designer and intended only for use by the expert, so he himself may be achieving his goal. In the other cases described, consequences depend very much on the context in which computer use takes place. All in all, computer-aided design is in the process of widespread introduction; it could have harmful effects but not if we seek to avoid them. There is still some choice left.

References

Arnold, E. (1981) *The Manpower Implications of Computer-aided Design in the UK Engineering Industry.* Paper to British Computer Society Conference, 1-3 July, 1981 (Preprint).

Bechmann, G., Huxdorff, K., Vahrenkamp, R., Werle, R. and Wingert, B. (1978) *Auswirkungen des Einsatzes informationsverarbeitender Technologien, untersucht am Beispiel von Verfahren des rechnerunterstützten Konstruierens und Fertigens (CAD/CAM).* Ergebnisse der Pilotuntersuchung. Kernforschungszentrum Karlsruhe GmbH: KfK-CAD 114, September.

Bechmann, G., Vahrenkamp, R. and Wingert, B. (1979) *Mechanisierung geistiger Arbeit. Eine sozialwissenschaftliche Begleituntersuchung zum Rechnereinsatz in der Konstruktion.* Campus Verlag, Frankfurt/New York.

Cooley, M. J. E. (1980) *Architect or Bee? The Human/Technology Relationship.* Hand and Brain Publications, Slough.

Duus, W. and Gulbins, J. (1981) *CAD Systeme – Aufbau und Komponenten* (preliminary title). Springer Verlag, Berlin, Heidelberg, New York.

Feigenbaum, quoted in Rosenbrock, H. H. (1980) *Automation and Society.* Paper prepared for submission to 'Electronics and Power', 24. (Preprint).

Hatvany, J., Newman, W. M. and Sabin, M. A. (1977) *World Survey of computer-aided design.* Computer Aided Design, Vol. 9, No. 2, p. 93.

Kubicek, H. (1979) *Interessenberücksichtigung beim Technikeinsatz im Büro-und Verwaltungsbereich. Grundgedanken und neuere skandinavische Entwicklungen.* GMD-Bericht Nr. 125. R. Oldenbourg Verlag, Wein, München.

Kubicek, H. (1981) Die Automatisierung der betrieblichen Informationsverarbeitung im Spannungsverhältnis zwischen Rationalisierung und Humanisierung menschlicher Arbeit — Dargestellt am Beispiel der Qualifikationsproblematik. In E. Frese, P. Schmitz, & N. Szyperski, (Eds.) *Organisation, Planung, Informationssysteme.* Erwin Grochla zu seinem 60. Geburtstag gewidmet. Poeschel, Stuttgart.

Manager Magazin (1980) No. 7, pp. 119-121.

Maver, T. W. (1970) *A Theory of Architectural Design in which the Role of the Computer is identified.* Building Science 4, pp. 199-207.

Maver, T. W. (1976) *Democracy in Design Decision-making.* CAD Proceedings, pp. 313-318.

Mertens, P. and Griese, J. (1971) Industrielle Datenverarbeitung Bd. II: Informations- und Planungssysteme. Wiesbaden.

Mumford, E. *Participative Design of new Technology: Four Design Tools to Assist the Design Process.* Vienna Centre, n.d. (Preprint).

Noble, D. F. (1979) Social Choice in Machine Design: The Case of Automatically Controlled Machine Tools. In A. Zimbalist (Ed.) *Case Studies in the Labour Process.* Monthly Review Press, N.Y., pp. 18-50.

Rader, M. and Wingert, B. (1981) *Computer-aided Design in Great Britain and the Federal Republic of Germany: Current Trends and Impacts.* Kernforschungszentrum Karlsruhe GmbH: KfK 3065, March.

Rosenbrock, H. H. (1979) *The Redirection of Technology.* Paper at IFAC symposium in Bari, Italy, 21-23 May, 1979, p. 16f.

Rosenbrock, H. H. (1981a) *Engineers and the Work that People do.* IEEE Technology and Society, Vol. 9, No. 3.

Rosenbrock, H. H. (1981b) *Automation and Society.* Paper presented at the workshop on 'Feedback and synthesis of linear and nonlinear systems', Bielefeld/Rome, 22 June to 3 July, 1981.

Watts, J. and Hirst, M. *User Participation in the Early Stages of Building Design – Some Issues for the Architect and the Social Scientist.* ABACUS, Glasgow, n.d.

Wingert, B., Rader, M. and Riehm, U. (1980) Changes in Working Skills in the Field of Design Caused by the Use of Computers. In J. Mermet (Ed.) *CAD in Medium-sized and Small Industries.* North Holland, Amsterdam.

CHAPTER 15

The Impact of Information Technology at Work:
The Case of CAD/CAM and MIS in Engineering Plants

Arthur Francis, Mandy Snell,
Paul Willman and Graham Winch

Department of Social and Economic Studies, Imperial College, London

INTRODUCTION

DEVELOPMENTS IN THE APPLICATION of microelectronics technology to production processes in manufacturing industry have given rise to a variety of concerns — some theoretical, some related to policy and others of a more practical immediate nature. At the theoretical level, the long-running debate about the major influences on the shape of technological development is relevant; questions are posed about the extent to which developments are influenced by concern for managerial control at the expense of operative control, job satisfaction or even technical efficiency. Equally, theoretical questions concerning the motor for more general innovation can be examined in the context of the relatively rapid level of innovations in microelectronics.

Policy questions of some importance are those related to the impact of this technology on overall levels of employment and skill, and on what can be done by governments to stimulate the rate of take-up in their countries in order to remain competitive internationally. A question which is either a policy question or a practical question (depending on where you stand) is that of the trade union response to this new technology. For the trade union movement, this is a policy question of some weight. For managers, it is a practical question of how to respond to the position the trade unions may take up and, more generally, how to handle the various industrial relations aspects of these technical changes.

182

Finally, there are questions about the impact of the new technology on patterns of work organization. What is an appropriate and efficient organization to run the technology? The question also arises whether the technology allows a new range of choices about work organization and if so, establishing what these are and what costs and benefits each choice will bring to the various interested parties.

There has been much speculation, and some survey research, about these various concerns and, a clearer picture is beginning to emerge in some areas. However, it can be argued that to get to grips with some of these questions, it is necessary to examine individual applications at the case study level, to establish some of the processes at work generating the macro phenomena. To this purpose, a team at Imperial College, London, embarked on a research study, jointly funded by the Science and Engineering Research Council and Social Science Research Council in the UK. Some interim findings of this research are reported here.

THE RESEARCH

THE DATA reported comes from a variety of sources. Much has been collected in the course of writing-up substantial case studies on six companies who have made a significant investment in microprocessor-based production technologies — principally in computer-numerical-control (CNC) machine tools, computer-aided draughting equipment (CAD) and management information systems (MIS). However, in the course of the research, some Masters students have conducted field studies and the authors have visited a number of other companies on a one-off basis. A total of 18 UK plants have thus been studied in relation to their innovations, primarily in the two areas of CAD and CNC machine tools. Cases of a new management information system (MIS) and of robot-usage were also viewed. This particular bundle of applications (CAD, CNC, MIS and robots) was chosen because they form the building blocks of fully automated (or unmanned) integrated manufacturing systems in batch-production engineering and thus have something of a conceptual unity. The UK Government has also explicitly encouraged and funded developments towards this objective, through the automated small-batch production programme (ASP, 1977). In one of our case studies, wholly unmanned manufacture was a specific long-term objective, set by the chief engineer handling the innovation studied.

The method used for the in-depth case studies was to compile an extensive checklist of information required, covering such aspects as: what led to the decision to innovate; how this decision was made; the nature of the innovation; the financial factors; how the change was handled and its impact on occupational structure, work organization and industrial relations in the plant. These questions were used as the basis of fairly unstructured interviews with knowledgeable respondents at all levels of the company, including union representatives. Some full-time union officials were also consulted. In these studies, an average of ten people were interviewed in each case, with a total of about 50 hours spent in each compan. Other data reported here has not been collected systematically and is based on information sometimes from single sources, making it rather less reliable.

The results are interim; some of the case studies are not yet complete and more are being planned, but they may be indicative. They are presented in four sections:

(a) the reasons for, and barriers to, innovation;
(b) impact on employment levels;
(c) effect on skills;
(d) changes in work organization.

THE DECISION TO INNOVATE

STANDARD NEO-CLASSICAL ECONOMIC THEORY of the firm suggests that companies engage in extensive intelligence operations firstly to keep informed of available product-market opportunities and technical processes and secondly, to innovate products or manufacturing processes when this is likely to optimise profitability. This view has been modified by the behaviouralists, such as Simon (1955), who suggest firms only search for alternatives when they encounter a problem and stop searching when they find a satisfactory, though not necessarily optimal, solution.

A radical alternative view is that of the labour process school (Braverman, 1974), who suggest managers introduce innovations in technology in order to maintain or tighten control over the workers to ensure continued realisation of surplus value. This view implies that production processes will be developed which fragment jobs and separate the mental from the manual component of work, placing the mental component into the managerial hierarchy away from the operative, thus reducing the skills required by shop-floor workers. A weaker, less Marxist, version of this argument has been voiced by the movement concerned with the quality of working life (Davies and Cherns, 1975; Rosenbrock, 1977), who have suggested that fragmentation and de-skilling of work, perhaps done for reasons of apparent technical efficiency, are not in the long-term interests of either managers or workers, since reduced quality of work-life reduces motivation, increases conflict at work and so negates gains in technical efficiency.

Very few firms in our sample approximate closely to the neo-classical economic model of firms continuously searching their environment and constantly optimising. Most decisions to take up the new technology were triggered by specific problems. Two major triggers for a company to think about making new investments in its production processes are if growth in product-markets leads to the need for extra production capacity and if technical changes in the product, or new product opportunities, require new methods of manufacture. There is a third theoretical reason for investing in new production processes: when factor costs change, usually there is an increase in labour costs or a marked decrease in capital costs, often due to technical change. Microelectronics technology arguably provides an example of this latter case with, for instance, highly productive fast CNC machine tools markedly increasing the ratio of capital to labour costs in machining. However, firms are not always likely to invest in new production machinery on a straightforward replacement basis simply because it is more capital productive than present machines, because the capital cost of current machining is a 'sunk' cost. Usually some other trigger will be necessary to stimulate investment in new production technology if markets are static.

With static and, in many cases, declining markets facing manufacturing firms in the UK, why have firms taken up the new technology? Has CAD/CAM enabled them to enter new product-markets because they can now manufacture things that were either too expensive or impossible to produce with conventional equipment? Have factor costs changed so markedly that firms have been prepared to discard conventional machinery and so reduce other costs (especially labour) and still show a return? What other triggers can be identified which have led to innovation?

In only one out of eighteen cases we studied was new technology introduced because the company expected (mistakenly as it turned out) an increase in overall sales and so a shortfall in total production capacity. New capacity was thought to be required and it appears to have been generally accepted that production technology, with a strong microelectronics component, should be adopted. This decision was not, however, made on strictly financial grounds. Despite the best efforts of the accountants, it was impossible to demonstrate that, even at forecast levels of capacity utilisation, there was any financial advantage in using this technology compared with investing in the more labour-intensive conventional technology. Moreover, the return on investment (ROI) in the new technology was much more sensitive to the level of capacity utilisation than the ROI in the conventional technology. There is also reason to suppose that the company knew it was being optimistic in its sales forecasts at the time of the investment.

Two reasons were given by the company for deciding on the new technology. One was a general feeling that the industry would have to take the new technology route anyway in the future (as presumably the capital/labour costs would increase over time) and that it was important to invest in the future. The other was a strong preference for a less labour-intensive technology because it was felt that this would reduce management/industrial relations problems. On the first of these two reasons, it is interesting that the company appeared not to choose the most advanced technology available but took an option that had been tried elsewhere. Currently, there is some dissatisfaction that the company now have a system that is less flexible than it should be and hence, cannot be as responsive to the market as it would like. It also appears that there has been little learning-by-doing advantage gained. The technology currently under consideration for the next phase of the company's investment plan is markedly different from the 'new' technology currently installed and so there is only limited experience to carry over. In any event, there are few people who could transfer their knowledge because the majority of key personnel involved in the first set of technology developments have left the company.

On the second set of reasons for adopting the new technology — that of reducing labour *per se,* without there being a cost advantage — a number of reasons were advanced. There was the general feeling that there would be a more predictable level of output and that a higher reliability of operations would be achieved, as the machines were less likely to omit operations on a random, non-detectable basis. (With the new technology, if operations fail to be carried out because of machine malfunction, sensors detect this, signal it to supervision and log it.) On the other hand, the automated process could handle less variability in the workpiece and this led to considerable pressures to refine and change processes upstream.

In view of the sharp decline in numbers employed and the company's inability to justify the new technology, in short-run financial terms, it is perhaps surprising that the unions were willing to accept the new process. They shared the management's view that this was the technology of the future and that the company could not afford to remain with the traditional process; indeed, one management respondent claimed that it was the unions who pushed for this investment. No extra payment was made to those transferring to the new process. Volunteers were requested and management then selected people. Implementation must have been helped, of course, by the fact that, although there was a general shake-out of labour in the company, this particular investment was for a new product and represented new work.

Three of the companies studied were stimulated to innovate because of changes in products or markets. In two cases (each in the aerospace industry), new designs required components which could only have been handled with great difficulty by conventional technology. In one case, a block had to be machined in an extremely complex way requiring great accuracy with a batch size of about 50 pieces. To undertake this work, the company bought a number of new CNC machining centres. In the second case (not strictly within CAD/CAM arrangements but of interest in terms of impact on skill levels), a new design increased the number of holes needed to be accurately drilled in a drum by an order of magnitude. The machining was done on a CNC machine which the company already had, but quality control, which involved checking the dimension of each of the holes, posed an overwhelming problem for the inspection department. As a result, the company devised its own microcomputer-driven sensing equipment to do the gauging automatically. Both these cases led to a reduction in skill levels required by the direct operators/inspectors. But in both cases, the tasks continued to be performed after the innovation by people with the same formal level of qualifications and there was no suggestion that a desire on management's part for deskilling *per se* led to the innovation.

The third case of innovation in response to product-market changes was the company who installed a new management information system in response to Japanese competition. They were being undercut on prices and delivery times and responded by tightening their control of the whole production area by buying an off-the-shelf, production-planning package.

However, most of the innovations we looked at appear to have occurred for various, almost random, reasons. In some cases, machinery needed to be replaced because it was worn-out and so the most up-to-date machinery on the market (which happened to be CNC), was bought to replace it. In two or three cases, the existence of government grants, specifically for microelectronics technology applications, stimulated activity. Most of the companies studied had an 'innovation champion' in the organization pushing changes through; in one case, a move to CAD was triggered by the company chairman's son, who was studying computers at university.

The interim conclusion of our studies is that controlling the 'refractory hand of labour', which may have been a major motive for innovating production processes in the past, is of secondary importance today in most cases. Nevertheless, the particular variant of new technology used, the decision to go ahead being taken on other criteria, may be influenced by labour control considerations. What may in the end turn out to have a much more significant impact on the way of life of any group of workers will be a company's failure to take up the new technology and so become uncompetitive. It is therefore important to look at some of the barriers to innovation in the UK.

One barrier, which at an impressionistic level, looks very significant in our cases at the moment is the fragmented organization of the engineering industry in Britain. With only four exceptions, our cases were either large companies operating virtually a holding company structure, so that the plants studied were innovating in isolation, or the companies themselves were so small that their in-house expertise in the new technology was modest. This is probably a fairly accurate reflection of the mechanical engineering industry in Britain, which comprises a number of relatively small firms and large firms created by mergers, who have not fully rationalised their pre-merger structures. Thus, few companies seem able to field a large manufacturing engineering effort to develop new technology applications. It may also be that CAD systems and CNC machines tools (to say nothing of fully integrated CAD/CAM systems) have economies of scale much greater than that of conventional draughting and machining methods and that the present size of many manufacturing plants will soon be below the minimum appropriate scale size, if not so already. Certainly, in one of our cases, a company bought one CNC machine tool to carry out the functions previously performed by seven conventional machines. The capital cost of this one CNC machine was about equivalent to the replacement cost of the outmoded seven. But its rated capacity should mean that it could handle double the present volume of work on single-shift working. Meanwhile, elsewhere in the same town, a plant in another division of the same company is engaging in a parallel series of plant investments.

A second apparent barrier to innovation in the UK is the lack of adequate technical expertise and management capability. This is difficult to disentangle from the scale effect just discussed. Certainly the largest, most integrated companies we visited had an impressive line-up of engineering talent. But on the smaller sites, there was often at best an enlightened innovation champion, with very little technical support to draw on in the organization, and line management, who needed considerable persuasion and education to make the most sensible use of the new technology.

A third and much less important barrier to innovation (but one which has attracted much attention and speculation) is that of operative or union resistance. In virtually all the cases we examined, this was not a significant factor. Of course, our sample may be biased in that we could not have investigated case studies of new technology where such use had been prevented by worker resistance. But we have attempted to keep our ears well to the ground and are not aware of many cases where such innovations have been stopped. In three of our cases, introduction of the new technology was delayed (for a number of months in one case) because of worker reaction, but in each of these cases the issue was over what could be negotiated from the deal, rather than outright opposition in principle. In only one case are we aware of a significant change in working practice resulting from negotiation; this was over the use of team-working rather than dedicated operatives for the new arrangements. Both sides favoured the former method but the union would not change working practices without extra money. The company was not prepared to disturb company-wide differentials by making a special payment to this group and so the particular proposal, though not the technology, was abandoned.

The final significant barrier identified was, of course, the recession. In the UK, this has meant firms either not planning to invest in new equipment or cutting back investment plans half-way through the programme. This has meant some CAD/CAM schemes which were fully integrated in the planning stage being implemented in a partial or piecemeal fashion and, in some instances, this has made it harder for the production people to understand the overall logic of the investment.

EMPLOYMENT LEVELS

THERE ARE NOW a number of forecasts and surveys of the employment effects of new technologies but the reliability of these is difficult to assess in the absence of detailed study of how unemployment is generated at plant level. We are collecting details for each case on numbers employed before and after the introduction of the new technology, but these are not yet fully available. However, some observations are reported on the difficulty of making sense of this data.

One necessary distinction is that between actual and perceived employment effects. Actual effects are clearly important in the context of national planning but it is the perceived effects that are likely to influence behaviour at plant level. Actual employment effects of new technology are often difficult to isolate from other simultaneous changes. Most of the companies we visited had been shedding labour anyway, partly because of a reduction in output because of the recession and partly because of previous over-manning. Some companies were also making other technological or organizational changes at the same time as introducing CAD or CNC machine tools. Some of these involved extending the range of services that various departments provided. Thus, fewer staff were being released than might otherwise have been the case. 'Before and after' measures would not therefore have been illuminating, even if the appropriate datum points for 'before' and 'after' could be satisfactorily established. The only firm estimates we could obtain were from management forecasts of the direct employment effects of the change. These are obviously unsatisfactory on at least two counts. They were from management, who had to adopt negotiating strategies to fit the particular circumstances and present figures which reflected them. This might involve a tendency to overestimate the job-loss implications if they were trying to convince the company's main board of the cost-reduction effects or a tendency to underestimate if trying to persuade unions to accept the change. The second count on which these data are unsatisfactory is that they were forecasts. We did not come across any *post-hoc* evaluation of the employment consequences of any technological changes, partly because of the difficulties outlined in doing such an exercise. This does not mean that the use of new technology was not closely monitored. Computer-aided draughting (CAD), for example, enables management to measure how many times a draughtsman enters data on the screen per minute — though this surveillance, if used, can easily be subverted by the draughtsman.

Regarding perceived job loss, important in terms of union and operatives reaction, two points can be made. One is that if the new technology is introduced when there are other changes and/or a high rate of natural wastage, then the job reduction implications of the new technology are less obvious. Most of our cases involved some direct job loss but in no case were any of the redundancies attributed to the new technology. Indeed to put a perspective on it, one of the firms was reducing its workforce by tens of thousands over the period of introduction of the technology we were studying; this technology required under one thousand operatives less than the type of technology it replaced and the new technology was an addition to production capacity, introduced for a new product.

A second point about perceived job loss is that it may be less if a company is first in the field with an innovation. That way, the management can argue that technologically induced job losses can be reduced by the company increasing its markets, as a result of better price or product performance due to the new technology. If this is so, then companies, or whole economies, innovating as followers may suffer a double disadvantage — the first that of losing market share because they have failed to innovate; the second, the difficulty of persuading the operatives/unions to adopt the new technology in the face of heightened perceptions about the likelihood of job losses. However, the contrary could be argued, namely that the technology is developing so fast that it may be a disadvantage to get in very early and that, in any event, operatives are more likely to accept new technology if they perceive a severe competitive threat to their company. Evidence from at least two of our cases points towards this second set of hypotheses.

EFFECT ON SKILLS

WE HAVE FOUND NO EVIDENCE so far of deskilling, in the sense that tasks previously done by skilled craftspeople are now, with microelectronics technology, being performed by those with a lower level of formal qualifications. All the CNC machine tools we have seen (with one exception) were operated by skilled men. The one exception was a set of CNC machines which had replaced conventional machines, doing large batch production, where operatives had always been semi-skilled. All the CAD applications were used only by draughtsmen who had previously been at the drawing board. We found one example when the introduction of microelectronics technology had been the occasion to negotiate a reduction in the number of skilled trades to two (broadly, mechanical and electrical) and the question of how to organize the functional specialisation of maintenance is under active consideration in a number of firms.

Much more contentious is the question of actual skill usage. Does the level of skill required to be used decrease with increased use of microelectronics? The answer depends partly on how the technology is used. In certain maintenance departments where there may be one CNC machining centre used for a variety of purposes, this may be programmed by the tool-maker. The more usual situation appears to be the use of CNC in production where there is union agreement on formally strict demarcation between craftsmen and part-programmers (those who write the programmes which drive the machine to produce a particular part). Often, the arrangement is that the craftsman is not allowed to do any programming and the programmer is not allowed to touch the machine. Thus, if an error is discovered in a programme on the shop floor, the craftsman has to call in the programmer who decides on the modifications to the programme, the craftsman then punching the appropriate buttons to input the alterations. Given the similarity between the two tasks of part-programming and machining, it is not surprising that many part-programmers are ex-craftsmen and perhaps inevitable that craftsmen on CNC soon learn basic programming and unofficially make adjustments to programmes. In some companies, this is discouraged. Craftsmen may have to learn programming in their own time, at their own expense at the local technical college (and some have done this). In one or two companies, the programming controls are blanked off or locked up, so that unauthorised alterations cannot be made. One manager expressed the following view. He felt that many machine-tool manufacturers had misread the market and were promoting CNC machines with too many 'bells and whistles', affording the operator a great deal of control over the machine and the programme. His company did not want such machines as they led to a loss of control on the shop floor. Programmes were being altered without record and without the part-programming office being informed; this meant that the company lost control over the specification and duplicability of the product.

Some other companies encourage craftsmen to learn programming and to exercise more complete control over the machines. These seem to be in work situations where the jobs are one-off or have high value added. In one case, where the typical transfer price of a piece after machining was £250,000 and the company's pricing of the machine's time was over £150 per hour, management had taken the view that enhancing the craftsmens' skills was an appropriate response.

CHANGES IN WORK ORGANIZATIOIN

THE DEBATE ABOUT THE IMPACT of microelectronics technology on the organization of work has been whether it has a centralizing or decentralizing effect. This technology is of course, basically an information technology and makes the collection, transmission and collation of data easier at the centre. Hence, some argue, decisions which previously had to be made at local level, due to the previous difficulty and cost of getting accurate data to the centre, can now be centralized. Others argue that because monitoring is now easier, decisions which were previously taken at the centre (because those on the periphery could not be trusted) can now be decentralized but monitored. This latter view is supported by the correlation observed in bureaucratic organizations, between the degree of bureaucratisation and decentralization

— as formal structures are instituted, so decisions can be delegated further (Child, 1972).

From the case studies it appears, however, that for the impact of new technology on peoples' experience at work the centralization/decentralization dimension may not be the most significant variable. We have identified two others important effects — one stemming from increased capital intensity and the other from the impact of information technology on organization structure.

As one production manager explained to us, ten years ago his concerns were with maintaining labour productivity, reducing absenteeism and turnover, maintaining close supervision, paying close attention to the operation of the bonus system and so on. The other side of this coin was, of course, the operatives' experience of tight control and pressure to produce. Now, with high levels of automation, output is not directly dependent on immediate operator performance and the focus of the manager's job is overseeing a complex network of interrelationships between the various functions within his department and between his and other interdependent departments. This interdependency is higher now because of the faster throughput of materials and product and because the more complex machines require a higher level of support from a number of other functions. This particular production manager was making very large batches in a light engineering factory. But the same phenomenon appears to obtain in small-batch production at the heavy engineering end of the industry.

When the machines are actually turning, production is automatic and at a high level of output. Setting-up and maintaining the machines, on the other hand, now requires a number of different skills working interdependently — the draughtsman, part-programmer, production engineer and machinist for one function, fitters and technicians of various persuasions (electronic, electrical, mechanical, hydraulic, pneumatic, and software engineering) for the other. Moreover, the precision — and lack of ability to handle random variations in the raw material or part-finished component being machined — of CNC introduces great interdependencies between departments. The production manager's job is now much more that of managing these interdependencies rather than leaning on subordinates to produce faster. And for the occupants of the various functions, their job experience is now more that of joint problem-solving than of maintaining standard routines.

It is not only the shift in the ratio of capital to labour which has introduced more complex organization. The increased use of information technology itself appears to have a similar effect. Galbraith (1977) takes the view that organizations are basically information-processing systems and suggests that as the amounts of information needing processing increase, then the requisite organization structure shifts to a more complex form, ultimately taking on a matrix structure with various integrating functions to handle the complexity. With the enhanced information-processing capacity inherent in CAD/CAM and MIS, we would predict a shift in organization form in the direction suggested by Galbraith. We have, however, little evidence of this happening in terms of changes in formal, management-planned, organization structures in the cases studied. But we have identified situations where a lack of organization change appears to have led to co-ordination difficulties in plants with new technology. There is also some impressionistic evidence of informal adaptations in the predicted direction.

CONCLUSIONS

LACK OF SPACE prevents us from providing full case-study material for each of our plants and, in any event, our research is in mid-term, the interim findings only being tentative. However, we have sought to show that as far as the impact on the way of life is concerned, CAD/CAM and MIS, as specific examples of the new information technology, have a number of effects.

Firstly, any influential impact on the way of life will be indirect, with the general standard of living depending on how successful firms are in any one economy in adopting the new technology. We have suggested some particular constraints facing UK firms. A second impact is on the changes in the pattern of occupations and level of skills required. Our evidence so far is that labour-process-type arguments, that managements choose particular technologies partly to deskill and exercise tighter control over labour, gain only limited support. We did not find a great deal of evidence either of this intention by management or of this effect. Though there appears to be some tendency in this direction, there are also many countervailing pressures.

For a third impact, that on employment, the case studies cannot provide data for projections, but they have indicated to us some of the difficulties in generating reliable data that a survey could be based on. Fourthly, an implication of the changes in work organization that we are beginning to see is that the experience of work at all levels in the organization will increasingly be that of managing and coping with complex relationships and problem-solving in collaboration with others. This, in turn, implies substantial training of both managers and operatives in how to organize and work with appropriate structures for handling this complexity and also in the interpersonal skills necessary for sustaining the complex and possibly conflicting relationships that these new forms of organization structure imply.

References

ASP (1977) *Automated Small Batch Production: Report.* Mechanical Engineering and Machine Tools Requirements Board (MEMTRB), Automated Small Batch Production Committee, London.

Braverman, H. (1974) *Labor and Monopoly Capital.* Monthly Review Press, New York.

Child, J. (1972) *Organization Structure and Strategies of Control.* Administrative Science Quarterly, 17, pp. 163-177.

Davis, L. E. and Cherns, A. B., Eds. (1975) *The Quality of Working Life.* Free Press, New York.

Galbraith, J. R. (1977) *Organizational Design.* Addison-Wesley, Reading, Mass.

Rosenbrock, H. H. (1977) *The Future of Control.* Automatica, 13.

Simon, H. A. (1955) *A Behavioural Model of Rational Choice.* Quarterly Journal of Economics, 69, pp. 99-118.

PART III

Urban Structure, Regional Development and Transportation

Hugh Williams, Paul Jeffrey and Frank Joyce provide a review of the likely impact of microelectronics and telecommunications on the urban structures of Europe. The authors initially examine the concept of urban structure, before discussing the likely impact that the new technologies might have. They emphasise that transformations in urban structures are realised by a multitude of factors, technology being but one of these.

The possibilities for delocalization of work activities and their likely consequences is the theme taken up by Mario-Rivas Espejo and Jean-Claude Ziv. They distinguish between the concepts of decentralization and delocalization, the former involving the diffusion of decision-making while the latter refers only to the physical deconcentration of activities. Alternative work situations (such as working at home or in community centres) are described, together with the effects on everyday life that such work practices might entail.

Michael Bannon looks at the growth of the services sector in the Irish economy and its geographical dispersal. In his view, new information technologies will serve to perpetuate regional disparities and reinforce the dominance of Dublin, unless enlightened policies are adopted.

The substitutability between the transportation and communications systems is considered by Marilyn Dover. The potential for decentralized work organization is examined, giving rise to a transformation of the demands on existing transportation systems and a possible reorganization of urban structures.

CHAPTER 16

Information Technology
and Urban Structure
in the EEC

H. E. Williams, P. N. I. Jeffrey and F. E. Joyce

Joint Unit for Research on the Urban Environment, University of Aston in Birmingham, UK

INTRODUCTION

A GENERAL DISCUSSION is presented here on the likely impact of microelectronics and telecommunications (referred to as 'information technology') on the urban structure within the proposed EEC-12 during the remaining years of this century. Our analysis has been undertaken in two broad phases. Firstly, we examine the concept of urban structure and the existing trends within the EEC, isolating the components of change. Secondly, we investigate the current and future applications of microelectronic/ telecommunication technology and suggest the likely impact on urban structure in the context of our findings on existing trends. The main argument examines the link between this new technology and urban structure. Other issues (for example, the social and manpower implications of new technology) are included only when they have direct bearing on urban structure.

Microelectronic and telecommunication technologies have evolved over time. Current developments in microelectronics are rooted in the post-war evolution of the electronics industry. At the same time, telecommunications is a well-established industry. The telephone, for example, has been in widespread use for many years. What we have now is a convergence of technologies, the creation of an information or post-industrial society (Bell, 1979). The most important development has been the increasing reduction in both size and cost of components, allowing widespread applications of new technology in previously unfeasible areas. Such changes may well have an impact on urban structure. However, the potential effects of these technologies must be assessed within the wider context of current trends in urban structure and the full range of influences that affect urbanization and all systems of cities.

197

URBAN STRUCTURE

THE NUMEROUS DEFINITIONS of urban structure will not be debated here. It is sufficient to state that the concept of urban structure used here is predominantly spatial and is primarily concerned with urban systems — the location of industry and population. Our interest lies in the distribution of industry and provision and, therefore, in the distribution of urban areas throughout the EEC. Whilst recognising the complexity of urban structure, it would be useful to make some generally applicable comments.

(1) Urban structure is not a static concept; it evolves over time. Urban structure will change regardless of 'information technology', which in itself may influence the rates and directions of change.

(2) Urban structure at any given point in time will show influences and remnants from a previous period (Foley, 1971).

(3) The rate of evolution will vary between countries and, indeed, between and within individual urban areas. The rate of change will be dependent on a number of variables, such as cultural, technological, economic, physical and political.

(4) Evidence suggests that despite the complexity of urban structure and the varying manifestations of change, a pattern emerges from which general conclusions can be made.

Before attempting to analyse any future changes in urban structure, it is imperative to understand current urban systems and prevailing trends within the EEC and to identify the determining factors. Drewett's detailed research (1980) on European urban structure has allowed him to produce a framework that demonstrates the evolutionary process of the determinants of urban change. In Drewett's model, change occurs in four broad phases (see Table 1):

(1) *Urbanization:* The concentration, for predominantly economic reasons, of population into urban or nodal areas. This period normally coincides with rapid industrialization and increases in population.

(2) *Urbanization – Suburbanization:* The core areas (cities) consolidate. Technology allows expansion to be channelled upwards (e.g. via the telephone and elevator) and outwards (e.g. via the telephone, roads and rail links) (Gottman, 1977).

(3) *Suburbanization:* Diseconomies of scale and congestion in the central area lead to migration to the outer rings or suburbs. Migration from peripheral areas into the suburbs continues, albeit at reduced levels. Urban sprawl results.

(4) *Desuburbanization – Intermetropolitan Decentralization:* Congestion problems (e.g. traffic, high land costs, loss of amenity) will encourage decentralization to the urban hinterland. Governments concerned about core-periphery inequalities will encourage and, in some cases, organize dispersal (e.g. New Towns). Traditional locational factors will become less important with the value of 'amenity' as a

Table 1
Evolutionary process of determinants of Urban Change

	Characteristis	Agents of Change	Examples
Urbanization	Creation and expansion of urban centres (at Historic, Resource, Communication Centres)	Industrialization	UK, West Germany (19th Century), Southern France, Spain, Greece, Southern Italy, Ireland (post-1945)
	Migration from peripheral hinterland to the core	Population Increase	
Urbanization-Suburbanization	Consolidation of Urban Core, Development of Suburbia, Continued migration into the core	Technology (e.g. automatic, rail, telephone) Economic Expansion	UK (mid-20th Century)
Suburbanization	Urban Sprawl	Decentralized services to suburban rings	France, Italy, Denmark (1960-70)
	Migration into the urban areas but at a reduced level	Changing industrial structure, tendency away from traditional large-scale infrastructure/labour-intensive, resource-based industries	
	Congestion, high costs in the inner areas resulting in outward migration from the inner areas to the suburban rings	Diseconomies of size (see below) leading to outmigration	
	First signs of decentralization as a result of congestion	Shift from industrial to service-based economy	
	Growth of suburban services (e.g. Retail Units)	Provision of infrastructure (e.g. houses, roads, drainage)	
Desurburbanization/ Intermetropolitan Decentralization	Containment of metropolitan areas	Government promoted ecentralization	Belgium, Netherlands, Denmark, parts of West Germany, UK, France (now)
	Decentralization of business and population to hinterlands areas	Diseconomies of size (congestion, land costs), loss of amenity, space)	
	New Towns	Increased wealth and leisure time allowing certain groups to move to areas of high amenity. Stabilizing/declining population. Restrictions of migrant labour who would normally concentrate in urban areas	New and extended towns in the UK/France, decline of large cities (e.g. Glasgow, Liverpool, London, West Berlin)
	Inner city decline		
		Availability of communications, continued changig industrial structure	

location factor increasing. The ability to disperse will be significantly linked to wealth and, in the declining cities, 'ghetto' areas will remain, characterised by increasing social and economic problems.

As far as Europe is concerned, Drewett (1980) claims that "deconcentration and counter-urbanization have now replaced urbanization as the dominant force shaping the settlement system in most Western European countries." There are a number of trends that support this claim. Without exception, the population growth rates of the large conurbations (over 500,000 population) are now no higher, and in many cases lower, than the growth rates of their surrounding regions. Indeed, many of the major urban regions in Europe are now characterised by outmigration or population decline (EEC, 1981), for example Hamburg, Bremen, West Berlin in Federal Republic of Germany; the south-east in UK; Ile-de-France, Nord-Pas-de-Calais, Lorraine in France; even the high growth of northern Italy, compared to the south in the 1960s, has altered since the 1970s and was even negative in some of the northern regions. Drewett's work shows that urban regions with the lowest growth rates (in all but a few cases negative) are dominated by the larger cities in Britain, Belgium and Germany with, since the 1970s, urban regions in the Netherlands, and Genoa and Trieste in Italy. By contrast, the urban regions with the highest growth rates of all urban regions are dominated by smaller cities and it is noticeable that a number of places have attracted new technologies (for example Toulouse, Reading and Eindhoven).

·The areas which are growing at the expense of the large conurbations are the hinterlands of most conurbations and cities, for example East Anglia, the south-west and south-east in the UK; the regions around Rome and northern Italy; the regions around Brussels; the Paris region; and the Netherlands-West German border. In addition, the high amenity areas of the Mediterranean coast and Alpine regions of France and Italy are also growing. With the exception of the latter group, growth still remains close to the core regions of the EEC. The peripheral regions (such as Wales, Ireland, Scotland, south-west France and the eastern border of Germany) are not growing from the decentralization of the major urban areas. Indeed, the ten regions which have the lowest population density of EEC-9 had the same share of the community's population in 1977 as they did in 1961 (53 per cent). By contrast, the ten most densely populated regions saw their share of population fall from 18.4 per cent in 1961 to 17.8 per cent in 1977.

These figures indicate that, although there may now be a fairly well-defined trend of decentralization away from the old, urban core areas of the EEC to their hinterlands and the high amenity regions, the scale of change is not very large. However, there is evidence from British cities that it is the younger and more highly skilled members of the population that are mobile and hence any trends of the kind outlined will have a disproportionately large impact upon these groups — increasing the proportion in the 'growing' areas and leaving a higher proportion of older and less skilled people in the older urban areas. The so called 'inner city' problems of UK cities are a manifestation of this.

Before discussing some of the factors that may underline these trends, it is important to note a contrary trend towards the centralization of industrial/commercial control which, although it does not outweigh the population and employment trends, consolidates the importance of the major capital cities. For example, in the mid-1970s, the head offices of 62 per cent of the largest UK manufacturing firms were located in London; 78 per cent of these in France were located in Paris; 65 per cent of the largest corporations in Italy had their head offices in northern Italy and the concentration was similar in the Netherlands. However, there is a clear distinction between the growing concentration — both nationally and internationally — of such high-level functions and the dispersion of routine tertiary activities and functions.

The causes of these processes of urban decentralization cannot be dealt with here in any detail. Suffice it to note some of the underlying factors related to such trends. Table 1 has alluded to some of them already. Although changes in population are important, the key motor for the location of urban development is primarily economic activity. But what influences the location of economic activity? Certainly, there seems to be evidence of both 'push' factors — the problems of congestion and obsolescence in the older urban conurbations (Keeble, 1976; McIntosh and Keddie, 1979; Williams *et al*, 1980), and 'pull' factors — easier opportunities for expansion and better physical environments (Fothergill and Gudgin, 1980; Keeble, 1976). However there may also be other issues involved such as changing production methods, reducing or increasing the need for economies of scale; the effects of public policy restraining growth in large urban areas and promoting hinterland development (the New Towns around London and Paris); and the impact of industrial restructuring and requirements of many high-technology firms to be close to universities or other centres of research. Finally, there are important 'enabling' factors that have allowed these trends to become manifest. The provision, usually through public agencies, of good transportation linkages has enabled industry to be less tied to the specific locations of suppliers or markets, whilst social infrastructure has enabled population decentralization to occur. Clearly, the development of telecommunications has also been a vital enabling factor in loosening the need for proximity and also enabling the concentration of control and the possibility of running branch factories/offices to expand into new market areas by the production of goods or provision of services in the new area, whilst allowing the head office to remain in its initial location.

It is through its influence on these factors that information technology will have its effect upon urban structure. Quite clearly, telecommunications developments may have the effect of reducing the cost of transmitting information and hence, allow linkages for *information* to be cast across a wide area. Secondly, the ability to process large amounts of data/information or to control processes through microprocessors may alter the production functions of different activities and hence, the economies of scale available. Finally, the firms producing and using information technologies may find the need for new kinds of agglomeration economies. Clearly, these aspects will vary between different types of economic agents and information technology will be applied and have an impact on urban structure only within the context of other, possibly more important, factors such as public planning policy, transportation infrastructure provision, trends in the locational requirements or desires of firms and trends in company structure/management (for example, centralization/decentralization of control; expansion through the establishment of branches in new areas, etc).

We will now review the likely implications of information technologies for different kinds of economic activity and agent. Some of the associated employment issues are also discussed since, as previously suggested, it is the nature of the groups that are to be found in different parts of the urban system that are at least as significant (if not more so) than the spatial distribution of physical development.

INFORMATION TECHNOLOGY AND ECONOMIC ACTIVITIES

WE INDICATE in Table 2 the likely effects that information technology will have upon the major groups of economic activities insofar as these are relevant to urban structure — the effects on economies of scale, on agglomeration and on the reduced cost of handling/transmitting information. We have also included a note on possible labour trends since, as pointed out, it may be that the nature of the groups involved in any change in urban structure is more important than the scale.

The producers of information technology are likely to exhibit some tendency to concentrate their activities — especially the manufacturers of microchips, large computers and telecommunications equipment. This tendency will result from the need for scale and agglomeration economies to be near pools of highly specialised skilled labour and research/higher education establishments. However, they are not bound to the older industrial centres (except through historical accident of having telecommunications-manufacturing facilities there); hence, examples of these activities are located in areas which have research establishments, good accessibility and better environments — the south-west and south of England, the south of France, etc. (Steven, 1980). The smaller computer assembly firms and software companies, are, of course, even more free to locate where they wish. If anything, the trends in this sector will reinforce the current decentralization processes from the core conurbations to the hinterland/high amenity areas.

In terms of employment, the manufacturers that use and apply information technology (numerically controlled machines, process control, computer-aided design and manufacture, robotics, etc.) are more significant. It seems unlikely that these technologies will markedly alter the production functions of many manufacturing industries and hence, the economics of scale are unlikely to be affected. Similarly, agglomeration economies are more likely to be related to the need for access to the markets and factors of production. But

Table 2

Economic Activities and Information Technology

Activity	Technological Scope; Rate/ Location of Use	Impact on Economies of Scale	Impact on Agglomeration Economies	Impact on Cost/Ease of Information Flow	Labour Trends	Comments
Primary Industries	Limited scope except for mining	Limited	None	None	Possible Threat	Will not affect location of activity
Producers of Information Technology						
(a) Micro-chip producers	Few firms only	Require large-scale production	Require access to skilled manpower/ research resources	Key is skills/ new ideas in practice	Few very highly trained; few unskilled	Small impact on jobs overall. Locationally free apart for need to be near research expertise
(b) Computer Manufacture	Few large firms many small ones	Scale economies reduced — especially for component assemblers	Require skilled manpower	Give wider choice of locations	Few highly trained; few assemblers	Possibility of few very large firms and many small ones. Locationally free. High quality environment/pool of highly skilled computer engineering desireable
(c) Telecommunic- ations Manufacturing	Produced by few large firms	High cost to develop, thus large firms only	Design functions required in areas of high skill/ expertise	Give wider choice of location, both design/HQ and manufacture	—	Unlikely to effect new locations of industry since it is already well-established
(d) Software	Variety of firms in the field	None	Require highly skilled analyst	Locationally free	Few high-skilled jobs	Growing number of small firms in this area. Locationally free although partly tied to areas where product is bought

——— *Table continued*

Activity	Technological Scope; Rate/Location of Use	Impact on Economies of Scale	Impact on Agglomeration Economies	Impact on Cost/Ease of Information Flow	Labour Trends	Comments
Users of Information Technology Manufacturing Activity						
(a) Continuous processes (e.g. food processing, chemicals, printing, textiles, energy, metal manufacturing)	Gradual application in existing plant. Large scope for use. Plant usually large and expensive	Makes possible larger plant	Require high-skilled maintenance personnel	Gives wider choice of location from information viewpoint	Little impact on most since already well advanced. Threat to textile and printing workers	Unlikey to see major change in location because some over-capacity and current plant investment is large, thus representing an asset that will be used
(b) Mass production (e.g. cars, domestic appliances, electronics, some mechanical engineering)	Medium to high scope. Robotics, remote engineering, NC Machines, CAD-CAM. Large companies can afford this; however small companies need joint ventures	Variable but helps to achieve economies of scale	Require skilled maintenance/set-up personnel. Require fewer craft skills. For smaller firms, industrial parks with centralized CAD facilities	Eases setting up of branch plants	Many large companies already highly automated. If not, high impact on skilled/semi-skilled, increased demand for technicians as opposed to craft skills	Larger firms will introduce, possibly piecemeal. This in current locations. Smaller companies if they introduce it become free to move. Possibility of small/medium firms joining together to share CAD/CAM facilities
(c) Batch production (e.g. mechanical engineering, shipbuilding)	Not high scope	Little	Few/none	Eases setting up of branch plants	Few	Limited Effects

Table continued

Activity	Technological Scope; Rate/ Location of Use	Impact on Economies of Scale	Impact on Agglomeration Economies	Impact on Cost/Ease of Information Flow	Labour Trends	Comments
Users of Information Technology Service Industry						
(a) Office functions of manufacturing industry	Large scope for use of data/ information/ word processing	Enables larger scale activities to be handled	Fewer clerical/ admin. traditional skills required. Need for ability to handle 'automated' office and maintain, such as fibre optics; links may attract HQs	Allows easier/ cheaper handling of centralized accounts/control data. Allows management to be remote from branches. Or managers of small firms to have access to wider market information	Fewer clerical/ admin. jobs available. Demand for some with new skills	The new technology will allow the continuation of trends of control being centred in a few major cities. Will reduce demand for lesser skilled clerical/admin. staff
(b) Banking/ insurance and finance	Large scope for office use, potential long-term scope for customer use	Enables larger scale activities to be handled. Also enables small branches to have access to sophisticated central data	Agglomeration effects related to skills as above. Major institutional HQs may be attracted to locations which have advanced telecommunic-ations infrastructure, such as fibre optics	Customer services can be delivered in small towns/ villages (through small branches, cash dispensers and eventually in the home). Sophisticated information transfers only available where necessary infrastructure provided	Fewer clerical/ admin. jobs	Two trends are possible: (a) reinforcements of the central importance of a few national centres (e.g. London, Paris, etc.) for financial/commercial activity; (b) dispersal of lower level service provision

— *Table continued* —

Activity	Technological Scope; Rate/ Location of Use	Impact on Economies of Scale	Impact on Agglomeration Economies	Impact on Cost/Ease of Information Flow	Labour Trends	Comments
(c) Other professional services (e.g. research, legal, accounting, architect/ engineering computing services)	Scope for office use and increasing sophistication of information used. Long-term scope for 'home-based' office	Possibly allows smaller units to be competitive since they can handle/access large amounts of data/ information	Only requirements access to skills for maintenance of equipment	Makes data/ information more generally available, hence loosens locational ties	Not large	The technologies will enable these tertiary activities to continue to locate in a wide variety of places
(d) Distribution (warehousing)	Stock accounting/ control/ automated warehouse handling, etc.	Automated handling most sensible in large units	As above	Limited	Not large, reduces demand for unskilled warehousemen	
(e) Retail distribution	Electronic tills, stock control, automated storage. Long-term possibilities of 'teleshopping'	Likely to increase scale economies of large shopping units (hyper-markets)	As above. Required to be located near areas of potentially high-consumer expenditure	Limited initially	Not large, except for less jobs in smaller shopping centres	Will reinforce current retail trends towards large single unit shops
(f) Social/ personal services training, health/ social services)	Use of telecom-cumications for 'distance'; data processing for improved services (diagnostics/ programmed learning, etc.)	Allow centraliz-ation of preparation of learning materials, dispersal of face-to-face services	May reduce need for companies to locate close to training institutions	Allows dispersal of teaching/ training, even home-based learning	Not significant	The trends in 'distance-learning' have reinforced home-learning via the use of TV

there may be some reduction in the need to be close to sources of traditional craft skills. However, for most of the larger firms, the new technologies will be introduced into existing plant since these represent considerable existing assets. Furthermore, the rate of capital replacement is unlikely to be so rapid that total renewal of complete plants, raising the possibility of relocation, will occur. The effects of introducing information technologies into the existing plant are that some manufacturing employment is likely to be threatened. Although there will be an increase in demand for skilled technicians to set-up and maintain the new equipment, this is unlikely to outweigh the drop in demand for craft skills. The continued improvement of telecommunications will, of course, continue to enable firms to expand by setting-up branches (if they are engaged in activities whose scale economies allow this). It will also allow firms to keep informed of market conditions and competitors' products and pricing changes, without necessarily being located in the areas where these markets are found. Hence, the branch plants and smaller firms (who may more easily relocate on expansion or when re-equipping) are likely to be less tied to traditional manufacturing centres. Smaller companies may consider joint ventures, where high-investment, new technology facilities are shared. This would result in a number of industrial units possibly linked to a computer-based design centre. This process, similar to Hottes 'autonomization' (1978), would result in new-style industrial estates. Autonomization is a logical future development, even though current evidence of its existence is sparse. There is little to indicate whether such estates would centralize near existing urban centres or decentralize.

The final locations of manufacturing plant will, of course, be a function of their location requirements, influenced by government policies and the availability of sites suitably provided with transport infrastructure. To some extent, their tendency to relocate out of the congested, older industrial centres to the hinterland areas lies behind the trends previously discussed. There is no evidence to suggest that the information technologies will do anything other than enhance such trends. The impact on the older centres is likely to be a reduced demand for labour and hence, an increase in their social problems.

It is in the office that the potential development of the information society is most likely to bear fruition. Currently, we are seeing the development of the automated office *via* the word processor, electronic-filing systems and the mini-computer. The move towards automation could lead to more compact offices with reduced infrastructure requirements, although in existing office units, as well as in factories, new technology is being applied initially in a piecemeal fashion. The standard office block, instead of housing numerous clerks, could combine a reduced labour force with a diversity of function; *Willis Faber and Dumas* in Ipswich for example, have combined work with leisure functions (Duffey and Pye, 1979). This could lead to a centralization of services and facilities under one roof.

Automation is likely to replace many clerical and typing duties if the increased usage of information continues. Many commentators predict adverse employment effects (Bird, 1980; Sleigh *et al,* 1979; McLean and Rush,

1978). The influential Nora-Minc Report forecast a 30 per cent reduction in banking and insurance employment in France, whilst APEX predicted (in 1979) a loss of 250,000 typing and clerical jobs by 1983 in the UK (Bird, 1980).

Reduced employment will alleviate congestion in the office centres (and urban areas generally), reducing the extent of commuting and ultimately effecting the provision of public transport and communication infrastructure. Such changes, however, would not occur overnight but evolve gradually. As with industry, it may well be that some of the more significant changes in urban structure are manifested in the decline of existing centres, as the supply of office employment decreases.

The service sector has, of course, been involved in the process of decentralization. Government intervention, diseconomies in the existing centres and the environmental benefits of decentralization have all played their part. The forces of dispersal are likely to be further strengthened by the application of telecommunicative technology that can, in theory, reduce the importance of face-to-face business contact. Business meetings can be conducted by videolinks (such as confravision, UK), whilst viewphones would cater for other face-to-face exchanges. Information services (for example, Ceefax, Prestel, UK) and electronic mail would allow rapid transmission of information. In theory, these developments would make the need for office concentration redundant and allow for complete dispersal, with the subsequent dispersal of office workers. Advanced and efficient telecommunications would negate the importance of space (Abler, 1977) and ultimately lead to the 'dissolution of compact cities' (Gottman, 1977). The city as a meeting place would no longer exist.

Such a scenario should only be seen as a long-term possibility for, although the technology exists, investment costs (notably in telecommunication infrastructure) will be extensive. At present, telecommunication providers in the EEC are committed to the increased penetration of the existing telephone network, for example Plan X, UK (DOE & T, 1978). This in itself will have notable implications for urban structure (Clark, 1978). The provision of office infrastructure (such as optical cables required for video links) will take secondary importance, although experiments in optical-fibre infrastructure are and will take place on a limited scale. Improvements in computer hardware, visual display units and information services are altogether more rapid.

Selected workers (like architects and journalists) already use their homes as work bases. The adoption of home computers and video-display units connected to the telephone network would allow functions normally under-taken in the office environment to be carried out equally well at home (Abler, 1977). Alternatively, they could be carried out in neighbourhood centres, equipped with terminals and telecommunicative infrastructure, owned by one or a consortium of companies. Widespread application of these schemes would have radical implications for urban structure. The office as a physical unit would become obsolete; the city as a collection of such units would be redundant.

Such a possibility may at first seem not only unlikely but also undesirable. However, all of the technological developments so far listed are not only feasible, but becoming increasingly cost-effective. Experiments are underway in the development of neighbourhood work centres and already there are examples of successful home-based office work. In the UK for example, one company *F. International (The Guardian,* 1981a) employs 600 plus, the majority of which are home-based programmers dispersed over an area; the neighbourhood centre has been explored in the USA (Duffey and Pye, 1979). The initial costs of office dispersal may be high (individual VDUs, etc), but as prices of telecommunication and computer hardware decrease, the advantages of dispersal will become more apparent. The office worker based at home will not be faced with problems of commuting, child-minding or choice of residence. The company will not be faced with the infrastructure costs presented by a large office block and may, indeed, move to a looser employer/ employee relationship.

Governments would have reduced influence over office location if the home-based or the smaller automated office becomes widespread. These offices would not have to rely on government infrastructure provisions and would escape restrictions and incentives, aimed at locating offices in development regions. Office functions dispersed in this way would tend to be the administrative, clerical and information-processing functions, together with some selected management functions and professional services. Multinational headquarters, the management function of manufacturing outlets and the headquarters of financial institutions are less likely to radically disperse in the foreseeable future due to necessary contacts with each other, the concentration of the control of many branches in a few central headquarters and the prestige and investment represented by major city locations (like central London and Paris). This may even be reinforced if more advanced telecommunications infrastructure (such as fibre optics) is installed in these centres.

As for other services, the introduction of information technology in distribution allows automated handling of stock in warehouses (for which there are likely to be some economies of scale) and better stock control in shops through automated checkouts. Investment costs required to undertake these developments will reinforce the existing tendency towards economies of scale in retail outlets. In the very long term, 'teleshopping' may reduce the need for access to outlets by consumers but this would merely reinforce the tendency to larger warehouse-based units, as is already the case with mail-order firms. The use of home-based facilities is a long-term possibility. However, in one field of personal services (training), it is already in use. The use of television for the *Open University* in the UK is an extension of the correspondence-course idea and disperses the training function. More generally, the development of 'distance-learning' through the use of video-tapes for training may loosen the spatial links between firms requiring training and training centres (as at Stanford in California), as well as the impact on the individual's place of education.

A POSSIBLE SCENARIO

IT SHOULD BE emphasised again that information technology is only one small factor that might influence the location of economic activities and hence urban structure. Other more important factors are transport infrastructure, the location of existing industrial investment, government policy and input and market links. Nevertheless, this discussion has indicated that there are few cases in which information technology inhibits the trends towards the decentralization of the core urban regions of the EEC; on the contrary, it is likely to enable this process to occur more easily, all other things being equal. Furthermore, its impact on the nature of jobs that may be offered in different parts of the emerging urban system could suggest that the nature of that structure is, in social terms, more significant than would be apparent at first sight.

If the current trends continue and are enhanced and enabled by the effects of information technology, then it is possible to suggest the following scenario for the future of urban structure in the EEC. At a regional scale, there will be little impact on the peripheral regions, which will remain with low-density populations. Since innovation is slow to diffuse from the centre where initial development occurs, it will be increasing the economic disadvantages of the peripheral regions. The central regions (with the possible addition of the high-amenity areas along the Mediterranean coast and near the Alps, particularly in France and possibly in northern Italy) will continue to be the areas which have most economic activity and population. However, within the central regions, deconcentration from the older industrial agglomerations will continue. There will be a tendency for a continuation of current trends, in which growth of employment, industrial floorspace and population is now found to be most vigorous in the towns of the high amenity regions and in the smaller towns in the hinterlands of the older industrial agglomerations. These smaller towns themselves display some features that are of higher environmental quality than their nearby industrial conurbations or centres. It is here too that smaller, medium-sized and branch-manufacturing enterprises have been growing and to which many service activities have been, or are being, decentralized. Because they are areas of new investment, close to the core and with tertiary and research/educational facilities, innovation and high-technology industry is likely to be found in such locations. For some, this may begin to set-up economies of agglomeration because a pool of labour with the skills in new technologies will be developed in such areas. By such processes, a dynamic situation is set-up, in which these locations become increasingly successful economically, with all the attendant employment opportunities, levels of income and provision of services.

In contrast, the older industrial core cities and conurbatioins will decline in population, but probably more quickly in employment as the large manufacturing firms tend towards automation and the service activities centralize in headquarters in a few major international cities or become dispersed to smaller centres. The trends in employment demand will probably switch away from craft and clerical/administration skills to unskilled operatives and a few more highly skilled technicians and managers. At the same time, the migration out to the more prosperous towns in the hinterland will consist of the more mobile and skilled members of the population. Thus, increased 'inner city' problems may occur, with higher concentrations of unemployment in these older centres than elsewhere in the core regions, concentrations of less able and skilled people, and an eroding financial base as population and economic activity stabilises or declines.

The introduction of planning constraints to protect the environmental advantages of the towns in the hinterland or such cores — or indeed, as a means of restraining growth as one element in an attempt to redirect it — may result in more severe competition for space (housing or industrial), increasing land and property values and hence, ironically, increasing the social barriers between the successful areas and the declining, industrial urban centres.

This scenario is, the authors hope, drawn in exaggerated tones. Current and future conditions are likely to be much more varied from country to country and will, of course, be affected by both urban and regional policies and the general level of economic activity in the EEC. Nevertheless, the seeds of such a scenario can be discerned in current trends, with all that this implies for continued economic and increased social imbalance between peripheral and central regions and the older industrial urban centres and smaller towns in their hinterlands and the high amenity regions. Such a pattern would certainly represent a problem on a community, regional and urban scale.

SOME POLICY ISSUES

CLEARLY, in the light of the foregoing discussion, the policy issues relate to urban and regional problems. As stressed throughout, information technology is only one element in the trends discussed and is more of an enabling than a causal factor. Hence, discussion of policies for the use/development of information technology, that have as their focus urban and regional problems, must recognise that any such policies would be ineffective if they were not part of a wider package of regional and urban planning, economic and industrial policies.

In this context, a classic response to urban and regional disparities has been to divert economic activities by means of incentives to relocate in less-favoured areas and constraints upon development in expanding zones. To the extent that information technology makes some activities less tied to specific locations, it may make such policies easier to effect, although the key issues will often be associated with other locational factors, such as infrastructure, environment and economies of scale. It may be that some of the aspects of agglomeration economies identified could be created in less-favoured areas making one element in a package of attraction-measures. For example, the provision of the right kind of training facilities so that the necessary skills can be developed quickly in an area or the location of demonstration applications of information technology (such as fibre optic links or communal CAD/CAM facilities) in the less-favoured areas may add to the attractiveness of such areas.

The diversion of growth from one area to another, although a powerful policy, has a number of difficulties and costs associated with it. An alternative, but not mutually exclusive, approach is to pursue policies that focus upon ways of making the industries in less-favoured regions more competitive and to encourage the growth of indigenous economic activity. It is a noticeable feature of the more peripheral areas that innovative ideas take a long time to diffuse outwards to them and to be applied. This, in part, increases the competitive disadvantages of such areas. It implies that policies to ensure the more rapid diffusion of innovation would be helpful. Hence firms can keep up with new ideas and approaches to production, management and products. Closely related to this is the need to encourage not just the ideas, but also the application. It may be that firms in the less-favoured areas are slower to adopt and exploit existing technologies (for example NC machines, general use of microprocessors in control, data-handling, etc.). Thus, schemes to provide incentives to carry out feasibility studies of application in firms, or even to subsidise installation, may be helpful. In connection with this, training facilities to ensure that local firms/employees have the requisite skills will be of some importance.

Finally, if firms in such areas are to compete in major markets, then they require information not just on new ideas, but a continual flow on market conditions, potential gaps and areas for development, competitor behaviour, pricing, and product and process developments. This is particularly true of small and medium-sized firms that are not linked to large groups and are not in the favoured areas where such information may be easier to find. Hence, there is a need to concentrate not upon the provision of or improvement in information technology, but rather in the provision of information itself. It is, of course, the information which is also the key element in training and improving the diffusion of innovative ideas. It is, perhaps, fitting that in the context of a conference on *The Information Society,** some of the most important policy approaches towards the community's spatial imbalance in economic development are concerned with the provision of information itself, rather than the technology of information provision.

---

*EEC Conference on *The Information Society,* organized by the (Irish) National Board for Science and Technology and held in Dublin, 18-20 November 1981.

References

Abler (1977) In *The Social Impact of the Telephone,* P. I. de Sola (Ed.), MIT Press, Cambridge, Mass.

Barron, I. and Curnow, R. (1979) *The Future with Microelectronics.* Frances Pinter Ltd., London.

Bell, Daniel (1979) The Social Framework of the Information Society. In *The Computer Age: A Twenty Year View,* M. L. Dertouzos and J. Moses (Eds.), MIT Press, Cambridge, Mass., pp. 163-212.

Bird, Emma (1980) *Information Technology in the Office: The Impact on Women's jobs.* Equal Opportunities Commission.

Blowers, Andrew, Hamnett, Chris and Sarre, Philip (1974) *Future of Cities.* Open University, Milton Keynes, UK.

CIS Report *The New Technology.* CIS.

Clark (1978) In *Impacts of Telecommunications in Planning and Transport.* Research Report 24. Depts. of Environment and Transport, HMSO, London.

Clark, D. and Unwin K. I. (1980) *Information Services in Rural Areas: Prospects for Telecommunications Access.* Geo Abstracts.

EEC (1979) *European Economy – Changes in the Industrial Structure in the European Economies Since the Oil Crises 1973-8.* Commission of the European Communities.

EEC (1981) *The Regions of Europe.* First Periodic Report on the Social and Economic Situation of the Regions of the Community. Commission of the European Communities.

DOE&T (1978) *Impacts of Telecommunications and Planning and Transport.* Research Report 24. Depts. of Environment and Transport, HMSO, London.

Dosi, Giovanni (1980) *Structural Adjustment and Public Policy Under Conditions of Rapid Technical Change. The Semi-conductor Industry in Western Europe.* Sussex European Research Centre (SERC), University of Sussex (Draft).

Drewett, Roy (1980) *Changing Urban Structures in Europe.* Annalys AAPSS 451, September.

Duffey and Pye (1979) *Paper Factory or Room with a View.* Architects Journal, July.

ETUI (1980) *The Impact of Microelectronics on Employment in Western Europe in the 1980s.* European Trade Union Movement.

Fife Regional Council (1980) *The Electronics Industry in Fife, Scotland.* Fife Regional Council, Scotland.

Foley, Donald (1971) An Approach to Metropolitan Spatial Structure. In *Explorations into Urban Structure,* Melvin M. Webber (Ed.), University of Philadelphia Press.

Fothergill and Gudgin (1980) *Urban and Regional Policy.* Cambridge Economic Policy Review, Vol. 6, No. 2, July.

Goddard, J. B. and Thwaites, A. T. (1980) *Technological Change and the Inner City. The Inner City in Context 4.* SSRC, Inner Cities Working party.

Gottman (1977) In *The Social Impact of the Telephone.* P. I. de Sola (Ed.), MIT Press, Cambridge, Mass.

Green, K., Coombs, R. and Holroyd, K. (1980) *The Effects of Microelectronic Technologies on Employment Prospects. A Case Study of Thameside.* Gower, London.

Guardian, The (1981a) *Programmers get a new boss* (5.10.81).

Guardian, The (1981b) *Prestel selling knocked* (7.10.81).

Holland, Stuart (1976) *Capital versus the regions.* Macmillan, London.

Hottes (1978). In *Contemporary Industrialization; Spatial Analysis and Regional Development,* F. E. Ian Hamilton (Ed.), Longman, Essex.

Keeble, David (1976) *Industrial Location and Planning in the United Kingdom.* Benham Press.

Llewellyn, Michael (1981) *Telecommunications: Resolution no substitute for initiative.* Economist Intelligence Unit. Economic Trends No. 66, February.

Lloyds Bank Reports (1980) *Selected EEC Countries.*

May, G., Ed. (1979) *The impact of new technology on the regional economy.* One day conference, Leeds Polytechnic, 15 July, 1979.

McIntosh, A. and Keddie, V. (1979) *Industry and Employment in the Inner City.* Inner Cities Research Programme Report, Dept. of the Environment, London.

McLean, J. and Rush, H. (1978) *The Impact of microelectronics on the UK. A suggested classification and illustrative case study.* SPRU Paper No. 7, University of Sussex.

Moseley, M. J. (1973) *The impact of growth centres in rural regions – II.* Regional Studies, Vol. 7.

NEDC (1981) *Industrial Trends and Perspectives.* National Economic Development Council.

Rothwell, Roy (1981) *Innovation, Small Firms and Regional Development.* Workshop of Regional Innovation Policy, SPRU, University of Sussex.

Scottish Development Agency (1979) *The Electronics Industry in Scotland.* Booz Allen, Management Consultants.

Sleigh, J., Boatwright, B., Irwin, P. and Stanyon, R. (1979) *The Manpower Implications of New Technology.* Depts of Employment, HMSO, London.

Steven, T. (1980) *Which regions benefit from the chip?* Planning, May.

TUC (1979) *Employment and Technology.* TUC General Congress, London.

Williams, H. E. *et al* (1980) *Industrial Renewal in the Inner City.* Inner Cities Research Report No. 2, Dept. of the Environment, London.

CHAPTER 17

Communication, Delocalization of Work and Everyday Life

Mario Rivas Espejo
University of Paris X and XII

Jean-Claude Ziv
Paris Town Planning Institute

THE EMERGENCE OF A COMMUNICATIONS SOCIETY

FOR SEVERAL YEARS NOW, new applications of information technologies have given rise to major changes in the technological and economic fields and also in the social structure. The upheavals brought about by new products and services connected with the progress made in informatics, tele-communications and the electronic media are creating the conditions which precede the advent of an 'information society', which is one of the main aspects of post-industrial society.

This technological revolution, the main feature of which is the development of a 'quaternary' sector of activity (Little, 1980) — the communication-information sector, which accounts for almost 50 per cent of the working population of industrialised countries — will bring significant changes in the localisation of activities, urbanisation, environment, consumption of energy and raw materials, training of people, information and forecasting and, consequently, everyday life. The various methods of organizing work, born of the industrial society, will be radically changed and will give way to new methods of management and co-ordination, which are better suited to the requirements of economic and social development. The application of the new technologies, which enable activities to be decentralized, constitutes one of the factors likely to produce significant changes, both in the field of work and in family life, social relations and leisure time.

Several issues, concerning the impact of working-at-a-distance on the forms

215

of social organization (with the exception of the work function) are considered here.* It is a question of determining the situations in which the introduction of the new information technologies can give rise to decentralization of activities, in order to highlight the ensuing effects on people's behaviour in their everyday life. Since the field is so vast and space is so limited, we have paid particular attention to three aspects, which seem to us to have priority: social cohesion, saving on travelling and the time budget. Before describing the techniques and types of changes which may arise out of the application of the new information equipment, enabling work to be done at-a-distance, certain concepts should be defined to facilitate the approach to the particular set of problems in hand.

DELOCALIZATION — DECENTRALIZATION

DEFINITION OF THE CONCEPTS of delocalization and decentralization is essential to the understanding of the nature and significance of the changes which may occur, insofar as erroneous confusion of the two is common. The experiments carried out in this connection show that the concept of delocalization refers to the geographical dispersal of activities, while the concept of decentralization concerns the transfer of decision-making powers from managerial groups to delocalized bodies.

The studies carried out by the 'Employment-at-a-distance' group at the *Institut Auguste Comte* show that both the delocalization of activities and working from home can fit in with varied forms of organization of work. The types of relations created between teams working at a distance and the units which federate them may vary significantly (Bakis, 1979). In other words, power, both in the form and the method of management, may remain highly centralized or may, on the contrary, be decentralized and delegated to each working unit.

Several quite separate scenarios enable us to establish that there is no correlation between the delocalization of activities and the decentralization of power. In different cases, we can observe firms in which power is delegated to a very great extent; teams which are relatively autonomous but all located in the same place; firms with teams which are scattered far and wide geographically but in which power, management and control remain highly centralized; and lastly, firms split-up into small teams with genuine decision-making powers. This brief classification shows that employment-at-a-distance can cover very varied forms of organization, ranging from hierarchical, centralized and, in some cases, dictatorial methods, to highly autonomous management methods.

*The authors wish to thank Vincente Sanchez Leighton, candidate for a Doctorate in Mathematics, and Christian Hourde, Assistant at McGill University, Montreal, for their co-operation.

Professor Goddard of the University of Newcastle, in a study of the decentralization of London firms, emphasises that the delocalization of certain types of employment leads to the strengthening of the central power of the organization. Indeed, the decision-making centres are increasingly located in the London area, even if the office work is distributed throughout the country (Bakis, 1980a). The conclusions of the various studies and reflections on work-at-a-distance make it reasonable to assume that the concepts of delocalization and decentralization must be understood according to two different types of analysis: the concept of delocalization refers to the form of production, while the concept of decentralization accounts for the political decisions which are taken within a form of development (Bakis, 1980b).

The delocalization of activities is becoming one of the constituent factors in the worldwide expansion of the Capitalist Mode of Production, the main feature of which is a process of internationalization of production. The requirements of international competition and greater mobility in the expansion of firms and services render geographical dispersal of activities necessary. This phenomenon must not be confused with a transfer of decision-making power from the managerial groups to the subsidiaries or units working-at-a-distance; it meets the requirements imposed by the reproduction of a mode of production.

The decentralization of work does not therefore appear to be a necessity which is inherent in the logic of the operation of the Worldwide Economic System. It is dependent on a political dimension, determined by the specific procedures for change within each type of society. The emergence of genuine decentralization of work depends on the advent of participation techniques, determined by the action of pressure groups or by the implementation of State policies to widen social consensus through greater access for workers as a whole to information and decisions.

COMMUNICATION AND DELOCALIZATION OF WORK

THE TREND TOWARDS delocalization of work is not a consequence of the 'informatic revolution'. Well before this event, a concern for greater efficiency and more flexible working environments had, *inter alia,* nurtured this trend. However, the very specificity of the new information equipment has resulted in marked quantitative, if not qualitative, progress in this direction. These new technologies combine a spectacular increase in the speed of transmission of information, with a greater capacity for processing and handling data.

An analysis of these two aspects in some of the more important information technologies will demonstrate their delocalizing potential. Tele-communications networks are a prerequisite for the transmission of information. At the present time, there are three types: general-purpose switched networks, leased line networks and specific networks. Large-scale technological developments are anticipated (Bernard, 1980). At the pinnacle of the communication networks are found the instruments for transmission-reception and handling-processing of information. (For a list of the instruments permitting working-at-a-distance, see Annex 1.)

The Delocalizing Potential of Information Technologies

Information technologies therefore combine rapid communication and great processing capacity. These two aspects embody their delocalizing potential. There are three types of working-from-a-distance: work at home, work in a delocalized unit of the firm and lastly the community work centre, an invention made possible by the new technologies and a compromise between the first two (Bernard, 1980).

The first two methods are already familiar but have been improved by the new technologies. The third type symbolises and synthesises everything which information technology offers as potential for social change. There are several ways of introducing the new methods among workers' handling information. Transport of a product, typing and translation of a text, programming and teaching — all can be replaced by, for example, a telematic routing. Furthermore, communications between geographically dispersed working teams can advance — using faster and cheaper transportation — possible with the emergence of new techniques such as meetings-at-a-distance, electronic mail and access to data banks. However, there has not as yet been any widespread development of these techniques in France, the authors' country. Government initiatives are attempting to remedy this situation — Antiope and Teletel systems of videotexts and experiments with optical fibre cables in Biarritz. The almost total absense of computer-aided teleconferencing and the supremacy of the United States in the microelectronics and data bank fields is proof of the substantial leeway which has to be made up in this area.

Work at home: Information technology improves forms of work already being performed at home, due to the swifter transmission of information which it offers. But it also brings in new forms and will enable everyone whose main occupation is in the information-processing field to work partially or completely at home.

Delocalization of units: Unlike work at home or in a community work centre, this form of delocalization is only a remedy for the problems posed by over-large teams. It only applies to situations where concentrations are not justified by the very nature of the work, but rather by the quality of the information to be processed. It does not bring about a change in the organization of the firm but may, however, meet a desire to bring staff nearer to their homes. This is what has happened in the case of the Directorate-General for Taxes in France, which has delocalized part of its programming department to Nantes. As the

'Employment-at-a-distance' group from the *Institut Auguste Comte* observes: "The splitting-up has been carried to the point where teams are divided between Paris and Nantes, those in charge being equally in one or other of the cities."

Community work centre: This is the most interesting and innovative of the types of employment-at-a-distance created by the information revolution. Indeed, it introduces new types of relations *vis-a-vis* work and the workers who share the same workplace. These centres consist of an office block, housing about fifty people and providing communal communication, data processing, security, catering and cleaning services. The centre is near the workers' homes. Employees from various firms, with no hierarchical or official contact among them, work there side-by-side. It is even conceivable that people of different social status will use the same premises and equipment.

The planned community work centre of Marne la Vallee, prepared by the *'Centre d'etude et d'experimentation des systems d'informations'*/CEESI (Centre for studies and experiments on information systems), will enable the question of the viability of such a form of work to be evaluated. It is conceivable that such a work centre will group together teenage friends, who are normally separated when they enter the working world, thus safeguarding ties which are important for the development of the individual. It will also involve widespread sub-contracting by information processors' co-operatives. It is fairly clear that for many human activities, the substitution of telematic communication for personal communication is not recommended. However, there is some attraction in thinking that the informatization of the working world can humanise the other world — the non-working world.

Experiments in France

A number of experiments have been carried out in France, in particular those by the Directorate-General for Telecommunications. Nonetheless, in the sociological field (or at least in those which have sociological implications), there is a terrible dearth of data and case studies. Indeed, the only large-scale employment-at-a-distance project which has been made public is that of Marne la Vallee. Unfortunately, that project is still only an experiment.

Delocalization of units, such as those of the Directorate-General for Taxes (DGT), throws no new light on our analysis. There is no need to reiterate the urgent need for simulations relating to the impact of the new telematic technologies. Countries such as the United States are already well ahead in this field. It is also clear that these experiments require conceptual 'breaking new ground' work beforehand (CFDT Magazine, 1981).

THE EFFECTS OF EMPLOYMENT AT A DISTANCE ON EVERYDAY LIFE

SIGNIFICANT DEVELOPMENT of employment-at-a-distance is made possible by information technologies and will lead to changes as important as the spread of electricity, the telephone and the railways. We will briefly describe some of the sociological changes that may occur in everyday life.

A definition of the concept of everyday life

The words 'everyday life' prove very ambiguous, defined as they are on the basis of concepts whose inadequacy or rigidity make comprehension of their true significance difficult. Everyday life cannot be conceived of in a partial or rigid fashion since it is conditioned by all the changes which occur within a type of society and give rise to new economic, social and cultural practices. If a global definition is used, everyday life appears to be the result of all the activities connected with production, consumption, family life and cultural practices, determined by norms, patterns of behaviour and values specific to each social structure. This enables us to differentiate between everyday life in, for example, the USA, France or the Soviet Union.

Nevertheless, the maintenance of an equilibrium of the unequal and thus, of the existing differentiation between various social groups, prevents everyday life from being thought of solely with reference to the alleged homogenization of the predominant social norms. People's attitude towards change or consumption in the broad sense depends not only on their socio-professional class (a somewhat rigid concept), but also on their access to culture or information. Such access is not conditioned strictly by income but, for instance, by the accumulation of cultural wealth transmitted within the family.

The difference which has to be established between the values corresponding to the social structure and the behaviour patterns of the various social groups allows us to put forward the theory that the changes which will occur in the working world, as a result of the development of microelectronics, will alter people's habits heterogeneously.

Delocalization of work and everyday life

The repercussions of the delocalization of work on everyday life may be very different, depending on the employment-at-a-distance scenarios. Study of the sociological impact of information technology on work must take into consideration the fact that it is a double-edged weapon, since it is the policies of the firms and services that condition the result of its application. Although it is used to delocalize, it can help to decentralize power or concentrate it, to curtail liberties or help them flourish, to broaden or weaken interdependence.

For there to be a proper understanding of the extent of these changes, many experiments and simulations need to be carried out. The inadequacy of the data available makes it difficult to give an accurate definition of the changes brought about by employment-at-a-distance and of the ensuing effects on everyday life: we shall therefore amplify a few thoughts on the subject for guidance, in order to give a general picture of some of these changes.

Delocalization of work assumes many varied forms, depending on the arrangements for employment-at-a-distance, as previously outlined. This explains its multi-dimensional effect on the social structure. In order to envisage the possible scenarios, we must first clarify the links which exist between employment-at-a-distance, the variables we have selected and everyday life.

The introduction of new telecommunications equipment will lead to significant changes in the geographical distribution of activities: the time budget, control or management will result in the emergence of new procedures for organizing work. As pointed out in the introduction, the multiplicity of factors open to analysis and the complexity created by their interdependence has forced us to pay particular attention to certain changes which may have a direct effect on people's behaviour patterns in their everyday life.

Social cohesion

Understanding the structural or destructural effects of information technology applied to work is one of the primary concerns of researchers studying its effects on everyday life. The acceptance or rejection of these new technologies depends mainly on their repercussions on the various forms of social cohesion. The effects of employment-at-a-distance on the social fabric may be very different in kind, depending on the procedures used and the specific nature of the forms of organization of work. We shall describe various situations in which employment-at-a-distance can produce new forms of social cohesion and reinforce or weaken pre-existing ones.

The delocalization of activities, in an 'at-a-distance' framework, may help to integrate new strata into the working world. Work at home will enable disadvantaged groups of people particularly to be slotted into the national production system with no technical difficulties, thus reinforcing overall social cohesion (housewives, the disabled, the elderly and people living in mountainous regions). Nevertheless, the process of integration does not depend solely on technical potential, as the incorporation of these new sectors must not run counter to firms' profitability criteria. The participation of housewives could take place through the use of piecework, enabling a complementarity between phases of paid work and phases of household activities (which are a form of non-paid and sometimes socially recognized work). The success of this innovation would depend upon prior training and also proper redistribution of the time allotted to work, home and leisure activities, in order to avoid the family disputes which might arise in the initial adaptation stage.

This change, which will undoubtedly reinforce economic and social integration and family interdependence, may on the other hand have a negative effect on the integration of housewives into social life. Increasing the number of tasks carried out in a single space will, in certain cases, lessen their connections with the outside world, thus contributing to their isolation. The integration of the disabled and elderly in these circumstances will give rise to fewer problems. These sectors are on the fringe of the working world and, in certain cases, of associative life. The incorporation of these disadvantaged strata into the working world can only exclude their integration into national life. Slotting these groups into leisure activities and the various forms of associative life should be attendant upon this integration, but not via information technology.

The working population living in mountainous rural areas (for example, the Ardeche and Haut Jura in France) have no access to work. This is due to a lack of commercial activities in the area, agricultural underdevelopment, distance from centres of activities or inadequacy of transport facilities. These workers are forced to uproot themselves and emigrate to big urban centres or to remain in their own area, generally working in small-scale cottage industries. Employment-at-a-distance might enable them to be employed in several capacities, some of their activities being traditional and connected with the country, others being considered as extra pay from office work, which they could carry out in their own time, probably on a piecework basis.

Having described the potential for integrating fringe sectors into working life through employment-at-a-distance, it is interesting to deal with situations in which delocalization of work may produce new forms of social cohesion. Several everyday life scenarios show that immediate space, at the level of work or housing, does not necessarily constitute a relational space which is likely to reinforce social cohesion. Two examples justify this assessment.

In most establishments, affinities are stronger within groups than between groups. Furthermore, the main features of housing in the big conurbations are, in most cases, a lack of contact with neighbours, isolation and sometimes conflict situations in relationships. These features of everyday life help to maintain urban anonymity. The delocalization of activities may reverse this trend and create the conditions which are prerequisite for the emergence of new forms of social cohesion.

Employment-at-a-distance may bring about a reconciliation between firms and rural areas, which is the complete opposite to all historical developments since the beginning of the industrial era; vast parts of regions, currently styled 'Assisted Economic Areas', may thus be revitalized. One of the solutions envisaged is that adopted by the *Legrand* firm in Limoges. An employer, who wished to expand his business but could not find any local labour, set up workshops in the countryside (Charreyron, 1981). This type of experiment could be developed with the help of telematics. Employment-at-a-distance in its various forms (work at home, collective workshop or delocalized firm) could not only give a new impetus to activities in rural areas, but could also reintegrate to their home regions people who are working in geographically distant conurbations and are thus separated from their families. Bringing home and work closer together, made possible through information technology, can enable such workers to lessen their sense of being uprooted from their surroundings and help them regain their individual and collective identities. The delocalization of units and the setting-up of community work centres will enable employees to be nearer their homes, with the foreseeable consequences of, for example, a saving of time, less travelling and a return to nature.

Given present structures, these formulae are the easiest to tackle and therefore the most suitable for rapid expansion. They may give rise to a strengthening of family interdependence, to deeper ties of friendship among people working on the same premises and living in the same places and to greater integration of community life. Bringing people nearer to their place of work and their place of residence may lead to revitalisation of local life — expansion of the role of community associations, more detailed knowledge of local problems and wider participation in management and decisions. In Britain, experiments of delocalization of work have given rise to greater investment in the community, thereby reinforcing the various forms of social cohesion (Crochart, 1980). Work at home also enables certain strata to choose housing on the basis of affinities, thus strengthening associative life.

The structural effects of the delocalization of work may be accompanied by destructural effects on overall social cohesion. The splitting-up of services, delocalizing units and creating community work centres may led to atomization of the social body. Delocalized teams will probably be scaled-down in size and will therefore be difficult to mobilise by means of mass movements. Furthermore, home workers will have difficulty in remaining closely connected with the organization as a whole and may as a result feel isolated, detached from their normal environment and lose the 'house' spirit which unites most firms. This dispersion may substantially curtail inter-group relations and weaken the power of trade unions, which will have further constraints imposed upon them in contacting the staff as a whole. Furthermore, the methods of organization required by employment-at-a-distance (namely, making people responsible for tasks, management by objectives) are conducive to direct negotiation with the managerial groups, a dialogue which excludes the unions. This lessening of the effectiveness of unions may condition the formation of corporative groups, or a new trade unionism, connected with specific problems.

Since these scenarios are hypothetical, we are unable to specify the extent to which the decision-making power of the managerial groups will be strengthened or whether, on the contrary, controls will be eased; this will depend largely on the ways information technology is used. Although delocalization of work seems capable of damaging overall social cohesion as we know it, it may also change it, by strengthening, for instance, organic interdependence in the local dimension. The multiplicity of factors which may intervene in this field make it difficult to establish any definitive hypothesis. Clearly, there will be progressive adaptation between the changes brought about by the new technologies and their social acceptance.

Saving on travelling

Transport is a prerequisite for certain activities. Without travelling, work, purchases, social relations and leisure time will all tend to dwindle. Thought must therefore be given to the effects which information technology might have on everyday life, particularly its impact on travel.

A few significant figures: People who have lived in the Ile de France for more than six years make on average two road journeys of six kilometers as the crow flies every day of the week. The one-hundred-million kilometers covered are divided out equally between private cars and public transport. Eight million hours are lost every day. Home-to-work trips account for 31 per cent of travelling time and 41 per cent of the kilometers (Glowinski, 1980).

Two of these figures enable us to describe the problem a little more specifically: 31 per cent of the travelling corresponds to 41 per cent of the kilometers. The inhabitant of the Ile de France therefore covers more kilometers when travelling from home to work than when travelling for any other purpose. It is easy to check that this phenomenon is due to the home/work change-over between increasingly distant suburbs and the centres of conurbations.

Work-at-a-distance and travelling: As the setting-up of services and businesses is not the main subject of any planning, geographical co-ordination between place of work and place of residence is almost non-existent *a priori*. As things stand at present, delocalization of administrative departments, firms or services seems to be a matter of urgency. However, it is important for this delocalization to be accompanied by real decentralization of decisions, both for reasons of efficiency and for social-balance requirements. Employment-at-a-distance is also included in this course of action. Assuming that these forms of working-at-a-distance were accompanied by genuine delegation of decision-making power, the improved quality of life and the saving of time would compel and fashion irreversible changes in everyday life.

The development of telecommunications has never prevented transport from developing. The information revolution will in no way change this fact; the complementarity between telecommunications and transport seems to be a sociological constant. Two types of contradictory effects are to be expected from the reduction in travelling between work-home and work-work: firstly, the amplification of certain travelling tendencies and the creation of new reasons for travelling, if the sociological constant is accepted; secondly, a falling-back on the home, created by the disappearance of the constraints of travelling to and from work. These effects should be analysed mainly in terms of behaviour groups.

Changes in the equilibrium per category of trip are to be expected. The time saved in decreased work-home and work-work trips will be used for more leisure trips, in the broad sense of the word. With this in view, transport will have to offer services of a new type, effectively competing with the prices of car journeys. A centralized rail network, such as the SNCF (French national railways), will have difficulty in meeting the new requirements. Thus, three key ideas dominate this development: delocalization and work at home can save time and alter the reason for a trip; the transport services must offer means suited to the new requirements; and lastly, advantage can be taken of this development to produce an effective energy-saving policy.

Saving on travelling and everyday life: People can expect reduced transport costs in their everyday life. All the travelling imposed on private citizens, for reasons other than social life and leisure, account for 40 per cent of oil consumption in transport as a whole. Greater flexibility in people's daily routine will make it easier to avoid 'urban stress', and strengthen ties in families or social groups; on the other hand, it may reinforce the feeling of isolation and urban solitude through the dwindling or disappearance of the social relations arising out of work. As the social and structural inertia of the system can be added to the latter, the change-overs may sometimes be distressing. Indeed as Clavaud (1981a and b) writes: "travelling enhances the junior manager by enabling him to set himself apart from the clerical worker or workman, who never travels 'on business'. It also enables him to break with the monotony of his work and to meet up with his colleagues, with whom he exchanges information about the state of the firm, which is generally screened out in teleconferencing because of the presence of a person of higher rank on the line."

Teleconferencing also does away with the social activities which form part of any business trip — ties of friendship, lunches, nights out, unexpected meetings. These perks seem to be essential at the present time; social events and the occupation of managers seem to be quite inseparable. The comments under one's breath to one's neighbour during a meeting, the client or potential colleague whom one meets on a train or plane, and the possibility of combining a business trip with a few days leisure are all outstanding features of current work-related intercommunication procedures. However, assuming that sufficiently well-developed information networks will come into being, several alternative solutions can be anticipated. During a teleconference, it will be possible to send person-to-person messages whose confidentiality will be ensured. As for contingencies, it will be enough, for example, to initiate a message on the network to whoever will accept it and answer it. These are, of course, only simulations. But great adjustments will have to be made before such technology becomes widely accepted.

The information worker will require compensation relating to his natural contacts: these compensations will be connected with housing, the neighbourhood and his closest colleagues. A parallel with Citizen Band (CB) radio may be relevant. Relationships are created through radio waves, frequently with no visual contact. There is much solidarity among CB users due, perhaps, to their being on the fringe, which is rare in our big cities. Here is an example where an instrument, through the will of its users, is conducive to improvements in social cohesion.

One must, however, bear in mind the example of another communication instrument, the telephone, whose role in terms of deepening social relations is controversial. Along these same lines, the public relations and marketing trades promoting travel will slow down the widespread expansion of information technology. At the dawn of the industrial revolution, dealings between manufacturers and customers were very direct, but soon, there was a tendency to multiply the number of intermediaries, thus ending the original concept of customers. The transfer of the centre of social cohesion from the workplace to the home is to be compared with the reverse phenomenon which occurred during the industrial revolution. The difference will lie in the choice of a decentralization which is the opposite to the strengthening of centralism currently practised in firms. We will illustrate our contention by giving three examples:

   (a) People living in mountainous areas will be able to be integrated into the working world through new information technologies and adequate training. For these people, the world and social life will be opened up to them as a result, which will then mean that the present inadequate transport facilities in these isolated areas will be more keenly felt.

   (b) For the executive who travels frequently and who feels the full effect of uncomfortable air travel and night trains, the teleconference will have the advantage of avoiding the fatigue of travelling and repeated absences from home.

   (c) Information technology seems to leave out the worker. Only the planning of industrial locations co-ordinated with the siting of housing can provide solutions to transport problems, which especially effect the quality of life of the most disadvantaged classes. However, technologies such as robotics are seeking to give back to the machine the work which belongs to it.

These examples provide a glimpse of the complexity of the changes in the use of time. Alterations to everyday life connected with travelling are to be expected in each of the various behaviour groups, particularly changes to the 'where' and 'when' of work. Work-related considerations will have less influence on the choice of housing and on various relationships — marriage, friendships, family, etc.

The time budget

The time budget is the most important variable in an analysis of the transformations to the social structure brought about by employment-at-a-distance. The changes in the distribution of the time allotted to work and to reproduction, in a broad sense, reflect the alterations which occur in everyday life. Due to a lack of statistical data, it is not possible to identify the types of daily routine which may be produced by the delocalization of work, especially considering that these changes will undoubtedly lead to transformations of a qualitative kind in individual and collective habits. A few thoughts on the subject may help to elucidate this set of problems.

The changes to living conditions which have taken place in France over the last fifteen years have had no major impact on the time budget. A comparison of the time budgets made by INSEE in 1966 and those calculated on the basis of the programmes of activities collected by LET in 1978 shows us that there is very great rigidity in activities of a mandatory nature (IDATE, 1980). Changes in activities have not upset the sequence corresponding to essential duties — work is the factor which most structures the organization of the day. The development of the various forms of employment-at-a-distance, with the features already outlined (time-saving as a result of less travel and geographical distribution of housing and the possibility for certain strata to organize the working day as they wish), may put an end to this rigidity and give rise to more flexible apportionment of the time devoted to work, leisure and family life.

The main basis for the remuneration of wage-earning work is output and hours. Of the two, hours are still given preference today. Work-at-a-distance will reverse this state of affairs. It is the usefulness of the skill provided which will be remunerated, however many hours it takes the person who is in possession of the skill to produce the desired effect within a given deadline. Working hours will lose their significance as the need for physical presence disappears (see *La revue de l'entreprise,* 1978). The lessening of the importance of work as a factor which structures the day will lead to greater flexibility in time budgets, giving rise to new behaviour patterns for people in their everyday life. More harmonious management of the time devoted to various activities may indeed entail a number of constraints which are determined by certain habits of a mandatory nature (such as work), thus creating the conditions for the emergence of new procedures for organizing the day.

One of the first signs connected with the lack of rigidity in the time allotted to paid activities may be the appearance of leisure in everyday life. Furthermore, the time saved on work, travelling and the rearrangement of housing will perhaps encourage a greater investment in associative life, such as neighbourhood meetings, participation in sports clubs and socio-cultural activities. This flexibility in the time budget will produce a new mobility, which is likely to lessen the existing separation between social life and personal life, a phenomenon which may be one of the main features of the information society.

The development of employment-at-a-distance will not affect all the socio-professional classes homogeneously. Man has constantly sought to reduce the amount of time required to satisfy his economic requirements and to increase his freedom of choice. Nevertheless this prerogative is always determined by the opportunities for each social class of gaining access to the benefits of development. For engineers, executives, certain groups of clerical workers and, as a rule, the liberal professions, opportunities will be immediate; other classes, however, among them industrial workers, will have to await developments in robotics and automatics. In the long term, this differentiation may seem somewhat rigid since, if the scope of the coming changes permits it, certain socio-professional classes will disappear and new activities will be established.

Time-budget studies for each socio-professional class, on the basis of employment-at-a-distance arrangements, will have to take into account the differences which exist between the distribution of time among the members of the family whose main activity is work and those who have other tasks.

Changes in the time budget will have major repercussions on everyday life. The flexibility of working hours and places will help to curtail alienation, which is determined by people's rigid subordination to the activities which guarantee their tangible reproduction. The transformation of the conditions for carrying out the work function will give people greater freedom of choice in their everyday habits. They will be able to apportion their time so as to satisfy a wish rather than a need, to earmark travelling for a purpose other than work or to participate in the various events which make up associative life. This lack of rigidity may lead to certain norms, patterns of behaviour and values conditioned by work being superseded, thus benefiting the revitalisation of other habits connected with leisure. The disappearance of certain binding principles, which govern the behaviour of social groups, will result in the creation of new forms of interdependence which will make everyday life more relaxed. The carrying out of experiments and simulations on the behaviour patterns of groups and individuals working-at-a-distance is essential in order to ascertain the foreseeable effects on everyday life of altering time budgets.

The feature of each society is a conception and use of time which accounts for its rationale. The defining of the links which may be established between the changes in daily routine for each socio-professional class and the ensuing effects on everyday life is therefore fundamental to understanding the extent to which the transformations brought about by the delocalization of work, may lead to the establishment of another type of society. Nevertheless, elucidation of this set of problems requires others factors of a political and economic nature to be taken into consideration, in order to determine whether all the social groups will actually be able to take advantage of the benefits of working-at-a-distance.

CONCLUSION

THE IDEAS presented here reflect an optimistic view of the foreseeable effects of working-at-a-distance on everyday life; we have attempted to define the beneficial aspects of information technology, while at the same time considering it as a double-edged weapon. This discussion by no means exhausts the implications of employment-at-a-distance for the three aspects selected (social cohesion, saving on travelling, and time budgets); but further reflection is needed, for future social equilibrium may be at stake.

The actual implementation of the transformations described will necessitate a lengthy period of adaptation, which should be preceded by awareness at all levels of the social scale.

We are nowhere near the stage yet where people will go to work using hertzian roads rather than ring roads. More detailed studies will help in the search for a social consensus, to cope with a new revolution which should not have the same grievous effects as previous ones.

References

Bakis, Henry (1979) *Elements pour une geographie des telecommunications. Quelques pistes de recherche.* Journees d'Etudes de l'Institut d'Urbanisme de Paris, December. (Paris Town Planning Institute Study Days).

Bakis, Henry, (1980a) *The communications of larger firms and their implications for the emergence of a new world industrial order. A case study: IBM's global data network.* Contributing Report, 24th International Geographical Congress. Pre-congress meeting of the Commission on Industrial Systems, Chuo University, Japan, August 1980.

Bakis, Henry (1980b) *Le Travail a distance. Outils, experimentations, reflexions.* Fundacion, para el desarrollo de la function social de las communicaciones. SIMO, November 1980, Madrid.

Bernard, Luc (1980) *La premier experience francaise de teletravail.* Secretaires d'aujourd'hui, No 247.

CFDT Magazine (1981) No 49, April.

Charreyron, Anne (1981) *Impact des Techniques de l'Information sur les modes de vie. Evolution des modes de vie dans les societes ouest-europeennes: quelques enjeux.* Rapport interimaire No 10 (Interim Report No 10), Centre d'Etudes Sociologiques. Centre d'Etudes sur le Bien-Etre.

Clavaud, Richard (1981a) *Les reunions au bout du fil.* Le Monde Dimanche, 12 April.

Clavaud, Richard (1981b) *Les premiers pas du teletravail.* Le Monde Dimanche, 4 January.

Crochart, Karl (1980) *Information et conditions de travail.* Apres-Demain, June.

Durrieux, Claude (1981) *La grande bataille des telecommunications.* Le Monde, 12 February.

Glowinski, Albert (1980) *Telecommunications, objectif 2000.* Collection scientifique et technique des telecommunications, CNET ENST. Ed. Dunod, Paris.

Institut August Comte (1980) *L'Emploi a distance. Reflexions et Propositions.*

IDATE (1980) *Le Teletravail: Premieres reflexions.* Preparatory document for the Journees d'etudes de l'Institut pour le developpement et l'amenagement des Telecommunications et de l'economie, October.

La revue de l'entreprise (1978) *Le controle politique des effects sociaux de la technologie.* No 19, July-August.

Lefevre, Bruno (1979) *Audiovisuel et telematique dans la cite.* E.P.C.

Le Monde (1980) *La telematique.* Dossiers et documents No 77, January.

Le Roche Delupy 1. (1980) *La telereunion.* IDATA, Montpellier.

Little, A. D. (1980) *Business Equipment: Technology that forces executive decisions.* In *Demain, le teletravail,* E. Monod and N. Alter (Eds.), Revue des telecommunications, No. 37, October.

Message des PTT (1981) Revue No 303, April.

Plassard, Francois *La vie quotidienne: Rigidites et flexibilities. La vie quotidienne et ses representations.* Interim documents from the Laboratoire d'Economie des Transports, Universite de Lyon II.

Quiniou J. C. *Telematique, mythes et realites.* Collection of ideas, Gillimard.

Traverses (1979) Quarterly Review, September, Ed. de Minuit.

Touraine, Alain (1976) *Les societes dependantes.* Ed. Duculot.

Voge, Jean (1981) *Des telephones sur les remparts.* Le Monde Dimanche, 15 March.

Annex 1: The Instruments enabling Work-at-a-distance

At the pinnacle of the communications networks are the instruments for transmission, reception, handling and processing of information:

(1) **Telephone stations:** These are becoming increasingly well-adapted and easy to use.

(2) **Telephone-answering machines and automatic message recorders:** Only recently developed, especially in France, they allow, *inter alia,* questioning-at-a-distance, listening to the message during the recording and amplification of the telephone signal. Numerous improvements making them even more useful are to be expected.

(3) **Radiotelephones and mobile (car) telephones:** New technologies will enable the overcrowding of the hertzian waves to be combatted, which is the main obstacle to the development of the radiotelephone in urban areas.

(4) **The computer, micro-computer and big computer:** with which everyone is already familiar.

(5) **Computer terminals:** A computer terminal is what allows contact to be made with the computer either on input/keyboard or on input/screen, printer, control signals.

(6) **Remote copiers:** The picture of a document is read by the machine, then transmitted by telephone line and reproduced on arrival. Remote copiers are classified according to speed of transmission of a standard format (20 seconds to 6 minutes); the quality of reproduction (2.5 to 8 lines/mm); and the method of transmission (analogue or digital). They may have local use as a photocopying machine, transmit and receive simultaneously or transmit automatically on a programmed basis. They all use a special paper; research is being conducted on the use of ordinary paper.

(7) **Tele-writing (Remote facsimile transmission):** This reproduces at-a-distance, via the telephone network, the movements of a pen on a special tablet instantaneously on a sheet of paper or television screen. The colour can be chosen, a punctuation mark obliterated or indicated. It is used with audio teleconferencing.

(8) **Videophone and other similar systems:** These consist of a microphone, a loud speaker, a television screen and a film camera which can be turned towards the speaker or document. Like all the processes using the video picture, it requires very high information throughput links, such as the coaxial cable, which prevents interference, and optical fibres. But on the telephone network, it is possible all the same to get what is called slow television to flow — pictures which recur line by line every 5 to 20 seconds, thus enabling, for instance, the remote surveillance of premises. There are also systems using the video picture for consultation of documents from a distance. The use of remote-controlled very-high-picture resolution TV cameras enables tiny details to be observed, but they also require very high throughput links, which makes these systems unsuitable for use over long distances.

(9) **Audio-teleconferencing:** This enables there to be a conference between two

or more groups of interlocutors, in specially equipped studios. The studios have six microphones, loud speakers and indicators identifying the person who is speaking and the studio where he or she is. Remote copiers and telewriting may also be made available.

(10) **The telemeeting:** This is an audioconference which does not use a special studio, but 'free hand' telephone stations which are linked by a central post office device. Insofar as tele-writing may be used via the telephone, this system will be able to deal with it.

(11) **Computer-aided teleconferencing:** The main contribution of this system is that via the computer, messages intended for an interlocutor who is not available at the time of transmission can be stored. The existence of portable computer terminals makes their use even more flexible. This is a system which fits in with the rhythm and density of work of each of the speakers. It is the first system in our list which actually combines the memory and management capacity of the computer and the transmission system.

(12) **Videotex:** This is a keyboard and screen terminal, similar to a television set, giving access to a number of data banks which are made available to it by the network to which it is connected: telephone hertzian network etc. Thus, it quickly makes accessible a large quantity of information. By combining it with a remote copier, 'electronic mail' becomes possible.

(13) **Teleprocessing services:** A terminal on the user's premises is linked up by telephone line to the computer of a teleprocessing company; they thus have available a very large information-processing and storage capacity, but only when the need arises; 'wastage' of the computation capacity is thus avoided.

(14) **Word processors:** By differentiating between the typing and printing of a text, these machines enable texts to be corrected and amended before the final version is produced. They have a keyboard similar to a typewriter, a screen which may be limited to one line, a store, correction software (internal programmes), retrieval of the information stored and a printing unit. It can also be connected to a computer or another word processor by linkage with the telephone network or a leased-line network.

(15) **The video-disc:** This is a disc on which television pictures have been stored in the proportion of 40,000 to 50,000 pictures per side. As the registration of the pictures is numerical, the video-disc can be combined with a computer which would manage the pictures.

Chapter 18

The Information Society: Implications for Regional Development, Decentralization and Urban Policy

Michael J. Bannon

Department of Regional and Urban Planning,
University College, Dublin

TECHNOLOGY, including information technology, is one of many factors influencing the location of people and activities in space. There is now considerable evidence that existing and foreseeable information technologies can help to bring about substantial changes in the pattern of life and the quality of human existence (Martin, 1978; Sweeney, 1980). However, concern with technological aspects may obscure the wider and more important context of the 'information society' which these technologies should serve and facilitate. Attention is drawn here to the worsening regional disparities within the European Community (EEC, 1981) and within some member states, as peripheral areas and lagging regions fail to participate fully in the transformation to an 'information society'. This trend, it is suggested, will continue, intensified by technological change, unless there are enlightened regional and urban policies to take advantage of new possibilities outside the developed areas.

GROWTH OF THE INFORMATION SOCIETY

THE TERM information society bestows a measure of belated recognition upon a process of labour specialization which has continued at an accelerating pace for almost one hundred years now. This process entails ever-increasing levels of investment in human capital and a shift from production of goods to provision of services. The results of these changes in the skill levels of the working population are most easily seen in the occupational changes within the labour

233

force of all developed countries; blue-collar and unskilled occupations have contracted severely, while white-collar occupations have, to date, continued to expand (Parker, 1981).[1] In the case of the thirteen countries listed in Table 1, all have witnessed a large-scale growth of jobs in information; this growth has been most rapid in the more developed economies, with countries such as Ireland and Greece both having a small proportion and a relatively slow expansion of white-collar occupations. Most encouraging has been the importance of managerial and professional occupations in this expansion, if we accept the validity of Adam Smith's belief that the wealth of a nation depends upon the skill, dexterity and knowledge of its people (Smith, 1976).

The processes of continuous labour refinement and job specialization, which underlie the growth of white-collar employment, underpin every aspect of modern lifestyles and they have generated new specialisms, providing unforeseen and valuable services. They have also generated a host of new firms which have contributed substantially to economic development and employment expansion. Despite periodic alarms about the adverse implications of new technologies,[2] there is no real evidence that, in the medium term, this process of job specialization and innovation will not continue. Information-related jobs are likely to continue to expand and to offer secure and well-paid employment, both in the production of technology and in the handling and use of information throughout the economy as a whole (NBST, 1981a). In addition, access to and control over information sources will increasingly act as a catalyst to innovation and determine the pace and location of new development.

Inequality of information availability

Table 1 has demonstrated the rapid expansion of information-related labour, while Porat (1976) and other researchers (Canadian Economic Services Ltd., 1977; Pettit, 1979) have calculated the contribution of an information sector to Gross National Product, incomes and employment. However, the importance of information is neither uniform between countries nor between regions within countries — large or small. By and large, information activities have concentrated in the capital cities and the capital-city regions, particularly in the more centralized economies where "no Member State appears to have succeeded in offsetting the powerful forces tending to centralize such activity in the private quite as much as in the public sector" (Marquand, 1980). Increasingly, research findings confirm that backward and lagging regions are characterized by poor information sources and a limited share of white-collar jobs, particularly in the professions, management and research; since these are

---

[1] Parker suggests that in the United States "the expansion of information occupations has reached a point of diminishing returns."

[2] In the Irish context, see *Microelectronic Technology: Consultation or Chaos* (1979), ASTMS, Dublin.

Table 1

Occupational Changes in Labour Force of selected countries (1960-1979)

Country	White-collar Employment c.1960*	White-collar Employment c.1978*	Growth in White-collar jobs Number	Growth in White-collar jobs Percentage	Percentage in White-collar jobs 1960	Percentage in White-collar jobs 1978	Change in Total Employment
Canada	2,476,066	5,192,000	2,715,934	109.7	38.0	46.4	+ 4,689,644
United States	27,268,896	48,852,000	21,583,104	79.1	39.0	47.7	+ 32,659,524
Sweden	1,069,202	1,909,900	840,698	78.6	32.9	45.8	+ 929,616
Belgium	1,154,714	1,406,808	252,094	21.8	32.9	38.7	+ 125,355
Denmark	558,370	840,059	281,689	50.4	26.7	36.3	+ 219,656
Greece	516,742	697,876	181,134	35.1	14.2	21.6	− 403,605
Ireland	268,969	376,300	107,331	39.9	24.3	32.9	+ 35,792
Italy	4,717,000	5,395,577	678,577	14.4	23.6	27.2	− 190,000
Luxembourg	38,817	46,456	7,639	19.7	29.9	35.9	− 465
Netherlands	1,374,744	2,322,000	947,256	68.9	33.0	45.9	+ 889,374
Germany (W)	8,076,700	11,674,000	3,597,300	44.5	30.1	43.3	− 130,900
United Kingdom	8,270,980	10,433,490	2,162,510	26.1	33.6	41.7	+ 404,460
France	5,717,398	8,712,500	2,995,102	52.4	28.8	40.1	+ 1,944,835

*Canada 1961 and 1979; USA 1960 and 1978; Sweden 1960 and 1977; Belgium 1961 and 1976; Denmark 1960 and 1970; Greece 1961 and 1971; Ireland 1961 and 1977; Italy 1963 and 1971; Luxembourg 1960 and 1970; Netherlands 1960 and 1977; Germany 1961 and 1978; UK 1961 and 1971; and France 1962 and 1975.

Source: ILO Year Books

the occupations associated with control of development, innovation and diversification, these regions remain disadvantaged; they continue to lack self-sustaining growth and the resources of the area are managed from cities outside the region. (For a discussion on the role of communication in development, seen Bannon and Eustace, 1977).

Within the European Community information, and hence innovative activity, is highly concentrated in the Brussels-Amsterdam-Dusseldorf-Paris conurbation. To illustrate the extent of this information concentration, Sahlberg and Engstrom (1973) devised a 'Contact Potential' index, based on the spatial pattern of decision-makers and information sources in relation to travel-time between centres. Thus, information availability and business-contact possibilities were clearly concentrated in Brussels and the central conurbation, while even capital cities on the periphery (like Copenhagen, Athens, Rome, Madrid or Dublin) were distinctly isolated and disadvantaged. Since the pace of innovative activity is closely related to the volume and rate of information exchange in an area, it follows that there exists a distinct variation in the pattern of innovations; this works to the advantage of the centre, intensifies regional disparities and ensures an increasing measure of external control over the economies of peripheral states. Similarly, within many countries, the advantages of highly centralized capital-city regions have intensified over time despite existing regional policies. For isolated countries like Ireland, there is a serious danger that, in the absence of relevant policies, the expansion of an information society could worsen their relative position in the European development league.

THE CASE OF IRELAND

WITHIN A EUROPEAN CONTEXT, Ireland is a small remote island with a relatively low standard of living. With a population of only 3.4 million persons, Ireland is one of the smallest countries in the European Community; it has the lowest density of population, the smallest *per capita* income and the second highest dependence on agriculture. Within the country, there are acute variations in income and opportunity; the urban system is dominated by the rapidly growing capital city (Dublin), which is the focus of an extremely centralized system of administration in both the public and the private sectors (Bannon, 1979). Outside Dublin, development opportunities decline with distance from the capital and large parts of the Midlands and West lack any major urban centre, being highly dependent upon Dublin for services and social and employment opportunities. In general, physical infrastructure is inadequate and poses a serious development constraint.

Unlike most EEC countries, Ireland has a very young population, over half being under 25 years of age. It is also one of the few member states facing the prospect of sizeable population growth and rapid urban expansion during the remainder of this century. While population growth is clearly a valuable resource, the scale of social provision to meet this growth is daunting, given Ireland's inadequate resources. These problems are further compounded by Ireland's very low participation rates in Third Level education, its continued dependence on foreign capital, the inadequate level of self-generating growth in the country and a traditionally low level of investment in Research and Development (NBST, 1981b).

Employment Restructuring

As indicated in Table 1, Ireland has undergone a process of labour transformation in favour of white-collar occupations, albeit at a slower rate than in the more advanced countries. These changes have been reflected in the growth of service sector employment, from 33.6 per cent of the 1926 labour force to 48.0 per cent in 1977. More directly, Table 2 shows that the shift from blue-collar into white-collar occupations, evident in the 1960s, has accelerated between 1971 and 1977. Apart from the continued decline in agriculture and the lack of growth in producer occupations, this table illustrates the rapid decline of unskilled and service occupations, while while-collar occupations continued to expand employment.

Table 2

Occupational Changes in Employment, Ireland (1971-1977)

Occupation	Numbers employed 1971	1977	Employment Change Number	Percentage
Agricultural	288,753	219,700	– 69,053	– 23.1
Producers, makers, repairers	230,941	231,400	+ 459	+ 0.2
Labourers and unskilled	88,840	52,000	– 36,840	– 41.5
Transport and communications	83,828	75,600	– 8,228	– 9.8
Clerical	103,214	111,800	+ 8,586	+ 8.3
Commerce, insurance & finance	108,720	108,500	– 220	– 0.2
Service	80,458	71,100	– 9,358	– 11.6
Professional & technical	103,316	128,700	+ 25,384	+ 24.6
Others	31,416	44,500	+ 13,039	+ 41.4
Total all occupations	1,119,531	1,043,300	– 76,231	– 6.8

Sources: *Census of Population* (1971); EEC *Labour Force Survey* (1977)

Table 3 shows the regional distribution of while-collar jobs in both 1971 and 1975 and confirms the importance of Dublin as a location for such jobs.

Table 3

White-collar Employment by region, Ireland (1971-1975)

Regions	Numbers employed		Change 1971-1975		1975 Percentage share	Number of white-collar workers per 1,000 population	
	1971	1975	Number	Percentage		1971	1975
East and North East	179,771	198,000	18,229	+ 10.1	53.8	146	151
South East & South West	75,809	81,900	6,091	+ 8.0	22.3	95	98
Midlands & Mid-West	43,896	49,900	6,004	+ 13.7	13.6	87	97
West, North West and Donegal	34,681	38,100	3,419	+ 9.9	10.3	78	87
Total	334,157	367,900	33,743	+ 10.1	100.0	112	119

Data is not available for individual regions for 1975 and may not always be exactly comparable to 1971 data.

Source: *Census of Population*, (1971); EEC *Labour Force Survey* (1977).

Table 4 shows that even the manufacturing jobs in electronics show a distinct concentration in Dublin and also in the Mid-West region, where the Limerick National Institute of Higher Education is a distinct attraction. Thus, most of the new employment in Ireland is in white-collar jobs, with a concentration of all grades in Dublin, particularly higher level jobs.

Table 4

Regional Distribution of companies and employment in Electronics, Ireland

Region	Number of Firms	Employment
North West	2	273
West	7	1,797
Mid-West	25	3,654
South West	13	684
South East	7	1,785
Midlands	1	700
East	33	4,883
North East	7	1,272
Total	95	15,048

Source: *Microelectronics,* NBST (1981), Dublin, Vol. 11

Regional Implications of Concentration

A variety of adverse social, economic and organizational disadvantages derive from a lack of information-related jobs in the regions. These include a limitation of the region's occupational structure, lack of adequate local employment, loss of spending power and its associated multiplier effects. Instead, outward migration to the capital is promoted. However, if the peripheral regions lack professional and managerial expertise, the results are likely to adversely affect a region's capacity to innovate, attract investment capital or generate self-sustaining growth. The resultant loss of local leadership affects the social as well as the economic life of an area. Furthermore, where decisions affecting a region are taken outside that area — whether in the public or private sectors — the benefits of local branch-plants and sub-offices are exported out of the region (Bannon and Eustace, 1977; Bannon, 1978).[3] Regions lacking leadership and control functions are likely to permanently lack the dynamic impetus of self-sustained growth.

---

[3] A study of Waterford showed that many of the benefits of local industrial and service units were lost to the local region as a result of external control.

On the other hand, continued concentration in Dublin may bring with it serious diseconomies in terms of land costs, transport and infrastructural developments,[4] while the public sector will have to bear the additional cost of promoting renewal and development in regional and local centres. In addition, the scale of Dublin's growth poses serious planning and social problems. Of particular concern also is the complete failure of persons from the lower socio-economic groups to enter the white-collar labour market (Bannon *et al,* 1981).

The Need for new policies

If Ireland is to benefit from the information revolution and its associated technology, development policies must become much more positive towards the information industry, with an emphasis on comprehensive self-sustaining growth and a reliance on indigenous strengths and the retention of multiplier benefits within the country. At the community level, inter-regional variations are liable to remain unless investment in research and development and in higher education in the lagging regions occurs *at a substantially faster rate* than in the more prosperous regions. This requires the support of both member states and the Community.

Within Ireland, new telecommunications technologies, especially telematics, can prove a positive force for change and can be harnessed to support the emergence of new and desired settlement patterns, provided the country has a clear strategy for future development. In the absence of any realistic alternative, office and information activities have concentrated in Dublin, with the advantages of proximity to a centralized administration, research facilities and other office firms. In general and in the absence of relevant policies, new technologies will serve to reinforce this dominant position and to perpetuate regional disparities.

The elimination of regional disparities within Ireland involves the promotion of a comprehensive programme with the following major elements:

(1) the designation of selected centres as centres of innovation, research and wide-ranging higher educational provision;

(2) since all decision-making is interlinked, the dismantling of the present highly centralized Government bureaucracy, preferably in favour of strong urban-centred regional units;

(3) the enlargement and development of current 'service industry' programmes to attract into these centres more head-office and research functions of firms from abroad with plants in Ireland;

(4) the relocation of public sector decision-making from Dublin to these centres, as well as the encouragement of private relocations;

(5) investment in a programme of telematics to facilitate and support the urban-based regional strategy.

[4] For a general discussion of diseconomies of urban size, see Evans (1972).

The problems of regional development are multi-dimensional and their solution requires a multi-dimensional response. Without a clear and comprehensive policy for future growth and the location of development, new technologies on their own may well intensify regional disparities while facilitating more dispersed patterns within city regions. But without careful direction, these new developments may discriminate both against disadvantaged areas and the lower socio-economic groups within society. The use of the new technologies requires careful and detailed advance planning if they are to prove socially desirable.

References

Bannon, M. J. (1978) *Office and White-collar Activities: The role of Waterford.* South-East Regional Development Organization (SERDO).

Bannon, M. J. (1979) Office Concentration in Dublin and its consequences for Regional Development. In *Spatial Patterns of Office Growth and Location,* P. W. Daniels (Ed.), John Wiley, London, pp. 95-126.

Bannon, M. J. and Eustace, J. G. (1977) *Service-type Employment and Regional Development.* NESC Report 28, Dublin, Chapter 5.

Bannon, M. J. *et al* (1981) *Urbanisation: Problems of Growth and Decay in Dublin.* NESC Report 55.

Canadian Economic Services Ltd. (1977) *Issues in the Analysis of the Information Sector of the Canadian Economy.* Ottawa.

EEC (1981) *New Regional Policy Guidelines and Priorities.* Commission of European Communities, Com. (81), 152, p. 3.

Evans, A. W. (1972) *The Pure Theory of City Size in an Industrial Economy.* Urban Studies, Vol. 9, pp. 49-77.

Marquand, J. (1980) *The Role of the Tertiary Sector in Regional Policy.* Studies, Regional Policy Series No. 19, EEC, Brussels, p. 71.

Martin, J. (1978) *The Wired Society.* Prentice-Hall, New Jersey.

NBST (1981a) *Microelectronics: The Implications for Ireland.* National Board for Science and Technology, Dublin 3, 3 Vols.

NBST (1981b) *Science Budget 1981.* National Board for Science and Technology, Dublin.

Parker, E. B. (1981) *Information Services and Economic Growth.* The Information Society, Vol. 1, No. 1, p. 73.

Pettit, A. (1979) *Information Employment in Ireland 1926-77.* Institute for Industrial Research and Standards (IIRS), Dublin.

Porat, M. U. (1976) *The Information Economy: Definition and Measurement.* US Dept. of Commerce, 9 Vols, Washington, DC.

Sahlberg, B. and Engstrom, M. (1973) *Travel Demand, Transport Systems and Regional Development.* Lund Studies in Geography, Series B, No. 39, pp. 133.

Smith, Adam (1976) *The Inquiry into the Wealth of Nations.* Clarendon Press, Oxford (1976) Edition), Chapters 1 and 2.

Sweeney, G. (1980) *The French Revolution and the Irish?* Technology Ireland, January, pp. 20-22.

CHAPTER 19

Signposts of Change:
The potential impact of new
technology on travel patterns*

Marilyn Dover

Technology Policy Unit, University of Aston in Birmingham, UK

INTRODUCTION

IN ANTICIPATING the impacts of microelectronic technology in its various forms, much of the research to date has reflected our current concerns with, on the one hand, ailing economic activity and, on the other, the social inability to keep pace with rapid technological change. The two dominant perspectives — economic and sociological — tend on the whole to offer disconcertingly different accounts, optimistic and pessimistic respectively, although these are the logical consequences of our originally stated concerns.

This is curious since the prime focus of both of these perspectives is the world of work, which is both an economic and sociological phenomenon. There is a strong entanglement between economic organization and social organization. The relationship of the two governs, and is governed by, our attitudes. Our willingness to adapt to change, social or economic, is often modulated by the influence the one will have on the other.

It is not surprising, therefore, that the subordinate foci of research attention — on leisure, education and, naturally, unemployment — should be defined in terms of their relationship to work: leisure is what you have when you are not working, education fits you for a particular kind of work and unemployment is the state of being anxious to get work. Most of us would agree that these are preconceptions that must change and yet we cannot lose sight of the pivotal nature of work. Nearly every activity we undertake has involved someone working: such is the interdependence of our society today that if enough

*The author wishes to acknowledge the support of the Science Research Council and Lucas Industries in funding this research.

people took to climbing mountains in their leisure time, whole new industries with their associated economic and social patterns would spring up to serve their needs.

The conceptual centrality of work is almost inescapable, the more so in this present case, since the new technology is primarily to be applied to work. The great drawback arising from this is that we are rarely able to develop any *characterization* of the future. Such research, while vital, presents us with the dots on a virgin map; what we need is a method to fill in the connecting lines.

Perhaps to discover the less direct impacts, we need a more oblique approach. Transportation is not in itself a sociological process; nor is it a direct activity, in the sense that it is a means to various ends. Yet, it is certainly an important part of our daily lives. Within the nine member states of the EEC, the average annual distance travelled by private road vehicle per head of population exceeds 7,000 km. For those countries where comparable data are available,[1] mileage by the private road vehicle greatly exceeds that of all other modes of passenger transport put together, generally being about 70 per cent of all. For the whole of the EEC, the number of road vehicles of all types has risen by almost exactly 50 per cent between 1968 and 1978, while for the same period the number of cars and taxis has increased from 46.5 million to 78.5 millions. The number of motorcycles and mopeds has also risen overall by about 7 per cent, although there are wide variations between countries. In West Germany, the number has doubled, while it has fallen elsewhere. Not only are there more vehicles, but in some countries mileage per vehicle has also risen. In Great Britain, for example, cars and taxis as a group averaged 13,695 km per vehicle in 1968 and 15,361 in 1978. All this despite a near-tripling of the retail price of 4-star petrol, from an average for the EEC of US$18.3 per hundred litres in 1970 to $53.27 in 1979 (Department of Transport, 1980). This price-inelasticity of demand demonstrates the importance we attach to personal transportation, especially to our cars.

The Potential for Technological Substitution

With the growth of the 'information sector' (Porat, 1976), the possibility of substituting telecommunications for transportation has been gaining currency over the last decade. Following early work by Nilles *et al* (1976), various groups have examined some facet of the 'telecommunications/transportation trade-off' — or T^3 for convenience.[2]

---

[1] France, Ireland and Luxembourg excluded in this instance only.

[2] This useful abbreviation was coined by Jussawalla *et al.* of the East-West Communications Institute, Honolulu.

Already, with the current state of the art and sufficient investment, it is technologically possible to substitute telecommunications for travel to and from work; travel in the course of work; education; shopping; social visits; booking holidays/flights/theatre etc.; mail; library-book renewals; primary health care and counselling; meter reading; newspapers; entertainment; playing chess; making a blind date; and looking for a job. The danger is that as these have become possible, or even highly probable, we will make the quantum leap to a scenario where no one ever actually leaves home.

What is needed is some more intimate profile of our everyday movements so that we can see where the real impacts of T^3 lie. Even for one country, such data are not always readily available and where they are, they are not always satisfactory to our purposes.[3] The analysis which follows deals with Great Britain and may or may not resemble other national profiles.

PATTERNS OF MOBILITY IN GREAT BRITAIN

ADOPTING THE CLASSIFICATION used by the UK's Department of Transport, journeys may be categorised by the following purposes: to and from work; in course of work; education; shopping and personal business; eating and drinking; entertainment/sport (spectator); day trips/playing sport; holidays; escort; and other. These have recently been superseded, but are used here as they are more illustrative of mobility patterns, being less aggregated than the newer categories (which are listed in Table 2).

Table 1 shows journey purpose as percentages of all journeys and all mileage, regardless of how short or how travelled (i.e. including walking). It can be seen that as a percentage of all journeys, the major categories, in descending importance, are shopping and personal business (28 per cent), to and from work (22 per cent), social (15 per cent) and education (10 per cent). In terms of the percentage of all mileage, however, the most important category is 'to and from work' (23 per cent), followed by social visits (18 per cent). Shopping and personal business accounts for only 16 per cent of mileage, indicating that such business may be conducted over shorter distances. Three categories then account for 10 per cent: journeys in the course of work, reflecting the greater distances involved; day trips/playing sport; and holidays, which commonsense decrees are taken at some distance.

---

[3] Because certain tables are not produced for all years, it has been necessary here to adapt data from different years.

Table 1

Journey Purpose as a percentage of	(a) all journeys	(b) all mileage
to and from work	22	23
in course of work	4	10
education	10	4
shopping and personal business	28	16
eating and drinking	3	2
social visits	15	18
entertainment/sport (spectator)	4	4
day trips/playing sport	7	10
holidays	1	10
escort and other	5	4

Source: Transport Statistics Great Britain 1968-1978

Modes of travel are show in Table 2, using the more recent aggregation of categories. Attention is concentrated primarily on the modes 'walking' and 'by car', partly because they are the two most important means of mobility and partly because of their trade-off value. The new grouping is problematic in terms of the category 'other' which here includes travel in the course of work and of which 54 per cent of journeys are by car. What is most interesting is that for the purposes of education, shopping and personal business, and leisure excursions, walking predominates over the car as the main mode used.

Another truth which has to be borne in mind when we discuss mobility patterns is the higher frequency of journeys at shorter distances and the comparative rarity of long-distance journeys. Lack of space precludes a full analysis, but statistics show that 89 per cent of all journeys for whatever purpose are of less than 10 miles and a third are of less than one mile.

When the main modes of transport are examined against all journey lengths, for journeys of not over 2 miles, walking accounts for 36 per cent, bus for 17 per cent, pedal cycle for 9 per cent, motorcycle or moped for 2 per cent and employers' transport for 6 per cent. An amazing 29 per cent of all journeys of 2 miles or less are made by car. At the other extreme, for long-distance journeys by car, 24 per cent are for getting to and from work, 17 per cent in the course of work, but 67 per cent of all such journeys are for non-business purposes.

In general it can be said that the choice of mode varies with the distance to be travelled: walking is more common for the shorter distances, the car becomes the dominant mode with an increase in distance and is rivalled by the train for even greater distances. The exceptions to this are in journeys to and from work, when the workplace is located in Central London (where commuter trains, the underground and buses are predominantly used) or in other city centres. The choice of mode of travel also varies with (a) income, (b) age and sex, (c)

Table 2

Journey Purpose by Main Mode of Transport 1978/79 (percentage)

	Mode		
Purpose	Car	Walk	Other
to and from work	46	20	34
education	14	61	25
shopping and personal business	36	46	18
leisure (1) social/eating, drinking/ sport/entertainment	48	34	18
leisure (2) holiday/excursion	28	63	9
other (includes in course of work)	54	30	16
all purposes	40	39	21

Source: Transport Statistics Great Britain 1969-1979

geographical location *vis-a-vis* amenities, and (d) access to personal transport. (In Britain, 58 per cent of all households have one or more cars.)

THE POTENTIAL FOR SUBSTITUTION FOR TRAVEL

FROM THE FOREGOING some pointers to the potential extent of change emerge. These, taken in conjunction with the most likely developments in the new technology may offer a glimpse of possible trends. Information technology is expected to diffuse more quickly in the non-domestic field (Cawkell, 1980). Thus, decisions to implement information technology systems will be taken in the main by firms with reference to the firms' perceptions of economic and functional efficiency. As a result, T^3 would be incidental. If, however, transportation itself began to be viewed as problematic (as it well might with rising oil prices and severe shortages) or if non-oil-producing countries wished to defend their vulnerability, then T^3 offers one alternative in a range of 'technological fixes'. We must look at potential changes then in two ways: firstly, how they might happen incidentally and secondly, which uses of transportation might be optimally suited to bring about change by substitution.[4]

[4] Changes in transport technology could achieve similar goals.

The expression 'trade-off' implies some benefit to be gained on both sides of the equation. Journeys which are walked have no trade-off value except in the saving of time. Most such journeys are for non-business purposes and their nature in the main gives little indication that individuals might wish to invest in technology to save such travel time. Firms would only invest to save consumers' time if it were in their own interests to do so.

It is not intended that this discussion be a comprehensive review of technological developments. Rather, assuming widespread familiarity and acceptance of information technology, we ask the question: Given current patterns of mobility in Great Britain, where do the potential impacts for technological substitution lie? In terms of our list of journey purposes, some can be dealt with summarily. For eating and drinking, day trips/playing sport, holidays and journeys to escort another, there is no possibility of technological substitution. There is some potential for T^3 in entertainment/watching sport (compare TV coverage of soccer and falling attendances at matches). In most of these instances, the percentage of mileage involved is too small and too local (thus walked) to make them a target for policy. If new technology has an impact in these areas, it is more likely to be to increase their importance. The journey purpose 'social visits' is already substituted in some cases by the telephone, but improved telecommunications services, perhaps with vision added, and lower costs could increase the level of substitution. But many social activities would not be amenable to substitution, for example visiting the sick, dining with friends, parties and so on. As with other social activities, these may increase if, as is predicted, people have more leisure time.

This leaves four major categories of journey purpose which require further consideration:

(1) **Travel to and from work:** T^3 could not come about as an incidental effect of new technology, except where new firms based on the new technology originated new trends in location patterns. If, at the outset, such firms were operated from employees' homes or from local work stations, then travel to and from work would be affected for those employees. However, to have an impact on the mileage travelled to work, this would need to become a major new sector in the economy. If employees of such firms were drawn from those social groups which are not at present economically active (such as housewives), then no major impact on current mobility patterns would result. Only if people who currently travel to work some distance by transport (particularly by car) were to begin to work at home or locally would T^3 be seen to be effective as an instrument of policy.

Travel to and from work might come to be seen as a target for policy if T^3 became a policy objective. To supplant or modify such travel requires conscious decisions to relocate; certain types of industry cannot relocate, (such as coal mining). The type of work has to be suited to technological substitution. Some areas of commerce, education, ancillary services to industry or central and local government may be amenable to T^3. But a rough calculation suggests that at most only a quarter of current jobs could be considered for T^3 in Britain (CSO, 1980). Of these, accountancy, clerical and similar functions would be the obvious choice. The vigour with which such a policy would be pursued would depend on the reasons underlying the policy goals. Should policy ever dictate restrictions in travel to work, firms would seek other ways out of the dilemma besides relocation. Finally, the most immediate prospect of modification to travel to and from work lies not in T^3 but in unemployment.

(2) **Journeys in the course of work** form a very small percentage of all journeys and only 10 per cent of all mileage. Incidental or planned T^3 is probable here. Studies by the Post Office and others (Tyler *et al,* 1977; Depts. of Environment and Transport, 1980) have shown that teleconferencing (even with vision, facsimile transmission facilities etc.) is costly and less satisfactory than face-to-face meetings. It seems, however, that T^3 will have a wide impact here.

(3) **Education** is one of those areas most amenable to T^3 and has a great potential for the use of information technology within it. Yet the profile of mobility suggests that as education stands at present, there would be little point in T^3 here. Even if, as Stonier (1980) advocates, the education sector were greatly expanded, educational facilities are widely spread throughout the community and journeys are generally short. Few journeys at present are travelled by car. Face-to-face teaching is considered educationally preferable and a large component of education is the social contact it brings. Remote learning might be more suited to higher education, for more specialist learning groups and for courses whose students are geographically dispersed.

(4) **Shopping and personal business** is probably the most likely aspect of our daily lives to be affected by information technology. Although much of it is conducted locally and many journeys are walked, much also involves the use of a car, such as visits to the supermarket to buy groceries. Personal mobility has been taken for granted in many areas of planning but even now, motoring costs are reaching levels where there are signs that people are cutting down on journeys. The technology already exists for remote shopping, using a variety of systems. Although there are some items which people would prefer to buy personally, there are many standard repeat items in a family grocery list which could be readily bought remotely. With rising transport, labour and other costs, it would make sense to organize retailing so that the customer keyed in an order through the telephone network, the packing, delivery-routing and payment of which was handled by computer.

Much personal business deals with handling personal finances. In one major respect Britain already lags behind Europe: 50 per cent of employees are still paid in cash rather than into a bank, compared with 5 per cent in West Germany and 2 per cent in France (Jones, 1981). Automatic teller machines will become widely used in the workplace. Point-of-sale credit and point-of-sale banking facilities are already in existence and should become widespread in the 1990s.

While shopping and personal business seems likely to be widely affected by the application of new technology, the extent of the impact on travel patterns is likely to be less, but still significant.

CONCLUSION

WE SHOULD BE CAREFUL not to think that the 'information revolution' is inevitable; technology by itself does not demand to be used, we have to choose to use it. We choose according to several decision criteria — availability of technology merely being one. There are no technological imperatives and the technology itself is neutral. The possibility that the penetration of new technology will reach a stage where it becomes 'irresistable' will not of itself ensure that the new systems will do any more than replace existing systems — regarding patterns of mobility, they need not generate new modes of activity (for example work at home instead of work in central offices); for all that the potential is there. In-building or intra-firm LAN's would affect the micro-social networks but not public mobility patterns.

Another difficulty which arises when attempting to forecast the effects of new technology on society is that society is subject to change from other sources. It will not be static; many social forces are at work concurrently with technology to bring about change. Changes in expectation levels, sectoral configurations in employment or unemployment, land-use, the distribution of wealth, resource depletion, political stability, rising population and other demographic changes — all will work through to alter society.

Travel is an integral part of our daily lives and helps to bind society together. Although information technology is likely to become widely used, its impacts on travel will perhaps be more limited than one might at first imagine. Even in those areas where its impact could be greatest, it is likely that other factors will play a deciding role in the extent of its substitution for personal transportation, with possibly the greatest influence being centrally directed policy, motivated by wider technological and social considerations.

References

Cawkell, A. E. (1980) Forces controlling the Paperless Revolution. In *The Microelectronics Revolution,* Forester (Ed.), Blackwell, Oxford.

CSO (1980) *Social Trends 1980.* Central Statistical Office, HMSO, London.

Departments of the Environment and Transport (1980) *Impacts of Telecommunications on Planning and Transport.* Research Report 24, HMSO, London.

Department of Transport (1979) *Transport Statistics Great Britain 1968-78.* HMSO, London.

Department of Transport (1980) *Transport Statistics Great Britain 1969-79.* HMSO, London.

Jones, Keith (1981) *NCR aims at wages by cash dispenser.* Computer Weekly, March.

Nilles, J. M. *et al* (1976) *The Telecommunicatioins Transportation Trade-off.* John Wiley, New York.

Porat, M. U. (1976) *The Information Economy.* US Dept. of Commerce, Office of Telecommunications, Washington, DC.

Stonier, T. (1980) The Impact of Microprocessors on Employment. In *The Microelectronics Revolution,* Forester (Ed.), Blackwell, Oxford.

Tyler, M. *et al* (1977) *Prospects for Teleconference Services.* Long-range Intelligence Bulletin 9, British Post Office Telecommunications.

PART IV

New Technology and the Changing Role of Women

The significance of technology as a factor in changing sex and occupational roles is considered. Tarja Cronberg analyses the impact of new information technologies on the social situation of many women. She argues that women are excluded from the design process and are largely consumers of technological products. The possibility for greater decentralization in work organization could breathe new life into communities if this is accompanied by a decentralization of power. Only then could such a development be advantageous to many women.

Terri Morrissey and Eileen Drew are optimistic that the new information technologies will allow greater freedom for women, insofar as they involve a potential breakdown of the traditional rigid distinction between wage labour and domestic labour.

On a different level, Cristina Bianchi, Alessandra de Cugis and Graziella Falaguasta argue that it is not simply a case of the new technology affecting lifestyles; rather, technological development should be actively subjugated to people's needs. An example of the inability of technology to satisfy social needs is given in the case of women, whose needs are not considered in the development of technology.

CHAPTER 20

A Word Processor in her living room? The impact of Information Technology on the way of life and work of women

Tarja Cronberg

Danish Building Research Institute, Hørsholm

THERE ARE MANY REASONS, why it is of special importance to study the impact of information technology on women:

(a) A widespread application of information technology will eliminate many of the jobs that women have today, especially low-paid routine administrative jobs in the office, with *unemployment* for women as a result.

(b) Women, who in many European countries have only recently left home and entered the labour market, will probably be the first group to face the possibility of *working at home.*

(c) Information technology will no doubt have an impact on the organization of *child care* in society. In many countries, the potential for savings is discussed — if women will work at home, fewer daycare facilities are needed.

(d) Information technology will not only have an impact on the amount of leisure people have, but also on how they actually spend this time. This, in turn, will affect *family life* and the role of women.

(e) The development of the new information technology and the proposals for its use have been *worked out by men.* Evaluation is carried out by groups consisting mostly of experts on technology. Their knowledge about the daily life and problems of women is limited.

While it is difficult to estimate (and the estimates generally disagree) how much unemployment there will be and how many people will be working at home in the next ten to twenty years, all estimates agree that the groups first to be affected are those with routine administrative tasks — those tasks performed in offices today by women. Even if the estimated 30 to 50 per cent of these administrative tasks were to turn out less, and if the 30 per cent of today's work force being employed in the home were to prove an overestimate, already a transfer of 10 to 20 per cent of the labour force into the home would mean a radical change both in the role of women in the labour force and in the life of the family.

The discussion here is concentrated upon the impact of information technology on women concerning two vital questions:

(a) How will the working situation of women be affected, particularly as a consequence of the potential of working at home (the possibility of transporting information rather than people); and

(b) what impact will the changes in the working situation have on the daily life of women in the home — on the relationship between work, child care, house work and leisure.

While much of the debate so far on the impact of information technology on the home has assumed that the nuclear family structure will remain the same, and that the new technology will be applied within this structure, there is nothing in the new technology that implies this kind of use. Therefore, it is important to provide some alternative scenarios, based on the application of the new technology in different kinds of social organization in the neighbourhood and community. In order to sketch some of these scenarios, I have selected three alternative ways of using the new technology in order to study the impact of these alternatives on the life and work of women:

(1) *A word processor in her living room* — work at home or what happens, if nothing else changes?

(2) *Neighbourhood centres,* the half-way house between headquarters and work at home.

(3) *The electronic community* — another organization of production and consumption, a new type of local community.

A WORD PROCESSOR IN HER LIVING ROOM

WORK AT HOME, as such, is nothing new. On the contrary, one could claim that work outside home is a recent innovation and the result of the industrial revolution. Today, home is the most important working place for many women, even if the working hours spent there are unpaid. Many others, mostly men (such as artists, freelance journalists and consultants) work at home. The new aspect of the electronic working place at home is the type of work to be performed and the groups to be involved. Authors and experts, who talk about the impact of the new technology, always elaborate on the idea of working at home. Alvin Toffler (1980) in his book *The Third Wave* talks about the 'electronic cottage' and the way work at home will enrich family life and solve the present crises of the family. In an experment carried out in the United States *(International Management,* October 1979), a secretary describes her new life after the US Bank Continental, Illinois, has set-up a word processor in her sitting room:

> *I travelled normally by bus and then by train. It was necessary to stand up. Nowadays I can sleep longer in the morning. During the day, I can have the household machines on and at five o'clock, I am finished with both my work and the housework, so that the evenings can be free.*

She now has more time for her hobbies (such as ceramics) and is less tired. The headaches she used to suffer from have completely disappeared; the stress has decreased, "there is no one looking over my shoulder as I am working."

The positive sides of this alternative are always highlighted. The individual will have more time, be under less strain and can do several things at the same time. Society will save resources and energy, as well as investments in infrastructure, such as roads, public transportation and so on. The need for real estate and office space will decrease. The housing areas, which are empty today, will be populated in the future. The negative sides, however, are less often discussed and written about. The feeling of community that many have in their working places, will gradually disappear. Many people, especially women, have gone out into the labour force not only for the money, but also in order to meet other adults. For many women, even hard industrial work or routine tasks in the office are preferable to staying at home, in order that they can have a sense of meaning and structure in their lives.

A common working place is also a prerequisite for the work of the labour unions. If the type of work to be first moved into the homes is low-paid administrative work, this will directly affect the unions, whose members are mainly women. This, in turn, will give them less power and potential to improve the working conditions of women.

When word processors are installed in offices, there is a time limit on how long one can work at a terminal. Even if the woman in the article claims that her headaches have disappeared, those having worked with terminals have the opposite experience. The health risks attached are far from established.

Work at home will not only affect the work situation but also child care. Not surprisingly, voices are already raised, proposing that women — since they are at home anyway — could also take care of their children during the day. Work at a terminal and a simultaneous use of household machines may be one thing. But looking after children as well must be a stress factor not only in relation to the work, but also for the children. Even if it is desirable that children should have more contact with working life than they have today, it is questionable whether the kind of work to be carried out at a terminal, and to see one's mother sitting in front of a home operator all day, will really meet this need. In addition, this implies a lot of contact with other children and adults, a contact normally supplied by a daycare centre.

What then will be the impact on family life? Professional data magazines abound in descriptions of the new family life: the mother planning the dinner for the family at her terminal, the children doing their homework at theirs and the father playing computer games with some of his distant friends. The new family life is carried out in front of terminals. If everyone has his own, there will be no more conflict in the family — and both husband and children will stay at home! Not a word is said about the questions of personal development or social contact. Last, but not least, present-day dwellings are hardly adapted to the new everyday life in front of home terminals.

NEIGHBOURHOOD CENTRES — SOMETHING IN BETWEEN

THERE IS NO IMMEDIATE REASON why the new technology should absolutely be brought into the home. The telephone and TV, of course, are already there and all experiences support the statement that the diffusion of new technology is easiest if no changes in infrastructure or organization are needed. But there are other possibilities: an alternative would be to establish small working places with facilities in the housing neighbourhoods. It is astonishing that while the international experts elaborate extensively on the alternative of work at home, the question of small, decentralized working places in the neighbourhood is either not explored at all or barely mentioned.

The small neighbourhood centres should be located close to where people live. Work would be centralized in the housing areas, either by several employers sharing a neighbourhood centre or by one employer establishing small satellite offices in selected neighbourhoods. Since work at a terminal is neither polluting nor noisy, it would be possible to scatter this type of working place in all neighbourhoods. The planners' dreams of integrating housing and work could finally come true. In the same way as the electronic home-working place, the 'electronic neighbourhood centre' would also save both time and energy due to the decreased need for commuting. Savings in real estate would not be as great as in the home alternative, since either the employers, the municipality or the housing corporation would have to invest in either rearranging existing space or building new workshops.

For women, this alternative would have the advantage of providing proximity between home and work, something that would make women's daily lives easier. The time spent in commuting between work, home and daycare centres would be decreased and access to shopping and other facilities would be easier. Instead of being isolated at home women could now meet each other at their new workplace, even if they are working for different employers. The question of labour unions would probably be equally difficult to solve as in the work-at-home alternative. The fact that more people would be spending their time in housing areas would probably bring new life into those areas and could prove the starting point for a dynamic development of neighbourhood organizations. New facilities could be built in relation to the new working places, such as meeting halls for the residents, restaurants, facilities for leisure activities and so on.

Compared to working at home, the advantages of neighbourhood centres are many but there is a great danger. A neighbourhood centre with only women working on routine administrative tasks could easily become a ghetto for them. The important decisions about the organization and content of the work would be made at headquarters. Women could thus risk being isolated with each other (and housework and childcare) in the neighbourhoods without any influence on society as a whole.

THE ELECTRONIC COMMUNITY — THE THIRD ALTERNATIVE

THE NEW INFORMATION technology could, at least in principle, be applied in order to realize a third type of development: a development towards a decentralized, resource-conscious, small-scale local community — a community not isolated from the world, but one with a more independent and self-governing structure than today's housing areas. The thought is not new but it has not been possible to realize it, except by retreating into the countryside. With the new information technology this thought could be realized on a new material basis and in a new organizational form. It could also be realized not only in the countryside, but in the cities and suburbs also.

The new information technology could support this type of development in several ways:

(a) increased productivity in production and administration will reduce the need for labour and extricate free time for other activities, such as activities within the 'informal economy' in the community;

(b) the new microelectronic technology is presumed to make small-scale production more competitive than large-scale centralized production units, thus creating a new material basis for both production and consumption in the local community;

(c) the local community would no longer be isolated in relation to the rest of the world. Organizational structures and new decision-making processes could be established to allow for participation at all levels.

What would this type of 'utopian' development mean for women? If everyone were to share the work in the formal sector, this could guarantee an equal participation for both women and men in the labour force. The restructuring of production in the informal sector in the neighbourhood/ community (such as homework and childcare) could both free time (as compared with carrying out these tasks within the nuclear family), as well as providing for a new social network in the neighbourhood. Opening-up of the family could also imply a more evenly shared burden of home work between husband and wife.

Organizing consumption in groups larger than the nuclear family would also imply a less resource-consuming way of life, while not decreasing the quality of life. Last but not least, this type of community would be less exposed to the negative risks of the new technology, namely the mass-consumption of TV-games and programmes isolated within the individual dwelling.

CONCLUSION

WHILE THE POSSIBILITY of working at home may immediately seem attractive to many women, the long-term consequences should first be analysed and discussed. Work at home should, at least in the beginning and possibly even in the long run, only be established as a supplement to a working place in the office. During this period, the long-term consequences for the organization of childcare, the role and working methods of labour unions and so on could be established.

If neighbourhood centres are experimented with and built, it should be guaranteed that a mixture of working places will be created in each case to counteract the segregation of women. New types of organizational structures should be developed in order to guarantee their influence on decisions to be made; similarly, for those working in a neighbourhood centre at a distance from headquarters.

Finally, more attention should be paid to the potential impact of the new information technology on the development of the community as a whole. Questions such as what production activities currently within the formal sector could in the future be carried out in the community, how care functions ought to be organized in the community, and how the relationship between the community and society as a whole should be structured—such issues need to be analysed and alternative proposals worked out. It is likely that only the third alternative (electronic community) will in the future be able to counteract the isolation of women within the dwelling, with professional work at their home terminal, combined with childcare and housework in between.

References

Cronberg, T. and Sangregorio I. L. (1981) *The Brave New Everyday Life.* Prisma, Stockholm (In Swedish).
EEC (1980) *Employment and the New Microelectronic Technology.* EEC Commission, Brussels.
International Management, October, 1979.
Toffler, A. (1980) *The Third Wave.* William Morrow, New York.

CHAPTER 21

Work in an Information Society: Converging Sex Roles and the Re-definition of Work

Terri Morrissey and Eileen Drew

Human Resources Study Group, Dublin.

THE ADVENT OF the microchip revolution has been simultaneously dreaded, as implying massive unemployment, and heralded, as an end to work as such. Historically, there has been no fixed idea as to what constitutes work. Work has always been an integral part of society and as society changed, so the conception and performance of work underwent fundamental change. Theories of work have been developed to accommodate contemporaneous social, cultural, religious, economic and political conditions and indeed to reinforce them. Technological developments have been a further and important influence on how work is performed and who performs it. Information technology is but one in a series of technical catalysts which have affected society and the performance of work in that society. It is furthermore only one factor which will influence the work of individuals.

The meaning of 'work' and the evolution of current work roles of men and women are examined here. We look at emerging definitions of work, particularly those which are sex-defined, as influenced by changing cultural values and by technological developments. In conclusion, a view of the future of work is presented in its broadest sense in an Information Society.

THE PREDICTED IMPACT OF INFORMATION TECHNOLOGY

INFORMATION TECHNOLOGY has caused considerable controversy about its likely effect on society. It is seen as a 'meta technology' which will radically alter how work is performed. Stonier (1979) suggests that "it is highly probably that by early in the next century, it will require no more than 10 per cent of the labour force to provide us with all material needs." Less apocalyptic predictions have emerged, which relate recent technological advances to the series of developments which have taken place in the past few hundred years. A recent report by the National Board for Science and Technology (1980) doubts, in the Irish context, the likelihood of large-scale unemployment resulting from the adoption of information technology.

In general terms there are three approaches to the probable impact of information technology, which may be categorised as optimistic, pessimistic and humanitarian. While the optimistic and pessimistic approaches appear to be in direct opposition about the future, they both accept a form of technological determinism, whereby technology directs society rather than the reverse. The third position, represented by Schumacher's humanitarian view (1980) emphasises that technological change is neither good nor bad *per se,* but can be controlled and/or utilised to improve the quality of life. This view allows for the impact of other factors, such as shifting attitudes and demands, in shaping society.

TOWARDS A RE-DEFINITION OF WORK

IN ORDER TO CONSIDER the future of work in an Information Society, it is necessary to examine what the term 'work' means. It was only with the industrial revolution that work came to mean employment. This narrow view of work is no longer appropriate for a post-industrial Information Society.

According to the Concise Oxford English Dictionary, work is defined as "expenditure of energy, striving, application of effort to a purpose . . . task to be undertaken . . . things done, achievement, things made . . ." Only one of the definitions related to work as "employment especially the opportunity of earning money by labour". Yet, as remarked by Jenkins and Sherman (1979, p. 140): "Work is inextricably entwined with income in industrialised societies and thus clearly has a value as income equals goods equals standards of living equals status." This comment highlights the major problem faced by society at a time when new technological advances would appear to threaten the way in which work is performed and hence, the living standards and status of individuals.

The view expressed by Jenkins and Sherman (*ibid,* p. 40) that "work became important in the industrial revolution" clearly ignores the contribution of individual effort to the economy prior to industrialisation and today in non-industrialised countries. Their statement also ignores all work performed at present outside employment in the formal economy. For example, the contribution of housewives is not considered, nor voluntary services, nor do-it-yourself activities. The narrow view that work equals employment is commented upon by Moss (1978) when he asks: "Must work involve some reward, either in money or material kind? . . . Does satisfaction or pleasure count as reward — as in work done for charity? Often what one person considers to be work is another person's leisure."

Current thinking on work also regards leisure activities as a reward from work, ignoring the fact that many individuals spend their time (when they are not sleeping or employed in a job) working in the home, garden and at various other pursuits. Therefore, to equate 'unemployment' with being 'workless' may be one of the disabling fallacies of this age: clearly the two may coincide but not automatically.

Already there is a growing awareness that a broader conception of work is needed. Walley (unpublished) of the Irish Foundation for Human Development questions industrial society's concept of work. He urges a re-examination of work, particularly in the technological society. Work should have a broader meaning as "those activities which go into maintaining the set of relationships which make up society — all the activities necessary to maintain and develop a culture."

Terkel (1975), in his study of working individuals, quotes Ralph Helstein of the United Packinghouse Workers of America as saying:

> *Learning is work. Caring for children is work. Community action is work. Once we accept the concept of work as something meaningful, not just the source of a buck, you don't have to worry about providing enough jobs . . . The problem is going to come in finding ways for man (sic) to keep occupied so he's (sic) in touch with reality.*

Illich (1978) holds the view that work as paid employment is too narrow a concept. Work in our present society acquires meaning only through its productivity and contribution to GNP. Thus, work no longer means the creation of value, but a job, and unemployment means idleness rather than "the freedom to do things that are useful for oneself or for one's neighbour." Scott Burns (1976) in his predictions of things to come, considers that over the next 25 years, paid work in a job and unpaid work in the home will take equal amounts of time — $5\frac{1}{3}$ hours per day. He suggests that as the market economy expands it forces the growth of the household economy. Dahrendorf (1975) refers to the artificial distinction between education, work and leisure and argues for the opportunities for individuals "to develop some of their dormant capacities elsewhere". He recognises that it is often in 'black work' or moonlighting that people find full expression. Along with advocating shorter working hours in employment, Dahrendorf considers that more people should be given the opportunity of sabbatical leave for further education or simply to pursue alternative work activities.

The implication from all these sources is that work has many forms; it exists in an employment and non-employment context and its value cannot be seen solely in economic terms. This is particularly important at a time when through new technology and worldwide recession, unemployment is mistakenly seen to create 'worklessness'.

WORK ROLES OF MEN AND WOMEN

JUST AS THE industrial revolution brought about a divergence between the work roles of men and women, so the information revolution may lead to a convergence of these roles. The clear distinction between men's work, performed primarily in employment, and women's work, performed mainly in the home, is a relatively recent one. In her research on women workers, Pinchbeck (1981) states that "in every industrial system in the past, women have been engaged in productive work and their contribution has been recognized as an indispensible factor." She notes that it is a mistaken notion that women only became industrial workers with the industrial revolution.

The industrial revolution changed the location of production. Instead of being involved in home-based work, women were forced to choose between home and production outside the home. By the beginning of the twentieth century, a woman's role was predominantly that of housewife and so dependent upon a male provider. As Oakley (1976, p. 4) states:

> Industrialisation has had three lasting consequences: the separation of the man from the intimate daily routines of domestic life; the economic dependence of women and children on men; and the isolation of house and childcare from other work.

Since work has come to be equated with paid employment, unpaid work (which is performed mainly by women) tends to be seen as 'non-work'. This is despite the fact that housewives spend an average of 77 hours per week at housework (*ibid*, p. 59). As a consequence of this, value is placed on being employed and to be unemployed means a lowering of self-esteem and the feeling of being a parasite on society. Illich (1981) sums up this cultural development as follows:

> But no matter how much we search other cultures, we cannot find the contemporary division between two forms of work, one paid and the other unpaid, one credited as productive and the other concerned with reproduction and consumption, one considered heavy and the other one light, one demanding special qualifications and the other not, one given high social prestige and the other relegated to 'private' matters.

Present indications are that this situation is undergoing major revision in terms of both male and female roles. An increased rate of re-entry to the labour force by women, particularly married women, has occurred during the last 25 years. In line with recent demographic trends — earlier marriage, a falling birth rate and planned families of smaller size — employment of married women in Sweden rose from 11 per cent in 1945 to 53 per cent in 1971 (Eurostat, 1977). In the UK, married women formed 23 per cent of the labour force in 1971 compared to 13.7 per cent in 1951 (Novarra, 1981). However, these figures mask the fact that part-time employment predominates among women. According to the 1966 UK Census, 88 per cent of part-time workers were women (Oakley, 1976, p. 78). A study carried out in Ireland on women clerical workers showed that 51 per cent would prefer to work part-time or marriage (McCarthy, unpublished). In the area of training, more women are participating than ever before. In Ireland, according to figures issued by the Industrial Training Authority (AnCO), the proportion of women in training rose from 10 per cent in 1975 to 30 per cent in 1980, with an increase in female participation in what have been known as traditionally male courses (AnCO, 1981).

Women's desire to play a wider role in society would, on initial reaction, appear to exacerbate the already excessive demand for jobs. However, once work is viewed in its broadest sense, it becomes possible to see a convergence between the paid work performed by men, almost exclusively in a job, and the generally unpaid and unacknowledged work done by many women in the home. An Information Society must recognise that future sex roles will be less differentiated and that this will bring with it benefits for men and women.*

CONCLUSION: THE FUTURE ROLE OF WORK

ALONGSIDE THE DEVELOPMENTS in technological know-how, there has been a fundamental rethinking in political and even in bureaucratic circles about work and its role in society. Although some experts still argue for 'work for all', there is also the realization that employment as now performed in jobs is not satisfying individuals. This is recognized by the EEC Directorate-General for Research, Science and Education which is funding research on attitudes to work at a time when "work crisis, allergy to work (and) the end of work is being discussed" (EEC, 1980). Similarly, the European Centre for the Development of Vocational Training (CEDEFOP) is engaging in studies to explore new paths where continuing training — when integrated into individual or community development projects — can provide an effective and convincing support to the creation of employment and new activities. In the section of the report drafted for CEDEFOP on 'new work' in Italy, there is recognition of the importance of the secondary market of "work in small decentralized units, home work, moonlighting, part-time work, second jobs, and independent craft work" (CEDEFOP, 1980).

The politician Shirley Williams (1981) also recognises that:

Young people in particular are attracted to other styles of work, for instance in co-operatives, communes or self-employed groups, engaged in everything from making rock music to cleaning offices. But the rejection of formal industrial structures is not the same as the rejection of work.

---

*There are some indications from men which suggest a reduction in sex differentiation. Calls have been made for shorter hours in jobs, increased opportunities for part-time work and phased retirement. In Sweden, leave is now available to both parents, upon the birth of a child (Chetwynd and Hartnett, 1979; Jenkins and Sherman, 1979, pp. 164-165; Koller and Reyher, 1980).

She argues for more flexible working arrangements, longer holidays and intermissions in working life.

The move towards a self-service economy as predicted by Gershuny (1978) is already taking place. A shift in work concepts is not only possible, but in fact essential for the future development of society. The re-design of the household is the first step towards achieving this.

We are approaching a post-economic era where functions in the formal economy will be reduced and functions in the informal economy (such as the household) will increase. The time has now come to investigate the possibilities inherent in information technology for a re-design of workplaces, particularly the household. The 'dual economy' approach would aim to improve the quality of both work and leisure and the distinction between them would become less clear cut. The reorganization of the household, coupled with a radical shift in the concept of work, could give rise to a situation advocated by many women (and some men) for more humanitarian work, greater flexibility in the use of time, work-sharing inside and outside the home and an integration of work and leisure.

Already the traditional work roles of men (wage earner/provider) and women (dependent/housewife) are increasingly being questioned. A radical re-thinking about work is required to ensure that both men and women have access to the same opportunities, so that work can consist of a balanced contribution to the three main spheres of activity in adult life — the home, the community and employment.

References

AnCO (1981) *Annual Report and Accounts 1980.* The Industrial Training Authority (AnCO), Dublin.

Burns, S. (1976) *The Household Economy.* Beacon Press, Boston, pp. 176-177.

CEDEFOP (1980) *Role of Training in Setting-up New Economic & Social Activities.* CEDEFOP, Berlin, p. 320.

Chetwynd, J. and Hartnett, O. (1979) *The Sex Role System.* Routledge and Kegan, London, p. 91.

Dahrendorf, R. (1975) *The New Liberty.* Routledge and Kegan, London, pp. 73-76.

EEC (1980) *Science and Technology Policy, FAST: Sub-Programme Work and Employment Research Activities.* Directorate-General for Research, Science and Education, Commission of European Communities, Brussels.

Eurostat (1977) *Social Indicators for the European Community 1969-1975.* Statistical Office of the European Communities, Luxembourg, pp. 104-110.

Gershuny, J. (1978) *After Industrial Society? The Emerging Self-Service Economy.* Science Policy Research Unit, University of Sussex. Macmillan, Surrey, pp. 151-151.

Illich, I. (1978) *The Right to Useful Unemployment and its Professional Enemies.* Marion Boyars, London, pp. 83-84.

Illich, I. (1981) *Shadow Work.* Marion Boyars, London, p. 22.

Jenkins, C. and Sherman, B. (1979) *The Collapse of Work.* Eyre Methuen, London, pp. 40, 140, 164-165.

Koller, M. and Reyher, L. (1980) *Working Time Over Life, Participation in the Labour Market and Economic Growth – The Effects of Changes in Working Time Patterns.* Institute for Labour Market and Employment Research of the Federal Labour Office, Nurnberg, for the Commission of the European Communities, pp. 6-7.

McCarthy, E. *Womens' Roles and Organisational Change: A Study of Interactive Effects.* Unpublished Ph.D. Thesis, Department of Psychology, University College Dublin, 1979.

Moss, P. (1978) *Work and Leisure.* Counterpoint 6, Harrap, London, p. 5.

NBST (1980) *Microelectronics: The Implications for Ireland. First Phase Report.* National Board for Science and Technology, Dublin, pp. 69-70.

Novarra, V. (1981) *Women's Work, Men's Work – The Ambivalence of Equality.* Marion Boyars, London, pp. 91-92.

Oakley, A. (1976) *Housewife: High Value and Low Cost.* Penguin, Hammondsworth, pp. 4, 59, 78.

Pinchbeck, I. (1981) *Women Workers and the Industrial Revolution 1750-1850.* Virago, London.

Schumacher, E. F. (1980) *Good Work.* Abacus, London, pp. 23-65.

Stonier, T. (1979) *Technological Change and the Future.* Paper presented to the British Association for the Advancement of Science, Annual Meeting, September 1979.

Terkel, S. (1975) *Working.* Penguin, Norwich, pp. 12-13.

Walley, P. *Technology and Work in Europe.* Irish Foundation for Human Development, Dublin, 1978 (unpublished), p. 7.

Williams, S. (1981) *Politics is for People.* Penguin, Hammondsworth, p. 77.

CHAPTER 22

The Impact of new ways of life on Information Technology

M. Cristina Bianchi

Management e Informatica Magazine, Milan

Alessandra de Cugis

Architect, Milan

Graziella Falaguasta

Management e Informatica Magazine, Milan

CONSEQUENCES OF A SUPPLY-ORIENTED APPROACH TO INFORMATION TECHNOLOGY

"INFORMATION TECHNOLOGY: IMPACT ON THE WAY OF LIFE", the title of this book, assumes a relationship between technology and life: that technology influences the daily lives of people. The inverse relationship is not considered — how daily life can have an impact on information systems design and, consequently, the future information society.

Servan-Schreiber (1980) believes that informatics is the only alternative resource capable of solving the crisis which industrial society is undergoing at all levels (production, employment, education, health, etc). He quotes examples of the Japanese experience, one of the most advanced countries in terms of microelectronics' applications. The consequences of such an approach are evident in the general plans for 'informatisation' of education and health services, which limit the scope for personal inter-relationships as the authorities provide services through the mediation of computers.

In the authors' opinion, informatics is not only a technological develop-ment, but also a social one; we believe it should be oriented towards producing models of social organization of a progressive nature which depend on the participation of a wide spectrum of society. Our conclusion is that research and development must pay more attention to the demand side of the economy

The report of the FAST* workshop, *The potential of information technologies for job creation,* held in Brussels in March 1981, contains as one of its recommendations: "Research and development (R & D) should be seen in the broad sense. In particular, with a time horizon of 15 years, one should not take the traditional view of considering merely R & D in technology (supply), but also consider R & D related to demand, to the family (daily life, consumption), to the labour force and the mechanisms which relate these factors" (EEC, 1981). Unfortunately, the research on technology during the past 30 years has concentrated exclusively on the supply side (manufacturers) and, only more recently, on the side of public administration.

The debates of the 1950s and '60s and consequently the resultant research on the new technologies, have developed on the unquestioned assumption of the 'positive' nature of technological development, in terms of both economic and social impacts. But in the 1970s, the international context has substantially changed and many of the hypotheses on the effects of the new technologies look rather thin. Since that time, the diffusion of technological innovation through society has reached its highest level, whilst social problems have developed in a reaction to the oversimplified model of relations between 'technology' and 'work organization'. A new quest has thus started for greater protection against pollution and a better quality of life, provided by social services. Among the different factors that have caused the current crisis, the introduction of microprocessors and the consequent employment displacements are the most important ones.

Microelectronics offers great possibilities, both today and for the coming years. On the positive side, there is the potential for substantial improvements in productivity in the production of goods and services. There are also possibilities in the development of new services, designed to improve the efficiency of production and sales, to satisfy the new demands of social consumption and improve the efficiency of public administration (Momigliano, 1980). But the greatest problems concern the contraction of the workforce, modified only by the potential creation of new jobs (connected to the development of the new technological processes), and the changing nature of work organization. New technologies (both in the industrial and services sectors) cause an excessive division of productive processes and procedures. This phenomenon causes a loss of professional skills with jobs being reduced to mere checking procedures. It is possible that in the next few years the demand for more participation in the design of technology will become more widespread. Public policies should not just assure the development of new technologies but should seek to develop sectoral plans which follow social planning and not market criteria. The State should also study the consequences of informatics and microelectronics in society. Such studies should be collective and include the participation of lay people and scientists.

---

*Forecasting and Assessment in the field of Science and Technology (FAST).

TOWARDS THE DEVELOPMENT OF A DEMAND-ORIENTED
APPROACH

NEEDS MUST BE distinguished from wants and desires, which express themselves in the market as demand. We must distinguish between the pursuit of needs through the market system and the pursuit of needs through social policy; free markets take needs as given, whereas social policy must attempt to characterize the needs it is designed to meet. Need is a relative concept. As Harvey (1973) points out: "Needs are not constant for they are categories of human consciousness and as society is transformed, so the consciousness of needs is transformed."

Concepts of need have evolved from being described as "the possible differences between the expertly ascribed descriptions of need and the felt needs of potential recipients of social services" (Plant *et al,* 1980), to the idea that needs may be felt, but not expressed on the grounds that the power structure of society stifles some demands at birth (Bacharach and Baratz, 1970), to the idea that the power structure of society so moulds individuals that they become unaware of their 'real' needs, and consequently express 'false' needs. A further point is that the whole of society expresses false needs, that we mistake desires for needs, since the system as a whole is geared to the induction of desires rather than needs. According to this theory existential needs are neglected and people are encouraged to seek 'passive stimuli' rather than 'active stimuli' and final satisfaction in using and possessing rather than doing and creating (Fromm, 1973). As a result of this, whims and caprices get converted into needs and natural human needs, such as self-expression and self-improvement, become dispensable.

An obvious example is the way in which it is often not thought necessary that paid work should be fulfilling, so that many people accept without question that their true lives begin when they leave the workplace (Plant *et al,* 1980). Another example, discussed by Marcuse (1964), is the way in which certain social forces stimulate the need for physical sex while at the same time discourage the need for love.

It is in this context that we characterize woman as a social subject. In the 1950s and '60s, women expressed a very significant 'demand' for consumer goods (Friedman, 1964). We think that the situation today, partly as a result of processes in daily life, does not allow the need for a different 'living environment' to be expressed as a 'demand'. Women have already expressed the need for a different method of providing for physical and psychological well-being. This hypothesis is summarised in Figure 1.

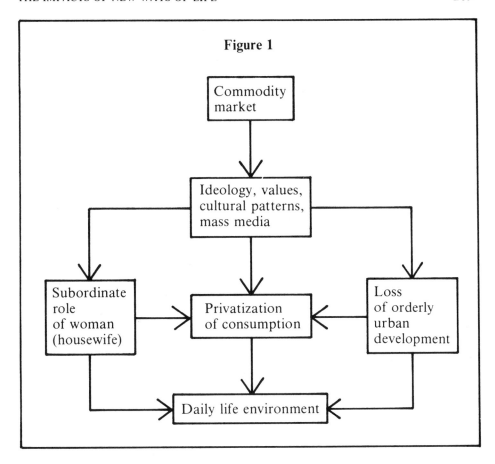

Figure 1

THE CASE FOR A DIFFERENT FORM OF URBAN SETTLEMENT

POWER (1966) points out that: "Women's condition has often been considered a test by which the civilization of a country or of an epoch can be evaluated. It is a difficult test to apply because of the difficulty of describing what has been the condition of women in different periods. Because the condition of women is one thing in theory, another in legislation and yet another in daily life." The daily life conditions of a period can only be discussed by attempting to generalize from different national situations. We will attempt this briefly, by describing the general subdivision of the world into poor and rich countries, western democracies and socialist countries, etc. The problems arising in such an attempt are those which arise in attempting any comparative work. Our hypothesis is that there are greater similarities in women's daily-life experiences than there are in most other fields of cross-national comparison. It is interesting in this respect to read *I want to go back home* by Christiane Collange (1979) and *A week as any other* by Natalija Baranskaja (1977).

In this sense, we can compare women's daily-life experiences in Western Europe more easily than we can, for example, compare planning experiences, as one can argue for a long time over what planning is, whereas most women would readily recognize the nature of the problems facing women in other countries, even those who live in an apparently completely different urban context. In Western civilization, there would be a peculiar linkage existing between the current role of women as prime consumers and their specific experience as the final recipients of the consequences of a consumer-oriented society, particularly as expressed in its urban form (De Cugis, 1981). The absence of planned development in urban settlements, which becomes apparent in the process of transformation of towns into cities, reflects the growing contradiction between the essentially social character of the emerging new mode of production and the individualistic nature of bourgeois society.

This process becomes more apparent in the development of a capitalistic economy and the expansion of production and consumption towards mass production and mass consumption — the development of the commodity market (Salzano, 1969). If 'consumerism' is an essential element in determining urban forms, then we must investigate the specific role which women play in it. We are concerned here with a process that can be subdivided into two: one by which women have become housewives — performing unpaid housework and having a subordinate role, being excluded as far as possible from wage labour in the economic interest of capitalistic-bourgeois society (Oakley, 1974); the other by which the environment of daily life (as opposed to working environment) becomes a product of the historical contradiction between social production and bourgeois privatization in the making of the modern city (Salzano, 1969).

In this hypothesis, women's liberation becomes a necessary condition for urban planning to be able to produce an orderly human settlement; this is because women's liberation would have to coincide with a general transformation of the commodity market into a system of social consumption. This process can only occur as a result of an alternative 'cultural project' in the direction of social consumption, based on a deeper understanding of human needs that cannot come about in a mechanical evolution, as Alvin Toffler would seem to suggest when he states: "The dawn of this new civilization is the single most explosive fact of our lifetimes . . ." (Toffler, 1980). What therefore is needed is the full development of a demand-oriented approach in the conscious planning of a possible living environment, as opposed to the unplanned consequences of the present supply-oriented approach. Such a project would profoundly change the ideology, values and cultural politics which are transmitted by the mass media and produced by a supply-oriented commodity market.

THE CASE FOR A DIFFERENT QUALITY OF PHYSICAL AND PSYCHOLOGICAL WELFARE

The Self-Help Movement in Italy

According to Servan-Schreiber (1980), new technologies could help form a national integrated network for health assistance, whose main starting points should be:

(1) the wide use of informatics in hospital analysis equipment that would provide for quick diagnosis;

(2) use of long-distance information control networks to provide services for those areas having limited medical services;

(3) emergency treatment facilities through an alarm system covering the whole country; and

(4) quick intervention to assist old people.

Foucoult (1969) states that as the passage from popular medicine to an official health system, using new techniques and practices in the 18th century, did not modify the imbalance between people's individual welfare needs (demands for better services) and the health system (increasing number of services), it does not now look likely that the new microelectronics and informatics technology will automatically solve this problem. We fear that the use of new technologies could once again reinforce the power of medical professionals, who generally exert great authority over patients and do not pay sufficient attention to their real needs.

We think that discussion on the possibilities of the application of new technologies must not be centred solely on the technological aspects, but must take into consideration people's demands for physical and psychological well-being (Illich, 1981). As an example, the women's health movement in Italy, as well as in many other countries, concentrates its attention on the subjectiveness of need and on the quality of the service provided (Illich, 1977). Today, women's lives are deeply marked by the presence of professionals (obstetricians, gynaecologists, paeditricians, etc) because their reproductive function has been heavily medicalized.

The rise of the women's health movement in Italy goes back to 1970-73 but, while at the beginning, its strategies were more specifically geared to alter, improve or drastically change routine obstetrical and gynaecological care for women, these strategies have recently been viewed as a model of how change might be effected in other fields involving routine medical care or treatment. By examining this movement, we found out how clients as a group can reshape institutions to meet their needs (Boston Women's Health Book Collective, 1979). Discussions inside the movement were carried out by small groups all over the country and focused on sexuality, contraception, abortion, gynaecological care and many other women's health concerns which troubled them but were not understood by male doctors. Women perceived that, when attempting to make their own decisions about standard medical procedures, they face deeply ingrained attitudes as to what women are like and what is 'appropriate' for them to do or say. When women seek medical care, physicians often fail or openly refuse to give them enough information to discuss medical procedures or to make decisions in a reasoned, competent manner (Mitchell, 1977).

The 'invention' of self-help gynaecology more than any other event transformed the movement into a separate social entity. Self-examination and self-help gynaecology have become revolutionary concepts, for they provided women with the opportunity of reclaiming that part of themselves which was controlled by male professionals. But self-help is not simply self-care, which focuses solely on the individual. Women's self-help groups differ from self-care groups because one of the problems women share is their relationship to a sexist society and the health care system, rather than a personal disability or behaviour problem (The Boston Women's Health Book Collective, 1979). We know that the tendency of medicine has always been to medicalize women's life through different sophisticated techniques which transform natural events like childbirth into a technological experience — ever-more alienating and akin to suffering from a weird disease. But in spite of these 'modern' practices, the infant mortality rate in Italy was 17.6 per cent in 1977 and still among the highest in the developed countries (Sonnino, 1979). Some practices, like foetal monitoring, create more problems then they solve when used in normal deliveries; they inhibit spontaneous birth and, in so doing, increase the need for all types of medical-surgical intervention, to the detriment of both mother and child. New methods conceived by male physicians, like Leboyer and Lamaze, try to create artificial rituals to substitute the natural ones women could create if they were not denied the opportunity. In fact, no 'method' is needed. Human needs may be to some extent universal but the way they are responded to is as varied as the people who respond. Women realized that their attempts to gain equal rights in education, politics, employment and the family would not be successful unless they were able to control their fertility.

As a matter of fact, birth control research performed by the medical establishment has produced no significant improvement in safe, accessible birth control (although many poor women, particularly in the Third World, have served as unfortunate guinea pigs in the 'search' for better methods) (Reed, 1973). Although many millions of women take oral contraceptives and use intrauterine devices, no one knows how safe these methods are; the great need for abortion can only diminish when birth control is improved and universally available. Until then, women will have abortions when contraceptives fail. In Italy self-help practices have been useful to the women's health movement in understanding how the social service called *consultorio* (established in 1975) should be; unfortunately even now *consultori* have not been organized as women have requested (and in some regions they still do not even exist).

Another aspect of women's analysis about physical and psychological well-being concerns the presence of women in the workplace. The two main concepts for a new science are 'no delegation' to doctors and 'recovery of subjectivity', which stresses the idea of prevention, not only as lack of disease but also as promotion and protection of health (Maccacaro, 1979). In this sense, the hypothesis that the application of new technologies to some routine medical care practices (i.e. laboratory analysis and diagnosis obtained through computers) really represents an important form of prevention, seems to us too restrictive. What the women's health movement realized about health risks in workplaces was the influence of external factors on their daily lives. These factors are represented not only by the lack of social services, but also by psychological problems (i.e. the wish or the fear of maternity, the fear of getting old, the control of emotions, etc.) (Bocchio, 1977). In this sense, the demands put forward by women are much wider than the demands of any other social strata. They centre on real physical and psychological well-being and thus create general struggles in the workplace, in the urban context and in the family. The question then is asked again: Will the new technologies be able to meet these fundamental needs and satisfy these demands?

References

Bacharach, P. and Baratz, M. (1970) *Power and poverty.* Oxford University Press.
Baranskaja, N. (1977) *Una settimana come un'altra.* Editori Riuniti, Rome. (Orig. title *Nedelja kak nedelja*).
Bocchio, F. (1977) *Donne, salute e lavoro: appunti.* Medicina Democratica, No. 5, March.
Boston Women's Health Book Collective (1979) *Noi e il nostro corpo.* 16th Edizione, Feltrinelli, Milano. (Orig. title *Our bodies ourselves*).
Collange, C. (1979) *Voglio tornare a casa – il riposo della guerriera dopo dieci anni di battaglie femministe.* Bompiani, Milan. (Orig. title *Je veux rentrer à la maison*).
De Cugis, A. (1981) *Città: dal consumo al progetto sociale.* Casabella, No. 467, March.
EEC (1981) *FAST B-2, Ten General recommendations.* Report of Workshop held in Brussels, 3-4 March 1981. Commission of the European Communities, Brussels.
Foucoult, M. (1969) *La nascita della clinica.* Einaudi, Torino.
Friedman, B. (1964) *La mistica della femminilità.* Edizioni La Comunità, Milan. (Orig. title *The feminine mystique*).
Fromm. E. (1973) *The anatomy of human destructiveness.* Basic Books, New York.
Fromm, E. (1981) *Avere o essere?* 20th Edition, Mondadori, Milano.
Gasbarri, G. (1981) *Salute e sanità.* Uomini Computer Come, No. 51.
Harvey, D. (1973) *Social justice and the city.* Edward Arnolds.
Illich, I. (1977) *Nemesi medica – l'espropriazione della salute.* 3rd Edizione, Mondadori, Milano.
Illich, I. (1981) *Per una storia dei bisogni.* Mondadori, Milano.
Maccacaro, G. A. (1979) *Per una medicina da rinnovare.* Medicina e potere, Feltrinelli, Milano.
Marcuse, H. (1964) *One dimensional man.* Routledge & Keagan, London.
Mitchell, J. (1977) *Women's estate.* 5th edition, Penguin Books, Manchester.
Momigliano, F. (1980) *Una nuova tecnologia per una nuova politica, intervento al convegno "Liberare il lavoro o liberarsi dal lavoro?"* Held in Milan, 31 Oct-1 Nov, 1980.
Oakley, A. (1974) *Housewife.* Penguin Books, London.
Plant, R., Lesser, H. and Taylor Gooby P. (1980) *Political philosophy and social welfare.* Routledge and Keagan, London, Boston.
Power, E. (1966) *Donne del medioevo.* Einaudi, Torino.
Reed, E. (1973) *Sesso contro sesso o classe contro classe?* Savelli, Rome.
Rockart, J. F. (1979) *Ha un segreto la bravura del capo: sa proprio tutto.* Harvard Espansione.
Salazno, E. (1969) *Urbanistica e società opulenta.* Laterza, Bari.
Servan-Schreiber, J. J. (1980) *La sfida mondiale.* Mondadori, Milano. (Orig. title *Le défi mondial*).
Sonnino, E. (1979) *Aspetti e problemi di demografia sociale e di politica della popolazione in Italia.* Università degli Studi, Rome.
Toffler, A. (1980) *The Third Wave.* William Morrow, New York.

PART V

The Changing Media – New Forms and Uses

The final section of this book includes both general analytical discussions on the nature of media technologies, together with case studies on particular aspects of the media industry.

Michele Mattelart takes a critical view of the passive nature of media usage, contrasting this with the descriptions of new products pushed by their promoters. In a similar vein, Nicholas Garnham analyses the tight commercial control exercised by a few multinational companies over the powerful media industry.

Chantal de Gournay provides a sharp critique of the concept of 'leisure', while developing an integrated evaluation of the impact of information technology across a variety of daily activities. Jon Fitzgerald takes the specific case of education, arguing that the new technologies are unlikely to alter dramatically the nature and structure of education.

Research results on the changing pattern of media usage in the Netherlands, based on a time-budget study, are presented by Wim Knulst. Jean-Claude Baboulin, Philippe Mallein and Jean-Pierre Gaudin outline the results of a recent study of video-cassette recorders (VCRs) in France. They suggest a profile, both for the users of VCRs and their patterns of usage.

Finally, Irving L. Horowitz and Mary E. Curtis examine the publishing trade in some detail and the likely impacts that information technology will have on this industry.

CHAPTER 23

Provocative Questions about Communications Today

Michele Mattelart

University of Paris VIII

MASS COMMUNICATION AS AN ELEMENT OF
THE POLITICAL SYSTEM

THE TERMS we are accustomed to use in conveying our reflections and analysis of the phenomena of media and mass-cultural production suffer from a certain ambiguity. Nevertheless, in one way or another, at one time or another, we have to use them in order to communicate the results of studies which call them into question and to establish common reference points with the person addressed.

Ambiguity begins with the very term 'means of mass communication'. This is not really a means of communication but a means of distribution. Brecht (1976), the first critic of radio, understood this well in 1932 when he claimed another social use for this technology:

> *Radio has only one aspect when it should have two. It is a simple distribution apparatus, it just transmits. To speak positively now (that is, to trace what's positive in radio), here is a proposition intended to transform its function; it must be changed from a distribution apparatus into a communications apparatus. Radio could be the most marvellous means of communication you could imagine for public life, a huge system of pipelines, or rather it could be, if it could not just broadcast but receive, not only make the listener hear but make him speak, not to isolate him but to put him in contact with others. So, radio must abandon its activity of provider and organize supply by the listeners themselves.*

Need one add that in our liberal society, the restriction of concepts and practices to the terrain of consumption, and the silence reigning over the order of production, are perfectly compatible with the idea that these political systems are based on the democratic participation of citizens.

References to an undifferentiated 'mass' are equally ambiguous. Moreover, there exists 'low range' and 'high range' series, in other words, so called popular products and quality products. This is a concept borrowed from the Anglo-American vocabulary, more and more used in 'marketing' circles and of course, immediately denied by media planners. The ambiguity continues with the expression 'mass culture', which empiricist manuals define in tautological fashion: "Culture which is born with mass communication which makes possible the almost simultaneous delivery of identical messages, through rapid reproduction and distribution mechanisms, to a relatively huge and undifferentiated number of people in anonymous relations."

To have culture requires accumulation and memory. But since Adorno and the Frankfurt school, everything tends to define this mass culture as a vast enterprise of memory deprivation. This characteristic of industrialized culture (noted by this school of philosophy since the end of the 1940s) has grown considerably. Is it possible today to analyse the radical mutations of a mode of production of knowledge, of know-how, but also of non-knowledge, leading us back to the term culture, indicative of continuity, heritage or surpassing of heritage?

This risks, among other things, leaving expressions like 'mass communication' and 'mass culture' in the shadows; it is politics which describes this particular mode of production of commodities. As an expression of a relation between broadcaster and receiver, producer and consumer, this mass culture is, in effect, the prolonging of a concrete system of liberal democracy. As an essential element in the production of opinion and in the manufacture of concensus, it reflects the necessity for the bourgeoisie to open up to other classes and thus follows the ups and downs of its project for social co-option. It is also a response to pressures exercised by the other classes.

In the context of the confrontations and alliances inside and outside the nation-state, the evolution of communication technologies becomes an evolution in the relations between social groups and social classes — a contemporary question to an epoch whose liberal societies worry at the 'excesses' of democracy.

It appears to be generally conceded that structural crises put the necessity to re-organize the production of material goods at the top of the agenda, while at the same time revealing the difficulties encountered in this re-organization, especially when one considers the number of research projects which try to focus on redeployment operations in the economy in general. That these same crises would also put the global restructuring of the mode of production of symbolic goods or cultural commodities onto the agenda is less obvious.

A NEW PHILOSOPHY OF PROGRESS

PUBLICITY SPEECHES on new communications technology are as ecstatic as ever. It is not an exaggeration to say that communications philosophy is in the process of assuming the role played in the nineteenth century by the philosophy of progress, through the voice of political power and electronic companies, to judge by the accents of these new social prophets. The extension of communication technology is the touchstone by which one measures the degree of evolution and harmony in a society. The satellite, cable TV and computer are installing the global village, electronic democracy, the return of the Greek forum.

Since their first appearance and social application, networks based on technical supports interlock a vast human community with consequences for the conquest of isolation, time and parochialism. They have invariably appeared as being the basis of a new type of exchange between men, of a new democracy — indeed, of a social revolution. In 1852, the book *The Silent Revolution* envisaged the social harmony of humanity on the basis of a "perfect network of electric threads". Count Birkenhead, in his futuristic work, *The World in 2030,* proposed even in 1930 the installation of an "Industrial Arcade" and the "revival of that form of democracy which flourished in the cities of Ancient Greece" (Carey and Quirk, 1973).

The magazine *All Electronic* (January 1979) stated, on the occasion of the VIth Audiovisual Communications Exhibition:

> *'Information' (the almost magic word) is immediately thrown up when one asks oneself what could constitute one of the major changes of Westernised society . . . what is fundamental is not so much that we are in the information century, but rather that we are getting there at the moment when what was élite is becoming popularised . . . Audiovisuals are in this regard special means, because they can impose themselves by the magic of the TV set into every home and every mind. Television, like modern televisual techniques, will tend to make the television receiver an active link (even interactive), rather than a passive mirror. We can certainly consider ourselves on the threshold of an important and beneficial evolution or revolution, when the master image will be the servant of all men.*

When one visits the Audiovisual Communications Exhibition, however, one gets a quite different impression — that of technological discoveries at the service of what exists and especially at the service of consolidating what exists. The application of these technologies seems certainly on the crest of a wave, in regard to capital flow, surveillance systems, management operations and authority transmitting operations. One can see during such visits that these social uses are certainly bound to greatly benefit the filling of orders, with rapidity and efficiency.

These viable markets play a decisive role in determining the types of application likely to be developed. As Blake and Perlmutter (1977) remark:

> *There will inevitably be more clients ready to pay in business circles than in*

other sectors of the population. Furthermore, these users (business users) are encouraged . . . The time spent on the collection of information is beginning to get concentrated on the paying clients and the training of the team is oriented to satisfying the models of these users.

One knows the difficulties experienced by various authorities with responsibility for installing telex networks in European countries. Witness the proposals put forward on various occasions during the discussions leading to the Belgian videotext experience:

In the first phase, only 'neutral' information (administrative, legal, financial and transport information, for example) will be used, which poses no political or sociological problems.

The orientations followed in these first experiences in telex in Europe, based on existing uses, run obviously counter to another demand, noted by the same director of audiovisual services at the Ministry for the French Community:

The target public, for me, should be the public who are disadvantaged at the level of information. We know that in the present social and cultural system, a part of the population is under-informed and incapable of decoding information, of research and, as a consequence, incapable of utilising it by turning it into action. If the new system of telecommunications is, in effect, financed by the public authorities, it should attempt to redress this situation, even if the pubic thus aimed at are precisely the least solvent! And if such is the choice, this implies that one should insert information on the development of unemployment in the various sectors and detailed information on social welfare into data banks. People will soon be able to obtain information at the touch of a keyboard. Will they be better informed, qualitatively, when technological development allows this? This way of looking at things, admittedly, I haven't seen anywhere and that's my worry. That's what's at stake for the next two years, during which we will be attempting to define for ourselves the best way of experimenting with telematics. (Reflections of Henri Ingberg in Mattelart and Piemme, 1980).

Can the notion of public service be expanded generously enough to embrace such propositions? The crisis suffered by this expression, so often evoked and manipulated — is it not visible here also, when commercial logic is introduced into of the concept of public service?

As for the interactivity which new technologies will allow — will it not be too often restricted to immediate commercial transactions: mail-order purchase, booking seats etc. Two authors of a report on the Velizy videotext experience in France, which was for associations, commented:

The information producers, basically administrations and companies with big resources (SNCF La Redoute), use videotext to present a catalogue of their services. The Velizy experience allowed 400 associations to use the network. Looking closely at this, what was supposed to counterbalance the omnipotent commercial companies ended up merely reproducing their procedures. Some associations used it, like tennis clubs. They were satisfied to use it to reserve tennis courts! (Le Monde, 1981).

The same question turns up at every level. Confronted with technological innovation (observe, for example, the appearance of video-recorders, electronic games, video-discs and home computers on the public sales circuit), we are bound to note a nothingness, a chasm, a creative void, a lack of content, form, values, of new uses. "What shall we put," they ask "into these machines which call for more and more input?" Thus, alliances are born, Philips or IBM with MCA, the giant American cinema company, which makes its film library (containing more than ten thousand films) available to these video-discs. Thus are born also incitements to get the maximum profit out of the video-recorder, to tape programmes from the TV.

Just read the advertising of one European producer:

TV viewers – free yourselves! Has a TV viewer the right to be anything more than a TV viewer. Of course he has! But how? Thanks to the ideal compliment to your television: the new Philips (VCR) NI 700 long-playing video-cassette recorder. You watch a programme and – at the same time – you record another, any other. You want to see an important match. But the wife absolutely insists on watching the latest episode of her favourite soap opera! A problem no longer! You watch the programme you want. And during that time, your Philips VCR will record another, any other, which you can see later – and re-see when you feel like it.

To comment on this advertising patter, one should first underline the notion of individual freedom which is subsumed into the possibility of better managing one's viewing hours of the same programme; this new flexibility which allows you to satisfy divergent tastes; and especially, the discrimination between roles and status (soap opera/femininity; sport/masculinity), each sex in front of the little screen being promised that they can stay locked in prescribed values by an order which is more than ever the image of traditional order, confronted with attempts at technological change! It is equally significant that the home is constantly validated as the unit destined to be the almost exclusive priority investment area for a so-called social revolution.

With every crisis of the models of expansion of capital, the authorities have asked technology to supply an additional burst of life, which as often as not is transformed into an additional spurt of normality.

The social uses of the existing media (compatible with a specific concept of social relations and daily life) has, in fact, swept aside other possible uses, thereby strangling the revolutionary promise inherent in the mobility of the productive forces. To imagine other social uses is equivalent to calling into question the relations of production or the particular conditions assumed by the development of science and technology in our societies.

CONTRADICTIONS AND TENSIONS IN
THE COMMUNICATIONS SYSTEM

THE STRUCTURAL CRISIS of the 1970s precipitated a re-definition of industrial/ cultural/technological relations of communications in the industrial field. At the end of the '60s one could observe a definite interest by big monopolies in diversifying into the area of cultural production. One could see numerous instances of the drawing together of hardware (heavy-equipment manufacture) and software (programmes), as well as multi-media alliances. This phenomena of concentration and diversification worked under the pressure of many factors, among which was the necessity for the aerospace and electronics industries to throw themselves into the civil field of electronic warfare technologies, after the closure of the space race and the end of the South-East Asian conflicts. In a perspective of civil reconversion, the culture and educational markets seemed promising. It became stagnant however, despite the promises, throughout the whole decade of the '70s. Today, CBS is a huge conglomerate, uniting electronic toys, educational products, cable TV networks, one of the most important Hertzian TV stations, records, publishing, etc; one of its managers noted in 1980:

> In the sixties, many companies saw the arrival of the 'knowledge explosion' but got their fingers burnt. Promises came before technology; now technology is there and it is important that we don't miss the boat" (Business Week, May 1980).

This 'knowledge explosion' has adopted the expansionist dynamism of the big transnational conglomerates and is broadcasting under the symbol of internationalism. It runs the risk of aggravating the expression of true and conflicting differences, based on regional cultural identities. It also runs the risk of concealing new sources of inequality and new forms of confrontation, based on the mastery of information, thereby aggravating the chasm between small and big industrial nations, small and big underdeveloped countries, a developed world and a third world.

The 'explosion of knowledge' will give preference to channels which can only be defined within the constraints implied in the crisis of the Welfare State. This crisis includes a re-definition of the relation between the State and its citizens and, at the same time, a re-definition of the notion of public service, which has presided over the installation of the majority of huge, audiovisual information systems in Europe.

Through the crisis of the Welfare State has emerged the tensions between the public and private sectors. But it is also the notion of pluralism, on which these public services and monopolies are built, which explodes under the pressure of sectors and social movements not represented in this notion of pluralism, which over-identifies with established and recognised apparati and organizations. Such is the case with the women's movement. Today a multiplicity of interests which make up civilian society can be seen trying to burst in on a system of information which has too often mistrusted them:

regional movements, anti-nuclear movements, consumer movements, cultural movements and many more, according to the specifics of each country and its social groups.

The 1980s are, in fact, marked by a movement of refusal to accept the standardizing effects of all forms of central power and representation which it legitimises. Tension (local/central; local/national; and a variant of the latter, national/ multinational) is translated into a struggle to win back one's identity and expression — the little facing the big, the micro facing the macro.

At the level of communication technologies, this tension translates into the greater esteem attributed to what is 'decentralized' and 'local'. Decentraliz-ation is only one word but it covers very different projects. It can mean an attempt at adjustment of power, which tries to legitimise from the periphery rather than from the centre, from the micro and not from the macro. It can mean, and does mean, the search for new forms of expression and interaction, or the search for new democratic forms. It can, and does mean, at the level of communication technologies, an active user, no longer confined to the consumer function. This struggle for decentralization, intended and experienced as a supplement to democracy, is a good occasion to remind ourselves: "One does not ask for freedom, one wins it."*

References

Blake, F. M. and Perlmutter, E. L. (1977) *The rush to user fees: Alternative proposals.* Library Journal, Vol. 102, No. 17.

Brecht, Bertolt (1976) *Theorie de la radio.* L'Arche, Paris.

Carey, J. and Quirk, J. (1973) The History of the Future. In *Communications Technology and Social Policy: Understanding the new 'cultural revolution',* G. Gerbner, L. P. Gross and W. H. Melody (Eds.), John Wiley, New York.

Le Monde, 30 September 1981.

Mattelart, A. and Piemme, J. M. (1980) *Television: Stakes without Borders.* Presses Universitaires de Grenoble.

*This phrase, incidentally, serves as the preface to the first report of the Mitterand Government in France on Audiovisuals (Meinto report).

CHAPTER 24

The Information Society is also a Class Society

Nicholas Garnham

School of Communication, Polytechnic of Central London

PERHAPS, in a brief discussion such as this, the best way to assess the likely impact of the new information technologies on our cultural life is to concentrate upon the medium that now massively occupies the centre of the cultural field — television. TV-viewing occupies between 30 and 50 per cent of most people's available free time and is their major source of information and entertainment. In addition, it also provides 'their main point of entry into other sections of the entertainment industry and the arts' (Murdock, 1981). Moreover, precisely because TV occupies this strategically central position in cultural consumption, it is the main focus of efforts to introduce information technology to the domestic consumer. On the hardware side, the electronics industry, faced by saturation of the TV-set market, is attempting to construct new markets around the TV-set, by turning it into a multi-purpose video-display unit (VDU), the core of a home-entertainment and information-processing centre, by offering a range of plug-in peripherals, such as video-cassette recorders, video-disc players, teletext and viewdata decoders, etc. On the software side, the introduction of information technology essentially involves attempts by a range of cultural producers (by means of satellite, cable, cassette and disc) to find new means of delivering audio-visual products for viewing on the domestic TV set which circumvent the control of that supply at present exercised by the broadcasting institutions. Furthermore, one of the effects of information technology in the cultural sphere is the shift across the whole range of cultural production from older media, such as printed paper and celluloid, into a common electronic mode.

The advocates of the benefits of information technology in the cultural sphere argue that it will usher in a new era of cultural freedom, diversity and abundance. Smith (1980) claims that it will mark 'a great shift from producer to consumer sovereignty in Western European societies', creating 'an Alexandria without walls'. Hyman (1980) claims that cultural freedom will be secured 'by making information in every form cheaply and conveniently available'. In particular, the argument is couched in terms of deregulation, the need and opportunity to sweep away what they present as the stuffy, bureaucratic, confining, censored, old world of public-service broadcasting in favour of the exciting new world of market provision. As another advocate put it:

> Once the technical pretext for electronic publishing has gone, the whole inverted pyramid of regulation and control must be dismantled. Those who care passionately for freedom in communication and publishing, whether print, electronic or simply oral, need now to gird themselves for a prolonged struggle against old habits and vested interests to ensure that new freedoms, which new technology will make possible, are translated into real freedoms for both producers and consumers.*

The purpose of this discussion is to challenge this view and to show that we are here in the presence of ideology in its pure, classical form; that is to say, a social analysis that not only misrepresents its object of analysis by focusing on its surface rather than its underlying structure and by denying its real history, but also misrepresents it in such a way as to favour the interests of the dominant class. In this case, the trick is played by concentrating upon the technical potentialities, rather than upon the social relations that will determine the form in which those potentialities are realized and by denying history by exaggerating the novelty of the process in question.

I would not want to deny either the manifold failings of public-service broadcasting or the marginal increase in individual freedom offered by a video-recorder, in terms of the ability to watch the offerings of the broadcaster at times of your own choosing, rather than those of the scheduler. But what we are in fact being offered is not a more socially responsive, politically accountable, diverse mode of cultural interchange in the electronic sphere but, on the contrary, the expansion of price and profit, of commodity exchange, as the dominating mode of organization in yet another area of cultural production and consumption as though this were a new phenomenon. We are witnessing merely the latest phase in a process integral to the capitalist mode of production. This is a process referred to variously as 'the industrialization of culture' (Briggs, 1960) and 'the colonization of leisure' (Sahin and Robinson, 1981), by which 'massive market interests have come to dominate an area of life which, until recently, was dominated by individuals themselves' (Briggs, 1960). This is a process that goes back at least 150 years in Britain, part of a larger process by which commodity exchange invades wider and wider areas of social life as the private sphere expands at the expense of the public sphere, driven by capital's restless and relentless search for new areas in which to realize surplus value, thus introducing the 'dull compulsion of economic relations' to more and more spheres of social life.

Therefore, in assessing the likely impact of information technology on our cultural life, we are not entering entirely uncharted waters. We have a lot of accumulated historical experience to work with — the dynamics of the cultural

*Speech by Peter Jay at the Edinburgh TV Festival, reported in *The Times*, 27 August 1981.

sphere in a capitalist mode of production. When we hear the Peter Jays of this world arguing that the new technology gives us the opportunity to fight for 'freedom of the press' in the field of electronic publishing, we need to remember that the actual history of the press is not one of developing freedoms but, on the contrary, that the growth of an advertising-financed, commercial mass-circulation press destroyed the independent working-class and radical press (as was the intention), steadily reduced the range of available views and information, incorporated nascent oppositional movements, helped to de-politicize our society and placed control of the channels of information in fewer and fewer hands (Curran, 1977). We need to remember that we live in a class society and that not all producers and consumers are equal. In deciding the characteristics of the future 'information society', the preferences of the members of the board of AT&T and IBM, and their corporate clients, weigh somewhat heavier than those of any member of the European working-class. Indeed, it may at present be regrettably true that their preferences weigh more heavily than even those of the whole of the organized European working-class.

Let us look in more detail at the structural dynamics of the cultural sphere within the capitalist mode of production. The first point to stress, against the grain of the ideological discourse that dominates cultural analysis (a discourse of individual taste, creativity, etc. inherited from a pre-industrial era), is that cultural relations are in general dominated by normal capitalist market mechanisms and most culture is produced and distributed by what have come to be known as cultural industries, under conditions similar to those reigning in other economic sectors.

However, the sphere of cultural commodity production does have certain specific tendential characteristics that need stressing (Garnham, 1977 and 1979; Murdock and Golding, 1977). Firstly, because there is a sense in which each cultural product is a prototype, the cost of production (known in the newspaper industry as first copy costs) tends to be high relative to the cost of reproduction and distribution. This means that there are exceptionally high returns to economies of scale leading to a constant push towards audience maximization, since the marginal profit from each additional consumer is high relative to marginal cost.

Secondly, because demand is highly elastic (in the sense that for any one cultural commodity, it is impossible to predict whether it will be a hit or a flop), profitability depends upon being able to offer a repertoire, so that the very high profits from the few hits can subsidize the need to write-off most of the rest of the product. In the record industry, for instance, only one single in 9 and one LP in 16 makes a profit; in a typical company, 3 per cent of the output can account for 50 per cent of the turnover (Huet et al, 1978). Similarly in the film industry, in a typical year the top 10 films out of 119 in the US market took 22 per cent of box-office receipts and the top 40, 80 per cent (Garnham, 1980). This has two consequences: (a) that the risks of cultural production can only be lowered to an acceptable level by a high and sustained level of investment in a whole production programme. The small independent producer in general and in the long run has no chance; and (b) reinforcing the high returns to economies of scale, it makes control of distribution rather than of production *per se* crucial. As the history of the US film industry amply demonstrates, a small group of companies has been able to retain tight control over both the US and world markets for over half a century without retaining control of exhibition and while actually reducing their direct involvement in production. Control of distribution, however, enables a wide range of 'independent' productions to be assembled into a programme and then offered to the widest possible range of audiences. Or rather, as the history of broadcasting shows, control of distribution allows the very construction of an audience out of disparate groups and individuals. Indeed, there is a growing tendency in the cultural industries, legitimized by an ideology of creative freedom, for the profit centres founded upon control of distribution to maintain a network of dependent and exploited production satellites, often themselves partially sustained out of public funds through cultural and educational budgets, onto whose shoulders can be shifted the costs and risks of research and development.

The result of these tendencies has been to produce culture industries characterized by a high level of oligopolistic control, not only in national markets but across the world market. In the record industry, 5 firms control 67 per cent of the world market; in the film industry, 7 firms control 90 per cent of the US domestic market and 70 per cent of the world market; in Britain, 4 groups control over 80 per cent of daily newspaper circulation. Culture industries are also characterized by a high level of horizontal integration — the development of conglomerates, such as Thorn-EMI in Britain and Warner Communications in the US, with an important market share across a wide range of different media. This enables the principle of the repertoire to operate not just in one media market but across markets, so that a firm can typically offer a package involving film, TV-series, book and record, with merchandizing such that each advertises the other and the risks can be spread.

These characteristics of the international culture industry are further reinforced by the specific structure of the consumer market in which the cultural distributors must compete to realize surplus value and maximize profit. This market is constrained by two factors, availability of time and availability of money. The free time available to the average working person has only marginally increased in recent years. US figures show an increase for men from 34.1 hours per week to 39.3 hours per week between 1965 and 1975, virtually the whole of the extra time being taken up by TV-viewing. Intense competition for this limited time-market has two consequences: (a) a tendency for one media to partially supplant another — the cinema to replace music-hall, TV to replace the cinema, and newspaper circulation declining in the face of TV; and (b) a tendency, as a recent Swedish study has shown (Ivre, 1981), for the cost to the consumer of each unit of consumption time to rise in real terms because each new media service (especially the ones that depend upon domestic investment in the technological delivery system), involves an increased investment which cannot be matched by an increase in consumption time.

At the same time, the discretionary expenditure available for cultural consumption is also strictly limited, having grown in the UK since 1968 from 5 to 6.5 per cent of total consumer expenditure (National Income Expenditure, 1979). If real diversity is to become a reality, it can only be produced by either a concomitant growth in that expenditure or by redistribution of expenditure by fiscal means. Present figures show in particular how, over the last decade, increases in consumer expenditure on electronic hardware, especially TV, has exceeded the increase in available discretionary expenditure, leading to a marked fall in real terms in expenditure on printed matter. Furthermore because, owing to what is known as Baumol's disease, the real costs of cultural production have been rising, markets have had to be expanded to support a given level of production, reinforcing the oligopolistic and internationalizing tendencies in the sphere of production itself.

This is particularly clear in both TV and book publishing. Rising production costs and the intense competition for this narrow consumption market has led to a rapid acceleration in the rate of obsolescence of cultural products. In the film industry, for instance, a high proportion of a film's total box-office receipts are earned in the first few weeks of release, in nine major metropolitan areas during twenty key weeks of the year (Garnham, 1980). It is now estimated that the shelf-life of the average paperback in the United States is five weeks. Barriers to entry to these markets are being continually raised by rising promotion costs. It is now estimated that the promotion of a feature film costs as much as the initial production investment.

The lack of discretionary consumer spending power has also led to a tendency right across the culture field to make up the short-fall from advertising expenditure. While this too is not a source of income that can be expanded endlessly (indeed it may, in the UK, already be reaching its limits as a proportion of GNP), it also has serious distorting effects on cultural provision (Curran, 1981). In particular, it reinforces the class stratification of cultural consumption that is already present in the structure of the market.

The class determination of cultural consumption takes place at two mutually reinforcing levels. It is firstly directly determined materially by the differential availability of both time and money. Members of lower socio-economic groups generally work longer hours in more tiring conditions than those higher up the social scale. In addition, consumption of cultural goods and participation in cultural practices increases in range and amount over virtually the whole spectrum of activities, except TV viewing, as income rises. This is hardly surprising. It is just normally ignored in discussions of cultural policy. The higher level of TV consumption among the poorer sections of the community is attributable to the higher proportion of their total discretionary expenditure tied up in the relatively fixed investment of the TV-set and licence. Once this investment is made, subsequent consumption is virtually free, making them a captive audience. This material hierarchization of cultural participation is matched at a second level by the distribution of what Bourdieu (1979) has called 'dispositions and competences' (Garnham and Williams, 1980). Dispositions refer to the internalized cultural norms acquired during childhood, within the family and the immediate social environment, which relate given modes of cultural participation to a given lifestyle and class position, such that those modes, which are objectively unavailable for material reasons or because of lack of competences, are de-legitimized and rejected as 'not for the likes of us'. Competences refer to the skills necessarily required for the consumptions of certain forms of cultural product. For instance, literacy for reading, but also and more subtly, a range of interpretive and social codes for painting, music, live theatre, art galleries and so on. Such competences are acquired both inside the family and at school and thus reflect and pass on the differential endowment of cultural resources in families of different social classes and the class-based differential participation rates in education. The growing Information Gap in Western societies, between the information-rich and the information-poor, points to the existence and importance of these dispositions and competences.

Thus, not only does the nature of cultural production and distribution under capitalist market conditions tend to increasingly limit diversity of provision and to place control of that provision in fewer and fewer hands and further and further from the point of consumption, but the structure of the market also distributes what choice there is available in a highly unequal way. There is a tendency, in fact, towards a two-tier market structure in which choice, being increasingly expensive, is offered to upper-income groups, while an increasingly impoverished, homogenized service is offered to the rest. This tendency is reinforced by advertising, which differentially subsidises media going to the rich and the poor (Curran, 1981). We can see this tendency clearly in the British press, where middle-market newspapers, such as the *Express* and the *Mail,* are slowly being squeezed out.

Many will at this point want to argue that the current experience with cable TV in the United States contradicts this view. Not at all. The significance of the cable TV explosion in the US is that the linkage of cable systems by satellite has made it possible to bring together scattered pockets of upper-income cultural consumers, who were not viable as separate local markets, into one national market which it is now economic to service. But even then, Home Box Office which controls about 40 per cent of the Pay TV market is only delivering feature films to a market that, for complex social reasons, had been lost to the cinema. It in no way threatens the basic structure of the international film industry. After all, for 1982 total US film-industry revenue from cable and video is estimated at 500 million dollars. So far as the all-news network is concerned, two points need to be noted: (a) that the US has no truly national newspapers with which such a service would compete; and (b) that even if there is a place for such a service in the US market, economically viable with a 5 to 10 per cent audience share, there is almost certainly not room in the long term for more than one. Thus, there will be a monopoly of·news on cable and only a small addition to the diversity of provision across the nation as a whole. So far as the recently announced cultural channels are concerned, it has been concluded (Winston, 1981) that most of them are unlikely to last and have been launched by the networks to pre-empt satellite channel space while they fight anti-trust prohibitions on entering the entertainment cable-TV market. The real danger of the US situation is that the history of the US film industry will repeat itself and the US cable industry will use its large home market as a base for the invasion of the European market, now that the technology is there to create the networks.

Thus, the impact of information technology will not, as its advocates claim, lead to consumer sovereignty and greater choice. Such a claim can only be made if one looks at the technical determinants in the audio-visual field rather than the economic ones. If information technology is introduced (as its advocates propose and as seems likely) as part of a move of broadcasting out of the public sphere and into the private sphere, then it will have different effects at different class levels, reinforcing existing tendencies to create a two-tier market with increased choice for the rich and decreased choice for the poor, no longer protected by the need for licenced financed broadcasting to make a range of provision available for all and thus, exposed to the full force of the international market. If one looks at British television over the last 20 years, it has made available a far wider range of cultural experience to a far wider range of people than the cinema or the popular press during the same period. I believe the same is true to a greater or lesser extent throughout Europe. For all its failings, European public-service broadcasting has represented a real step forward in the attempt to create a common culture. The introduction of information technology is likely to represent a massive retreat. Recently announced plans for the BBC to offer a specialized Pay TV service are indications of this.

Similar tendencies can be illustrated in the sphere of information as well as entertainment. As Dordick (1981) and Schiller (1981) have recently shown, the introduction of on-line information systems in the United States has led to a shift of information out of the public sphere and into the private, where price barriers to access are making that information less freely available than it was before and where decisions, on what information to make available and in what form, are made on the basis of market considerations or other corporate interests, rather than on the grounds of public interest. This whole development is seriously threatening the public library movement, with its commitment to make information freely available to the whole population. What we are witnessing is a struggle to turn all information into private property and therefore, a source of private profit rather than, as is claimed, the development of a system to provide information widely and cheaply to all. The recent shift in Prestel's marketing policy is a symptom of a similar development which is leading in many spheres to a division not only between the rich and the poor in the sphere of private consumption, but also between the business and domestic markets, such that developments of new information services are privileging corporate use rather than public use.

A further advantage claimed for the new information technologies, as compared with over-air broadcasting, is their interactive capacity; the QUBE experiment in the US is cited. Such interactive capacity may indeed be useful for financial and commercial transactions. However, claims that it allows the consumer in some way to talk back or the voter to be more fully involved in political decision-making are highly misleading. Such systems still place control over the agenda and questions in the hands of the controller of the network. Moreover, it reinforces other tendencies in our society to what Sartre called 'serialization' (Sartre, 1976); that is to say, a social structure within which isolated individuals only relate to each other statistically. It is the model of the consumer rather than the citizen which privileges privatized forms of knowledge and experience, as opposed to group participation. The privileging of the domestic TV-set by all these developments is part of this wider and deeper social development. Even with existing conventional media (the press and broadcasting), there has been a steady tendency towards depoliticization, the down-grading of the political party and programme in favour of issue politics and related issue constituencies — a general development which is expressing itself in all Western industrial societies in falling political participation rates and a decline in the legitimacy of politics and politicians.

In my view, this is a serious development. Eventually, we will have to choose between two social forms. On the one hand, we can choose a society which primarily fosters social relations, based upon the Aristotelian notion of men and women as essentially social animals, based therefore upon notions of social reciprocity and interchange, upon the public as opposed to the private as the essence of humanity. Without such a notion, politics in any true sense is unthinkable. On the other hand, we can choose (or more likely have forced upon us) a society which is merely a social structure within which atomized, privatized individuals interrelate, primarily through commodity exchange, and by so doing necessarily reproduce the dominance of the capitalist mode of production and of those who control it, namely the owners of the means of production. Such a society will necessarily subordinate the public to the private sphere and destroy politics in favour of a manipulative form of elite control if we are lucky — what Bertram Gross has dubbed 'Friendly Fascism'. These latter tendencies will be powerfully reinforced in the cultural sphere by the introduction of information technology under market conditions. Such introduction should therefore, as far as possible, be opposed.

References

Bourdieu, P. (1979) *La Distinction.* Paris.

Briggs, A. (1960) Fisher Memorial Lecture. University of Adelaide.

Curran, James (1977) Capitalism and Control of the Press 1800-1975. In *Mass Communication and Society,* J. Curran *et al* (Eds.), Arnold.

Curran, James (1981) *The impact of advertising on the British Mass Media.* Media, Culture and Society, January.

Dordick, H. (1981) *The Emerging Network Marketplace.* Ablex, Norwood, N.J.

Garnham, N. (1977) *Towards a Political Economy of Culture.* New Universities Quarterly, Summer.

Garnham, N. (1979) *Contribution to a Political Economy of Communication.* Media, Culture and Society, April.

Garnham, N. (1980). *The Economics of the US Motion Picture Industry.* A Report for the European Commission.

Garnham, N. and Williams, R. (1980) *Pierre Bourdieu and the Sociology of Culture: An Introduction.* Media, Culture and Society, July.

Huet, A. *et al* (1978) *Capitalisme et Industries.* Culturelles, Part 2, Chapter 3, Grenoble.

Hyman, Anthony (1980) *The Coming of the Chip.* New English Library.

Ivre, Ivar (1981) *Mass Media: Costs, Choices, Freedom.* Intermedia, September.

Murdock, Graham (1981) *Programming: Needs and Answers.* Paper delivered to the Conference on 'New Dimensions in Television', Fondazione Rissoli, Venice, March 1981.

Murdock, G. and Golding (1977) Capitalism, Communication and Class Relations. In *Mass Communication and Society,* J. Curran *et al* (Eds.), Arnold.

Sahin, H. and Robinson, J. P. (1981) *Beyond the Realm of Necessity.* Media, Culture and Society, Vol. 3, No. 1.

Sartre, J. P. (1976) *The Critique of Dialectical Reason.* New Library Books.

Schiller, H. (1981) *Who Knows: Information in the Age of the Fortune 500.* Ablex, Norwood, N.J.

Smith, Anthony (1980) *Goodbye Gutenberg: The Newspaper Revolution of the 1980s.* Oxford University Press, Oxford.

Winston, B. (1981) *Showdown at Culture Gulch.* Channels, Aug-Sept.

CHAPTER 25

Leisure and Cultural Activities in the Information Society

Chantal de Gournay

Paris Town Planning Institute

INTRODUCTION

THIS DISCUSSION PINPOINTS the role played by the technologies connected with information and telecommunications in changes to lifestyles and to the organization of the temporal cycles of everyday life. The non-work-related applications of these technologies are analysed, with special emphasis on the use to be made of people's free time in the context of the information society; 'leisure' may become as important a social activity as work, given the prospect of the impossibility of guaranteeing full employment in the present economic situation.

This inability of the productive system to provide full employment for all the working population is not, however, a short-term phenomenon and brings every society face-to-face with two alternatives: either endemic unemployment for a large section of the population or a substantial reduction in working hours for the whole of the working population. These are basic structural facts, which in themselves justify the urgency and relevance of reflection on the re-organization of free time and the informal economy (all activities which are non-commercial or not included in a formal economic network). This process whereby formal employment is reduced involves radical changes in lifestyles which may be analysed independent of the effects of the development of microelectronics and its role in creating jobs. Indeed, there is no positive proof that this sector creates more jobs than it does away with through automation. This means that henceforth, one can work on the assumption that the professionally recognised and paid hours worked by each working member of the population will be on the decline; the progress made in microelectronics can only reinforce this trend but will in no way be sufficient to stem it.

Combined with these structural changes in the organization of work are the technological transformations connected with microelectronics and telecommunications. It seems doubtful whether the functional division between the sphere of production and that of reproduction will continue in its current kind and form, in view of the advent of the information society and the new communications systems. The work/home spatial ratio is bound to change. One need only mention working-from-a-distance and working-at-home. Of all the applications of the new technologies, it is working-at-home which is most likely to have a dramatic effect on lifestyles. The result will be a substantial saving in time spent on travel.

A LEISURE SOCIETY OR AN INFORMAL WORK SOCIETY?

TIME FREED from productive activities is not necessarily spontaneously and entirely changed into leisure time or into time given over to consumption. The aim of this discussion is to show that people's so-called 'free' time may in actual fact constitute a sort of secret work (or 'phantom work' as Illich, 1981, puts it) which contributes to the vitality of social and economic organization at three quite separate levels: organization of work; education and training; and social relations.

The organization of work

There is no longer any break between work and outside work in the sectors of activity which are connected with the production, processing and exchange of information — the sectors involved in the production of scientific and technological knowledge, the technical-sales sector and the distribution sector, to mention only the most representative. This means that it is becoming increasingly difficult to establish a system of remuneration for work actually done on the basis of the hours worked on the firm's premises, since the productivity of the intellectual worker can no longer be quantified according to his attendance at the workplace alone, but more according to his ability to keep his knowledge permanently up-to-date and to establish contacts with persons likely to supply him with relevant, up-to-the-minute information. Some of these tasks, therefore, are carried on outside the working hours entered in time sheets, in particular through the reading of specialist newspapers and magazines, but above all through keeping up 'social connections' on a regular basis. These two programmes of activity have to date come under the heading of 'leisure' or 'free time'.* Fashionable cocktail parties, business lunches and dinners, scientific symposia, private viewings in

*The word 'leisure' comes from the Latin 'licere', meaning 'to be permitted' or 'to be free to'. Yet the activities in question here are more activities which people are forced to indulge in for social reasons.

the arts world or high-level seminars really do form part of the daily work of a not-inconsiderable class of workers, whether they are intellectuals, businessmen or technical-sales representatives. These meetings are the places where information circulates and any worker in the service industries has to exercise the strict discipline of regular attendance at gatherings for persons-in-the-know, if he wishes to further his career.

In other words, the information society will produce an increasing overlap between the two temporal cycles of everyday life — work and outside work — by reinforcing the requirement that work-related knowledge should be kept permanently up-to-date (it is difficult to do so without encroaching on free-time) and by developing an activity which consists of capitalising on social connections ('making new acquaintances' also requires an investment of free-time).

In today's context, the introduction of flexible working hours is in no way equivalent to a reduction in work. Data-processing workers, for example, are often compelled to work outside standard hours (after 18.00 hours and at weekends). Indeed, in order to make a computer profitable, which represents a very costly investment for the firm, it sometimes has to be operated outside the standard eight hours, to ensure that each employee has optimal machine-time and to avoid the overloading of transmission circuits at peak times. Contrary to what might be imagined, shift work is no longer only in operation in manufacturing industries but would seem to be spreading more and more among workers in the service industries. There are now over a million shift-work jobs in the service industries in France, mainly in distribution (Cotta, 1980). These are effects of a type which are difficult to quantify since working hours are less often formally counted these days and the arrangement in some firms is for certain managerial staff to agree to work overtime in exchange for a larger salary. This forms part of the informal practices which elude statistical analysis, but which represent nonetheless a state of affairs which is bound to become more widespread. Already in the technical-sales sector, work is paid not so much on the basis of hours worked, but rather on that of sales made, through a system of bonuses.

Education and training

School life, although it is always being extended, is no longer sufficient nowadays for the necessary knowledge to be absorbed and adapted to enable occupations to be carried out in a productive system which is in a state of constant technological development. The problem tackled here is that of skills, in the complex process of under- and over-qualification of the workforce, which our productive system is now experiencing. An analysis shows that part of training and education, which was under the schools' monopoly, should in future be undertaken by the media and that the post-school and post-university self-educated will become a widespread phenomenon, with people taking charge of their own education during their free time. Here is a second definition of 'phantom work'.

Organization of community life at local level and the reorganization of the public service

Self-organization and associative living have become the major themes in modern political debate and are articulated chiefly through the question of decentralization and self-management. It is to be noted that these new demands from the social body coincide with the progressive State disengagement from the social sector, which is resulting in a deterioration in public services. This can be explained by the increasingly unbearable, onerous cost of social security and by the excessive growth in public expenditure which can no longer be offset by contributions from wages. It is therefore becoming increasingly likely that part of the socialized consumption sector (health, education and collective urban facilities) will be the responsibility of people themselves and that consumers' and users' associations, neighbourhood associations and other associative movements will replace the State and take over the organization of collective services such as crèches for the children of working women, cultural activities, mutual-aid systems for the elderly, the disabled or tenants in difficulty. This social change marks the transition from a society based, up to now, on the mandatory consumption of institutional services (social-aid systems) to a 'self-help' society, the convivial keynote of which is the associative movement. At lifestyle level, it is therefore to be expected that tasks of arranging and organizing local public life will replace some leisure activity, a sort of civic service, the virtues of which are undeniable since they amount to making citizens assume responsibility for these matters. However, the practical implications deserve criticism, insofar as this civic service is supplied by a form of specific work undertaken by people who receive no payment for their services and which, for the time being, is akin to a sort of voluntary work that hardly differs, despite being a form of political commitment, from Christian charity work. This is why we define it as a third form of phantom work, until new arrangements for payment of this labour are introduced, either by allowing people to deduct a few hours from the time spent working for their firms, in order to participate in the activities undertaken by the associations, or by paying these people out of the budgets of the associations themselves with State subsidies.

As a result of these three development processes, people's free time is becoming the ground for multifarious activities which are no longer connected only with consumption and recovering one's working strength. Although the FAST (Forecasting and Assessment of Science and Technology) programme has chosen to take an interest only in the changes likely to occur in the reproduction sphere (that part of everyday life which is given over to domestic activities, leisure, education and social contacts), it is nevertheless preferable to abandon the concept of 'reproduction' and adopt in its place that of the 'informal sector', which is less rigorous but more accurately reflects current trends. Within a framework of the advent of the information society, it is the very concept of 'productivity' which is shifting outside the firm, since, during their leisure time and thanks to interactive systems, people are no longer doomed merely to consume information, but are capable of producing and exporting it.

It is because of the increasing importance of this informal sector — and I would even go so far as to say, its increasing productivity — that the family unit must be more closely integrated into its social environment; this is precisely the role which falls upon the new communication systems. If consumers' and users' associations prove to be capable of organizing, on a small scale, what an overgrown bureaucracy manages inefficiently at a centralized level, the State would not hesitate to finance these associations and to place at their disposal sophisticated information and communications systems. This would, of course, be on condition that limits, other than its own reproduction, are defined for the State.

By analysing the informal sector in greater depth, this discussion is diametrically opposed to works which may have contributed to the myth of the 'leisure society'. Contrary to the latter, we do not believe that the post-industrial society corresponds to a stage where work is reduced and idleness and play flourish (even though in actual fact, it does lead to a real reduction in formal working hours). But, as far as is known, a reduction in compulsory working time has never resulted in increased leisure for the groups which are not included in formal work — women constitute the living proof. Certain sociological studies even tend to show the opposite: non-workers are the least solvent groups for 'dealers in leisure', for travel or winter-sports agencies, clubs or sports associations etc. Everything points, on the contrary, to the quantity of the leisure (if not its quality) increasing progressively, the more one invests in work and professional success. This means that the organization of leisure activities remains closely dependent on the socialized conditions created by work (this is why non-working women have no leisure), on the material or financial conditions achieved through work (certain categories of workers only go on holiday or to the theatre because there are work councils to organize everything for them at low cost), and on the need to 'let off steam', to compensate for or to exert oneself after the strain of work.

In short, leisure only exists as the negative of work and as a social phenomenon, it has only assumed its full importance and significance in societies where work has been set-up as the sole dominant value, to the exclusion of all others, whether religious, family or community. In non-industrialised societies, leisure, with its own budget for consumption, does not exist. This does not mean that people work more, but quite simply that beside work, and in place of leisure, there are other social activities which are as important as work, namely religious rites, festivities tied to local customs and symbolic exchanges. This is why all Western political theories, which aim to abolish work — after having set-up work and productive capacity as the basic values of humanity — err through lack of imagination (and Marxism does not escape this criticism), in that they are unable to envisage any substitute for work other than its negative — leisure.

The hedonistic ideas on the progress in microelectronics do not avoid this failing: the technical utopia arrogates two finalities to itself, the abolition of work and the production of leisure, as if the discontinuance of the one did not by the same stroke lead to the disappearance of its double or counterpart, the need for leisure.

THE POTENTIAL ROLE OF THE MEDIA IN THE INFORMAL SECTOR

SO FAR, we have examined the need for greater integration of the domestic unit into the communication networks. This analysis was based on a diagnosis of recent trends in the organization of work and in social organization, which may be summarised as follows:

(a) the outgrowth of work or diffuse work, which is not limited by a specific time-space. With work in the home, interference will be witnessed between mandatory working time and free time, within the same space. There will no longer be a clear break between work and outside work;

(b) the ending of the schools' monopoly of education: the widespread phenomenon of the self-educated and of permanent education for which the family is responsible;

(c) lack of investment by the State in the social sector (health, education, housing, amenities etc) and the end of a specific conception of public service. Hence, the need to find new methods of managing social relations (self-organization, self-supervision, development of voluntary work and mutual-aid systems based on associative movements).

To these trends must be added a fourth, not yet mentioned. It relates to the enhanced role of commerce in our productive system — it is no longer productivity which poses a problem, but sales.

(d) the disproportionate growth in the role of commerce in the productive system, together with a need to make use of information systems far more complex than mass advertising to win over potential consumers. Advertising has reached the point of ineffectiveness using the means of mass communication, insofar as the latter do not enable consumer targets to be specified. The diversification of goods corresponds to an extreme fragmentation of the consumer population.* In order to sell, it is no longer sufficient to make oneself known through advertising; it is also necessary to ascertain the tastes

---

* An advertisement in *Elle* (a woman's magazine) sells more beauty products than one in women's magazines with a larger circulation. The reason is that the women who read *Elle* go out to work in most cases and have an independent and larger budget at their disposal.

and habits of certain socio-professional classes, so as to adapt the product and style of the advertising to them. In short, the commercial role of information must be to inform the consumer about the product, as well as to inform the producer about the consumer. Advertising information will be interactive.

This is exactly what the videotex system is designed for. Every time the consumer fingers his keyboard to select a brand or supplier of services, the film he wishes to watch on his cable television that evening or the travel agency which will organize his holidays, he leaves a mark showing his preferences which, if put together, will sketch a very accurate outline of his identity. This capacity for diagnosis or permanent sampling, peculiar to the new media, could moreover be used for things other than market research, by contributing in particular to a transparent society in which administrators will be increasingly better acquainted with the people under their jurisdiction.

With interactive systems, what is called social communication strongly resembles social sounding: 'listening in' has become the watchword; the trader listens to the consumer, the mayor to his voters, the actor to his audience. Television is changing targets and is saying to its viewers: 'you are the information'. In this context, how will the time spent in communicating and in operating keyboards be computed? Will not the time saved on travelling in any case be taken up by compulsory communication, constant demands being made upon people by their social environment?

Given these major approaches to economic and social organization, the functions of the new media can be defined.

The work-related (work-at-a-distance) communication function and the reproduction of occupational knowledge function: Without anticipating the effects of work-at-a-distance, we may note that the informatisation of society, and of the domestic world in particular, obliges people to update their knowledge at the expense of some of their leisure time, for at least a generation, since not everyone has had the opportunity at school to become familiar with the logic and language of the computer. The first stage in the penetration of the home by microelectronics is specifically to take the shape of recreation and creativity, as these are the most attractive forms of learning. Through the introduction of sophisticated recreational equipment in the home, games are bound to become indistinguishable from learning; in actual fact, it is becoming one of the most effective pedagogical forms for the widespread dissemination of a certain technical know-how. The setting-up of *Microtel* clubs by the PTT (French Post Office and Telecommunications service), where certain data-processing professionals or amateur fans come to tinker during their leisure time, illustrates the educational nature of these associations, despite their avowed purpose — that of recreation and creativity. What appears questionable in these public initiatives — which in the end are only subtle marketing manoeuvres, hiding behind the noble mask of social experiments in a new creativity — is that they very clearly reveal one of the most predictable consequences of the information society: the increased hold of the productivist rationale over the part of people's everyday existence which has been most under their control to date. The real question is this: when a father who is a data-processing executive buys for his son electronic games or other intelligent little machines and spends most of his leisure time teaching him how to use them, is he really contributing to the blossoming of the child's personality or to the development of a skill which only managers will be able to use? What basis have we for stating that mastery of machines and technology is more enriching and forms the personality better than the handling of a musical instrument or initiation into theological discussions? This Promethean ideology (the basis for the ideas about the benefits of computerisation of leisure — the mastery of technology by the user and the democratisation of knowledge, where people no longer submit to technology but dominate it) must now allow us to overlook the fact that people's time budgets are not elastic and that the gradual erosion of free time by machines which communicate and inform means giving up other activities and gifts which need to be developed — such as the beauty and mastery of the body, the dexterity of the hands, the magic of human language (as opposed to the instrumentality of machines' language) — in short, everything which is given prominence by a specific humanist culture.

The educational function of the media or their didactic task: This function is different from the previous one, in that it extends the role of the school within the family unit, whereas the former is more of a link from the firm to the domestic space, aiming to reproduce operational knowledge and a logic specific to the discipline of work. The didactic role of the media in question here might reinforce the importance and autonomy of the family unit, by restoring to it some of the responsibilities confiscated by schools at the parents' expense. Through the technical assistance provided by the media (out-of-school television, 'mediatheques', editions of school textbooks on video cassettes etc), parents might become full educators again. This new division of powers between the family and the school represents such a turning-point in the processes leading to the socialisation of children and the conditions of ideological reproduction that it requires special analysis and will be discussed later.

The Capacity of Mobilization: Very often, the absence of information networks may inhibit action. In new residential areas on the outskirts of towns, housewives sometimes feel the need to be active, to participate in local decisions and in neighbourhood administration. This desire is often deterred by ignorance of the procedures to be followed to join groups or of the existence of associations or of people engaged in various activities. The contribution of the media in this field can be very positive, particularly through the setting-up of information networks at a local level.

The most recent illustration of this new role of the media is to be found in the example of mobile radios (citizens band/CB). Devised at the outset for work-related use (long-distance lorry drivers and taxis), this equipment has developed into a special craze in France among the dynamic fringe who wish to rediscover a sort of 'primitive' communication. Using CB radio-sets, new forms of solidarity have emerged, even going so far as to demonstrate capacities for organization in the case of specific actions: CB users have indeed saved lives by appealing for blood doners in emergencies. This use of the media can contribute towards making citizens assume responsibility and help to remove them from a way of live conditioned by the passive use of television.

The 'Social Diagnosis' Function: With increased media feedback capacity, we will witness an expansion of the polling phenomenon, the importance of which in current political life we are all aware. The public will be constantly called upon by various public authorities to justify or approve such and such a policy; the ratings will become the sole criteria for evaluating the quality of such and such a cultural programme — in short, public opinion will be sovereign, with the risks which that involves: the domination of a majority, of its tastes, its values, its norms.

The Control of Consumption: This function makes use of the same technical features of the new media — the feedback capacity peculiar to the interactive systems. It is known that telematics enables purchases to be made from a distance, invoicing to be done from a distance and products and selling points to be selected from a keyboard at home. This will no doubt revolutionise consumer habits. It is not yet known whether this change will foster more selective consumption (and therefore more qualitative consumption, since the consumer will have information at his disposal to enable him to make his choice), or whether it will merely be conducive to more consumption (increased effectiveness of advertising). It is known at present that detailed invoicing (keeping the consumer constantly informed of the real price to pay for a service) constitutes rather a positive factor, which is an incentive to the user to rationalise and even curb his consumption. This is the case in particular with energy consumption and in the use of the telephone. With the development of pay television or *à la carte* television (feasible only with coaxial cables or optical fibres), people may perhaps begin to choose their television programmes with more discernment and may even watch less due to the fact that they will have internalised concepts of cost.

These, briefly defined, are the five functions which the domestic applications of the information technologies are destined to fulfill. It remains for us to examine in greater detail the concept of lifestyle through special analysis of the leisure habits of each social class. What is fundamentally at stake with the introduction of the new media into the domestic scene can be summarised by two questions:
(a) Will the computerisation of leisure and the new methods of communication result in the desocialisation of leisure, with the family retiring within itself, thus increasing the isolation and anonymity experienced in big urban housing

estates? This is the scenario of the self-sufficient house-terminal, depending
very little on the surrounding area and the social environment.
(b) Will the availability of more extensive technical capacities stimulate
tendencies towards creativity and autonomy in seeking an improved situation,
or will it, on the contrary, reinforce dependence on commercial logic, which
governs the satisfaction of needs and cultural production? In other words, will
the telematic invasion artificially create communication needs which will
enable increasing amounts of electronic equipment and cultural merchandise
to be sold, or will it be conducive to people putting together their own
equipment and producing their own programmes? The video-cassette recorder
is a typical example: is it used to watch television more and differently, with the
possibility of storing programmes broadcast simultaneously, or is its purpose
to screen films which the user himself has made?

The answers to these two questions are not given. In our opinion, the action
of the new media can only reinforce existing trends. The two forms of leisure —
socialised/unsocialised; active/passive — are unevenly distributed among the
various social classes and this is worth analysing.

LEISURE AND LIFESTYLES

IT IS THROUGH the observation of leisure habits that socio-economic
differentiation between lifestyles can best be understood; the standardisation
of the same level of comfort across all social classes no longer makes it possible
to perceive class differences through physical indicators, such as the number of
consumer goods. It is thus necessary to return to more qualitative concepts,
such as how free time is used, in order to perceive the differences; for time, in
the information society more than elsewhere, has become a rare possession,
not to say a piece of merchandise. The time which you spend watching
television no longer belongs to you completely, since it is sold to advertising
firms, so that they can occupy part of the viewing time. Similarly, the time
which you spend looking for goods in a large store and then packing them after
you have paid at the check-out adds value to the article purchased, which can
be measured against the wage which a sales assistant would have been paid to
do all this for you.

The alienation of time — this is the reality of life for the underprivileged: for
those who have to wait for buses when there is an increasingly poor service in
the suburbs after nightfall, for those who are subjected to mandatory and
passive consumption of television or of institutional services, who have to
queue up for treatment or for social security benefits to be paid out.
Conversely, the privileged person in modern society makes it his business to go
about outside the rush hours so as to avoid traffic jams, rarely watches
television, knows a private doctor who can see him outside peak hours, who

has at his disposal at home a communication cut-out switch to filter unwanted calls when he is busy (an answering machine) — in short, he is a man who knows how to organize his time and who definitely saves time.

The Criteria for Socio-Economic Differentiation of Lifestyles

The Socio-Professional Class: If the purpose of recreational activities were only the pursuit of pleasure or of rest or the battle against boredom, why then do people wish, at all costs, to abide by a model of recreational modes of behaviour which they consider worthy of the class to which they belong. Why has watching television become discreditable, compared with other activities such as tennis, reading or bridge? Is TV not a good way of combating boredom also? To explain away this hierarchy of the various types of leisure by snobbery or the desire to show-off is not adequate. The fact is that recreational activities are not purely gratuitous — free time has become as precious as working time because it can be 'made profitable' and must be invested in. Yet, what is the nature of this investment? The grading of the various types of leisure and of lifestyles would seem to result from the fact that people, according to the position occupied in society, have at their disposal unequal conditions for turning this free time to advantage. To answer the question, use must be made of the concepts developed by the sociologist Pierre Bourdieu (1980) who, besides 'economic capital', has developed two other concepts: 'social capital' and 'cultural capital'. Let us look at what he has to say:

> To return to social capital, to construct this concept is to create the means to analyse the logic where this special sort of capital is accumulated, transmitted, reproduced, the means of understanding how it is transformed into economic capital and, conversely, how much work it takes to convert economic capital into special capital, the means of perceiving the role of institutions such as clubs or the family, the main place where this type of capital is accumulated and transmitted. Social events cease to be, as is generally believed, model manifestations of the idle life of the leisure class or ostentatious consumption by the rich and appear instead as a special form of social work, which involves expenditure of money, time and a specific skill and which tends to ensure the reproduction, simple or extended, of social capital.

From this quotation, it is clearly apparent that luxurious idleness or laziness, is not, as many believe, the prerogative of the rich. The members of the dominant class are, on the contrary, people who are always busy, especially during their leisure time. They cannot allow themselves to waste time, as it can be devoted entirely to accumulating a social capital (having as many social contacts as possible at one's disposal) and a cultural capital (having at one's disposal knowledge which cannot be transmitted by schools alone, initiating oneself into the highly elitist world of art). Leisure and culture are the two compulsory thoroughfares of this work, which cannot define itself as what it is:

the meticulous and progressive building-up of economic and social power. Those who make a good living prefer to spend an increasing proportion of their income on freeing themselves from domestic chores (housework, cooking or child care), which are considered to be less rewarding than social events and cultural activities. They would not do so if they did not anticipate obvious benefits, from an economic and social point of view.

Thus, it can be seen that the axis which we have traced between, on the one hand, socialised and active (or creative) leisure, and, on the other, unsocialised leisure (restricted to the members of the family) and passive leisure (given over to the consumption of goods or of cultural industries, such as shows) corresponds to another axis, which reflects the social differentation between lifestyles: the most privileged are those who have extremely socialised recreational habits and who are the least subject to consumption of mass means of communication (with the exception of the press and the cinema). The question is whether the introduction of the new media into the home, by reducing participation in social relations and physical encounters, will primarily affect those who are most under the influence of the current media (particularly television and radio).

Furthermore, participation in social relations would not be a strategic activity if there was an overlap between occupation and leisure — the personal contacts which one makes at fashionable gatherings in the evenings may always prove useful to one's career and, conversely, people who are high-up in one's profession are often the very ones whom one invites out. What gives the executive the advantage over the ordinary workman is the means at his disposal, enabling him to create some degree of continuity, some degree of permeability between the two temporal cycles of his everyday life, between work and outside work. He makes it his business to ensure that his occupation is the venue for intermittent activities not directly linked with productivity (meeting people, making contacts or attending business lunches and dinners). Conversely, he also ensures that the organization of his leisure time is a party to the reproduction of economic and social power, which, moreover, may be very profitable to the firm in which he is employed. The workman, on the other hand, does nothing but produce at his workplace and consume during his leisure time. For him, there is an unbridgeable gap between these two temporal cycles, between the types of people with whom he mixes in each case. This is why socio-professional class is a relevant criterion to explain differences in lifestyles.

All this takes us a long way from an approach based on time budgets since such an approach postulates that every activity has its own finality and is confined to this, whereas very often it is merely the pretext for underlying covert work which is a party to the social reproduction of the person who indulges in it; the aim of recreational habits often consists, therefore, of finding the link between one's working life and one's private live. The study of sporting habits, for instance, clearly reveals this relationship. Studies on sport (Duraic, 1974) have revealed that the privileged classes prefer games which do not require physical strength and a powerful physique and in which the mediation of objects avoids direct contact between bodies (tennis, for instance). Among workmen, on the other hand, physical strength is still a predominating value which encourages them to get more readily involved in the fray and the clash of bodies (football, for example). From this morphological distinction between sports, involving physical strength and contact or otherwise, springs a form of sexual segregation of sport. Among the working classes, the husband's sporting activities reinforce the sexual division of household roles, because of the wife's inability to participate in male-leisure activities. On the other hand, the practice of a less virile sport enables the wife and the whole family to join in the activities of the head of the household. The role of fee-paying sports clubs is precisely to ensure this integration of the family in a single recreational area. In these clubs, in addition to recreation, all aspects of social life are mingled, including working life. The husband thus finds an opportunity to re-affirm, *vis-a-vis* his colleagues or his boss, the virtues of his lofty morals, which only a united family can guarantee. Should the wife show how charming she is and demonstrate her skill at tennis, her husband's career can only be furthered. A drink after the match will provide an opportunity for an exchange of views on business and work. It is therefore becoming increasingly difficult for the privileged classes to dissociate work from leisure. All these habits determine a lifestyle. And it is this interdependence and interpenetration among all aspects of social life and recreational habits which is the main feature of the lifestyle of the privileged classes.

It should be noted that the wife's participation in her husband's leisure activities is an important basic fact for the higher social classes, whereas among the working classes recreation is often a pretext enabling men to be among men (*petanque* (bowls) and card games in France). This again confirms that bourgeois leisure time is not just a mere game, but a social game in which allurement or the art of being agreeable is an important rule, hence the indispensable presence of women.

These remarks are not neutral, taking the nature of electronic games into account. These are indeed individualised, not to say individualistic games: the keyboards are designed to be handled by only one person at a time. Most of the time it is the husband and children who find it easiest to handle these new tools because they have acquired some knowledge of data-processing at work or at school. Very often, electronic games create as many secret worlds as there are members in the family, even when they are all there, each being only too pleased that the others have found something to occupy them which enables him to be on his own. Buying gadget toys for one's children often amounts to ridding oneself of a feeling of guilt at one's inability to take part in children's games, through lack of time or inclination. Electronic games may, therefore, contribute to the collapse of the family unit, even if they are conducive to the increased presence of everyone in the home. Not to mention the fact that modern life, with working women, prevents members of the family from eating at the same time and together at the same table. These aspects can only reinforce the dichotomy between the dispersal of working-class families (which are exposed to clashes between the generations, further intensified by life in big urban housing estates) and the interdependence of middle-class families, which have the means to incorporate the leisure activities of all the members of the family into a harmonious whole.

To sum up, the main features of the lifestyles of the privileged classes are a high level of social integration of outdoor recreational habits and close involvement by all members of the family in the organization of leisure time and of domestic life.

Sex: We have already noted that sexual segregation of games, particularly sports, exists. Cotta (1980) describes three categories of games: physical games (sport, fighting), gambling games (lotteries, bets, games of chance) and strategy games (chess, draughts). It would be wrong to believe that the inclination towards games is dependent upon greater availability of time. The capacity for recreation and the right to recreation are determined entirely by social conventions and are dependent on the freedom which each person claims for himself *vis-a-vis* the norms laid down by his group. Recreation presupposes a freedom of body and mind, which certain social classes do not possess — a result of the status which history has imposed on them. This is the case for women in particular. Sometimes they were banned from physical games in societies where religion predominated (Islam, for instance) as it did not do to show the female body, which was only intended for physical love and reproductive purposes; sometimes they had no access to intellectual pastimes as they were not supposed to have any intellect (chess and other games of strategy). In most societies, children and men enjoy the privilege of recreational games. Even today, though women have gained access to sport and the so-called intellectual pastimes, an overwhelming majority of women are nevertheless to be found in games of chance and gambling games (lottery, bingo, bets), a phenomenon which is deliberately fostered by the media, which have always organized games on a huge scale on radio and television and aimed them at women, since the prizes to be won have always been household appliances. Doomed to be serious because their social role was eminently serious (since it concerned the reproduction of the species and the rearing of children), women had to remain serious even in their recreation: their games could not be gratuitous, they had to have usefulness as an alibi, to work towards winning money or a utilitarian reward (household goods, holidays). In short, female recreation is never as 'disinterested' as children's games or the pastimes of intellectuals. It is hardly surprising therefore that they formed the favourite target audience of the traditional media, as the games offered were mainly games of chance and gambling games.

It would seem that the new generation of media games are more akin to male games (games of strategy and sporting games). In addition, they involve more elaborate technical handling. Now women, whatever their level of education, always let men carry out operations as simple as fitting a plug, connecting the hi-fi set or changing the oil in the car. Any technical handling seems to be a deterrent to women and it seems that the communication involved in dialogue with a machine is less accessible to them than immediate and transparent communication, such as the telephone, for instance. This, we would repeat, is not attributable to the level of education, as the examples quoted apply to women who have had a university education too. It is more a question of a historical gulf between a technical culture and a culture of a literary type: it so happens that the special sensitivity of each sex inclines it more to one than the other, men being often the ones who benefit from the two cultures.

From these observations, it may be feared that women will have the greatest difficulty in adapting to the information revolution and that the creativity promised by the new media will hardly be accessible to them. These differences in behaviour due to the sexual roles seem to us to be more tenacious than those which are attributable to levels of education.

The level of Education: Where then is creativity — the promised land of the applications of microelectronics? Certain prophets of the communication era reduce it to merely a question of educational levels: the more people are trained in data processing, the more they will make creative and controlled use of it, as if the increasingly high degree of school attendance in our societies had prevented the masses from becoming besotted by television and increasingly dependent on the media to form their ideas and opinions, through tampered-with information.

In this field, accepted ideas are worth re-examining. Highly educated intellectuals were not automatically the first to make creative recreational use of the original audiovisual equipment. Very often, manual workers have a far more dynamic relationship with technical things. Firstly, do-it-yourself or the fact of being able, like a craftsman, to control the construction of an object from beginning to end enables manual workers to compensate for the alienation which they experience at work, as a result of the extreme compartmentalisation of tasks. Secondly, lacking mastery of technology, domination of the machine constitutes a virile value which is extremely deep-rooted among the working class, as it symbolises the domination of man over nature and arouses a feeling of power, which alone can give back dignity in his position as the victim of exploitation. This is why from adolescence, young working-class people do everything they can to get their first motor-bike, then their first car. This thirst for acquiring machines may subsequently spread to hi-fi equipment, then citizen-band or amateur radio. One is sometimes surprised at the way they can display detailed technical knowledge about mechanics or radioelectronics which they have acquired by themselves. Often veritable walking catalogues, they know everything about the hardware market — the makes and features of the various types of equipment. In short, this is undoubtedly the section of the population which has the greatest level of motivation for handling new audio-visual and data-processing equipment, provided that cost considerations are removed. There is no reason why some knowledge of data processing should be any more difficult to acquire than knowledge of mechanics or radioelectronics. The barriers attributable to levels of education are not therefore a major obstacle and to present them as such is to be party to deceiving people about the complexity of data processing. It also means overlooking the fact that the differentation between technical training and scientific training in our industrial societies adds to the gulf between the lower and middle classes on the one hand, and on the other hand, the privileged classes, which alone have access to the scientific training given by the universities.

This means that rudimentary technical knowledge is as widespread among the middle classes as among the elite, who have often been nurtured with a more classical and humanist culture. Practical commonsense is, for the time being, on the side of the less privileged and this is quite simply what is needed to operate a machine, however intelligent it may seem.

Towards productive or creative leisure?

The creative nature of leisure lies in the possibility of making the time allotted for this programme of activities to serve the exchange relationship. Associating with social acquaintances assumes additional importance in the information society, insofar as information circulates not only via machines but also via people; in an era when man has reached saturation point through over-production of information, it is discussion with other people which enables relevant information to be selected and synthesised, thus accumulating a cultural capital which cannot be acquired at school. As may have been noticed in today's society, the benefits of such an investment are passed on to the professional (career) and social (status) mobility of the individual, who has based the organization of his leisure time on the acquisition of these resources, which are both human and cultural. On the other hand, the social classes which are penalized are those for which leisure activities are directed entirely towards compulsory, passive consumption, towards the mandatory quest for the satisfaction of needs, under the undisputed influence of commercial logic.

By productive (or active) leisure, we also mean the capacity to create value, either for the physical requirements of domestic life (do-it-yourself, gardening, the maintenance of the estate) or for the cultural blossoming of the individual (taking part in the creation of works of art and no longer being consumers of the culture industries) and the fulfilment of his aptitude for action (participation in collective decision-making) — all while escaping as much as possible from the commercial logic which governs the satisfaction of needs.

At the present stage of our development (the main feature of which is the extreme complexity of society, economically, socially and politically), only the microelectronics revolution can provide the means of transcending the alienation brought about by the consumer society, by enabling people to have at their disposal the information necessary for them to act collectively, with full knowledge of the implications of their action. Is not *interdependence* the keyword of our era?

This means that every individual initiative mortgages the future of the community (energy consumption and the wastage of natural resources are examples of this interdependence). Whether one likes it or not, sophisticated information and communication instruments are the only means of regulating this interdependence, by reducing as much as possible, through more democratic knowledge, the margin of error and irresponsibility of individual actions. Hence the need to equip family units and not to reserve the benefits of the microelectronics revolution only for work-related and institutional applications.

However, technical means alone are nothing; the active and creative use of the media comes up against the inertia of behaviour patterns and outlooks. The belief that people will change their lifestyles when they work less and have more time at their disposal is a highly dubious assumption, not to say an assumption that has been invalidated by recent events: when workers in slump-ridden iron/steel and textile industries were given early retirement, it was noticed that the new jobless had a great deal of difficulty in finding an occupation which they considered to be of personal value. Men spent their days in pubs with other mates or doing manual tasks (do-it-yourself and gardening), which are traditionally masculine and quite clearly distinguished from the domestic tasks set aside for women. Conversely, women who ceased work in the textile industry very quickly went back to their traditional household chores, although their shift-work (at different times to their husbands) had up until then meant that the man and the woman had to share the housework. Thus, far from being an opportunity for everyone to regain some control over their own lifestyles after being released from productivist constraints, stopping work only reinforced a pattern of traditional and extremely normative behaviour (Gaulier; Chancel).

For many people, work is a means of becoming liberated, a way of breaking with the social conventions and traditions which weigh down lifestyles. It is this deep motivation which was behind the feminist demands for the right to work. The belief that change and freedom can be achieved through leisure is mistaken; leisure itself can only become an interesting activity if it is involved in social and economic matters, as Andre Gorz (1979) points out:

> *Spare time activity can only cease to be a pastime and a compensation, it can only have a cultural dimension (and hence a social one) if there is an extension, an outlet, scope for it in the main social activity: work.*

THE MEDIA AND EDUCATION

The connection between the technological developments in the productive system and the training of workers

Education, the responsibility of schools, and training (the acquisition of a skill or a qualification which renders the worker operational at his job), the joint responsibility of schools and undertakings, have ceased to be the monopoly of these institutions and are now incorporated into the activity of the media, which have contributed to the large-scale dissemination of popularised knowledge. It is thanks to the existence of the media that it has been possible to witness self-education becoming a widespread phenomenon (for example learning English, thanks to the BBC).

However, it is not possible to greet this extraordinary growth in educational activity (which is inherent in the information society) with proper enthusiasm, after the fashion of Ivan Illich in his *Société sans Ecole*. De-schooling society, far from having contributed to the fulfilment of the individual, has only subjected him to relentless competition, the rules of the game being dictated by the mode of production. It may indeed be wondered to what extent competition between the media and schools has contributed to the devaluation of diplomas. Each person's sum of knowledge and general education is consistently increasing, without these extra skills being recognised on the labour market, even if they are actually used at work. It thus becomes impossible to pay workers on the basis of the skill actually provided, qualifications and diplomas having become indicators outside the real value of their capacities and, in extreme cases, superfluous. In the end, the person who will have the most chance of being paid in line with his skill will be the one who has chosen to study the subjects which have been the least popularised (therefore, the least devalued) by the media — the exact sciences and technical subjects. On the other hand, the arts and social sciences are the field which have been most affected by the action of the media, therefore they are socially devalued: this is the case for history, geography, literature, linguistics, sociology, etc. In other words, there are various types of 'cultural capital' and the conditions for turning them to advantage are unequal, even if they have required the same investment in time and money. This is due to the fact that certain types of knowledge can be acquired outside of school with the assistance of the media. Democratisation of learning has its pitfalls and it is not just any type of learning which is being democratised: on television, for instance, the number of historical programmes far exceeds the number of medical ones.

Some people will object that too general an education does not meet the requirements of the labour market and that it is right that specialists should be better paid than other people because they are more efficient. This was true at one stage of our technological development, but it is no longer the case in the data-processing era. The current crisis in the education system is not attributable to its inability to supply sufficiently 'work orientated' and specialised knowledge. It arises more from the fact that schools have been unable to find a balance between technical training and scientific training and also from the fact that they are mutually exclusive. Now, with the information society, the technological processes introduced in production are developing at such a speed that there is always a timelag between the technical training given in schools and the situation in firms. Under these circumstances, a good scientific training provides workers with a greater capacity for adaptation and retraining. A typical example of this can be given: the difference between a computer operator (who only controls the language of the machine) and an electronics engineer, who dominates the internal functioning of the machine and its construction. The computer operator, who has spent three years of his life learning how to converse with such and such a system, can find himself unqualified overnight because the design of the equipment has changed. The electronics engineer, on the other hand, has adequate basic knowledge to enable him to adapt to hardware changes.

In view of the extreme mobility of the capitalist economy and of technological processes, it is in the interest of employers to have available, at the present time, wage-earners with multiple technical skills and a capacity for adaptation and learning new skills. The development of temporary work and the interdisciplinary mobility of workers proves that growing interchangeability in the forms of work will be observed. As Pierre Rolle notes:

> *Education prepares young people less for a particular job; rather it is conducive to their adaptation to varied duties. As a result, it creates as many permanent disqualifications as multiple technical skills . . . The scientific training of wage-earners ensures that the technical equipment, however it is developed, will always find its social partner (NON, p. 6).*

In this context, firms therefore prefer to retain a sufficiently versatile education, even though it may mean that they only control the final part of the training, that which is acquired on the job. The 'work orientation' of education is no longer, therefore, a question of current interest in the information society. The business of schools, more so nowadays than ever before, is to give a sufficiently versatile and interdisciplinary education. But, at the same time, saturation point has been reached as regards the sum of knowledge which can be assimilated during school life; introducing data-processing at school amounts to getting rid of history or economics. It is in relation to this constraint that the role of the media becomes clear.

The distribution of powers between schools and the media in dissemination of knowledge

The distribution of powers between these two institutions should, in the author's opinion, use as an intermediary the border which separates 'know-how' (which only involves technique) from 'knowing how to act' (which also involves an ethic and a mastery of the social environment). This means that part of what constitutes the specialist's field should be able to be taught *à la carte*, using audiovisual means. This concerns languages (data-processing languages, foreign languages etc.) and techniques. This also means that part of what constitutes the specialist's skill, and which is due to memory alone, should be able to be incorporated into machines. The aid to medical diagnosis from sophisticated systems is an example: this enables Third World countries, where there is a shortage of medical personnel, to train more doctors in less time — studies for personnel working in the field would be shortened, by making-up for certain gaps through technical aid supplied by skilled persons located in the capital.

On the other hand, schools should retain their monopoly over what can only be learnt by the comparison of identities in their diversity and by the wealth of experience. They must have control over the most important stages in the socialisation process and provide a place where teachers are not only custodians of learning (something which machines can do quite well in their place), but also 'educators' in the full sense of the word — a moral authority, however transitory and questionable it may be. This task can only be carried out through the presence of the various identities, which the media cannot provide within the family unit.

Lastly, schools should be the custodians of scientific training and leave part of technical training to the media. This seems all the more logical as the media have in their possession a capacity for permanent updating of the information which they transmit, which is not the case in schools and universies. The media are therefore the instruments which are the best suited to technical knowledge, which is constantly developing. Controlling scientific training means making some degree of epistemological dimension accessible to pupils.

The risks of out-of-school education

The problem raised by the role of the media in education goes far beyond the qualitative aspect of information. With courses on television, education at home and *à la carte* education using audio-visual means, will there not be a warping of the egalitarian principle introduced by the educational system, whose role in theory was to be that of distributing knowledge and culture fairly, tasks which have in part been sophisticated by the media? In short, are the media equally accessible to all, as are the schools, however imperfect?

In addition to the fact that audio-visual equipment is beyond some people's means, as is software (the programmes recorded on video-cassettes and video-discs), out-of-school education reinforces class determinism because it combines several effects:

   (a) that of family determinism connected with cultural heritage, which depends on the parents' level of education. With out-of-school education, the parents will again become the sole guides and counsellors available to the child;

   (b) that of the dwindling of dwelling space. Certain activities do indeed need a space allotted specifically to them to enable them to blossom. If rich people's children have the privilege of knowing how to play a piano, it is not only because they can buy a piano and afford music lessons, but also because they have enough space available to enable them to practise without deafening their parents in the next room. This also applies to audiovisual teaching, which is incompatible with the parallel activities of other members of the family in the same time space, which, in short, cannot tolerate promiscuity.

To sum up, before rejoicing at the possibilities of saving on energy and travel which could be achieved by bringing certain activities back into the home, perhaps some thought should be given to the fact that this flexibility of organization will initially benefit those classes which have sufficient space to accommodate them.

References

Bourdieu, Pierre (1980) *Questions de sociologie* (Questions of sociology). Les Editions de Minuit, Paris.

Chanel, Jules *Adieux a la Siderurgie* (Farewells to the iron and steel industry). Autrement, No. 29.

Cotta, Alain (1980) in *La Société Ludique* (The Recreational Society), Grasset and Fasquelle (Eds.), Paris, p. 260.

Duraic, Chantal (1974) *Les hierarchies sociales en fonction des depenses sportives et des pratiques sportives* (The social hierarchies in expenditure on sport and sporting habits). Toronto.

Gaulier, Xavier *Licencies a 50 ans, l'occasion de changer?* (Made redundant at 50, an opportunity to change?) Autremenet, No. 29.

Gorz, Andre (1979) *Le socialisme difficile* (Difficult socialism). Edition Le Seuil, p. 135.

Illich, Ivan (1981) *Le travail fantome* (Phantom Work). Edition Le Seuil, Paris.

NON *Aspects contemporians du travail* (Contemporary aspects of work). NON, No. 2, p. 66.

CHAPTER 26

New Information Technology: A Revolution in Education?

Jon J. Fitzgerald

*School of Industrial and Business Studies,
University of Warwick, Coventry, UK*

IF THE PROPHETS of 'post-industrial' or 'informational' society are anywhere near right, then over the next decade or two, the educational system in most advanced Western nations is due to be transformed by an unstoppable 'tidal-wave of electronics' which will create the need for more education and provide the means for its provision. After presenting examples of the kinds of future which now seem to be so widely accepted, some of these authors' underlying assumptions are examined and arguments put forward to those who see the revolution in information technology leading inevitably to dramatic and beneficial changes in the educational system.

Attempts to devise universally applicable scenarios for the development of European education in the 1990s can only be partly successful because, in spite of some convergent tendencies, educational systems in different European countries are the product of unique cultural and historical forces (Mallison, 1979). Moreover, any serious attempt at forecasting has to take into account that education has become the subject of many doubts and pressures for fundamental reform (OECD, 1973). It has come under fire from all directions (Illich, 1971; Reimer, 1971; Faure, 1972; Carnoy, 1974; Bowles and Gintis, 1976) and no longer enjoys the same uncritical support, from either the public or governments, which existed in the 1960s. Whether any of these reforms will be carried out and to what extent they will influence the overall structure of the education system remains to be seen.

INFORMATION TECHNOLOGY AND EDUCATIONAL REFORM

IN THIS CONTEXT, the eternal promise of painless technological 'fixes' for complex social problems never seems to lose its attraction. In modern industrial societies which have become cynical about politics and pressure groups, it has become common practice to justify unpopular social changes in the name of technological or economic 'inevitability' (Winner, 1977).

Innovation and diffusion of information technology in Europe has always been strongly influenced by government promotion and regulation. This applies most notably to telecommunications and, to a considerable extent, educational technology. Of the European nations, France seems most committed to large-scale spending on what Nora and Minc (1978) have christened 'telematique'.

The Technological Optimists' view of the future

In a number of books and articles, Daniel Bell has presented us with the most detailed scenario of 'post-industrial' society, in which education plays a central role:

The really major social change of the next two decades will come in the third major infrastructure, as the merging technologies of telephone, computer, facsimile, cable television and video discs lead to a vast reorganization in the modes of communication between persons; the transmission of data; the reduction, if not the elimination, of paper in transactions and exchanges; new modes of transmitting news, entertainment and knowledge; and the reorganization of learning that may follow the expansion of computer-assisted instruction and the spread of video-discs (Bell, 1979).

For Bell, like most of the visionaries of the 'information society', changes in education are just one of the many revolutionary social changes which will take place as industrial society is superseded by some form of post-industrial society. According to Bell, this transition has been underway since well before microelectronic devices made their first appearance. Microelectronics has merely hastened the change. The computer is only one of many information technologies which are combining to form a 'new information environment'.

The Promise of Educational Technology

Since the pioneering work of B. F. Skinner, with mechanical 'teaching machines' at Harvard in the early 1950s, educational psychologists have been extolling the virtues of 'programmed learning', based on a 'science of instruction'. By the time the drawbacks and limitations of these primitive devices had become apparent, they were in use in many schools and universities (Saettler, 1968). Computer-aided instruction (CAI) promised to overcome the obvious limitations of these machines and, by the late sixties, many optimists were already making predictions of an inevitable revolution in education (Kay, Dodd and Sime, 1968). For almost twenty years computers have been used in a variety of ways to assist in the learning process. (Some of these are reviewed in Lewis and Tagg, 1980.) Until recently, many CAI systems, like *Plato,* were very expensive. With the advent of best-selling personal computers like *Apple* and the availability of the standard CP/M operating system, there is now something approaching a mass market for off-the-shelf software. Moreover, personal computers have a number of characteristics which make them ideal for educational purposes. They have colour graphics of adequate quality, quick response time, reasonably effective, removable storage media (floppy discs) and can be enhanced with a large number of hardware and software accessories. In most optimistic scenarios, existing calculators, chip-based teaching toys and personal computers are only the first wave of a whole new generation of effective 'teaching computers'.

The Teaching Computer

The late Chris Evans, one of the most eloquent popularizers of the information technology revolution, saw portable teaching computers leading to major changes in the teaching process. The pressure to develop these new products, he predicted, would come mainly from commercial organizations, who in their efforts to profit from these vast new markets, would pump large sums of money into software development and research on human learning processes. As Evans (1979) states:

> *By the mid- to late-1980s, their research will probably begin to make headway and, for the first time, Man may develop a true Science of Education and with it a real understanding of the nature of learning . . . the world is about to move on from the era where knowledge comes locked up in devices known as books, knowledge which can only be released once the keys to their use have been acquired. In the era it is about to enter, the books will come down from their shelves, unlock and release their contents and cajole, even beseech, their owners to make use of them.*

The unrestrained optimism of many computer scientists is typified by Licklider of MIT, who in the 1960s was one of the first to conceive of a paperless society. He now sees computers as a prerequisite for attacking the problem of education:

> *The technological armamentarium will include devices and techniques to create a knowledge base for each field within the curriculum; knowledge-packaging programs that will convert cognitively structured knowledge into tutorial and exploratory interactions; interaction programs attuned to various ages and levels of mastery; consoles featuring speech input and output and graphical displays; endless varieties of computer-based models,*

> *games, projects, experiments, seminars, journals and competitions; and powerful prgrammed aids for human teachers . . . The problem is essentially, how to get laymen to see computer-based education the way computer scientists do, who are familiar with its potential and can envision the systems that could be created, given sustained support and dedicated effort (Licklider, 1979).*

Seymour Papert (1980), one of the most imaginative researchers in computer-aided learning, has a more romantic view:

> *I sympathize with Ivan Illich's vision of a deschooled and decentralized society but think that his proposals are totally utopian without a look at education through the prism of the computer culture... Dewey, Montesorri, Neill, all propose to educate children in a spirit that I see as fundamentally correct but that fails in practice for lack of a technological basis. The computer now provides it; it is time to reassess the practical possibilities for instituting what previous generations have dismissed as romantic.*

Papert attacks conventional 'drill and practice' where the child is 'programmed' by the computer. We ought to reverse this, he says (1980) so that:

> *... the child programs the computer and in doing so, both acquires a sense of mastery over a piece of the most modern and powerful technology and establish an intimate contact with some of the deepest ideas from science, mathematics and from the arts of intellectual model-building.*

Information Technology and Educational Reform

A number of educational technologists like David Mitchell see the new technology leading to a shift away from school-based education:

> *A global transformation of human affairs is beginning, one in which human information handling skills are being amplified much as muscle power was in the past... The emergence of interactive video-computer systems, cheap microprocessors programmed for a specific instructional procedure and increasing interest in distance-education schemes presage a radical shift to home- and job-based education (Mitchell, 1980).*

In *The Wired Society*, a classic of technological optimism, James Martin (1978) paints a breathtaking panorama where:

> *Many persons will learn two, three or four careers in a lifetime as telecommunications, automation and, later, machine intelligence will cause entirely different work patterns. Electronics will create both the need and the tools for lifelong learning.*

For technophiles like Martin, technology may be the cause of many of the world's problems, but it is only more technology that can solve them. Information technology makes it possible to:

> *... build a world without pollution, without human drudgery, in which destructive consumption patterns are avoided, and in which the human mind*

can be nourished as never before in history and can soar to new forms of greatness (Martin, 1978).

Are these optimistic forecasts plausible?

A more careful look at two of the leading assumptions which underlie these optimistic visions of the electronic future raises doubts:

Assumption 1: The demand for education and training will continue to grow rapidly. In the 'information society', education and knowledge are the new sources of wealth. Rapidly changing technology means that not only is there much more to be learned, but that a great deal of obsolete knowledge must be constantly replaced. Education is not something that will stop outside the school gate. For an ever-larger proportion of the population, it will become a 'lifelong' process. In addition, education will be an increasingly important leisure activity for the unemployed, underemployed and prematurely retired.

This assumption reveals a number of common misconceptions about the nature of the demand for education and depends on naive extrapolations from the recent past. Firstly, rapidly changing technology, as Berg (1970) and Braverman (1974) have argued, does not (with certain exceptions) require an ever-more skillful population. That employers have been demanding higher and higher qualifications for the same kinds of jobs does not prove that they actually require more education and training. Instead, it is the most obvious manifestation of credential inflation (Collins, 1979), which means that more and more people are overqualified for the work they do. One of the characteristic features of modern industrial society is not that skills are in short supply, but that most people are discouraged or prevented from developing and using the skills and talents they already possess.

Secondly the rapid expansion in the number of higher education places in the 1960s and early '70s has provided the main impetus for a supply-lead spiral of demand (Dore, 1976). As higher qualifications have become more common, employers and the professions have been forced to raise their entry requirements in the competitive bidding for the most talented applicants. This arbitrary raising of standards also serves to maintain the status of corporations, professions and other skill monopolies.

Thirdly, above a certain minimal level, education is not a universally beneficial product; it is a 'positional good' (Hirsh, 1977). One man's qualification tends to reduce the value of the next man's. The first man to stand on tip-toe in the crowd has to work harder but he gets a better view. When everyone does the same, they are all more uncomfortable and nobody is any better off. The educational system is significant not only for what it teaches overtly, but also for what it teaches through the 'hidden curriculum'. In modern industrial society, it acts as a social filter, which, unlike most other methods of distributing wealth, power and status, is accepted by a large majority as legitimate. Even if educational technology were to become cheap, effective and universal, this would to a certain extent be self-defeating, since it would tend to reduce the market value and status of the skills which could be most easily acquired in this way.

Fourthly, when it comes to choosing a school, most parents are more concerned that their children should acquire the right attitudes and beliefs and mix with the right people than with novel teaching methods. Apart from that, they want the school to place their child as high up on the ladder of competitive examinations as possible. This is demonstrated by the continuing popularity of church schools and private education. As a determinant of life-chances, where you go to school is still much more important than what you learn there (Hajnal, 1972). One of the main attractions of Oxbridge, the Harvard Business School, Ecole Polytechnique or most elite educational institutions is the network of social contacts they provide. For this reason education tends to be a very traditional product. Usually, parents and teachers are not very enthusiastic about innovation in either teaching methods or curriculum content (Oettinger and Marks, 1969).

Finally, computer-aided learning is unlikely to have much impact on recreational education. Most sports, crafts, artistic pursuits and social skills are very difficult to learn without a human teacher. Moreover, the opportunities for social contact are probably the most important attraction of this type of learning. Without the stimulus of certification, there would be comparatively little desire to study subjects like nuclear physics, statistics or Latin.

Assumption 2: Teaching computers, information utilities, video-discs and other education hardware, backed up with software and an adequate 'science of instruction', will be capable of replacing teachers in many circumstances and vastly increasing their productivity where they cannot be replaced. 'Technology-push' factors will attract private investment and force governments to take decisive action to promote the new technology.

There are four points to be considered here. Firstly, with a technology as dynamic and versatile as electronics, there is a natural tendency for forecasters to overestimate the importance of technology-push. Since the earliest days of teaching machines and educational television, there have been numerous comparative studies of media effectiveness. It is too soon to pass judgement on CAL, which has tended to be used in unimaginative ways. However, empirical studies continue to show that most people can learn most things fairly well with a mixture of simple media and face-to-face teaching (Gagne, 1977; Schramm, 1977) and that, contrary to McLuhan's famous slogan, the message is usually more important than the medium.

Secondly, educational technologists argue that the educational possibilities of computers have only just begun to be explored (Elton, 1977). In the longer term, this may well be significant. In the short term (over the next 20 years), computers, although they will become fairly common in educational institutions (and in better-off households), will generally be used in ways which create as little institutional change as possible. If anything, the technology will tend to reinforce existing inequalities and structural effects.

Wealthy schools are able to afford better laboratories, more teachers and better libraries. Educational technology will be the subject of fairly rapid development for a long time to come. Therefore, even if the cost effectiveness ratio tends to decrease over the years, only the wealthier institutions will be able to afford the latest and best. Far from overcoming inequalities, it simply adds another source of institutional inequality. The same applies to home computers or videotext systems. At present, large numbers of poor, handicapped and old people cannot even afford a telephone. Instead of constantly looking for new technological miracles, we ought to ensure that we are making full use of existing, albeit less exciting, technologies like the telephone and radio. Reid's research (1977) indicates how useful the telephone could be as an educational resource.

Thirdly, if the technical merits of teaching computers are not an automatic guarantee of financial support, then what about the economic attractions? The problem here is that, unless they can be shown to actually replace teachers or generate obvious improvements in productivity, they are simply an additional cost (Hooper and Toye, 1975). Where there is a choice to be made between spending money on improving the teacher/pupil ratio and spending it on teaching machines, previous experience suggests that teachers will win every time.

Fourthly and finally, the future effectiveness of teaching computers greatly depends on the quality, price and range of software available. The cost of hardware may continue to decrease. The same is not true for software, with the exception of off-the-shelf, mass-market software products. Low volume and bespoke software will become relatively more expensive. Existing European copyright laws are in considerable disarray and ignored by most educational institutions. Schools may well find themselves the subject of expensive legal actions. It is likely to take many years of legal wrangling before mutually agreeable solutions are found.

CONCLUSION

FORECASTS OF AN EDUCATIONAL SYSTEM transformed by interactive educational technology should be treated with a certain scepticism. The history of information technologies, like the telephone, radio and television, shows how social and political forces have been much more important in determining their rate of development and applications than purely technical factors. As Carey and Quirk (1973) point out:

> The 'third communications revolution' has within it the same seeds of miscarriage that have historically attended innovation in communications. Instead of creating a 'new future', modern technology invites the public to participate in a ritual of control where fascination with technology masks the underlying factors of politics and power.

Even if future technology is much more cost-effective than expected and is exploited on the widest possible scale, this will do little in itself to make education (whether inside or outside schools) more enriching or enjoyable. It will continue to be a major cause of relative deprivation and a confirmation of personal inadequacy for the many losers in the education obstacle race.

References

Bell, D (1979) The Information Society. In *The Computer Age: A Twenty Year View,* M. Dertouzos and J. Moses (Eds.), MIT Press, Cambridge, Mass.

Berg, Ivar (1970) *Education and Jobs: The Great Training Robbery.* Penguin, Harmondsworth, Middlesex.

Bowles, S. and Gintis, H. (1976) *Schooling in Capitalist America: Educational Reform and the Contradictions of Economic Life.* Routledge, London.

Braverman, H. (1974) *Labour and Monopoly Capital.* Monthly Review Press, New York.

Carey, J. and Quirk, J. J. (1973) The History of the Future. In *Communications Technology and Social Policy: Understanding the new cultural revolution,* G. Gerbner, L. P. Gross and W. H. Melody (Eds.), John Wiley, New York.

Carnoy, Martin (1974) *Education as Cultural Imperialism.* Longman Inc., New York.

Collins, Randall (1979) *The Credential Society: An Historical Sociology of Education and Stratification.* Academic Press, New York.

Dore, Ronald (1976) *The Diploma Disease: Education, Qualifications and Development.* George, Allen and Unwin, London.

Elton, L. R. B. (1977) Educational Technology Today and Tomorrow. In *Aspects of Educational Technology.* P. Hills and J. Gilber (Eds.), Vol. XI, Kogan Page, London.

Evans, C. (1979) *The Mighty Micro.* Hodder and Stoughton, London.

Faure, E. (1972) *Learning to Be.* UNESCO, Paris.

Gagne, Robert (1977) *The Conditions of Learning.* Holt, Rinehart and Winston, New York.

Gerbner, G., Gross, L. P. and Melody, W. H., Eds. (1973) *Communications Technology and Social Policy: Understanding the new 'cultural revolution'.* John Wiley, New York.

Hajnal, J. (1972) *The Student Trap: A Critique of University and Sixth Form Curricula.* Penguin, Harmondsworth, Middlesex.

Hirsh, F. (1977) *Social Limits to Growth.* Routledge, London.

Hooper, R. and Toye, I. (1975) *Computer-assisted Learning in the United Kingdom: Some Case Studies.* Council for Educational Technology, London.

Illich, I. (1971) *Deschooling Society.* Calder and Boyars, London.

Kay, H., Dodd, B. and Sime, M. (1968). *Teaching Machines and Programmed Instruction.* Penguin, Harmondsworth, Middlesex.

Lewis, R. and Tagg, E. D., Eds. (1980) *Computer-assisted Learning: Scope Progress and Limits.* Proceedings of the IFIP TC3 Working Conference on 'Computer-assisted Learning', Roehampton, England, 3-7 Sept 1979. North-Holland Publishing Company, Amsterdam.

Licklider, J. C. R. (1979) In *Computer Age: A Twenty Year View.* MIT Press, Cambridge, Mass.

Mallinson, V. (1979) *The Western European Idea in Education.* Pergammon, London.

Martin, J. (1978) *The Wired Society.* Prentice-Hall, New Jersey.

Mitchell, David (1980) *The Concept of Individualized Instruction in the Microelectronics Era: Educational Technology Comes of Age.* Presented at Educational Technology International Conference, London, April, 1980.

Nora, S. and Minc, A. (1978) *L'Information de la Société.* La Documentation Français, Paris.

OECD (1973) *Recurrent Education: A Strategy for Lifelong Learning.* OECD, Paris.

Oettinger, A. G. and Marks, S. (1969) *Run Computer Run: The Myth of Educational Innovation.* Harvard Studies in Technology and Society, Harvard University Press, Brighton, Sussex.

Papert, S. (1980) *Mind Storms: Children, Computers and Powerful Ideas.* Harvester Press, Brighton, Sussex.

Reid, A. L. (1977) Social Uses of the Telephone. In *The Social Impact of the Telephone,* I. Poole, (Ed.), MIT Press, Cambridge, Mass.

Reimer, E. (1971) *School is Dead.* Penguin, Harmondsworth, Middlesex.

Saettler, Paul (1968) *A History of Instructional Technology.* McGraw-Hill, New York.

Schramm, Wilbur (1977) *Big Media, Little Media: Tools and Technologies for Instruction.* Sage Publications, California.

Winner, L. (1977) *Autonomous Technology.* MIT Press, Cambridge, Mass.

CHAPTER 27

Time budget and Media usage in The Netherlands

Wim Knulst

Social and Cultural Planning Office, The Hague

DEVELOPMENTS IN THE USE OF MEDIA UP TO 1975

BETWEEN THE YEARS 1955 and 1970, television spread throughout the Netherlands. In the same period, the majority of Dutch households became car-owners. It has been calculated that the use of television and a car swallowed up more of the weekly leisure time of a worker than he had gained (weekly), thanks to the shortening of working hours. On balance, there was less free time for the existing pattern of leisure activities. Many households had more money available per leisure hour for other pleasures, taking the cost of the car and television into account. In general, this money appears to have been invested in sports, hobby or holiday equipment, hi-fi sets and subscriptions for periodicals and membership of associations. The time budget was 'burdened' with more hobbies, whilst (for those in employment) relatively little scope resulted from the shortening of working hours. In the Netherlands, it has been established that:
  (a) during the period of increased prosperity, the individual's leisure repertoire has become distinctly more varied;
  (b) various leisure activities which already existed for some time are less often performed; and
  (c) various pleasures are combined or have become accumulated.
The propositions that Linder posited in *The Harried Leisure Class* appear, to a great extent, to be correct as far as leisure activities in the Netherlands are concerned. Attendance at public performances or spectacles (cinema, dancing halls, theatres, football stadia) has shrunk considerably. This decrease

does not always coincide with the spread of the television set in Dutch homes. Thus, the growth of television does not appear to be the only factor in changing leisure habits. Television can, however, be regarded as the exponent of a more general development, whereby consumption in public places has shifted to consumption in a more private sphere and the use of common amenities has been increasingly exchanged for private facilities.

Figures from the Audience Research Survey indicate that the stage of 'getting accustomed' to television was completed in about 1975. Average interest in evening broadcasts no longer showed an increase, but remained stable or dropped very slightly. This was in spite of the fact that in the 1970s a considerable number of Dutch households were able, via the cable network, to receive 3 to 6 foreign stations, in addition to the two Dutch stations. On the eve of further expansion of television possibilities (Dutch transmissions during the day; more foreign stations; individual programming by means of video-sets and pay-cable, etc), the public's attitude appears to be reasonably adjusted to the television screen as an everyday object: the public no longer automatically gets excited about everything which appears on it.

The advance of television has had consequences both for the programmes and also for the use of *radio.* The radio became principally the purveyor of music and information as a background to other daytime activities (domestic tasks or work). Moreover, the information provided was more attuned to the specific interests of those at home (women's topics, social problems, minorities). The *periodicals market* showed a comparable development: a shift from general interests to special interests. In contrast to the radio, the use of periodicals rose considerably during the past period of increased prosperity. The largest growth took place in the gossip and hobby magazines and the technical and professional journals. Just as with listening to music (records), the common-reading interests of the family which formerly prevailed split up into a number of individual interests for members of the family. Apart from this individualisation of the consumption of periodicals, the periodicals market was also able to take advantage of a pattern of combined consumption which the increased prosperity permitted. Periodicals were produced for every current interest or hobby and were, moreover, edited in such a way that the leisure-spending reader, with his many and varied activities, could glean his information as rapidly as possible.

This pattern also characterises to a considerable extent the *use of books,* although the book market only covers about 50 per cent of the Dutch public. During the rise of television, books declined, just like other media. After people had got used to television, the reading of books returned to its former level and has since then remained remarkably stable. Thanks to heavily subsidised public libraries, the share of readers who obtain their books via the library has grown considerably. However, the sale of books did not keep pace with the growth of prosperity. The same applies to the *newspaper.* In contrast to periodicals, the sale of newspapers does not increase in a period of growing prosperity. Nevertheless, the daily papers also experienced a slight increase in circulation in the recent period. This development appears to be influenced above all by the increase in the number of households: there were more and more user units for the newspaper.

In general, it can be said that television has had important consequences for people's going-out habits and for the radio. The use of other media did not remain unaffected during the rise of television, but the development in their use has, for the rest, little to do with television and much more with general socio-cultural changes, such as the way in which leisure life has come more into the private and individual sphere and has become so diversified.

BACKGROUND TO THE TIME-BUDGET SURVEY OF 1975 AND 1980

TIME-BUDGET RESEARCH offers possibilities for analysing the volume of use of the media, in combination with the intensity of use. This enables more extensive research to be done than is possible in surveys into the relation between various forms of media usage, whilst it is also possible to examine the way in which the use of media combines with other activities. Thus, time-budget research can teach us whether so-called saturation point in media consumption exists or whether, on the contrary, with an increasing supply, the use of media will expand still further as a secondary activity (in the background or to occupy temporary lacunae in primary activities). It is also important to obtain data on the whole time budget in connection with research into the relation between working hours and the use of media or, more generally, between the volume of leisure and the use of media.

In connection with the recent rise in unemployment and plans to combat it by means of shorter working hours, there is great interest in the data concerning how increasing leisure hours are spent. (The Social and Cultural Planning Office also attaches importance to periodical time-budget research for other fields of research.) In the Netherlands, there had been a lack of integral or periodical surveys on how the population spends its time. Previous surveys had conducted an hour-by-hour record of how time was spent on evenings-off or during the weekend.

In 1975, a systematic enquiry was established to find out how the Dutch population spent its time during one whole week. The Social and Cultural Planning Office was one of six bodies that commissioned the enquiry. The way time was spent was examined by means of an extensive list of activities, which kept broadly to the categories used in the cross-national survey of 1965-66, which was carried out under the auspices of the European Co-ordination Centre for Research and Documentation in Social Sciences in Vienna. The time spent was registered per quarter of an hour. The first survey took place during 5-19 October 1975 amongst a representative group of some 1,300 Dutch people of 12 years and older. The respondent was asked to score his activities per quarter of an hour with the help of a structured list of some 200 activities, divided into 10 main categories. In 1980 a replication of the project took place. The 1980 enquiry was also held in the period 5 to 19 October but this time 2,700 Dutch people of 12 years and over were interviewed.

Let us take a brief look at the most important findings on the use of media from the budget enquiries of 1975 and 1980. By the 'use of media' is meant watching television, listening to radio, listening to gramaphone records or music cassettes, reading newspapers, periodicals and books. Since the use of media is discussed as an element of the weekly time budget, it is only considered as a primary activity. However, the use of television and radio has also been examined as a secondary activity; that is, as background to activities which the respondent has scored as a principal activity during a quarter of an hour (such as listening to the radio whilst working, watching television during a meal, etc). It was established that since 1975, the use of the radio has become to an increasing extent a secondary activity. In 1980, 94 per cent of the use of the radio took place in the secondary sphere and 26 per cent of the use of television. It is not surprising that these electronic media are forced more into the background as the individual's daily programme becomes fuller. In other observations, the use of radio and television only appears as a principal activity, partly because secondary use has not yet been fully analysed. It should be noted that pronouncements about the radio only cover a fraction of its use.

SOME GENERAL RESULTS (1975 AND 1980)

General patterns of how time is spent

Before looking at the shifts in the time-budget observed in comparing the results of 1975 with those of 1980, it would be useful to mention the basic patterns that emerge about how time is spent, both in 1975 and 1980:

(a) people whose time is, to a great extent, occupied during the day by work, domestic duties or schooling, do not greatly differ from one another in the time spent on these obligations. Moreover, there is a conformity in the amount of leisure they enjoy. However, women who have a job outside the home have less free time than men with a job and considerably less than housewives;

(b) men spend more time using the media than women;

(c) the percentage of free time reserved for the media varies from about 30 per cent in the case of working women, to about 45 per cent in the case of retired men.

Shifts in time usage

If one examines the shifts between 1975 and 1980 on how time was spent, the most striking facts to surface are:

(a) the average amount of working time for working men in 1980 is about 80 minutes less than that of working men in 1975. The time gained did not go into leisure activities — the time spent on media and other leisure activities decreased by a good hour, but shifted to work in the home and looking after the family;

(b) there were no striking shifts in how the working woman divided her time between work and household. There was a noticeable increase in the use of media at the expense of other leisure activities. The difference in the time spent on the media between working men and working women remains considerable, but was less in 1980 than in 1975;

(c) students and schoolchildren in the 1980 enquiry spent nearly 2 hours less on their study than the students and schoolchildren in the 1975 enquiry. The leisure time of the students/schoolchildren questioned in 1980 amounted to almost as much more as the time spent on study was less;

(d) retired men in the 1980 enquiry spent more time on media than those in 1975. With a score of 30 hours per week, they fill nearly half their leisure hours with the media.

A closer examination of the use of media (as a primary activity)

The time spent on the media by the whole population does not exhibit any striking change between 1975 and 1980. Moreover, the division of time over the various electronic and printed media remained broadly the same. There were shifts however in the level of use made of the media within population categories:

(a) men increased their ascendancy over women in spending time on electronic media and newspapers. The women's lead in spending time on periodicals and books decreased;

(b) with the exception of music records and tapes, older people spent more time on the media than the young. However, in the time spent on the electronic media, there was more convergence between the various age groups. The differences between the age groups in time spent on the printed media grew larger. The diminished interest taken by young people in daily papers and periodicals is particularly striking here;

(c) in general, people with a lower level of education spent more time on electronic media than people with a higher level. The latter spent more time on the printed media than the former. Convergence in time spent by groups of different educational levels occurred for television, music record/tapes, newspapers and periodicals.

Working hours and the use of media

The surveys show the following relations between work and media usage:
   (a) the total use of media by men drops from 28.4 hours with 0 working
       hours per week to 13.8 hours with 51 or more hours work per week.
       The drop is less pronounced for women: from 15.9 hours (with 0
       working hours) to 10.2 hours (with 51 or more hours work per week);
   (b) for men whose working hours are between 0 and 20, there is an almost
       elastic adjustment in the use of media. Between 21 and 50 working
       hours, there is scarcely any elastic reaction in the use of media to the
       number of hours worked, but above that number the elasticity
       increases again. For women, the adjustment in the use of media to the
       number of hours worked per week is not very elastic.

The difference between men and women must be ascribed to the fact that, as
far as women are concerned, they still have considerable obligations on the
domestic front between work and leisure, which men do not have to the same
extent. The difference in the ratio *work: use* of media between men and women
disappears when the use of media is related not just to work alone, but to the
totality of work and domestic chores.

The conclusion to be drawn is that, with the present unequal distribution of
obligatory activities between men and women, only in the case of men can the
number of hours worked be a suitable predictor of the number of hours use is
made of the media. On the basis of the results, it can be said that changes in the
number of working hours in the 40-20-hour zone do not have much effect on
the use of media. A possible official shortening of working hours from, for
example, 40 to 35 hours per week will scarcely effect the use of media in their
totality nor the use of individual media. However, a shift in the total
package of obligatory activities (redistribution of work and domestic chores
between men and women) would probably have a noticeable effect.
Moreoever, drastic alterations in working hours, such as unemployment and
retirement, have a considerable effect on the use of media.

The amount of leisure and use made of media

The extent of leisure hours (that time which remains after deducting time
spent on work, household, education, sleeping, eating and personal hygiene) is
more difficult to determine than the average amount of time spent on work.
The average working hours of various groups of employees are regularly
registered; in order to calculate leisure hours, a time-budget enquiry is
necessary. Nevertheless, knowledge of the development of the volume of
leisure hours provides the most reliable basis for pronouncements on the use of
the media. The use of the media forms 34 to 40 per cent of leisure activities and
grow almost proportionately with an increase in the volume of leisure hours.

Use of media by the economically active and the non-active

So far, we have established that the use of the media (for men) reacts very elastically in the 0-20-hours-work per week zone. Every hour which is worked less (or more) in this zone is accompanied by a shift of nearly one hour in the use of the media. This outline is naturally rather theoretical. People who have no paid work, such as the retired or unemployed, have in most cases left a 40-hour-week job, not a job in the 1-20 zone. In order to judge the effects of retirement or unemployment on the use of the media, it is better to compare the situation of working men, with a working week of more than 20 hours, with that of the non-active.

The comparison shows that the use of the media by economically non-active men (retired and unemployed) increases to a disproportionately larger extent than the amount of leisure which becomes available to them. If one compares the use made of the media by working women and by housewives, then it can be seen that shifts from work outside the home to work in the domestic sphere have scarcely any effect on media consumption (at any rate in 1980). It may be concluded that the increase in the number of economically non-active people has had much more drastic effects on individual use of media than the effects of women's participation in the labour market or the results of the shortening of working hours. To the effect of the growth in the number of unemployed and retired people must be added the effect of the autonomous increase in the use of the media by the economically non-active between 1975 and 1980.

Use of media and variety of leisure activities

The use of the media appears to claim a fairly constant portion of leisure time, which points to the fact that the amount of leisure in the individual's time budget forms an important factor in the distribution of time over media and other leisure activities. However, the proportion of use made of the media is an average and the fact that working women devote 32 per cent of their leisure to the media, as opposed to 46 per cent by retired men, calls for a separate explanation.

There are two other budget aspects to be considered: the degree of variety in the leisure budget and the degree of fragmentation. It has been noticed in various studies that people who make very intensive use of television have, on average, fewer other hobbies than people who do not watch much television. The assumption would seem to be justified that intensive use of the media need not necessarily be connected with an intensive interest in the media, but possibly also with the absence of alternative opportunities for leisure activities. This hypothesis is examined within the terms of the budget study (data on individual experience is however not available). It has been established that:

    (a) people whose leisure activities are not very varied make more intensive use of television and radio;

    (b) people whose leisure activities are varied score considerably higher

on reading books.
For the remaining media, there did not appear to be any connection.

Fragmentation of the leisure budget and the use of media

Both in 1975 and in 1980, women spent less of their leisure budget on the media than men. The difference even increased in 1980. An explanation of this is sought in the assumption that women, in the present distribution of roles, have fewer blocks of free time since their leisure activities are alternated with, or disturbed by, obligations in housekeeping or the care of children. On the basis of analyses of the budget data for 1975, this assumption appears to be correct for the electronic media. The fragmentary nature of women's leisure time offers no explanation for less use of newspapers.

RELATION OF TELEVISION USE TO OTHER MEDIA USE

IT IS OFTEN ASSUMED that television might compete with or even oust other forms of leisure activity. Put in these general terms, the assumption is incorrect. As previously mentioned, the development of leisure activities has been subject to influences other than television, whilst television scarcely appears to be relevant at all to some forms of relaxation and development of personal potential. However, people who watch television to a relatively great extent have a less varied pattern of leisure activities than people who make less use of this medium. Also in this case, the use of the media should not be labelled as the cause without further explanation, since there are other factors which influence both the extent of the use of television and also the variety of the leisure activities, such as age, level of education and so on. Since corresponding functions are ascribed to television, radio, newspapers, periodicals (information, amusement, etc), there is a great temptation to assume a direct relation between the use of the various media forms.

The time-budget enquiry of 1975 and 1980 makes it possible to register the further development of the relation between the use of television and other media. We have established the following points:

    (a) the more intensive the use of television, the more intensive the use of radio (both as primary activities);

    (b) intensive television-viewers score less time on periodicals, which show specific interests — hobby magazines, news and opinion weeklies;

    (c) intensive television-viewers score considerably higher on weeklies which are concerned with radio, television and show business; and

    (d) neither the use of books or newspapers appears to be affected by the extent to which use is made of television.

These ratios were not so very different in 1975. Moreover, the shifts were of such a nature that it was not the competition of television against the other media which grew stronger, but the cumulative pattern of time spent on the media. It must be remembered that these facts have been established at periods when the Dutch television stations do not transmit during the day on weekdays. This situation will change in due course. Thus, the possibility cannot be excluded that the ratios will change in a future situation where television is also the regular daytime competitor of the newspaper, periodical or book. However, this will mainly be of significance for people who are in a position to watch television on weekdays (the retired, unemployed and housewives).

To conclude, a warning should be given against too radical expectations of the results of technical innovations. We must be careful to avoid translating breakthroughs in the realm of communication techniques simply as revolutions in the lives of media consumers. New techniques often mean little more than a greater choice, more personal say in what appears on the television screen and the time that it appears. Expansion of the possibilities of filling the screen have not, to date, led to more intensive use. Intensive use would appear to be determined not so much by the possibilities offered, but rather by the characteristics of the users. The author doubts whether this relation will undergo any drastic change.

Chapter 28

Uses and Users of the VCR

Jean-Claude Baboulin
Institut National de l'Audiovisuel, Bry-sur-Marne

Philippe Mallein
University of Grenoble

Jean-Pierre Gaudin
University of Paris XII

THE DEVELOPMENT of the market for the video-cassette recorder (VCR) and its uses was the subject of a survey, conducted over a period of one year, by the Research Department of the French Institut National de l'Audiovisuel (INA). Before presenting the results of this investigation, it will be useful to review the methods used in the survey and the range of issues studied.

SUBJECTS AND METHODS OF THE RESEARCH

THE PURPOSE OF THE SURVEY was to analyze the various factors contributing to the growth in the social use of video in the consumer market and the influence that possession of such equipment might have upon social life. The analysis was made at two levels:

(1) *The supply level:* analysis of industrial, commercial and cultural strategies. The purpose was to verify the synthesis and appraisal of statistical data concerning the equipment market (hardware) and the programme market (software). This analysis of supply led us to carry out a survey concerned with home-video advertising, published in the French consumer press, so as to find out how the VCR was depicted and offered to the public by the leading newspapers since 1978. We wanted to know the extent to which the image fits the actual usage of video equipment.

(2) *The level of actual usage:* existing video statistics proved useless for an analysis of VCR uses. Though the market for video equipment is growing very quickly, it is still restricted. Most of the marketing surveys previously conducted appear to be quite incomplete, heterogeneous in their methods, unverifiable and too closely related to the sponsor's commercial targets. That is why we choose a 'qualitative approach', our purpose being to analyze the function of the VCR as a support and catalyst of psychological images and social behaviours, its social and cultural context. We analyzed three specifics fields:

- (a) *Domestic use* (individual or family use): based upon the analysis of a sample survey revealing the present structure of the market and including some 30 semi-directive interviews of home-video owners. We wished in particular to analyze the function of the VCR and its impact upon pre-existing patterns of cultural consumption (various leisure activities, TV, cinema and so on) and the relationships within and without the family structure.
- (b) *Uses within organized groups and associations with similar interests:* based upon the analysis of strategies and functioning of video clubs, non-professional associations and exchange circuits, emerging at the present stage of market development. We wished to define the impact of the VCR as a 'socialization factor', with regard to domestic use as well as 'social video' use during the 1970s.
- (c) *the use of the VCR in schools:* based upon an interministerial experiment called *Active Young TV viewer,* * in which several schools were equipped with half-inch cassette recorders, so as to enable the teachers and pupils to analyze televised programmes. In such a situation, video is used to confront one pedagogic institution with another — the school and the television.

The sectorial surveys have now been completed, but their analyses have yet to be finalised. Therefore, only an introductory analysis, concerning the impact of the VCR on the way of life, is presented here covering the following points:

- (a) the main function of the VCR is, to a certain extent, the 'mastering' of television;
- (b) the use of the VCR is mainly restricted to well-known cultural products;
- (c) the use of the VCR does not change behaviour or pre-existing social relationships to any great extent;
- (d) video socialization induced by the VCR only concerns a small part of the audience and is related to the present state of the market;
- (e) non-professional video production is still undeveloped and conforms to pre-existing uses (family cinema viewing and social video);
- (f) the use of the VCR within schools is an opportunity to confront one cultural pattern with another.

*Jeune téléspectateur actif.

Some basic statistical data about the market and the users

The VCR became a consumer good only when the half-inch cassette was developed by Sony and JVC in 1977. The VCR appeared on the market in 1978 and is thus only 4 years old. Today, this market has two features. Firstly, it is still a small market: in 1980, the highest penetration rate (between 6 and 7 per cent) was found in Japan and Sweden. It was roughly 2.5 per cent in the United States and 1 per cent in France. Quantitatively, the worldwide unit production was 10 million at the end of 1980, roughly divided into four equal parts between Japan, the United States, Europe and other countries. Secondly, the VCR market is growing quickly: Japanese production (representing 90 per cent of the world market) has expanded from 1.5 million units in 1978 to 4.5 million units in 1980 — an average growth rate of 100 per cent per annum.

The average user's characteristics reflect a growing market for up-to-date products:

(a) the user is generally between 30 and 35 years old (at this age one is still keen on technological innovation and, at the same time, a solvent consumer);

(b) his cultural, social and professional qualifications are above the average national level: two-thirds of the average users are management executives or belong to professional classes (they view television with a critical eye and are ex-cinema-lovers);

(c) he lives in a town: in France, 20 per cent of VCR users live in urban areas (60 per cent of these in Paris or its suburbs);

(d) two-thirds of the users are married couples with children (1 or 2) with the wives generally working outside the home.

Considering the 'way of life', it is obvious that the average user belongs socially to the upper classes and is keen on technological, cultural and social innovations. Let us now look at the influence of the VCR in this context.

The main function of the VCR is to master television viewing

All the existing surveys show that the possession of a VCR is closely linked with the possession of a colour TV set: in Japan and the United States, the colour-TV penetration rate reaches 97 per cent and two-thirds of the households own two TV sets. In the United Kingdom and West Germany (together representing 60 per cent of the VCR market in Europe), the penetration rate reaches 75 per cent. In France, it does not exceed 45 per cent. Still, it is important to observe the close connection between colour TV and VCRs, the percentage of their distribution being identical in these European countries (0.8%). Surveys also indicate that 85 per cent of VCR-owners simply use the machine to record TV programmes and thus, do not use pre-recorded cassettes or video cameras.

A closer look at the different social uses of the VCR with respect to TV reveals that the behaviour of VCR-owners towards TV is the same as it was previously — a 'reasonable interest' — he mainly views TV at prime-time hours (7.30-10 p.m.), but he also views later than the average audience, probably because some interesting programmes are broadcast later in the evening. Eighty-five per cent of VCR-owners are regular readers of a TV magazine, from which they chose their programmes and look at the reviews (as they used to when they were cinema-goers). This 'rational consumption' is shown in an American survey, which points out that VCR-owners are light TV viewers (in comparison with the average national audience). In the United States, the average national TV viewing is 45 hours per week, while the VCR-owners view for only 22 hours. Therefore, it seems that the user of the VCR is not a passive consumer of the 'televised flow' but, on the contrary, he acts as a cinema-goer: the user of a VCR has to make a choice, which is the result of a thoughtful decision. Most people use the VCR in the evening at hours when they are accustomed to viewing TV. Indeed, some people use the VCR for viewing video-tapes beyond regular hours, but at this time the audience is not much larger: housewives, older people and children.

This analysis enables us to assert that, contrary to what one might initially think, the use of the VCR does not imply heavy TV viewing — 60 per cent of VCR-users do not change their TV viewing habits: rather 20 per cent increase VCR-users do not change their TV-viewing habits: rather 20 per cent increase TV viewing and 20 per cent reduce TV viewing. The statistical data concerned with the weekly use of the VCR confirm this pattern of use. The VCR is used: less than once a week (7%), between 1 and 5 times a week (62%) and more than using the VCR:

(1) the recording of a TV programme occurs while the VCR-owner is away from home and thus he is able to free himself from TV-schedule restrictions;

(2) the recording of TV programmes occurs while the VCR-owner is viewing a programme on another channel and thus he is able to increase TV viewing (if all the video-recordings are viewed afterwards); and

(3) the recording of a TV programme occurs while the VCR-owner is viewing it and thus he is able to stock his favourite programmes in order to view them again.

More qualitative surveys reveal three notions, closely related to the use of the VCR:

(a) the control of time;
(b) the possibility of choice;
(c) the access to 'audiovisual knowledge'.

Therefore, what is at stake is the notion of a rational control of time and culture.

Use of the VCR is generally restricted to the consumption of well-known cultural products

Due to the characteristics of the VCR-owner, as we have already described them (a sensible TV viewer who is also a cinema-lover), motion pictures represent 90 per cent of TV-programme recording; next come the light entertainment programmes (40%), sports (35%), children's and cultural programmes. The statistical data show that the VCR serves as a substitute for going out to see a play or a motion picture (going out is rather expensive, it takes time and there are time-table restrictions). Even if, previously, the VCR-owner was not used to going out more often, the VCR now enables him to view more events at home.

This analysis of cultural consumption is one of the factors that enables us to understand the present state of the pre-recorded cassette market, but we must also take into account the inner logic of this market and particularly its financial and juridicial characteristics: motion pictures in video form represent 90 per cent of the consumer pre-recorder cassettes offered in the catalogues. Thus, the VCR, like the TV set, serves as a substitute for the cinema, but it concerns only a certain audience (people who are not interested in cinema as art): this type of audience does not mind viewing motion pictures a long time after their first showings nor do they mind visual quality being worse than the cinema or the more restricted choice offered.

There is a paradox between this demand concerning motion pictures in video form and the narrowness of the pre-recorded cassette market. The figures for pre-recorded cassette consumption per VCR are 2.8 in the United States, 0.10 in Japan and 0.8 in France. In the United States, where the consumption of pre-recorded cassettes is the heaviest, 76 per cent of VCR-owners do not view any purchased or rented cassette in a week and 17 per cent only once or twice a week. One of the reasons lies in the cost of the cassette (in France, it costs between 60 and 100 dollars). But the main reason is the nature of the product: a motion picture is intended to be seen once and is suitable for cinema exhibitions or broadcasting. That is also why the rental cassette business is rapidly increasing: today it represents 45 per cent of the market in the United States. And for the same reason, 70 per cent of TV-programme recordings are erased after having been viewed only once. The most popular products are pornographic films, which still represent 60 per cent of the sales, films with a symbolic value (classic films) and films for specific audiences (children, music-lovers, housewives and so on).

Use of the VCR does not change behaviour and pre-existing social relationships

Like all the new technical devices appearing on the market, the development of the VCR is emphasized by fine speeches foretelling it will 'revolutionize' the way of life. Advertisements have indeed played a great part in the image offered to the public. Let us try to appraise the relevance of this image.

Firstly, the VCR offers a symbolic participation in the history of technological advance and in the fascinating world of media: advertising presents the VCR as an up-to-date device related to space technology; the technological power of countries like Japan or the United States supports this futuristic approach. In some way, the VCR is Science Fiction itself turned into reality in everyday life. On the other hand, the user is always challenged as someone being able to become a 'media professional' by means of the VCR: 'Become a TV programmer', 'Become a TV-programme producer', 'Become a reporter of daily life' — the advertisements say. Yet all the qualitative surveys show that as soon as the VCR is used, it becomes a banal product taking its place among the normal domestic durable goods (household equipment, car, telephone and so on). In fact, the VCR-owner does not feel part of an elite at all nor does the VCR induce any particular fascination with technical, cultural or social matters. It is an almost well-known product, closely related to the pre-existing TV-set, tape-recorder and Super 8.

Secondly, the VCR also offers to free the user from time-table restrictions such as labour, leisures and TV programmes: advertising, as well as users, deal with this subject, pretending that VCR is freedom while labour, leisures and TV timetables are pure slavery. The VCR turns the notion of choice into a paradox; in fact, the choice of recording more or less TV programmes does not mean more or less TV-viewing, but is just filling a lack — the feeling of being frustrated by the flight of time. It is stated that the use of the VCR does not much change the usual timetable: it does not serve as a substitute for other spare-time activities, but enables a control of time, the flight of which is symbolized by the continuous flow of television.

Finally, the VCR offers harmony in family life, putting an end to the conflicts between members of the family, with regard to the choice of TV programmes. It is true that the VCR allows one to personalize the use of the TV set. This harmony in family life is not the result of an agreement, rather the respecting of differences between family members: every member is able to record his favourite programme and view it when he wants. In some way this harmony is also a paradox, serving as a substitute for evenings that people used to spend together. The TV set is now inducing a lonely enjoyment that cannot be shared.

We must add to this analysis an interesting discovery that we have made: the VCR has a certain erotic and emotional function. In fact, TV may be considered as representing a feminine and motherly form for the male, giving him almost an oral satisfaction. Even if the male denies it, he has less control over TV than the female who is more aware of the outside world, at least in the social class that we have analyzed (the female may also be attracted by more meditative activities as reading a book, listening to music or just thinking). The wife is often jealous of TV and feels aggressive towards the televised flow that keeps her husband under hypnosis. So, the male considers the VCR as an ally and a friend, the technical means of his power which enables him to juggle at will with the televised flow, recording it, cutting it up, diverting it, stocking it, liberating it again and thus gaining a better control of it, partly neutralizing the conflict with his wife.

Thus, it is obvious that the VCR plays a conciliatory role between contradictory demands. It is an up-to-date but easy-to-use device, banal but unusual, one which allows not only cultural products to be consumed, but also to control this consumption and, at the same time, to be passive and active, to choose and accumulate, to retire within oneself and improve relationships within the household.

Video socialization induced by the VCR only concerns a small part of the audience and is related to the present state of the market

As already stated, the development of new communication technologies is emphasized by ideologically fine speeches, foretelling that it will upset social relationships and revive traditional neighbourliness. This kind of talk was especially prevalent in the '70s, when the major industrial companies aimed at experimenting with uses of second generation, video-equipment (three-quarter and half-inch), the first generation being non-portable video equipment, intended for broadcasting. In the '70s, video was considered as a tool to 'democratize expression' by social groups having similar interests, social/cultural organizations and local collectives. But what is the situation today? Our research shows that generally the VCR does not induce socialization and when it does, only a small section of users are concerned, connected to the characteristics of this growing market. It has already been stated that the VCR serves to harmonize relationships within the household, allowing a mutual respect of differences; also that the VCR does not induce significantly more interest within the household towards the outside world, but rather promotes a kind of agreement concerning the control of time and social behaviour. For instance, the surveys show that only 10 per cent of users invite friends home for viewing films on the VCR; this mostly happens just after the VCR has been purchased.

However, the use of the VCR induces some social behaviour that reveals how the growing market is taking shape by means of new organizations and groups trying to promote the consumption of pre-recorded cassettes. We have already noted that this consumption is restrained by some obstacles: the relation of video to TV and the cost of cassettes. There are three types of organizations and circuits:

(a) commercial organizations, aiming to promote the rental cassette business; 90 per cent of such organizations call themselves 'video clubs' as if to suggest that they belong to an elite of connoisseurs and privileged people; they offer special advantages to their clients such as mutual-aid services and so on;

(b) non-professional associations, organized on a non-commercial basis (the well known *LAW 1901* in France), few in number but very active, offering special services to their supporters (training courses, advice,

loans, exchange of cassettes and so on) and trying to gain a legitimacy
as 'representatives' and 'protectors' of consumers;

(c) groups organized by similar interests, unstructured but numerous
and very active, each of them representing about 10 or 30 persons and
based upon friendly or professional relationships, sometimes by
means of classified advertisements. There are mutual-aid groups,
exchange groups and cassette-duplication groups.

In spite of the differences between their structures and functional aims, these
organizations seem to apply the same type of strategy. Firstly, they are
promoting an ideology based upon what might be called the 'pioneer spirit'
which appeals to enthusiastic users who feel they are doing pioneer work in
new technology and in cultural matters, coping with the technical, juridical,
commercial and artistic problems of the growing market. By different ways
and means, these organizations try to invent and experiment with uses,
practices and groups. Secondly, their activities represent what might be called
a 'strategy of cultural legitimacy': video is a practice that is especially
appropriate to those who are precluded from the 'official culture' but still
censure the 'mass culture', symbolized by television. Indeed, these social
practices within the framework of associations or groups with similar interests
come up against obstacles which restrain their influence as well as their future.
These obstacles are circumstantial, for instance, the juridical problems:
everybody knows about the temporary situation which restrains or even
prohibits the renting, exchange or duplication of video cassettes. Still, it seems
that more fundamental problems concern video practice itself and its
significance which is related to a process of individualizing cultural
consumption and social relationships.

Non-professional video production is still undeveloped and conforms to pre-existing practices (Family Super 8 and social video)

A survey carried out by JVC in the United States shows that 60 per cent of
the VCRs sold are home devices and 40 per cent are portable equipment.
However, video cameras only represent 20 per cent of the total equipment
sold: in 1980, there were about 2 million consumer video cameras in the
world. Other surveys show that the correlation between the practices of non-
professional cinema and video is a very slight one, the proportion being one-
third only. The remaining two-thirds represent 'new producers of images'. The
advantages and disadvantages of Super 8 and video are often compared,
showing that video allows not only smaller production costs, but also the
possibilities of erasing, recording in continuity and gaining better
luminosity. All these specifications are suitable for non-professional needs
based upon the 'continuity-shot'. The disadvantages are high initial
investment, weight and bulkiness, lack of autonomy and quick technical
development, which discourage the potential buyers. There is also a great

difference between Super 8 and video on psychological grounds: aesthetically, video refers to the televisual pattern, more heterogeneous and naturalistic than the cinematographic pattern which is of more cultural value and applies to an elite. For all these reasons and contrary to what is often said about video rendering the creation banal, it seems that, in fact, video should significantly democratize artistic expression and cultural communication. But consumer video will probably be restricted to such traditional family practices as photography and Super 8: a 'middle art' (in the words of sociologist Pierre Bourdieu). The non-professionals who apply to video-clubs or cultural associations are mainly going to benefit from practical services (training courses, loans of equipment, lower prices and so on). But the technique of editing, for instance, is still unknown to most of the non-professionals.

In the same way, the VCR with half-inch cassettes partly revives the social video practices of the 1970s, the advantages of the device allowing lower costs and the possibility of standardizing the equipment of different institutions. So, along with the growth in social and cultural associations or new services, we can notice a tendency to diversify the nature of the products: those who did not have access to non-portable equipment, and therefore to wealthy institutions, are now able to experiment with the possibilities, as well as the limitations, of audiovisual expression and social communication. The few non-professional video festivals, beginning to appear nowadays, also confirm this tendency to diversify producers and products.

The use of the VCR within schools is an opportunity to confront one type of culture with another

Although the school is not part of what we usually call the 'consumer market', it concerns our research for the following reason: an interministerial experiment called *Active Young TV Viewer (Jeune Téléspectateur Actif)* focused upon the education of the TV viewer (it is well known that children are heavy TV viewers) and aimed to equip numerous schools in France with half-inch consumer VCRs. Today, the situation is quite different from the 1970s when video was restricted to educational TV programmes, serving as a 'pedagogic aid' and to a few local productions. Now, school has changed its attitude towards TV, ceasing to reject it and admitting the social event it represents as well as its impact on children in everyday life. Moreover, such aims as the 'education of the TV viewer', to enable him to exercise more control over TV and to view it with a critical eye, correspond to the topics of advertising and the practice it proposes.

In fact, we have noticed that the VCR contributes to modifying the attitude of teachers: they feel less suspicious about TV and, even if it is challenging them, they are capable now of using it for educational purposes. It also prevents the children from rejecting school: TV is something familiar which enables them to escape from pedagogical formalism and boredom.

Teachers who take part in this experiment often utilize daily TV programmes that children are fond of: light entertainment programmes, cartoons, documentaries and so on. As for the children, they seem to be in a better position for a dialogue with the teachers since TV is part of their life and their culture, much more so than books. Therefore, without giving up their pedagogical function, the teachers integrate TV into their education programme at two levels:

    (a) teachers utilize some TV programmes as a source of information, a cultural document, an 'opening on the world' and an opportunity for discussions, adding to it their own knowledge; and

    (b) secondly, teachers utilize TV programmes as a tool for the analysis of television language, audiovisual narrative forms and the process of turning reality into images, so as to form a 'critical distance' with regard to the representation of the world offered by TV.

Such uses of the VCR enable one to confront two cultures which were dissociated until now: on the one hand, the educational rationalism essentially based upon the authority of the book and the teacher and on the other, the spectacular exhibition of the world essentially based upon the audiovisual capacity to captivate and to seduce.

CHAPTER 29

The Impact of the New Information Technology on Scientific and Scholarly Publishing

Irving L. Horowitz

Rutgers University, New Jersey

Mary E. Curtis

John Wiley & Sons, Publishers, New York

DISCUSSIONS OF THE NEW TECHNOLOGY and its impact on publishing have often centered on technical issues, such as how specific hardware can be incorporated into systems so as to maximize efficiency in the production and dissemination of books and periodicals.[1] Other discussions have been concerned with the implications for traditional book and periodical publishing. Issues have included xerography and its impact on copyright and word processing as a method to give publishers greater control over composition costs. The following discussion will emphasize the impact of new technologies not simply on the publishing business as it now exists, but with respect to its consequences for the social structure of the publishing business. How is the new information technology changing the fundamental character of author-publisher-marketplace relations?[2]

The common consensus, and the source of much concern, is that significant social changes, no less than technological changes, are underway. The dimensions of these changes can still only be surmised but the questions are at

---

[1]Such discussions often appear in trade periodicals such as *Folio* and *Book and Magazine Production*. For examples, see Frank Romano, *All Together Now: Standardization Helps Publishers Benefit from Photocomposition Technology,* Book and Magazine Production, September 1981, pp. 43-45; and *Demand Printing Could Provide Economical Reprints, Monographs.* Management Update, Folio, p. 4.

[2]"The extraordinary capabilities of information machines has tended to obscure the impact such machines are having on the very fabric of our economy-society" (Horton, 1979).

least becoming clearer. They include such issues as how the new technology affects the notion of property rights to intellectual material and the limits of copyright ownership in the publishing enterprise. How will decisions about what to publish in print format, what to archive or what is disposable be made in future years? Are these decisions being made wisely? What will be meant by a work being published? Will publishing be limited to mean the production of material in print or will it include output from the new technologies?

The Latin root of the term 'publish' is *publicare* — to make public. This simple meaning of publishing has grown more complex, since anyone can make anything public simply by affixing words to a piece of paper and photocopying it. If the same individual distributes the paper or adds it to a data bank, where it may be accessed by users, ownership of copyright and the means of communication becomes even more diffuse. Publishing can be performed by anyone who has the opportunity and ability to use the new technology to input and retrieve information, from librarians to researchers in industry.

The Copyright Law of 1978 began to acknowledge the implications of some of the changes imparted by technology by stating that copyright protection exists from the moment an idea is made permanent (Wagner, 1977). Permanence can mean affixing words to print or transcribing a document into some kind of machine-readable format, so that it can be introduced into and extracted from a data base. But the publishing community has yet to confront some of the legal implications of this broader definition of copyright. In fact, the new copyright legislation has moved a long way in the direction of considering ideas in relation to the creator, apart from mediating agencies such as publishers. Publishers gain few rights simply by virtue of having transcribed words into print, unless these rights have been explicitly transferred to them by the creator. Permanency can exist apart from any particular format, such as type. There is a strong presumption that since the work is now protected from the time of creation in permanent form, the relationship between author and publisher is different than it was in earlier times, when publishers automatically gained all rights by virtue of having printed the work in book or periodical form. The proprietary presumption is more heavily weighted on the side of authors than in the past.

In an age of xerography, simply affixing an idea to paper offers the possibility of dissemination. It is no longer essential to restrict the concept of permanence to setting words into type and then into traditionally printed and bound form. As technology influences publishing still further, the definition of what constitutes publishing will become more ubiquitous. There are now many ways to publish and disseminate information.[3] There are formats other than print, or in addition to it, through which ideas can be

---

[3]"The emergence of electronic publication does not resolve the confrontation between the First Amendment and its strong belief in the free use and exercise of information and statutory provisions for fair use under copyright protection. To be sure, such electronic transmission of copyrighted data and images, like the publication of hard copy itself, is coming under the increasing scrutiny of courts seeking not so much to inhibit consumer usage as in assuring proper payments to publishers and authors alike — whatever the forms may be of information transmission." See Oler (1980); Horowitz (1981).

disseminated. In a high technology environment, the publisher's traditional 'value-added' contributions of selection and evaluation, editing, typesetting, and proof reading may become less important in relation to some products and more important in relation to others. Marketing and promotion may become critical elements distinguishing publishing from availability. Certainly, marketing is a critical factor distinguishing publication by presumably legitimate publishers. So-called vanity press publication requires that the author assumes financial responsibility for production of the work, while the press assumes only limited responsibility for selling the work — with little or no investment in marketing or promotion.

Publishing has been moving toward greater emphasis on marketing and promotion for more than a decade. Such presumably marginal factors have become critical, even in scholarly publishing, partially because the market-place has witnessed a proliferation of published material. More books have been published since 1950 than in all the years prior to that and a great many of them have been scholarly in character. Those who participate in the complex system through which scholarship is produced and disseminated have consequently developed a growing awareness that publishing has commercial determinants. In textbook publishing, market research on consumer capabilities and demands plays an increasingly important role in the development and packaging of new textbooks. In scholarly publishing, the relationship between identifying and communicating with the market and responding to that market is more ambiguous.

Traditionally, the publisher runs a certain level of risk in selecting books and periodicals to compose, copyedit, print, bind and promote, but that risk is compensated by sale of those products beyond the level needed to recoup investment in those activities. In an environment where writers have increasing access to sophisticated technology, such as word-processing equipment, and where some responsibility for pre-publication activity can be transferred from publisher to author, the traditional author-publisher relationship may change (Esler, 1981).[4] As publishers yield certain responsibilities, they also yield control; and as authors invest more time and money in the preparation of copy prior to printing and marketing, their share of risks and rewards is likely to increase commensurately. Traditionally, authors take a small share of the return on investment, called a royalty. When a larger share of the initial investment is shared with the publisher, the royalty rates should increase. There are also other issues. As we witness more active participation in the pre-publishing process by authors, will publishers accept a decline in standards of editing and proof reading? Can authors maintain a press' standards?

In the pre-printing press era, people with ideas permitted others to copy their spoken words for a fee; human copiers recouped the fee by permitting others to copy their copy. In pre-commercial publishing times, authors simply

---

[4] A Wiley-author word-processing survey, conducted in the spring of 1981, reports that over half of Wiley's authors have some kind of word-processing capability available to them and 30 per cent use word-processing technology to prepare manuscripts.

printed their own work and tried to recoup their investment by selling that work. Historically, a number of commercial publishers began as printers. When they decided to back-up their judgment that certain works had commercial potential by investing in marketing and sharing the return on their investment with authors, they became publishers rather than printers. As printers began performing greater services for authors, advising them how to improve their work and helping them to do so, they indisputably added value to the author's work. It was not the same work that the author had originally presented to them. The value that publishers added to the work that an author creates has mainly taken the form of print-related activity — copyediting, typesetting, proofreading and so on. But now that the concept of publishing need no longer be restricted to print format, the publisher must rethink what value can be added to the work that the author creates. Publishers are uniquely positioned to perceive that work presented in one format could be packaged and sold in another; perhaps they can provide the means for transcribing the material into other formats or may offer to combine the material into another collection of material in which it has different applications and can be re-formatted.[5]

The possibilities are as limitless as our imagination. Publishers who continue to limit themselves to a print concept may experience economic difficulties resulting from the new markets created by the new technologies. Certain publishers, operating solely in traditional print formats, have attempted to reduce their pre-publication costs in the last decade by abdicating some of their traditional responsibilities for authenticating the merit and validity of a work. They will have to rethink those decisions. The publisher serves as a clearinghouse for specialized information; it is not simply a passive instrument transmitting ideas and information. If the publisher limits his role to production and dissemination and reduces his pre-publication contribution to a work, a more limited definition of role, coupled with the new technology, may make the publisher redundant.

Decision-making about what to publish and how to publish it will be of increasing rather than decreasing importance, especially in scientific and scholarly publishing. Organizing the decision-making process and incorporating some form of authentication into that process must remain one of the chief responsibilities of publishers. A publishing enterprise is known for a particular quality of book or periodical; its reputation rests on its publishing decisions. A publisher's reputation in a certain area can become a *bona fide* to prospective authors and customers alike and reputation will be a key factor ensuring credibility in the developing new technology markets. Specialization within the scientific community has encouraged smaller, more specialized forms of scholarly publishing and the development of specialized units within larger publishing houses. Both have close relationships with subsets of the scholarly community and their publishing activity both supports and is

[5]One advantage of having manuscripts in electronic form is that, given an age of the electronic dissemination of textual materials, publishers with words in machine-readable form will be able to sell their 'books' in either, or both, hard copy or disc form. See Paul (1981); Shotwell (1981).

supported by these subsets. The new technological environment will re-emphasize the role of the publisher in authenticating the work of an author to a select public of users. Even now in scholarly publishing, publishers do more than select information to make public; they validate it by the act of making it public, enhancing the value of the intellectual effort.

When professional societies are involved in a broad range of publishing activities, why is commercial publishing in that area needed? For example, both the American Chemical and the American Sociological Association are intensively involved in publishing. They publish journals, magazines, even semi-popular periodicals and newsletters. This situation can be replicated for many professional and scientific associations. Paradoxically, such professional agencies find it difficult to innovate. They must develop an internal consensus in order to act and this is a complex process, which is one reason why organizations, institutions and professional bodies need extension-arm services, as information technology provides. But this does not reduce the publisher's need to authenticate and disseminate.

Unlike a commercial organization, a Society has a presumption of collegiality and sees its responsibility as collective. Consequently, marginal areas of scientific inquiry seldom find expression in Society publishing. If all publishing were centralized, or grounded in professional societies, scientific communication could well be hampered. Even if a Society representing a disciplinary area did represent every legitimate field addressed by that discipline, emerging fields might not be covered, because a consensus about their merit had not yet developed. Such intellectual high-risk areas are best serviced by commercial publishers or independent university presses. In addition, subjects that are of interest across disciplines can be exploited by commercial publishers who already have established relationships in more than one discipline. Professional societies are reluctant to put their *imprimatur* on a work that may not be defined as 'serious' five years hence. Often, they are barely aware of the interests of those outside their own discipline or disagree about the merit of these interests. They are therefore conservative and reluctant to take intellectual risks. Commercial publishers, on the other hand, define intellectual risk in terms of business risk and cannot afford to be too conservative.

This suggests a corollary activity. Universities, no less than other large institutions engaged in research activity, do not define themselves as responsible for encouraging innovation outside that institution. Such organizations serve as initiators, places that provide supportive resources so that serious work can be done; they do not propagate such work once it is completed. The publisher of scholarly work, in the physical and social sciences, serves as a filtering agent. The publisher acts as an independent autonomous factor, able to permeate the university or scholarly environment as a whole, to sift through opinions and evaluations until it perceives a degree of agreement about what work is important. Publishing gives scholars and researchers a way to move beyond parochialism and organizational constraints. It is not only that organizations and universities are unwilling to make publishing decisions; rather, they are ill-prepared to propagate pioneering work they have helped initiate.

Publishing has a peculiar position in the scholarly world: it 'brokers' innovation. It cannot stimulate innovation, it can only respond. Without that broker, it would be difficult to verify scientific innovation or intellectual imagination. The publisher's interests in the verification of what it publishes derives from the fact that a publisher is defined not only in terms of the information it releases, but in terms of what it does *not* publish. How that information is sifted is one means by which the scientific endeavour is rationalized. The publisher, as part of the division of intellectual labour, performs unique chores. The publisher is that agent prepared to evaluate and market specialized data and ideas, as well as that agent uniquely equipped to provide a forum for the distillation and synthesis of those data and ideas. The new information technology, as it multiplies mechanisms for scientific communication, will make the mediating role played by the publisher even more important. The classical division of intellectual labour may shift, but the relationship will be enhanced rather than weakened by the new information technology.

Scholarly publishing is itself intended as an authenticating device. It is also a medium through which work can be further authenticated by a scholarly community. As such, publishing facilitates decisions about promotion and rewards. The publisher provides a medium for ideas to which other people can respond; the publisher creates an entity which exists apart from what the author alone creates. A book can be reviewed, receive an award, be cited and so on; it has a reality that is vouchsafed only by the publishing process. The resources a publisher commits to marketing its publications say something about how important the publisher thinks the work is and the kind of financial return it expects the publication to yield. Users perceive that fact and respond accordingly. As an adjunct to this process, communication among individuals interested in a particular area may be facilitated by publication. For example, if their names and addresses are captured (say on a subscription list or a book-buyers' list), development of a network may occur as the list becomes an instrument through which the publisher introduces new publications and products. Absent such instruments, as the network becomes refined, the difficulty of communicating with that group may increase. Precise targeted marketing itself becomes a central publishing function. The new technology both enhances and complicates this function.

Bibliographic data banks, containing comprehensive information about the existence (and sometimes availability) of scholarly books and periodical articles, enables users to search for everything on a particular subject that has been published over a defined period of time. In some cases, the user can scan large amounts of text and access specific pages of a work to determine whether or not it is relevant to his research. The user can go one step further and order the information, visible on his terminal, to be printed, if a printer is attached to the terminal or, if a large amount of material is desired, the researcher may order the material printed offline and mailed to him by a document-delivery service. The user need never go to the orginal.[6] In the United States, online services now permit searches of bodies of material published by *Dow Jones Inc., New York Times, Washington Post* and other newspapers. KIT (Key Issue Tracking) offers a constantly updated index of important and topical subjects. LEXIS provides searches of legal material. The Congressional Information Service is available online. But users' acceptance has been mixed. LEXIS is a great success among attorneys, partly because of an intelligent initial marketing strategy. Use will expand as faster terminals become more widely available and more scholars become familiar with using online searches as a supplement to traditional forms of scholarly research.[7]

The wider acceptance of such technology may also affect traditional ways publishers communicate with their customers. When searching of bibliographic data banks becomes routine, publishers may not be able to justify investing in extensive direct mail to bring certain categories of scholarly books and periodicals to the attention of a wide spectrum of professionals, particularly if only a handful of them will care about the work. When prospective customers are scientists and businessmen (groups which still comprise the majority of microcomputer owners), scholarly and professional publishers may find it cost-effective to set up free access to information about new products through existing telephone networks such as Telenet. The librarian of the future will be an 'information manager', skilled in knowledge of information storage and retrieval systems and able to provide information about where and how material of interest to researchers can be accessed (Bergen, 1981; Stueart, 1981). Publishers may confine their efforts, in some cases, to informing the librarian/information manager about a work; they in turn will direct users to that work. Marketing today involves informing large numbers about the availability of a book or journal, but selling to only a small peripheral group after one has sold to the core group — often less than one per cent of those informed. As the marketplace becomes increasingly segmented, reflecting the development of science and scholarship itself, technology may enable publishers to communicate effectively and at acceptable costs with the segmented marketplace.

Publishing itself may become redefined. Certain works are now produced in extremely limited editions, perhaps only 'on demand' or by means of xerography with loose-leaf binding. It is possible that information centres

---

[6]One serious source of potential, and actual, litigation amongst publishers is in the area of unauthorized abstracting services. *The New York Times'* KIT, for example, is embroiled in serious controversy with McGraw Hill's *Business Week,* the latter charging that such abstracting, based on exclusive copyrighted material, is being recycled and illegally sold; whereas the *Times'* position claims that there is no copyright on facts. This is an area of litigation that will grow as computer technology of the printed work expands. See Barry (1981).

[7]Given an annual worldwide market for information technology now roughly US$110 billion and expanding at ten per cent annually in real terms, the impact on publications will be substantial. Journals and books, especially those of a data-rich variety with highly refined audiences, are prime candidates for electronic counterparts to conventional journals. The mechanisms for publisher participation in such efforts are stil experimental, but quite real. See Seiler and Raben (1981); Singleton (1981).

(libraries) will produce needed material on demand, in addition to informing researchers about it, *de facto* assuming some publishing functions. Availability will become associated with a given centre of research. Aspects of the scholarly publishing process are beginning to take place in a non-commercial environment as part of the costs of performing research. The cost of publication is now more frequently built into specific allocation of funds to a project. In such cases, material is prepared with little attention to minimal standards of publication.

As this kind of in-house 'publishing' becomes commonplace, and as bibliographic data banks receive information and maintain records about the availability of such material, the 'informing' role of the publisher may become less critical to the dissemination of certain kinds of scholarly material. Those who seek specialized information may be required to take a more active and less passive role in the pursuit of such questions. As the information manager redefines his role, he will play an important part in this communication process. Conversely, the publisher of such material can become more passive with respect to traditional marketing. In the future, a publisher's decision to commit substantial resources to promote a work may be a key factor distinguishing active from passive publication and broadly important from technically significant work. The definition of a work's importance may be as simple as how many direct mail pieces are despatched and responded to or how many space advertisements, directed to how many discrete audiences, are placed in what periodicals. Promotional and advertising budgets will become a key definition of what constitutes significant publishing; commitment to a certain level of effort in an area, or clarification of an intent to promote aggressively, will become central to contractual negotiations between authors and publishers. A distinction will continue to be made between self-promotion by an author and promotion by a publisher addressed to the buying public.

The role of the marketing professional within publishing is changing dramatically. Authors have thought about marketing as a routine activity. Information about the work is given to a marketing person and that individual simply provides generic information to another generic entity, known as the public. Increasingly, marketing people are becoming involved in publishing decisions at earlier phases. They may point to a need for books on a particular subject because sales suggest there is demand for such books or journals. They are ideally positioned to filter information about acceptance of and demand for new technology-based products. The marketing role is not only limited to the satisfaction of letting people know that a work exists but, increasingly, it encompasses interpreting consumer needs, or the needs of scholars in a particular area, and helping to define what kinds of products might satisfy those needs. In most businesses, marketing people play a major role in product development, in figuring out how to shape a product that people will want to buy. To some extent, those involved in the marketing of scholarly information will also participate in shaping products that their customers will buy and these products will not be confined exclusively to print products.

Historically, producers and consumers of scholarship have been closely identified. In addition, a larger general interest audience bought some serious books, particularly on history, politics and social issues. This group still exists and an occasional book taps this market, but usually such success results from serendipity rather than careful planning. Certainly, the general-interest audience is much smaller than in the past, when it ranged from dillitantes to people who were simply curious about a particular subject. Our private and business lives increasingly require such a high level of specialization of interests, tastes and skills that the curious onlooker (the person curious about serious work in an avocational sense) is disappearing. Few book or journal buyers are seekers after truth, in a general non-heuristic, non-utilitarian sense. At the end of the twentieth century, everyone is part of a market. Even the buyer of antiquarian books is a distinct market. The marketplace is radically different from what it was even ten years ago. As the general-interest audience has declined, the market is increasingly limited solely to producers and consumers of information, who are fast becoming one and the same individual. The publisher, therefore, rarely can expand sales by innovative marketing techniques; success resides in identifying, with utmost precision, the actual potential of the market and achieving results in that scaled-down universe.

The market for scholarly and professional material is highly educated and technically specialized. When it is interested in a problem, this population wants to know everything that has been written about it. Depending on the problem, the researcher may be willing to pay a high price to avoid the possibility of missing even a small part of the available information about a particular question. In some areas — patent research, for example — the cost of overlooking even one item is unacceptably high. Unless a data bank is complete and current, patent researchers will not bother to search it. When the stakes go up in terms of time and reputation, consumers will pay a great deal and take the information any way they can get it. They may even be willing to pay for the same information twice. Many subscribers to online systems now subscribe to a backup system carrying the same data banks, to ensure that if one system fails they can get at the data through the other system. Users of online systems are even more likely to use them when someone else will ultimately be paying the bill. This truism may, in part, account for attorneys' acceptance of LEXIS. The high prices charged for scholarly and professional print information have gone far beyond what general-interest readers are prepared to pay. Publishers produce books and journals for the specialized reader rather than the general-interest reader. Scholars write for their peers, not the intelligent layman. This very fact has come to define what we mean by scholarly publishing. Books dealing with serious issues are no less plentiful than they were in previous decades, but they are rarely picked up by the general-interest reader. Journals are directed to segmented audiences.

The new technology may accelerate this process already underway, which is a kind of new feudalism. The scholarly publishing world is one of limited numbers, limited players and searchers for legitimation, with an extremely high personal investment in the results of the game. Authors and publishers share an interest in the same outcome, although for different reasons. Both hope to reach their target audiences so as to allow the information they have generated to be more widely used. Generally, the payoff for authors is recognition and the emoluments that accompany publishing. They are less concerned with general impact than with specific impact. Both the author and publisher realize that they cannot effectively communicate with the entire universe of persons who may be marginally interested in a work. It costs too much and 99 per cent of those contacted may not be interested. Funds that are spent in reaching the 10 per cent of the world that may be marginally interested in an author's work would be better spent in reaching those people who are known to be eager to know about the work. Resources are finite. Authors are being encouraged to become more realistic about the limited number of potentially interested people and to become active supporters of specialized marketing. Increasingly, questionnaires to authors require them to provide relatively sophisticated marketing information. Publishers know that probably no one in their firm can define the specific audience they want to reach better than the author. Certainly, questions about target audiences, major outlets and primary sources presume (and encourage) a high degree of sophistication on the part of authors. Publishers thus compel authors to accept the notion of the specialized marketplace; the questions evoke that awareness. If the post-printing press environment, like the pre-printing press environment, permits more direct interaction between the author and the marketplace, the scale will be different. Publishers exist and they are large. The scholarly world is diverse and geographically dispersed. Authors still need the resources publishers offer, but publishers must rethink their role and figure out exactly what they will do for authors in order to retain their value to them. We return to the medieval notion of the author, who was not only involved in the production of his work, but with its dissemination. How the involvement of authors in marketing will evolve in relation to publishing as we now know it and how it will interact with the new technology are fascinating questions. How they are answered may define conditions for success for professionals and the survival of some publishers.

Scholarly publishing addresses specialized audiences and it will be heavily impacted by the new technology. Even now, products can be delivered in microfiche, microfilm or discettes, in loose leaf, updates and on demand — as well as in traditional books and journals. By the late 1980s, online access to vast quantities of full-text material will become widespread as optical discs reduce the costs of storing online data, as computers become faster and as software becomes more sophisticated (Alder, 1981; Harmon, 1981). The inherent value of the information and ideas will increasingly determine pricing, rather than the cost of manufacturing the package. The new information technology, at least in its interim phases, may also compel us to move away from the notion of risk and liability as the sole province of publishers, to risk and liability as a shared responsibility of the community of scholarship.

Technology does not mechanically resolve itself into new social systems. A fully articulated, post-print publishing world awaits the resolution of a number of complex issues. These issues are as fundamental as what form of presentation of information will be defined as publishing. Will saddle-stitch reports, prepared by an agency or a campus with which a scholar is affiliated, constitute publication? What about the inputting of information into a data bank accessed by subscribers to an online system, when no hard copy at all is created unless the subscriber requests that information be printed? There may be works for which no physical inventory is ever created and other works that are published solely to satisfy an institutional need and receive no reviewing attention. Are these to be considered publications? Even now, a myriad of post-publication issues exist. The complexity of these issues will be intensified by the possibilities inherent in the new technology.

The scholarly environment has a number of feudal elements and publishing has taken on some of the characteristics of the scholarly world it serves. If scholarly publishers, as we now know them, are to maintain a primary role in this world of rapidly accelerating technological development, they must rise above a kind of cottage-industry approach to the way in which information is prepared, distributed and evaluated. The new technology offers the possibility of extraordinarily rapid accumulation and dissemination of information. Yet curiously, word processing and even information retrieval systems share characteristics of cottage industries. For example, composition, until the past decade, was performed almost exclusively in large print shops and factory settings. Increasingly, factory settings are being replaced by composition units in private dwellings, perhaps controlled by a central management that allocates work and processes magnetic or paper tapes on computers to create camera-ready material. Inputting typeset material into data bases at acceptable cost levels requires that the typeset material be captured in machine-readable format, together with knowledgeable people who can work with the online service to translate the composition codes and structure the format of the electronic product appropriately (*Nature,* 1981).[8] Publishers may have to make a short-term choice between goals. They may have to choose between buying composition at the lowest possible price, which will be especially important as the market for print material declines, or positioning themselves to create an electronic product by using full service (and usually more expensive) compositors, with a programming staff committed to help develop an electronic version of the product.

Technology is already affecting publishing. In mass-market publishing, tie-ins have been important for some time. A television show or movie seen alongside the first appearance or reissue of a paperback can ensure its success. What comes first is often transformed: sometimes the paperback is derived from the television show. Discette or video-cassette versions of print stories may become more frequent, as multiple forms of packaging the same entertainment for the mass market becomes common (Dahlin, 1981).

---

[8]The point is also forcefully made by Cuadra Associates, a Californian consulting group, in their formal presentations.

Educational publishers are developing software that will enable students to apply what they have learned in textbooks in real-life simulations of problem-solving. Similarly, scholarly publishing is developing new products in response to markets opened up by the new technology. Consumers of information and entertainment may have a variety of ways to receive the same content.

Those who are trying to develop and disseminate online data bases are at something of a crossroads in new product development. The general consumer market is clearly going to be a major user of the new technology but, so far, data bases directed towards the consumer market (such as the Source), have not been particularly successful. Data bases that are designed for specific professions or industries with a major commitment to research and development have been far more successful. More than half the nearly 1,000 data bases now available are source bases, containing raw data, summarized data or data in manipulated formats. Source data bases may be exclusively numerical (financial and stock quotations), textual/numeric (such as Disclosure, which manipulates data provided by the US Securities and Exchange Commission) and full-text (such as LEXIS offered by Mead Data and Weslaw offered by West). As terminals can more rapidly screen large amounts of material and as graphic terminals become available at a price users can afford, we may expect widespread acceptance of full-text delivery. Some of the former print products may be constructed solely for online, such as newsletters or frac and answer data bases. Video-discs hooked up with online services may enable people to retrieve visual as well as textual information on any subject without delay. Encyclopaedias and catalogues are prime candidates for this kind of electronic product.

This is a new publishing environment. According to the American Association of Publishers, nearly thirty publishing houses are trying to develop electronic versions of book products (Gallese, 1981). Bibliographic data bases now provide mechanisms for managing an incredible amount of information, especially technical information, that our society now generates (Freedman, 1981). One can define through use of 'key terms' the kind of information one wants to know about and immediately find out where work on that subject has been printed, screening out a great deal of information 'noise'. Information retrieval, through computer-based means, permits researchers instantly to get what is pertinent to their interests; the the usefulness of online services. Access to online terminals is still restricted and use of online services can be expensive. But as scholars become familiar with using terminals to access online data bases, the amount of research conducted may be transformed. Depending on the kind of research being done and who is paying for it, research can be performed on terminals at home, much as some authors now work at home on word-processing units. Of course, people will need to come together in public fora for certain purposes, but these occasions can be supplemented by work at home. We are moving into an era when people will be able to control and access the large quantities of information generated as direct and indirect by-products of business and scholarship.

Access will not be automatic. There will be a struggle to define who is allowed access to what kind of information. The nineteenth century was largely defined by the struggle for control of the means of production; the twentieth century is being defined as a struggle over the means of communication and information. The new technology forces us to come to terms with the social content of ideas: who controls the hardware, software and marketing, or information about the information, may ultimately control the information itself. What is released and in what quantity will itself come to define what we mean by big words like 'democracy'. We may begin to talk about democracy in terms of how widely a society permits access to information, computers or photocopying equipment. In totalitarian societies, the struggle is clearly on to limit all possible access to the means of communication. Thus, while there may be threatening or uncertain aspects of the new information technology, there are undoubtedly liberating aspects as well.

Potentially, every person is both a producer and a transmitter of information. In the past, information was the monopoly of the few. As access to control of the delivery of information itself becomes democratized, as more persons become involved in the publishing process, there is an opportunity to maximize information as a liberating, democratizing activity.[9] Authoritarian regimes restrict access to information, while at the same time they are plagued by the need to use advanced information. Whatever the short-term difficulties outlined, democratic societies will be advantaged by the new technology and by its openness to all. There are, after all, problems of abundance and affluence — issues that an open society can more readily cope with than a totalitarian society.

[9]"As publishers, we are opposed to the regulation of content in any form . . . Democracy cannot exist without unfettered freedom of speech and both government and private citizens must constantly be on guard against any encroachments and any forms of censorship." From the American Association of Publishers invited policy statement, filed on September 23 1981, in response to legislative efforts to rewrite the Communications Act of 1934. *AAP Newsletter,* 9 October 1981.

References

Alter, Nicholas A. (1981) *Microfilm: The Next Ten Years.* UMI International Reprint, June.

Berger, Mary C. (1981) *The Endangered Species: Can Information Service Survive.* ASIS Bulletin, October, pp. 12-14.

Berry, John F. (1981) *'Times' in Copyright Controversy.* The Washington Post (Business and Finance section), 8 Novembr 1981.

Dahlin, Robert (1981) *Consumer as Creator.* Publisher's Weekly, March.

Esler, Bill (1981) *The Printer Strikes Back.* Book and Magazine Production, July, pp. 39-42.

Freedmen, Henry B. (1981) *Paper's Role in an Electronic World.* The Futurist, October, pp. 11-16.

Gallese, Liz Roman (1981) *Publishers try adapting Print to Video Uses.* Wall Street Journal, 2 November 1981, p.1.

Harmon, George H. (1981) *Micrographics: Return of the 25-cent Book?* The Futurist, 18 October 1981, pp. 61-62.

Horowitz, I. L. (1981) *Corporate Ghosts in the Photocopying Machine.* Scholarly Publishing, Vol. 12, No. 4, pp. 299-304.

Horton, Forest Woody, Ed. (1979) *The Information Resource: Policies – Background – Issues.* Information Industry Association, Washington DC, p.1.

Nature (1981) *Making Journals fit for Readers.* New Journals' Review, Nature, October, p. 341.

Oler, Harriet L. (1980) Copyright Law and the Fair Use of Visual Images. In *Fair Use and Free Inquiry: Copyright Law and the New Media,* J. S. Lawrence and B. Trimberg (Eds.), Albex Publishing, Norwood, N.J., pp. 268-286.

Paul, Sandra K. (1981) *Roadblocks in typesetting from the Word Processor.* Scholarly Publishing, Vol. 12, No. 4, pp. 323-327.

Seiler, L. H. and Raben, J. (1981) *The Electronic Journal.* Transaction/Society, Vol. 18, No. 6, pp. 76-83.

Shotwell, Robyn (1981) *Getting into Data base Publishing: Some Possibilities and Pitfalls,* Publisher's Weekly, 11 Sept. 1981, pp. 45-46.

Singleton, Allan (1981) *The Electronic Journal and its Relatives.* Scholarly Publishing, Vol. 13, No. 1, pp. 3-18.

Stueart, Robert D. (1981) *Great Expectations: Library and Information Science at the Crossroads.* Library Journal, 15 October, pp. 1989-1992.

Wagner, Susan (1977) *New Copyright Law Primer.* Publisher's Weekly, 26 December 1977, pp. 37-42.

New Information Technology and the Individual in Future European Societies

Olav Holst

FAST Programme, Commission of the European Communities

THE STORM was raging. Various objects were thrown in different directions, dust and sand were stirred up and it was difficult to see at a distance. From time to time, it was even impossible to discover where one was. Such is the situation many conference participants find themselves in. But one the storm has spent its force and everything has calmed down, one can reconsider the landscape. It has certainly changed in several respects, but is the new one more attractive than the previous one? What remains after the storm has passed? Did the wind go in a certain direction after all or was it a whirlwind, creating a lot of noise and inconvenience but effectively only rotating objects?

These are the standard questions to be asked after every conference and the subject *Information Technology: Impact on the Way of Life* invites them for two particular reasons: it is very broad in its scope and the research related to it is still in its infancy.

This discussion does not try to make a 'before- and after-the-storm' assessment of the entire landscape, but it is a modest attempt, presumably biased, to identify a few trees and buildings which resisted the storm and some which were levelled to the ground. Let us begin by stating two general principles for approaching the new information technology from a societal point of view.

Principle I: The necessity of killing some myths on the information technology

Sorge *et al* state in Chapter 9 that: "The discussion of work and employment under new technology has suffered from a speculation where truisms, truths, half-truths and plain errors are strangely mixed." The only objection one feels tempted to make is on its limitation to the fields of work and employment, omitting such fields as leisure activities, education, transport and domestic tasks, just to mention a few which have also been subjects for the creation of a number of myths.

It is my impression that this Conference contributed significantly to the killing of some of the myths on the societal impacts of new information technology as I shall try to show later in the discussion. It must also be admitted that 'contributed' is the correct word because many of the myths only die hard. That the main characteristic of the new information technology is to devour jobs, or that we shall live and work in a wired house in a few years time, are myths which are fostered and kept alive by very powerful social actors.

Principle II: How to fly high yet keep one's feet on the ground

How can it be that the subject 'the future impact of new information technology' on one hand, has fostered so much speculation in Europe (or even 'wild phantasies') on what will more or less inevitably happen and, on the other hand, has resulted in very few visionary ideas about how the new information technology should be used?

Nobody can give the answer but it has established one fact, namely that we are inclined to reject visionary ideas as daydreaming when we are confronted with them. Such was the case in Masuda's visionary paper on *The Global Information Society* (see Chapter 3). Terms such as global education system, global health care system and global intelligence are not familiar to us, maybe because we are used to reacting to undesirable consequences of emerging technologies, as opposed to pre-acting according to some desired objectives.

Masuda's views tell us to become pre-active and not to maintain the present bias of the public and political debate by only discussing the negative consequences of the new information technology, even conducting the discussion in a fatalistic way. And weight is given to the message when it comes from one of the 'grand old men' behind the Japanese strategy for information technology. On the other hand, Martin-Löf suggests a more realistic appraisal of what the new information technology can do and cannot do on its own — it will not go as fast as promoters hope nor so badly as critics fear.

The two messages to be taken from Martin-Löf and Masuda are certainly not contradictory but complementary. They suggest, respectively, that we should be more down to earth about the impact and the power of technology, but we should try to fly a bit higher, which will also give us more vision when we set our wider societal objectives for the application of the new information technology. Martin-Löf calls for more empirical evidence on the relations between technology and society; Masuda calls for a wider public and political debate, which the Conference and this publication hopefully will stimulate. There are already good indications that this has happened in Ireland and we shall elaborate later on the need for strategic thinking and setting strategic objectives for the societal use of the new information technology.

On New Information Technology and its impact on society

The new information technology is not the source of a societal revolution but will only enhance trends in an evolutionary development of society. Several authors (Boddy and Buchanan, Hedge and Crawley, Radar, Sorge *et al*) have shown the validity of this statement for the working environment and others (Martin-Löf, Garnham) have expanded it to other fields of human activity. To clarify it, we can say that there are factors such as economic and social policies, labour market agreements and education policy on the societal level, and management structures and lifestyles on the micro level, which are more critical than new information technology in determining the future development of society. A logical consequence is that the generalisations about the impact of new information technology have hardly any value. Sorge *et al* have shown this in an Anglo-German investigation in the case of CNC-machine tools and suggest that:

> *Just as CNC has different effects, according to plant and batch size, type of cutting and machinery, so it also adapts to different societal environments. It is fitted into different institutions and habits of technical work, management and training. In our cases, it leaves Anglo-German differences in this respect, which has already been established, intact.*

One cannot generalise from CNC to the general societal impact of new information technology, but the results of Garnham point in the same direction. He has analysed leisure activities and has focused "on TV, both because it is the medium that dominates cultural relations and because, for that very reason, it is the focus of efforts to introduce information technology to the domestic consumer". He finds most forecasts, in particular those by the promoters of new technology, far too exaggerated and says that:

> *The trick is played by concentrating upon the technical potentialities rather than upon the social relations that will determine the form in which those potentialities are realised and by denying history by exaggerating the novelty of the process in question.*

Garnham sees two alternative future societies. The one will foster social relations and be based upon the public (as opposed to the private) as the essence of humanity, while the other will foster a social strucutre of atomized and privatized individuals subordinating the mass to a manipulative form of elite control. He concludes by saying:

> *These latter tendencies will be powerfully reinforced in the cultural sphere by the introduction of information technology under market conditions. Such introduction should therefore so far as possible be opposed.*

Other authors, who argue that 'technology has no impact *per se*, the impact depends on our use of technology and there are options available to us', suggest in my opinion a hypothetical openness of the future, if they do not in the same breath add comments on the need for long-term societal strategies. Without anticipative long-term actions, not many options remain valid.

Towards New Forms of Daily Life?

There is no evidence that we will be confronted with major changes in our daily life over the next 5 to 10 years. The few experiences so far suggest a smooth incorporation of new technological applications into present activities due to development determined by humans. The observation calls for a qualification: the reason for such apparently smooth introduction might be that only a tiny fraction (the elite?) has adopted the new technologies. The market for the general public has not as yet taken off. When it does, we may have to confront changes in daily life of quite a different order of magnitude. Today, information technology is in the factory and in some offices, but it is only in a few classrooms and, except for a few hobbyists, not in the home. The most important factor in major societal and economic impact of the new information technology and therefore the emergence of a real information society, is the way (time, speed and modalities) the general public will choose the way in which new information technology is used. A better understanding of how this can happen and its consequences is urgently required.

Time budgets, time-space budgets or activity programmes are tools available for such analysis, but they are rarely used and therefore there is only scattered information on the linkage between various daily activities and their development over time. The traditional weakness has been the lack of longitudinal data, which has also conventionally been by-passed by making a cross-sectional analysis. By taking a particular 'progressive group', one hoped to identify a pattern of behaviour which could be taken as representative of a more general future pattern for society as a whole. Gershuny and Thomas (1981) have shown that this approach is fundamentally shaky because it makes no attempt to identify the underlying factors determining how people spend their time. Without this, it is almost impossible for us to make forecasts and we have to rely upon retrospective or cross-sectional analyses.

De Gournay goes one step further by arguing that, for the privileged classes in society, the dividing line between leisure and work does not exist and "this takes us a long way from an approach based on time budgets, since such an approach postulates that every activity has its own finality and is confined to this". Keeping such fundamental weaknesses of time budgets in mind, the Conference revealed some interesting results. The discussions by Knulst, and by Baboulin *et al* put forward specific observations on time spend on the media and the effect of this on other activities. A general observation, albeit almost a truism, needs however to be mentioned: the cross-sectional differences in time budgets are much greater than the longitudinal changes — the differences between groups (employed men, employed women with children, employed women without children, etc.) are much greater than the differences one of these groups makes in their time budgets even over very long periods. There is another general observation which may appear less conventional to most readers: There is no reason whatsoever to believe that we are moving towards a leisure society. Knulst finds, for instance, that average working time for working men decreased by 80 minutes per week from 1975 to 1980, but "the time gained did not go into leisure activities ... but shifted to work in the home and looking after the family".

The point is further supported by de Gournay, who in her concept of lifestyle, goes beyond the time budget:

The belief that people will change their lifestyles when they work less and have more time at their disposal is a highly dubious assumption, not to say an assumption which has been invalidated by recent events: when workers in slump-ridden iron/steel and textile industries were given early retirement, it was noticed that the new jobless had a great deal of difficulty in finding an occupation which they considered to be of personal value.

An analysis of work activity as seen in the context of all daily activities of the individual gives further evidence to the belief that no significant changes in daily life are at hand. Let us take working-at-home as an example. 'Work' cannot change dramatically without having comparable dramatic repercussions on other daily activities of the individual for at least two reasons:

(1) the activity 'work' is to most people the centre piece in structuring their daily activities, partly determining the timing, duration, nature and place of other activities such as transport, leisure, shopping and social contacts;

(2) the activity 'work' has several functions other than merely producing a certain output. For the individual, it also means social contacts, personal fulfilment and a change of physical environment. Working-at-home will, in comparison with the way most people work today, affect all these functions and compensation will be looked for in other spheres of daily activity.

Thus, working-at-home on a large scale is not a minor ripple on the surface of daily life. It would mean a major rupture in our daily life and that is why we do not consider it likely to happen over the next 10 years. In the long term, it might well happen and therefore we need to look further into the question of alternative scenarios for working-at-home, the actors involved, the means at their disposal and so on. It is necessary to use a systems approach to analyse working-at-home and that is usually not done by those who promote working-at-home nor by those forecasting its spread. It has, for instance, often been suggested (to my knowledge, mostly by men) that working-at-home is a unique opportunity (for women!) to combine work and child care. Cronberg gently debunks this:

Not surprisingly, voices are already raised proposing that women (since they are at home anyway) could also take care of their children during the day. Work at a terminal and simultaneous use of household machines may be one thing. But simultaneous care of children must be a stress factor, not only in relation to the work but also for the children concerned.

There is also a very simple and real, but often forgotten, constraint on the use of working-at-home: the need for appropriate space. This point is well illustrated by the following quotations:

The dwellings we have are already adapted to the new everyday life in front of home terminals — Cronberg.

To sum up, before rejoicing at the possibilities of saving on energy and travelling, which could be achieved by bringing certain activities back into the home, perhaps some thought should be given to the fact that this flexibility of organization will initially benefit those classes which have sufficient space to accommodate them — de Gournay.

To summarize then on the likely spreading of working-at-home, there is no evidence at all to support the belief of a rapid spread of home work during the next 5 to 10 yers. On the contrary, there are physical and social constraints suggesting that only few groups will make use of it. As particular candidates for immediate use of working-at-home, Espejo and Ziv suggest the following groups: housewifes, the disabled, the elderly and people living in mountainous regions. At least these groups have a clear 'need' for working-at-home, but whether they will actually get the opportunity depends on our actions in, for instance, infrastructural investments and social and labour market policies. Thus Principle II, mentioned earlier, also applies to working-at-home: be more realistic as to what is likely to happen, but be more imaginative in the normative use of the new information technology.

On Communication and Spatial Structures

Let us continue the analysis from the previous section to see how new information technology may affect spatial structures. We have seen that changes in the location of work are not bound to a certain development but still open to 'alternative futures'. At that stage of development, it is important to outline options and to discuss objectives before elaborating details of specific plans. This is what Cronberg has done, in presenting three scenarios for working-at-a-distance: work-at-home, neighbourhood centres and the electronic community. Having found home work only rarely accepted by society, she analyses neighbourhood centres. They eliminate several of the drawbacks of working-at-home (loss of personal contacts, lack of basis for trade unions, health risks); but, according to Cronberg, one decisive risk remains — neighbourhood centres as 'a ghetto for women'. Therefore, she argues for the third alternative: "The electronic community, a development towards a decentralized, resource-conscious, small-scale local community, a community not isolated from the world, but one with a more independent and self-governing structure than today's housing area". This alternative scenario certainly deserves further technical, economic and political consideration and I hope my pessimism proves wrong when I cannot avoid thinking of the quotation by Peter Hall in his report *Europe 2000,* where he says: "As with resource-conserving society, so with a decentralized decision-making society, we cannot easily image what it would be like".

In fact, the 'electronic community' goes far beyond the activity of work. Analysing it, we must look at the fundamental relations between daily life expressed as activity programmes, transport and spatial structures. These three elements are intrinsically interrelated through the need for communication. Changes in one of the elements will inevitably, with delays of course, lead to changes in the two others. Consider these two particular phenomena: the interrelation between telecommunication and transport, and new information technology and regional development.

Dover suggests in her discussion on the possible impact of new telecommunications technology on urban-transport demand that "although the possibilities for telecommunications substitution exist for a wide range of activities, information technology may not in fact have as much impact as initially thought". Considering the various journey purposes in urban transport, her analysis suggests shopping and personal business journeys are most likely to be first affected by telecommunications, followed by journeys to and from work and journeys in the course of the work. The paper by Picot *et al* gives some empirical evidence on the last group of journeys. Data from four organizations, in two large private companies with some 30 locations in Germany, show that "about 8 per cent of more than 1,000 face-to-face contacts are perceived as suitable for new electronic media (tele-tex and/or fax)". The rather small figure of 8 per cent does not suggest a no-change development, but the main changes are *within* telecommunication between alternative media for telecommunication, not between telecommunication and transport. Picot *et al* say:

> *Telecommunication technology in general and new text-oriented media in particular can primarily take over those transfers of information which can be coded and whose content is not too complex. New technology can carry out those communications faster, cheaper and probably more reliably than channels previously used for that purpose.*

Thus, firstly there is only little scope for substituting travel by telecommunications. Secondly, even if the first effect would be to suppress travel for some specific purposes, there is good evidence (Holst, 1982 based on data from Javeau, 1972) that the time saved in the first place on transport will be spent on transport for other trip-purposes, such as going away for the weekend — thus not net saving.

On the question of regional development, how will new information technology affect the less-favoured regions of Europe? This is a question barely considered as yet, but which is of crucial importance to the cohesion of Europe. Some of the discussions of the Conference have thrown flashes of light on the issue. Bannon has analysed the implication for regional development in Ireland and he concludes pessimistically that the present trends of worsening regional disparities within the European Community "will continue, intensified by technical change, unless there are enlightened regional and urban policies to take advantage of new possibilities outside the developed areas". In particular, the knowledge-based industries must form part of regional development policies and, therefore, Bannon concludes that investments in research and development and in higher education in the lagging regions must occur at a substantially faster rate than in the more prosperous regions. Similar strategies for regional development are suggested by Williams, Jeffrey and Joyce who argue that:

Information technology is only one small factor that might influence the location of economic activities. Other more important factors are transport infrastructure, the location of existing industrial investment, government policy and input and market links.

Therefore, they argue, any policy for the use and development of information technology is pointless, if it is not part of a wider package of regional and urban planning, economic and industrial policies. They suggest the encouragement of the growth of indigenous economic activity as an extra objective for regional development policy; the application of new information technology is a powerful tool for pursuing such a policy, by allowing more rapid diffusion of innovation. "Hence, there is a need to concentrate not upon the provision or improvement in information technology, but in the provision of information itself". In my opinion, this quotation is more pertinent than the previous one. Information technology may only appear as 'a small factor' in location policy if viewed in isolation, but mastering the new information technology is a future basic asset, without which regions cannot survive economically. How could a region lagging behind the information technology, for instance, attract employment when 50 per cent of the labour force is in information jobs?

In summary, in spite of the many valuable specific findings on how to use new information technology to help regional development, one cannot but conclude that the philosopher's stone, as regards the response to the gloomy prospects for the less-favoured regions of Europe, has not been found. New information technology must certainly be part of the response, but we still need to find out how.

On New Information Technology and Equal Opportunities

New information technology can create more equal opportunities for people, in work, leisure activities etc. But it will do so only if public authorities are pre-active in research, education, training and regulation — anticipating possible consequences of new information technology. A *laissez-faire* policy, essentially leaving it to market forces to determine the introduction of new information technology, will most likely lead to new and increased divisions in society.

This view emerges from several of our authors. For instance, Garnham attacks those who consider "consumer sovereignty and greater choice" to come about almost by necessity due to the new information technology. On the contrary, he says:

It is to the existence and importance of (unequal) dispositions and competences that the evidence of a growing Information Gap in Western societies, between the information-rich and information-poor, points.

Also Mattelart aims a blow at the technology promoters who make us believe that "we are on the threshold of an important and beneficial revolution, a revolution in which the master frame (the TV-screen) will become the servant of everybody". But when "we visit the exhibition for audio-visual and communications equipment, we get quite another impression. Technological discoveries are more than ever put to the service of what already exists and in the hands of those who are currently in power". Pushing technology without corresponding education or social and economic policies aiming at the general public will, according to Mattelart, only give the elite, in each society and in the world, one more powerful instrument to maintain their privileges. The layman will not know how to make use of the new information technology because:

> We know that in the present social and cultural system, a part of the population is under-informed and incapable of decoding information, of research and, as a consequence, incapable of utilising it by turning it into action.

Also, de Gournay fears that an uncontrolled use of the new information technology will lead to increased divisions in society. However, she sees one reason why the new divisions might now follow the existing ones:

> Rudimentary technical knowledge is as widespread among the middle classes as among the elite, who have often been nurtured with a more classical and humanistic culture. Practical commonsense is, for the time being, on the side of the less privileged and this is quite simply what is needed to operate a machine, however intelligent it may seem.

The general analysis of Mattelart and de Gournay is well-supplemented by the more specific analysis of publishing and printing by Horowitz and Curtis. They suggest that those "who control the hardware, software and marketing, or information about the information, may ultimately control the information itself". This has hitherto been the domain of the publishing houses, but Horowitz and Curtis see the new information technology as opening up an alley towards opportunities:

> to maximise information as a liberating, democratizing activity . . . Whatever the short-term difficulties outlined, democratic societies will be advantaged by the new technology and by its openness to all.

But making forecasts and indentifying risks and opportunities is one thing. It is quite another to say what should be done in order to avoid the risks and to seize the opportunities. Here most of the discussions fade out; however, there are a few indications, one of the clearest being that the role of the State will have to be reconsidered. Mattelart wants "a re-definition of the relation between the State and its citizens and, at the same time, a re-definition of the notion of public service" because:

> The notion of pluralism, on which these public services and monopolies are built, explodes under the pressure of sectors and social movements not represented in this notion of pluralism . . . Tension (local/central; local/ national; and a variant of the latter, national/multinational) is translated into a struggle to win back one's identity and expression – the little facing the big, the micro facing the macro.

De Gournay anticipates a certain development of public services:

> It is becoming increasingly likely that part of the socialised consumption

sector (health, education, collective urban facilities) will be the responsibility of people themselves and that consumers' and users' associations, neighbourhood associations and other associative movements will replace the State and take over the organization of collective services such as, for instance, crêches for the children of working women, cultural activities, mutual-aid systems for the elderly, the disabled or tenants in difficulty. This social change marks the transition from a society based up to now on the mandatory consumption of institutional services (social-aid systems) to a 'self-help' society, the convivial keynote of which is the associative movement.

One cannot emphasize strongly enough the crucial role of the State in ensuring a societally successful transition towards an information society. The State can only assume this function if it is pre-active and takes a long-term view of the new information technology. Otherwise, the battle-field will be left entirely to 'technology pushers' and we shall, at the best, miss many opportunities.

A Particularly Exposed Group: Women

There are unfortunately all too many reasons to believe that women, forming 51.3 per cent of the population in the EEC, are particularly vulnerable to the consequences of the new information technologies. Let us first make a general analysis. When an individual wants to adapt to, or even better to command, the new information technology, she has essentially two tools at her disposal — her job and her training. The job supplies her with the financial, technical and political means to resist or induce changes, while the training is the personal asset for making use of the new technology in all spheres of daily life. Women are worse off than men in both respects. The female participation rate is 30 per cent, as compared to 54 per cent for men, and fewer women than men go to universities, as shown in Table 1.

However, Table 1 also shows that the situation for women is improving. If we concentrate on the technically oriented studies, we see from the bottom line of the Table that the percentage of female graduates is very low. To these general observations could be added several more specific ones, the most important being that the jobs which are most exposed to displacement or significant change by the new information technology (such as jobs in the office, banks, assembly and in primary schools) are mostly occupied by women. Thus, women are exposed to change and change implies risks and opportunities. There is therefore every good reason to investigate particular options in new information technologies and their impacts on women.

Working-at-a-distance (which might be in the home) is of particular importance to women. There may be pressures of various kinds — political, economic and male — to push women back into the home; several activities, such as child care, home surveillance and cooking, could then be partly combined with work. Public savings on child-care facilities, energy savings in transport and a more 'flexible' work-force would be some of the benefits, not to mention views on 'the right role of women in family life'. So why not encourage women to work at home? Cronberg points out some of the risks, or disadvantages, for women working at home in her discussion.

De Gournay warns us against believing in easy solutions to make women adapt to the new information technology. The source of the problem is deeply rooted in our society and is not attributable to simple factors such as, for instance, the level of education:

> It is more a question of a historical gulf between a technical culture and a culture of literary type and it so happens that the special sensitivity of each sex inclines it more to one than the other, men being often the ones who benefit from the two cultures. From these observations it may be feared that women will have the greatest difficulty in adapting to the information revolution and that the creativity promised by the new media will hardly be accessible to them. These differences in behaviour due to the sexual roles seem to us to be more tenacious than those which are attributable to levels of education.

De Cugis *et al* see similar risks (particularly for women) in the present development of technology, mainly because "the whole of society expresses false needs". But they also believe that the development can be changed. They see the activities of the Women's Health Movement in Italy, which was created in the early 1970s, as a proof that, if properly organized, groups in society can "reshape institutions to meet their needs". They argue that the many opportunities offered by the new information technology must be oriented towards the needs of society seen in the wider sense:

> Women's demands are in this sense much wider than any other social subjects. They request real physical and psychological well-being and these needs start general struggles in workplaces, in the urban context and in the family . . . Will new technology be able to meet these fundamental needs?

Viewed on the background of these quotations, Morrissey and Drew express a more optimistic view on the place of women in an information society. They say:

> In an information society, it should be possible to recognize the value of all work forms and to bring about an end to sex-role stereotyping in work . . . Just as the Industrial Revolution brought about a divergence between the work roles of men and women, so the Information Revolution may lead to a convergence of these roles.

This is certainly true. But it is just as true that it will not happen so easily. The pertinent question is what actions are required by whom in order to make it happen — a question which has unfortunately not been addressed either by the many researchers working on the consequences of new information technology for women or by politicians. This is astonishing, bearing in mind the number of women, particularly if one compares it with the attention attracted by much smaller, but much more powerful, groups such as printers,

Table 1

Participation of Women in Third-level Education in EEC Countries

	Germany	France	Italy	NL	Belgium	Luxembourg	UK	IRL	Denmark
Third level students as percentage of all students (1977-78)									
Female $\frac{f}{F}$ 100	7.6	8.5	8.0	6.0	8.0	4.0	3.7	4.1	9.5*
Male $\frac{m}{M}$ 100	10.9	9.4	10.2	10.3	10.0	5.0	5.3	5.8	12.2*
Female graduates as percentage of all graduates. All third level studies:									
1964/65	26.0		36.5	27.7	39.2	48.3	27.0	36.1	39.3
1965/66		38.2							
1966/67			43.2		29.8		29.3		40.0
1970/71				31.6		56.2			
1971/72									
1972/73	34.0	39.3	42.7	33.2	33.9	70.1	31.7	41.2	47.8
1973/74									
Engineering only 1973/74	1.3	5.3	0.9	8.7	2.3	—	3.2	4.5	4.2

*1976-77

$\frac{f}{F}$ × 100: females as percentage of all females in relevant age group.

$\frac{m}{M}$ × 100: males as percentage of all males in relevant age group.

doctors or steel workers. Maybe the reason is that women have always been underprivileged, so what's new?

WHAT FUTURE LIES AHEAD FOR EUROPEANS? WHERE ARE WE GOING?

IT IS NOT BY ACCIDENT that the title refers to Europeans and not to Europe. The key issue of the Dublin 1981 Conference was what would be the impact on the individual of the new information technology, an aspect often neglected in favour of what will happen in Europe. The challenge posed to Europe by the new information technology is a double one, with an industrial/technological competitiveness aspect and a societal aspect. Most studies and political views tend to consider one of them and neglect the other. Simplifying the matter, we might call the two extreme views the 'hard-nosed' and the 'soft'. The 'hard-nosed' present the problem as solely that of being as productive and as innovative as Japanese and American industry, while the 'soft' design a future utopian society — national, regional or local — as if it was isolated from the rest of the world. The reality is that in fifteen years time, European societies will still find themselves in a competitive situation *vis-a-vis* the world and they will still, hopefully, pursue ideals such as offering equal opportunities to all their people.

While the industrial challenge seems to have been recognised, even if the responses to it are slow in coming, the societal challenge (as regards the impact on the individual) seems much less appreciated. Hence, the emphasis on Europeans in the title. In spite of the variety of European cultures, which we usually refer to as the distinct characteristic of our continent, the papers of the Dublin Conference show that the regions of Europe and their people are facing the same kind of problems, albeit different in their size and consequences, with respect to the new information technology: un- and re-employment, a two-culture society, a re-definition of the public services, revision of the education and training system, to mention a few. Therefore, it is correct to talk about the societal problems of Europeans facing the new information technology and much is certainly to be gained from strengthening collaboration at European level on research and on exchange of empirical evidence relating to the societal impact of the new information technology. Only through such a European research and communication network can local, regional and national authorities create a sufficient knowledge and experience basis to elaborate their own responses to the new information technology.

Having said this, we must admit that the present discussion rarely transcends the national frontiers of the authors' countries. More, but still very few, transcend in their references their mother tongue, in particular if it happens to be English or French. Europeans do not know Europeans. I dare not think how much duplication of work takes place due to this lack of inter-European collaboration and communication.

Social experiments and exchange of the results obtained should be a top-priority activity for European collaboration. The urgent need to reduce the gap between the general public and the development, design and application of new technologies is evident.

The discussions also show that the question 'where are we going' cannot really be answered. Looking at the papers presented at the Conference, a wide range of possible alternative futures are offered. Roughly we might divide them into two groups. The first group presents an 'extrapolative' picture of the future, pointing out rather gloomy prospects for our societies being increasingly 'two-culture societies, a small elite and a great general public'. This group is, in my opinion, rather convincing in their analyses and identification of real risks calling for corrective measures. The second group sees the openness of the future as an alibi, either for guessing what the future *could* be like or what it *should* be like. Such discussions are absolutely necessary for opening up our vision about future uses of technology and options for future developments, but they have one possible risk embedded in them — they trick us into believing that such futures will come about by themselves.

If we want to seize some of the opportunities outlined in the various discussions (such as a more equitable distribution of opportunities between men and women, better use of information for everybody, skills enhancement instead of deskilling, job enrichment, social integration of the disabled, etc.), *a strategy is called for.* Such a strategy must be characterized by two key components: it must be long-term oriented, in its actions and in its perspectives, and it must stimulate collaboration between the most important societal actors: government, industry, the general public, universities and other research institutions. New information technology will have an all-pervasive impact on society. It will change systems, not only components, and its indirect impact will be just as important as its direct impact. Each actor, fortunately enough, controls only parts of any changing system and cannot control the whole development. Therefore, a collective effort of several actors will be required. The formulation of such a strategy will encounter several difficulties. Firstly, it will be quite a new experience for most actors involved. The presentations by Martin-Löf and MacBride show that almost no country in Europe has a strategy for new information technologies. Nor is it a common practice of industry to have a strategy as illustrated in the following quotation by Hedge and Crawley, taken from their study on electronic office systems:

> It is abundantly clear that at present most organizations still lack any general policy or strategy for managing technological change. In consequence, there is a real danger that the piecemeal acquisition of electronic office systems will result in technology determining, rather than fulfilling, the requirements of organizational change.

Secondly, we shall have to come to terms with the paradox embedded in 'the open society versus purposeful action': to what extent do we accept State intervention today in order to enlarge the future range of options and individual freedom? What is the acceptable trade-off between short-term costs and long-term benefits? (For a further discussion, see Cantley and Holst, 1981) In short, the need for a strategy, as a means for making technology fulfill rather than determine societal change, has to be weighed against two very good reasons for not going too far in specifying plans for the future:

 (1) the uncertainty of future developments and events; and

 (2) nobody has the wisdom to design the future of others.

Such trade-offs and compromises cannot be resolved once and for all, but only through a continuous participation of the majority of societal actors in the elaboration and implementation of the strategy. Maybe participation and strategy are the two key-responses to our desire to let technology fulfill rather than determine societal change.

I am convinced that nobody wants technological progress to go against, rather than behind, societal demand, as the Little Prince of Saint-Exupéry (1946) thought it did in the following example:

"Bonjour", dit le petit prince.

"Bonjour", dit le marchand.

C'était un marchand de pilules perfectionnées qui apaisent la soif. On en avale une par semaine et l'on n'éprouve plus le besoin de boire.

"Pourquoi vends-tu ça?", dit le petit prince.

"C'est une grosse économie de temps", dit le marchand. Les experts ont fait des calculs. On épargne cinquante-trois minutes par semaine.

"Et que fait-on de ces cinquante-trois minutes?"

"On en fait ce que l'on veut . . ."

"Moi", se dit le petit prince, *"si j'avais cinquante-trois minutes à dépenser, je marcherais tout doucement vers une fontaine . . ."**

---

*For those Europeans who do not know French, the passage quoted from *The Little Prince* reads:

'Hello', said the little prince.

'How're you', answered the shopkeeper.

The man was selling some very sophisticated pills which took care of peoples' thirst. A pill a week and you'd never feel the need to drink again.

'Why are you selling this stuff?', asked the little prince.

'Because people can save an enormous amount of time', replied the shopkeeper.

'According to calculations of experts', he continued, 'by using these pills, a person can save fifty-three minutes a week!'.

'And what would people do with these extra fifty three minutes?'.

'Whatever they liked'.

'Myself', murmured the little prince, 'if I had fifty-three free minutes to spare, I would slowly make my way to a big fountain . . .'

References

Note: Most references in the text are from this book and are not therefore not listed below.

Cantley, M. and Holst, O. (1981) Europe in a changing world: Open society or purposeful system? Collaborative R&D and the role of the EEC + FAST programme. In *Operational Research '81,* J. P. Brans (Ed.), North Holland.

Gershuny, J. and Thomas, G. S. (1981) *Changing Leisure Patterns, UK 1961-1974/5.* Science Policy Research Unit, University of Sussex, UK.

Holst, O. (1982) *European Transport: Crucial Problems and research needs. A long term analysis.* Series FAST No. 3, Commission of the European Community, Luxembourg.

Javeau, C. (1972) The trip to work: the application of the time-budget method to problems arising from commuting between residence and work-place. In *Use of Time,* A. Szalai (Ed.), Mouton, The Netherlands.

de Saint-Exupéry, Antoine (1946) *Le Petit Prince.* Gallimard, Paris.

371

List of Participants attending
Dublin International Conference on
Information Technology: Impact on the Way of Life
18-20 November 1981

Belgium

Biolley de Ines
Universite Catholique de Louvain,
Louvain-la-Neuve

David, Willy
Centre de Psychologie de Travail,
Universite Catholique de Louvain,
Louvain-la-Neuve

Falk, Thomas
European Institute for Advanced
Studies in Management,
Brussels

Gaussin, Jose
Universite Catholique de Louvain,
Louvain-la-Neuve

Grewlich, Klaus, W.
Commission of the European
Communities,
Brussels

Gryspeerdt, Axel
Universite Catholique de Louvain,
Louvain-la-Neuve

Huber, Roland
Commission of the European
Communities,
Brussels

Holst, Olav
Commission of the European
Communities,
Brussels

Laconte, Pierre
Universite Catholique de Louvain,
Louvain-la-Neuve

Laethem Van, Anne
Universite Catholique de Louvain,
Louvain-la-Neuve

Petrella, Ricardo
Commission of the European
Communities,
Brussels

Vandermassen, Kathleen
State University of Antwerp,
Antwerp

Van Rhijn, Arie Adriaan
Commission of the European
Communities,
Brussels

Canada

Sindell, Peter S.
GAMMA,
University of Montreal,
Quebec

Thompson, Gordon B.
Bell Northern Research,
Ontario

Valaskakis, Kimon
GAMMA,
University of Montreal, Quebec

France

Baboulin, Jean-Claude
Institut National de L'Audiovisuel,
Bry-sur-Marne

Bonnafous, Alain
Laboratorie d'Economie des
Transports,
Universite Lyon II,
Lyon

De Gournay, Chantal
Institute d'Urbanisme de Paris,
Universite de Paris — Val de Marne,
Paris

Dessein, Catherine
Development et Amenagement,
Paris

Marchard, Marie
Direction General des
Telecommunications,
Paris

Mattelart, Michele
7, Rue Payenne,
75003 Paris

Mercier, Pierre-Alain
Centre d'Etudes Sociologiques,
Paris

Monod, Elsbeth
Direction General des
Telecommunications,
Paris

Plassard, Francois
Laboratorie d'Economie des
Transports,
Universite Lyon II,
Lyon

Scardigli, Victor
Centre d'Etudes Sociologiques,
Paris

Greece

Carvas, Elie
Ministry of Exterior,
Athens

Ireland

Bannon, Liam
National Board for Science
and Technology, Dublin

Bannon, Michael
University College,
Dublin

Barry, Ursula
National Board for Science and
Technology, Dublin

Blennerhassett, Evelyn
Institute of Public Administration,
Dublin

Breslin, Robert
Northern Telecom,
Galway

Burke, Raymond
Stokes Kennedy and Crowley,
Dublin

Byrne, Fergus
Northern Telecom,
Galway

Byrnes, Tom
An Bord Telecom,
Dublin

Cahill, Anthony
National Institute for Higher
Education, Limerick

Christian, James
Thomond College of Education,
Limerick

Collins, Columb
Regional Technical College,
Dundalk, Co. Louth

Cooney, Sean
An Foras Taluntais, Dublin

Crotty, Niall
Bank of Ireland Head Office,
Dublin

Crowley, James A.
University College,
Dublin

Cullen, John
Irish Foundation for Human
Development, Dublin

Cullen, Paul
Dept. of Labour,
Dublin

Daly, Joe
Concept Teoranta,
Dublin

Daly, John
Dublin Meat Packers,
Co. Dublin

Daly, Peter
National Board for Science
and Technology, Dublin

Dillon, Brian
National Institute for Higher
Education, Dublin

Donovan, Finbar J.
Allied Irish Banks Ltd.,
Dublin

Drew, Eileen
Human Resources Study Group,
Co. Meath

Drummey, Michael J.
Inbucon Ireland, Dublin

Duffin, Andrew C.
Computer Automation Limited,
Dublin

Dunne, Paul L.
AnCO, Dublin

English, Michael J.
Dept. of Industry and Energy, Dublin

Fahy, Tony
Radio Telefis Eireann, Dublin

Finnegan, John W.
University College, Galway

Fitzgibbon, Michael
Institute for Industrial Research
and Standards, Dublin

Fitzsimon, Paula
Industrial Development Authority,
Dublin

Forsyth, Terry
Bank of Ireland Head Office, Dublin

Frain, Pat
National Board for Science
and Technology, Dublin

Gunnigle, Patrick G.
Shannon Free Airport Development
Co. Limited, Limerick

Hall, Patrick A.
Institute of Public Administration,
Dublin

Hannan, Damian F.
Economic and Social Research
Institute, Dublin

Hayes, Michael
Cara Data Processing Ltd., Dublin

Healy, Mel
National Board for Science
and Technology, Dublin

Hodnett, Liam
Regional Technical College,
Co. Cork

Holden, Paul
National Board for Science
and Technology, Dublin

Hyland, Bill
Dept. of Education, Dublin

Johnston, Edward C.
Confederation of Irish Industry,
Dublin

Kelly, Patrick
National Institute for Higher
Education, Limerick

Kennedy, Kieran
Economic & Social Research
Institute, Dublin

Lalor, Eamon
National Board for Science
and Technology, Dublin

McCurtain, Margaret
Senior College,
Ballyfermot Rd., Dublin

MacBride, Sean
Roebuck House,
Clonskeagh, Co. Dublin

McCarthy, Eunice
University College, Dublin

McGeachy, Catherine
Regional Management Centre,
National Institute for Higher
Education, Limerick

McGovern, Tom
Systems Dynamics Ltd.,
Dublin

McKechnie, Geoffrey
Trinity College, Dublin

McKenna, Anne
University College, Dublin

Maloney, Oliver
Agricultural Credit Corporation,
Dublin

Manahan, Michael
Dept. of the Taoiseach, Dublin

Martino, Vittorio Di
European Foundation for Living and
Working Conditions, Co. Dublin

Moran, Frank
Institute for Industrial Research
and Standards,
Ballymun Rd., Dublin

Morrissey, Terri
Human Resources Study Group,
Dublin

Murphy, Patrick
Regional Technical College, Carlow

Neill, Terry
Arthur Andersen and Co., Dublin

Nichol, Robert
Institute for Industrial Research
and Standards, Dublin

O'Conchubhair, Gearoid
Udaras na Gaeltachta,
Gaillimh

O'Conghaile, Wendy
European Foundation for Working
and Living Conditions, Co. Dublin

O'Connell, Maurice
Dept. of the Public Service,
Dublin

O'Connor, Donal
Dept. of the Public Service,
Dublin

O'Connor, Joyce
Social Research Centre,
National Institute for Higher
Education, Limerick

O'Deirg, Isolde
Instituid Teangealaiochta Eireann,
Dublin

O'Dubhchair, Kate
Regional College,
Dundalk, Co. Louth

O'Grady, Maurice
Nixdorf Computer Ltd., Dublin

O'Hannrachain, Padraig
Dept. of Education, Dublin

O'Kane, Philip
University College, Dublin

O'Keefe, Hugh
Electricity Supply Board, Dublin

O'Kelly, Michael E. J.
University College, Galway

O'Neill, Helen
University College, Dublin

O'Regan, Aidan
New Ireland Assurance Co., Dublin

O'Riagain, Padraig
Instituid Teangeolaiochta Eireann,
Dublin

O'Sullivan, Michael
An Foras Taluntais, Dublin

O'Sullivan, Noel
National Social Service Board, Dublin

Quillian, John
Electricity Supply Board, Dublin

Rabbitte, Patrick
ITGWU, Dublin

Redmond, Gay
Irish Management Institute,
Dublin

Robinson, Senator Mary
17 Wellington Pl., Dublin

Roche, James
Regional Technical College,
Co. Cork

Roseingrave, Thomas
26 Highfield Pk., Dublin

Salmon, Mary
Dublin Institute of Technology,
College of Commerce, Dublin

Sliney, Margaret
Lake Electronic Design,
Co. Dublin

Sweeney, Gerry
Institute for Industrial Research
and Standards, Dublin

Talbot, Pat
Coopers and Lybrand Association,
Dublin

Thornhill, Don
Dept. of Finance,
Government Buildings, Dublin

Timoney, Seamus
University College, Dublin

Walsh, Edward
National Institute for Higher
Education, Limerick

Wheeler, Timothy
National Institute for Higher
Education, Dublin

Whelan, Christopher
Economic and Social Research
Institute, Dublin

Whelan, Matthew
Dept. of Health, Dublin

Whelan, Noel
Dept. of Taoiseach, Dublin

White, Anthony
National Council for Educational
Awards, Dublin

Italy

Bistintini, Ilena
C.N.R., Turin

de Cugis, Alessandra
Milan

Drovetto, Loredana
C.N.R., Turin

Giuseppe, Richeri
Regione Emilia-Romagna,
Viale Silvani 6, Bologna

Lanzavechhia, Giuseppe
C.N.E.N., Italy

Michele, La Rosa
Instituto de Sociologia, Bologna

Pellegrini, Umberto
Tecnetra,
P. le R. Morandi, 2,
20121 Milano

Taiti, Fabio
Censis Foundation, Roma

Michel, Andre J.
Intergovernmental Bureau for
Informatics, Rome

Japan

Komatsuzaki, Seisuke
Research Institute of
Telecommunications and Economics,
Tokyo

Masuda, Yoneji
Institute for the Information Society,
Tokyo

Luxembourg

Mahon, Barry
Euronet Diane, Luxembourg

Netherlands

Boswijk, Rieks
STT, Gravenhage

Dirkzwager, Arie
Free University of Amsterdam

Demper, Hendrik
Ministry of Economic Affairs,
The Hague

Jonkers, Herman Louise
Ministry of Education and Science,
The Hague

Knulst, Wim
Social and Cultural Planning Office,
Ryswijk

Rondagh, Perry
Ministry of Economic Affairs,
The Hague

Van Trier, Anthony
Vesalinslaan 15, Eindhoven

Northern Ireland

Cairns, Edward
New University of Ulster, Coleraine

Martin, William J.
The Queen's University of Belfast

Smyth, Alice
Department of Commerce,
Co. Antrim

Norway

Godoe, Helge
Norwegian Telecommunications
Administration, Oslo

Portugal

Morais-Neves, Elina
Junta Nacional de Investigacao
Cientif. Tec., Lisboa

Spain

Chaparro, Francisco Ortiz
Fundesco,
Serrand 187, Madrid

Sweden

Löf-Martin, Johan
Ministry of Industry, Stockholm

Turkey

Ahmet, Esin
Instanbul University

United Kingdom

Allport, Richard
University of Leeds

Barnett, Ross
University of Lancaster

Bessant, J. R.
University of Aston in Birmingham

Boddy, David
University of Glasgow

Braun, Ernest
University of Aston in Birmingham

Buchanan, David
University of Glasgow

Campbell, Angela
Sisters of Notre Dame, Glasgow

Crawley, Richard
University of Aston in Birmingham

Dickson, Keith
University of Aston in Birmingham

Dover, Marilyn
University of Aston in Birmingham

Fitzgerald, J. J.
University of Warwick

Garnham, Nicholas R.
Polytechnic of Central London

Gershuny, Jay
University of Sussex

Halloran, James D.
Centre for Mass Communication
Research,
University of Leicester

Hedge, Alan
University of Aston in Birmingham

Hubbard, Geoffrey
Council for Educational Technology
for United Kingdom, London

McGhee, Kathleen
Sisters of Notre Dame,
Liverpool

McKenna, Eugene F.
North East London Polytechnic

Miles, Ian
Science Policy Research Unit,
University of Sussex

Morris, Ian G.
Scottish Education Department,
Edinburgh

Moseley, Russell
University of Aston in Birmingham

Nabavi, Annette
PACTEL, London

Newman, Julian
City of London Polytechnic

Nicholas, Ian James
Ashridge Management College, Herts

Paker, Yakup
Polytechnic of Central London

Robins, Kevin
Sunderland Polytechnic

Sweeney, James
Passionists/Coodham Conference
Centre, Scotland

Wheelock, Vernor
University of Bradford,
West Yorkshire

Wilkinson, Barry
University of Aston in Birmingham

Williams, Hugh
University of Aston in Birmingham

Williams, Robin
University of Aston in Birmingham

Winch, Graham
Imperial College, London

United States of America

Borrell, Jerry
The Library of Congress, Washington

Brownstein, Charles
National Science Foundation,
Washington

Leontief, Wassily
Institute for Economic Analysis,
New York University

Horowitz, Irving Louis
Rutgers University, New Jersey

Horowitz-Curtis, Mary Ellen
John Wiley Publishers,
New York

Robbins, Edward
Room 10-485,
M.I.T., Massachusetts

Jones, Thomas
7504 Holiday Tce., Maryland 22034

West Germany

Picot, Arnold
Universitat Hannover

Priebe, Klaus Peter
Universitat Dortmund

Rader, Michael
Kernforschungszentrum Karlsruhe

Henckel, Dietrich
Deutsches Institut fur un Banistik,
Berlin

FAST
Forecasting and Assessment in the field of Science and Technology

THE COUNCIL OF MINISTERS of the European Communities decided in 1978 to initiate a five-year experimental programme: Forecasting and Assessment in the field of Science and Technology (FAST), which was implemented early in 1979. The main aim of FAST is to contribute to the definition of long-term Community research and development (R&D) objectives and priorities and thus, to the formulation of a coherent science and technology policy in the long-term.

To this end, the programme has to highlight prospects, problems and potential conflicts likely to affect the long-term development of the Community, with an orientation towards defining alternative courses of Community research and development action to help solve or achieve them or to render concrete those possibilities. The programme has also to encourage the establishment of an *ad hoc* system of collaboration in the form of networks, as informal and flexible as possible, between Community centres specialising in forecasting and assessment in the field of science and technology.

FAST is not intended to predict the future but rather to study the possible sources of alternative development and hence to throw light on possible and desirable options for R&D policy. A central tenet of the programme is that the possible futures are not a matter of chance: they will be as our societies determine them.

Within this mandate, three sub-programmes, reflecting problem areas of three different time horizons, have been defined:

    (1)   Work and Employment
    (2)   Information Society
    (3)   Bio-Society

Fifty European research teams have been working for FAST on thirty research projects:

Work and Employment

— Prospects for the European chemical industry
— Prospects for the construction industry
— The future of repair activities
— The development of the environmental industry
— The future of employment in the services
— Regional prospects of employment in Europe
— Biomass, regions and employment
— Attitudes towards work
— Social innovations in the 1980s
— Productivity and progress
— Small enterprises, technical change and employment

Information Society

— Microelectronics innovations in the context of the international division of labour
— Job creation potential of the information technologies
— Long-term options and forecasts for transport in Europe
— Representation and sharing of power in an information society
— The impact of information technologies on the way of life: work, leisure, transport and communications
— Distribution of benefits and risks associated with microelectronics applications
— Man-machine relations: dangers and remedies

Bio-society

— A Community strategy for European biotechnology
— Biotechnologies in the production of chemical feedstocks and derived products
— Proteins: probable impacts and development strategies for bio-technology in European agro-food systems
— Community strategy for biotechnology: analysis of scientific disciplines germane to biotechnology
— Information technologies in the development of biotechnology (bioinformatics)
— Manpower and training implications of the expansion of bio-technology-based industries
— Social dimension of biotechnologies. Social and political choices that may be created by progress in biotechnologies
— Proteins: implications of biotechnologies for developing countries and international trade
— Implications of biotechnology for the Third World
— Technological forecasts of downstream processing in biotechnology
— Detoxification as therapeutic techniques, problems and prospects
— Environmental biotechnology: future prospects

Reports on these projects are available from the FAST-team at the provisional address: FAST, Directorate-General for Science, Research and Development, Commission of the European Communities, Rue de la Loi 200, B-1049 Brussels, Belgium.